T0235429

Lecture Notes in Computer Science **12528**

More information about this subseries at http://www.springer.com/series/7409

Joaquin Garcia-Alfaro · Jean Leneutre ·
Nora Cuppens · Reda Yaich (Eds.)

Risks and Security of Internet and Systems

15th International Conference, CRiSIS 2020
Paris, France, November 4–6, 2020
Revised Selected Papers

 Springer

Editors
Joaquin Garcia-Alfaro 🆔
Telecom SudParis
Palaiseau, France

Jean Leneutre
Telecom Paris
Palaiseau, France

Nora Cuppens
Polytechnique Montréal
Montréal, QC, Canada

Reda Yaich
IRT SystemX
Palaiseau, France

ISSN 0302-9743   ISSN 1611-3349   (electronic)
Lecture Notes in Computer Science
ISBN 978-3-030-68886-8   ISBN 978-3-030-68887-5   (eBook)
https://doi.org/10.1007/978-3-030-68887-5

LNCS Sublibrary: SL3 – Information Systems and Applications, incl. Internet/Web, and HCI

This Springer imprint is published by the registered company Springer Nature Switzerland AG
The registered company address is: Gewerbestrasse 11, 6330 Cham, Switzerland

Preface

This volume contains the papers presented at the 15th International Conference on Risks and Security of Internet and Systems (CRISIS 2020). Although it was intended to be held in Paris (France), due to the COVID-19 pandemic CRISIS 2020 was finally held virtually together with the satellite events of the conference (Post-quantum Cryptography Workshop, Intelligent Transport Systems Security Workshop, H2020 Project SeCoIIA Webinar, H2020 SeCoIIA Preparedness Workshop and H2020 SeCoIIA Information Security Workshop).

Each submission was reviewed by at least three members of the Program Committee (49 members from 14 countries and areas, complemented by 15 external reviewers). More than 130 reviews were submitted, followed by discussions over a period of two weeks. Out of 44 submissions (from 20 countries), 16 full papers were accepted, complemented by 7 short papers. The accepted papers cover diverse research themes, ranging from classic topics such as vulnerability analysis, intrusion detection, security protocols, access control and risk assessment to some more advanced topics such as security knowledge, neural networks, web protection, infrastructure security and malware detection. The program was completed with an excellent invited talk given by Roberto Di Pietro (Hamad Bin Khalifa University, Qatar) on new dimensions of information warfare.

Many people contributed to the success of CRISIS 2020. We warmly thank all the Program Committee members, as well as the additional reviewers, who volunteered to read and discuss all the submitted papers. We greatly thank the Advisory Board Chairs (Paul Labrogère and Frédéric Cuppens), the General Chairs (Reda Yaich and Nora Cuppens) and the Publicity Chairs (Mawloud Omar and Slim Kallel) for their efforts and support during the preparation phases. We thank as well all the members of the Organization Committee and the Sponsors. Our special thanks to Roberto Di Pietro, for accepting our invitation to open the conference with a keynote talk. Last but not least, we thank all the authors who submitted their research results and all the attendees.

December 2020

Joaquin Garcia-Alfaro
Jean Leneutre

Organization

Advisory Board Chairs

Paul Labrogère	IRT SystemX, France
Frédéric Cuppens	Polytechnique Montréal, Canada

General Chairs

Reda Yaich	IRT SystemX, France
Nora Cuppens	Polytechnique Montréal, Canada

Program Chairs

Joaquin Garcia-Alfaro	Institut Polytechnique de Paris, France
Jean Leneutre	Institut Polytechnique de Paris, France

Publicity Chairs

Mawloud Omar	ESIEE Paris and Université Gustave Eiffel, France
Slim Kallel	University of Sfax, Tunisia

Organization Committee

Mawloud Omar	ESIEE Paris and Université Gustave Eiffel, France
Witold Klaudel	IRT SystemX, France
Khalifa Toumi	IRT SystemX, France
Kalpana Singh	IRT SystemX, France
Ines Ben Jemaa	IRT SystemX, France
Farah Sophie Haidar	IRT SystemX, France

Program Committee

Jocelyn Aubert	Luxembourg Institute of Science and Technology, Luxembourg
Takoua Abdellatif	Polytechnic School of Tunisia, Tunisia
Esma Aïmeur	University of Montreal, Canada
Saed Alrabaee	United Arab Emirates University, United Arab Emirates
Michel Barbeau	Carleton University, Canada
Sébastien Bardin	CEA, France
Anis Bkakria	IMT Atlantique, France
Ismael Bouassida Rodriguez	LAAS-CNRS, France

Ana Rosa Cavalli	Telecom SudParis, France
Mila Dalla Preda	University of Verona, Italy
Soufiene Djahel	Manchester Metropolitan University, UK
Roberto Di Pietro	Hamad Bin Khalifa University, Qatar
Saïd Gharout	ARM Cambridge, UK
Mohamed Ghazel	Université Gustave Eiffel, France
Bogdan Groza	Politehnica University of Timisoara, Romania
Brahim Hamid	University of Toulouse, France
Philippe Jaillon	École des Mines de Saint-Étienne, France
Christos Kalloniatis	University of the Aegean, Greece
Sokratis Katsikas	Norwegian University of Science and Technology, Norway
Nesrine Khabou	University of Sfax, Tunisia
Evangelos Kranakis	Carleton University, Canada
Igor Kotenko	SPIIRAS, Russia
Marc Lacoste	Orange Labs, France
Luigi Logrippo	Université du Québec en Outaouais, Canada
Wassef Louati	University of Sfax, Tunisia
Ahmed Meddahi	IMT Lille Douai, France
Mohamed Mosbah	University of Bordeaux, France
Guillermo Navarro-Arribas	Universitat Autònoma de Barcelona, Spain
Melek Önen	EURECOM, France
Kai Rannenberg	Goethe University Frankfurt, Germany
Riadh Robbana	University of Carthage, Tunisia
Michael Rusinowitch	LORIA – Inria Nancy, France
Siraj A. Shaikh	Coventry University, UK
Natalia Stakhanova	University of Saskatchewan, Canada
Ketil Stølen	SINTEF, Norway
Qiang Tang	Luxembourg Institute of Science and Technology, Luxembourg
Nadia Tawbi	Laval University, Canada
Lingyu Wang	Concordia University, Canada
Akka Zemmari	Université de Bordeaux, France

Additional Reviewers

Bochra Bouchhima	Mariam Chaabane
Christopher Schmitz	Orhan Ermiş
David Harborth	Samir Ouchani
Hamida Belkhiria	Shahid Mahmood
Hoang Nga Nguyen	Vasily Desnitsky
Huu Nghia Nguyen	Vinh Hoa La
Katerina Mavroeidi	Wissam Mallouli
Katerina Vgena	

Contents

Risk Analysis, Neural Networks and Web Protection

Infrastructure Security and Malware Detection

Short Papers

Keynote Talk

New Dimensions of Information Warfare: The Economic Pillar—Fintech and Cryptocurrencies

Maurantonio Caprolu[1]([⊠]), Stefano Cresci[2], Simone Raponi[1], and Roberto Di Pietro[1]

[1] Division of Information and Computing Technology,
College of Science and Engineering, Hamad Bin Khalifa University, Qatar Foundation, Doha, Qatar
mcaprolu@hbku.edu.qa
[2] Institute of Informatics and Telematics, National Research Council (IIT-CNR), Pisa, Italy

Abstract. The fast-paced technological advancements of the last decades have led to digitizing an ever-increasing amount of information, processes, and activities. A wide range of new digital devices have made our lives easier, faster, and funnier, quickly becoming indispensable for both work and daily life. As a result, the digital realm has dramatically expanded its boundaries, replacing the physical world in several areas. Information warfare has found fertile ground to expand into this modernized electronic world, creating new scenarios and novel attacks on nations and citizens' virtual perimeter. The economic sector plays an essential role in this context, widely affected and profoundly changed by recent technological advancements. For instance, the rapid rise of fintech systems, on the one hand, has led to the globalization of markets, with evident benefits on industries and tertiary services. On the other hand, the financial sector's dependence on digital systems and information has increased dramatically, also introducing new digital risks. This paper explores the new threats opened up by the latest technological advancements to the national economy of a typical developed Country. After identifying two of the major targets of information warfare – cryptocurrencies and stock markets – we investigate possible attacks and evaluate their potential repercussions on the national economy, also highlighting promising avenues for future research and experimentation.

Keywords: Information warfare · Fintech · Cryptocurrency · Market manipulation

1 Introduction

The end of the Cold War and the collapse of the Soviet Union in the late 80' caused tangible changes in the world economy, that engaged in progressively internationalized trades that led to the globalization of today's economy.

© Springer Nature Switzerland AG 2021
J. Garcia-Alfaro et al. (Eds.): CRiSIS 2020, LNCS 12528, pp. 3–27, 2021.
https://doi.org/10.1007/978-3-030-68887-5_1

Theoretically, this approach pursued free trade principles and a gradual disengagement of states, thereby somehow adhering to the popular theory of Montesquieu that "commerce softens manners and encourages peace" (*The Spirit of the Laws*—1748).

Sadly, history has shown us that this phase of economic globalization has quickly diverged from the principles of Montesquieu. Admittedly, as of today, free trade has essentially imposed itself, while few states have given up their political and economic supremacy prerogatives. On the contrary, economics, banking, and trade are all increasingly seen as subtle, but sharp tools of leverage and power-gathering. Indeed the economy of a nation—intended as the total production, distribution, and trade of goods and services conducted by a nation's various economic agents—is central to the livelihood of the nation. The more a nation's economy thrives, the greater the capacity of the nation to provide the public services required for the well-being of its people, including public health, education, and infrastructure, as well as military spending, which is vital to safeguarding stability against both internal and external threats.

To make an example, let us take into account the conflict between the United States of America and the Republic of China. A merciless trade war is being fought by the two nations, with major economic interests at stake. Among their weapons, it is possible to find industrial espionage, technological hacks, custom duties, and legal tools; the same arsenal that, together with soft-power, has allowed the USA to enforce their political agenda—overall, successfully, so far. A further example of a nation's interest in economic war is given by France. In 1997, France established the École de Guerre Économique (School of Economic Warfare) as an academic institution of a renowned Parisian business school, called École Supérieure Libre des Sciences Commerciales Appliquées (Free Superior School of Applied Commercial Sciences). According to such a school, the economic war is a strategy and a process decided by a state as part of the assertion of its power on the international stage, being carried out through information on the financial, economic, technological, political, societal, and legal fields[1]. In the years following its creation, the School of Economic Warfare has been proposing a curriculum based on the following assumptions: (i) the economic conflicts have been increasing during the past 20 years; and (ii) both information warfare and management are the essential means used by contestants to be predominant in such conflicts. However, given the level of complexity, both companies and nations need to boast a vast range of skills to face information warfare on the economic battlefield.

The teaching of competitive intelligence is explicitly designed to examine and resolve economic conflicts shaped by states and private companies alike. In areas such as Policy and Economic Intelligence, Risk Management, International Security, and Cybersecurity, the school currently provides postgraduate training.

---

[1] https://portail-ie.fr/resource/glossary/95/guerre-economique (Last checked December 2020).

One of the foundations of its model, according to the school itself was "the transfer of methodology from the military world to the civilian world."[2].

External actors, such as foreign governments and terrorist groups, may target a nation's economy in various ways and for various reasons such as undermining defensive capabilities before a military attack, or simply destabilizing a country by causing population turmoil. Indeed, it is known that a country that is destabilized and fractured is more fragile and can be affected more quickly from the outside. In this respect, any economic asset important to the nation, such as individuals, companies, organizations, or the government itself represent the attack surface. New technologies, which are constantly applied to different sectors of the economy, lead, on the one hand, to developing, optimizing, and automating economic processes, thus reducing costs and increasing income. But emerging innovations, on the other hand, eventually introduce new vulnerabilities: they raise the reach of attack and expose the economy to unprecedented risks. Consider cryptocurrencies. They have recently gained tremendous momentum and attracted hundreds of billions in capitalization.

One of the first, short contributions related to the new dimensions of Information Warfare, including the above highlighted issues, can be found in [23]. Therein, new possible scenarios are sketched, together with a coarse grain analysis of the impact of new threats on the most sensitive targets exposed by every nation: the Society, the Economy, and the Critical Infrastructures. Instead, in [24] can be found a detailed, analytical, rigorous and—to the extent possible—complete treatment of the different domains characterizing the new dimensions of Information Warfare.

1.1 Motivations

The frenetic technological progress of the last few decades is radically changing our habits and lifestyle. The subsequent digitalization of an ever-increasing amount of data is expanding the boundaries of the digital realm, exposing our society to new security challenges and risks. In this new virtual environment, cybersecurity threats can jeopardize countless new private and public assets, with potential impacts on national security hardly imaginable just a score ago. Therefore, it is not surprising that information warfare is gaining more and more strategic importance and attention from public and private industries, governments, and various other actors. Hence the need to contextualize information warfare in the current technological scenario, investigating the attack and defense techniques existing in the literature, considering different possible scenarios, and identifying open research and technology problems.

1.2 Contribution

In this paper, we delve into the novel threats introduced by the new dimensions of information warfare, specifically targeting the economic sector. We first iden-

---

[2] https://www.ege.fr/index.php/l-ecole/presentation/economic-warfare-school-of-paris.html (Last checked December 2020).

tified two of the most critical targets of Economic Information Warfare, i.e., the cryptocurrencies and the stock market, significantly affected by emerging security threats. We then investigated the possible attacks against these targets and highlighted the current state-of-the-art concerning existing and future threats, proposing solutions, and identifying related research and technology problems.

Roadmap. The paper is organized as follow. In Sect. 2 we present the cryptocurrencies as a target of the modern Economic Information Warfare, discussing the possible existing and future attacks against its technological pillars (Sect. 2.1) and its IT infrastructure (Sect. 2.2). We then discuss the attacks against the Stock Market in Sect. 3, investigating market manipulation techniques (Sect. 3.1), new threats introduced by the rise of high-frequency trading (Sect. 3.2), and attacks against the market's availability (Sect. 3.3). Finally, in Sect. 4, we draw some final remarks.

2   Cryptocurrencies

Blockchain-based systems, in particular permissionless ones, have a large attack surface due to the distribution, complexity, and openness of the resources involved in their protocols. The most important cryptocurrencies, such as Bitcoin, Ethereum, and Monero, are public blockchain-based systems where all users have the same permissions. Anyone can join their network, access the distributed ledger, and participate in the protocol. As a result, any user could be a potential adversary and jeopardize the security of the system. The architecture of existing cryptocurrencies requires that the system's security and consistency are verified and guaranteed by its users, without relying on trusted third parties. On the one hand, this feature allows the development of transparent systems, where each user can verify the data's consistency. On the other hand, by design, the system's security is guaranteed as long as the majority of users behave honestly. All the most important cryptocurrencies are supported by a consensus mechanism that allows the network to agree on users' transactions validity. This mechanism is based on the resources, usually computational power, that each user offers to the network to guarantee its security. To successfully compromise a cryptocurrency, a malicious user would have to own and use the majority of the total resources available in the system, performing the so-called 51% attack. Consequently, a cryptocurrency is more vulnerable in the early stages of its life cycle, when its community is still young and unstable. In fact, during the first period after its release, a cryptocurrency usually is little known and used, like any other software. In this phase, when the community's size is still limited, an attacker could easily obtain 51% of the resources and use them maliciously, compromising the system's security and consistency. This type of attack does not need to compromise resources or exploit vulnerabilities. Since the consensus mechanism is based on the majority, it is sufficient to join the network with enough resources to make decisions independently, without even violating the protocol. The 51% attack is, therefore, very effective and challenging to detect. However, it is also hard to be performed, especially against cryptocurrencies with extensive, stable, and solid communities, such as Bitcoin and Ethereum. There are several other ways to attack a cryptocurrency, mostly exploiting the vulnerabilities of the individual modules of which they are composed. Cryptocurrencies are software systems consisting of different technologies, each of which plays a different role and allows different functions. For example, the blockchain is used to implement a distributed database that ensures data consistency through consensus among participants. In turn, peer-to-peer networks connect the nodes that make up the system among each other, enabling exchanging messages and data. In addition to their functionalities, all these technologies also introduce their vulnerabilities, increasing the attack surface. Consequently, an attacker could threaten a cryptocurrency not only by directly attacking its protocol. Malicious users could also exploit vulnerabilities or implementation errors in its software components, solve mathematical problems on which the security properties are based, and attack the underlying IT infrastructure.

The impact on a nation's economy of a possible successful attack on a cryptocurrency is highly variable. The assumption about cryptocurrency users' honesty is problematic for many people, who prefer to trust a single external entity, e.g., a bank, rather than half plus one of the other network users. The mistrust of new users towards cryptocurrencies is one of the main reasons this technology struggles to establish itself as a daily payment method, remaining much more used for investments and speculations. There are no nations that strictly depend on a cryptocurrency at the time of writing. This implies that, currently, the national security impacts of an attack against cryptocurrencies would be limited. In fact, the affected users would be companies and small investors scattered worldwide, hardly grouped in a single nation. However, several nations are dreaming about creating a state-sponsored cryptocurrency that can enhance or displace traditional fiat money. In such a scenario, the national currency would be exposed to several new cyber threats, with consequences ranging from short DoS to permanent damages to the national financial infrastructure.

In this sections, we describe some methodologies that could be used to attack cryptocurrencies, divided into two macro-categories: attacks against enabling technologies; and attacks against vulnerabilities in the underlying IT infrastructure layer. Then, we investigate how these attacks could be used to jeopardize the economy of a nation.

2.1   Vulnerabilities of the Technological Pillars

The most important cryptocurrencies, both in terms of users and capitalization, are based on blockchain. Introduced in 2008 by Satoshi Nakamoto, the blockchain is a peer-to-peer network that implements an append-only, immutable, and distributed database. The system's security is verified by its nodes, without resorting to a trusted third party.

In its original form, the blockchain relies on several technological pillars, mostly based on cryptographic functions. The Elliptic Curve Digital Signature Algorithm (ECDSA) is used, for example, to ensure that users can only spend their own funds. Cryptographic puzzles [1], instead, are used to implement the so-called proof-of-work, a consensus mechanism that manages new block's creation and validation. Finally, storing data within an immutable chain is made possible by hash functions that concatenate the ledger's blocks. These cryptographic functions are based on particular mathematical problems, considered difficult to solve by the international scientific community, from whose complexity derives the security of the protocol. In these cases, the attacker who manages to solve the mathematical problem can break the cryptographic protocol. Among the many possible attack strategies, we can identify two very effective methodologies: reducing the complexity of the mathematical problem and using new technologies to solve it efficiently.

Complexity Reduction. The ECDSA algorithm uses the elliptic-curve discrete logarithm problem (ECDLP), a mathematical problem based on the cyclic groups of elliptic curves over finite fields, considered hard to solve. The mathematical properties used in this protocol ensure that, given a public key $pubK$, the computation of the private key pK associated with $pubK$ is infeasible. Cryptocurrencies use ECDSA to secure transactions, allowing each user, identified with a public key, to spend only their own money through the corresponding private key. This system is considered safe because deriving pK from $pubK$ is computationally too expensive for any attacker. Here, "too expensive" means that, regardless of the attacker's capabilities, the computational time spent to break the protocol exceeds the usefulness window of the violated secret. This property has been formally proved valid, as long as certain ECDSA implementation conditions are met. The sufficient conditions, identified in [8], include the following properties:

– the underlying hash function must be collision-resistance and must have the uniformity property
– pseudorandomness in the private keyspace for the ephemeral private key generator
– generic treatment of the underlying group
– a further condition on how the ephemeral public keys are mapped into the private key space.

Nevertheless, at some point, someone could either simplify the problem underlying ECDLP or create a new computational technology capable of finding a solution in a much faster time. In both cases, the opponent would be able to calculate the other users' private keys, thus becoming able to spend their money. Victims would have no opportunity to get back the stolen crypto money, as transactions are irreversible in the blockchain environment. The possibility of anyone reducing the complexity of ECDLP is considered very unlikely. However, it would not be the first time that a mathematical problem, considered difficult for many years, has been solved. Fermat's conjecture, formally known as Fermat's Last Theorem, is a famous example of such an eventuality. This theorem, formulated in 1637, asserts that the equation $x^n + y^n = z^n$ does not admit solutions for integers $n \geq 3$. Although plausibly correct, this conjecture remained unproven for three centuries when in 1994, a British academic, Andrew Wiles, published a formal proof. Just as happened with this conjecture, advances in mathematics or technology could involve solving problems underlying Elliptic-curve cryptography (ECC) or ECDSA, exposing new vulnerabilities able to break the security of current cryptographic protocols.

Other examples of similar eventualities are the "baby-step, giant-step" algorithm, and Pollard's rho method. Although not aiming to decrease the mathematical complexity of the problem, these two algorithms have tried to solve ECDLP using "shortcuts" compared to classical solutions. Nevertheless, although significantly optimizing the resolution of the problem, these algorithms do not yet allow to attack ECDS in a reasonable time, i.e., fast enough to threaten the security of the systems that use this cryptographic protocol. Unfortunately, there is no way to predict if and when further optimization of these algorithms could be discovered and used to compromise cryptographic protocols, leaving tremendous uncertainty about these technologies' future security.

New Technologies. As discussed above, existing cryptocurrencies rely on cryptographic protocols to guarantee the security of the network. These protocols are proven safe against any adversary, regardless of their abilities. However, an attacker with unexpected computational power, not available at the time of cryptographic protocols' design, may be able to take an unfair advantage over other users. An example of such a scenario concerns cryptocurrency mining and the introduction of ad-hoc hardware: the Application-specific integrated circuit (ASIC). Before the advent of ASIC hardware, the computational power made available by users to secure the Bitcoin network came only from generic-purpose hardware. No user had a consistent advantage over the others. With the release of ASIC hardware, specifically designed to optimize mining activities, the Bitcoin network balances have changed. Users who started mining with ASIC have had such a massive advantage in computational power that mining activities with generic hardware has become ineffective and unprofitable. Since this hardware was created to be immediately distributed on the global market, the beneficiaries of this novel technology were numerous. Consequently, the new computational power is widely distributed for users and geographic areas, as depicted in Fig. 1, avoiding its centralization on a single entity.

Conversely, suppose this technology was not intended for the global market. In that case, its developer could have used it to gain a computational advantage over other users, jeopardizing the network's security. Therefore, the large-scale distribution of new computational technologies is essential to avoid problems of stability and security of cryptocurrencies. However, this may not always be possible. In the case of Quantum Computing (QC), for example, the high production costs could slow or prevent its distribution on the global market. As a result, the manufacturing company could be the only one in possession of such computational power, gaining such technological supremacy as to allow it to control current cryptocurrencies. At the time of writing, we are still a long way from

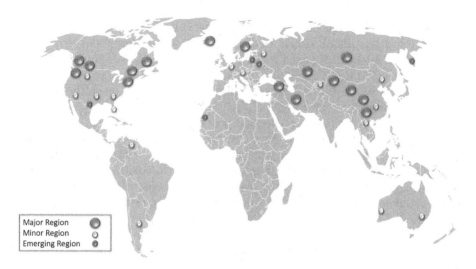

Fig. 1. Global overview of the Bitcoin mining regions. Data sourced from [6]

obtaining a quantum computer capable of endangering current cryptographic protocols. However, research is proceeding rapidly in this area, reaching increasingly important milestones. According to initial results, the incredible computational capabilities of quantum computers promise to perform tasks, infeasible in today's computers, efficiently. An attacker could use this technology to break current cryptographic protocols, seriously endangering systems, such as cryptocurrencies, which base their security on these mechanisms.

2.2 Vulnerabilities of the IT Infrastructure

Another type of attack against cryptocurrencies aims to exploit vulnerabilities in the underlying IT infrastructure, such as software modules or network infrastructure. Vulnerabilities in software modules, such as electronic wallets, blockchain management software, or the transaction validation system, can be exploited to harm individual users or the entire network. The vulnerabilities of the network infrastructure, on the other hand, can be exploited to compromise multiple functions, such as the consensus mechanism, by tampering with messages in order to alter interactions between users.

Software Vulnerabilities. Although the mathematical properties on which ECDSA bases its security have never been compromised, we can cite several examples of attacks that exploited vulnerabilities in its implementation. One of the most sensitive phases of implementing a cryptographic protocol is the choice of the security parameters. In ECDSA, for example, the choice of the elliptic curve and its domain parameters determines the robustness of the encryption keys produced. The scientific community has extensively studied different types of elliptic curves, releasing standard parameters universally accepted as safe when correctly used in the implementation of ECDSA. However, each developer is free not to use the standard parameters, replacing them with other customized versions. Besides, the scientific community has also studied the best practices to be followed during the implementation of ECDSA and other cryptographic algorithms. Some particular parameters, for example, must be chosen randomly at each execution of the protocol. Their static setting could introduce severe weaknesses in the generated encrypted material, as happened to Sony in generating their key pair used to digitally sign video games for their Playstation3 console [35]. They used a static parameter (rather than random) to implement the ECDSA protocol, making the resulting private key computable by analyzing few digitally signed files. This flaw was discovered by a group of hackers, known as *fail0verflow*, who was able to reconstruct Sony's private key and use it to distribute counterfeit video games.

Often, the software implementation of a cryptographic protocol could be vulnerable even if developers diligently follow the best practices suggested by the scientific community. Usually, one of the most significant problems is how to generate random numbers, especially on mobile device platforms, where the available resources are limited. There are several libraries capable of generating pseudo-random numbers. [41] provides an investigation on the most used Java libraries to generate random numbers, evaluating the methodologies used and the quality of the numbers generated. They found multiple flaws on entropy collector components, with different severity and probability of occurrence. In details, they showed that the Android PRNG's overall entropy could be reduced to only 64 bits. This flaw was exploited in 2013 to steal Bitcoin from accounts generated by electronic wallets in the android environment. The Java class SecureRandom, used by unsafe digital wallets, has been identified as the main responsible for the introduced vulnerability, generating collisions on the produced random numbers. The best practices require that the random number used to sign a private key in the ECDSA protocol cannot be reused. If the randomly generated number is used more than once, the private key could be easily computed by an adversary.

Another severe vulnerability discovered in 2011 enables a full key recovery attack against a TLS server that manages authentications with ECDSA signatures. As described in [9], a vulnerability in OpenSSL's implementation allows a timing attack affecting the generation of the encryption keys used for the digital signature.

Network Hijacking. In this type of attack, an adversary maliciously interferes with a cryptocurrency protocol manipulating the network traffic used by honest users to communicate. The attacker can be either an external or an internal user. In the first case, the attacker does not participate directly in the protocol but performs a passive attack. A classic example would be an attacker dropping network packets, preventing specific users from exchanging information with the rest of the network. In the case of an insider, however, the attacker joins the network and participates in the protocol as an honest user, interacting publicly with other nodes. Then, he begins to behave maliciously, sending false information, creating fake transactions, or acting in any other way that does not comply with the protocol.

Several factors influence attacks on the network infrastructure of a cryptocurrency, conditioned by the technologies used by the single protocol. Therefore, cryptocurrencies are not all affected in the same way by this type of threat. Furthermore, the vulnerabilities are often due to external conditions, not managed by the protocol or the technologies used by cryptocurrency, such as the Internet routing infrastructure.

By design, every permissionless cryptocurrency allows anyone to access the network without authentication. To participate in the protocol is sufficient to run a full node, from anywhere in the world, with an active Internet connection. For this reason, how ISPs manage their network directly affects cryptocurrency full nodes' ability to communicate with each other. It is also important to note that, although anyone in the world can join the network, it is very unlikely that the nodes are geographically distributed in a uniform way. As a direct consequence of this, full nodes are likely to be grouped in a few regions, hosted under the infrastructure of a few ISPs, that will be responsible for routing the entire network's traffic. In this scenario, multiple attacks may be carried out, either actively or passively, to threaten the cryptocurrency by targeting the ISP's network infrastructure. We list in the following a few malicious behaviors that may be executed either by an external attacker or by a malicious ISP:

- *Network traffic redirection:* by exploiting vulnerabilities in network protocols, i.e., bgp hijacking.
- *Network traffic filtering:* by maliciously dropping selected packets, causing DoS, i.e., Blackhole attack.
- *Network traffic manipulation:* to isolate specific nodes only, i.e., Eclipse attack.

These malicious operations, known as Internet routing attacks, could be used, alone or together, to carry out the following attacks:

- *Partition attack:* The goal is to split the peer-to-peer network of the targeted cryptocurrency into separate disjointed segments, such that the different sections are no longer able to communicate.
- *Delay attack:* The goal is to postpone the spread of new blocks through the network to enable multiple other attacks, such as double-spending.

All of the attacks listed above can be performed against any cryptocurrency that relies on public internet infrastructure to manage inter-node communications. The motivations behind these attacks, as well as the consequences, could be manifold, while the possible impacts vary according to the victim. For example, a storekeeper could be subject to temporary outbreaks that prevent his activities, as well as more severe issues such as the double-spending attack. If under attack, miners could waste the computational power that they provide to the network to guarantee its safety, facing lost earnings. Finally, a regular user would face DoS attacks that prevent the access and use of the payment services.

3 Stock Market

The majority of existing studies at the intersection of security and economics focused on problems of micro-security – that is, how to enforce security for specific applications and protocols, or how to protect data about users of a given service. This approach is orthogonal to that focusing on macro-security, which concerns with the security and trustworthiness of whole markets and technologies. While the former is of great importance and concern for individual users, the latter is instead primarily of interest for governmental actors and nations themselves, thus falling under the broader information warfare umbrella. This is due to the potentially significant influence that macro-security threats can exert on the national economies. Within the context of economic war, nations regard the economy as a worldwide arena and the latest technological advancements as sharp weapons with which to advance their strategic and political agendas. Here, the vulnerabilities inevitably introduced by such new technologies, such as those that contribute to the rise of fintech, combined with the weak regulatory frameworks, can be profitably exploited by malicious actors. The existence of many ways to directly compromise fintech services, or to tamper with their underlying technologies, means that an opponent nation could use the very same fintech technology as a weapon. Indeed, fintech services can easily become attack vectors that could lead to the compromise of critical economic resources of competing nations. In this regard, we can easily find a plethora of news on alleged state-backed actors and state-sponsored hacking on newspapers and information sites [21].

Among the paramount examples of the systems and technologies that contribute to the rise of fintech, are the national stock markets. Stock markets, or equity markets, are one of the most important economic assets of a nation and a constituent of national free-market economies. They refer to centralized physical or virtual spaces where equities or stocks of publicly held companies, bonds, and other classes of securities, are issued and traded. Given the central and crucial role that stock markets have within the economic processes of a nation, fair and secure operations should be guaranteed at all times. However, while in the early days of physical hectic trading floors this posed somewhat manageable challenges, the security risks introduced by the wide array of technologies that permeate current physical and virtual stock markets have escalated to new – dangerous – heights. Among them, are the risks related to the many different existing forms of market manipulation, aimed at artificially inflating or deflating the value of given traded securities. When targeted at country-relevant stocks or nation-critical firms, these forms of market manipulation are capable of endangering a whole national economy. Then, new rapidly-evolving technologies such as automatic trading (AT) and high-frequency trading (HFT) are responsible for a progressively larger share of market transactions. Their role within catastrophic flash crashes and their effects on market stability are still debated, so as their contribution to stock market security concerns. Finally, the recent COVID-19 pandemic sped up the ongoing virtualization and "remotization" of trading floors and stock markets. With always less manual intervention in favor of remote software-mediated operations, a new wave of security threats needs to be addressed.

In the remainder of this section, we investigate the different ways in which fintech and the stock market can be weaponized to attack a nation's economic assets, describing the current state-of-the-art with regards to both attacking and defensive means.

3.1   Market Manipulation Threat

The new market manipulation methodologies share the same objectives as their traditional techniques. However, efficiency has improved dramatically as new manipulation methodologies leverage the latest technological advances and operate in a different, faster, and highly interconnected digital market [57]. There are different forms of market manipulation. Some of these aim at marginal, low-value stocks, while the more aggressive aim to hit the heart of the financial market. These latest forms of manipulation have the potential to create massive shocks in national and global markets, making such activities a primary national security concern for any country.

Previous studies on this subject classified manipulations into two main categories: (i) information-based, and (ii) trade-based. Information-based manipulation consists of distributing false information or publishing fake news to have a specific effect on the stock markets. On the contrary, trade-based manipulation is based solely on shares' movement, without involving other publicly observable information such as disseminating fake news [57]. Some of these manipulation techniques have always existed. However, in recent years, they have become increasingly widespread, effective, and indistinguishable from legitimate actions, thanks to the recent technological progress.

Information-Based Manipulation. Traditionally, stock market forecasts were obtained by exploiting historical stock market data, for instance, by training statistical autoregressive models. In recent times, however, it has become clear that also other types of information could be used to predict future market trends. A new quest thus began to discover and exploit other informative data sources. Among them, textual data from official news outlets and spontaneous user posts in online social platforms showed great potential and predictive power [44]. For instance, news articles from Yahoo Finance are leveraged by the system proposed in [50] to predict future prices of S&P 500 stocks. As another example, asset volatility movements are predicted in [2] by processing information extracted from several news sources. The work in [25] applied text-based event detection to identify noteworthy events. Such events are then fed to deep convolutional neural networks to model both short-term and long-term influences of events on stock price movements. For what concerns data extracted from online social networks, it has been shown that the sentiment polarity of user posts holds great predictive power for forecasting movements in financial markets [7,54]. The system described in [11] is a notable example of this body of work, where authors trained a machine learning classifier capable of predicting the next day trend of certain stocks by only exploiting the sentiment value of stock-related tweets. In a similar fashion, opening and closing prices are predicted in [49] by leveraging sentiment analysis of social media posts. In addition to the mere textual data, also other types of data extracted from online social networks can be profitably used for market prediction. For instance, in [34] authors developed methods for market prediction and for portfolio selection by leveraging correlations between companies that co-occur in social media posts. Co-occurring companies are modeled via large networks of companies and results are obtained by the application of graph mining techniques.

All the previous examples highlight the growing importance of alternative online data sources for stock market prediction. However, serious concerns arise if we consider the possibility and the ease with which online data can be tampered with, manipulated and even outright fabricated [17]. Thus, on the one hand, many systems for monitoring and predicting stock markets are now heavily based on the analysis of online data. On the other hand, however, a significant share of such online data turns out to be fake, inaccurate and misleading, thus possibly leading such systems astray. Should this risk materialize, consequences in terms of market crashes and widespread financial losses would be dramatic, as it already happened in a few notable cases [27]. In recent years, this risk motivated an emerging stream of research on online financial disinformation, which already led to interesting – yet worrying – findings. Among the most striking results, is the detection and investigation of an online manipulation campaign carried out on the Twitter microblogging platform [16,17]. In detail, the authors analyzed some 9 million tweets mentioning 30,032 different companies traded in the main US financial markets (e.g., NASDAQ, NYSE, NYSEARCA, NYSEMKT, OTCMKTS). Within this dataset, they found suspicious co-occurrences between a few stocks with very high market capitalization and many unpopular stocks with very low capitalization. By applying state-of-the-art bot detection techniques [15], the study found that more than 70% of all users that tweeted about the low-capitalized stocks, were in fact bots – namely, automated accounts used for large-scale spamming [14]. Going forward, a subsequent study also analyzed the characteristics of such financial bots, concluding that their goal was that of luring automatic trading algorithms into buying the low-value stocks by exploiting the popularity of high-value ones [52]. The need for evaluating the credibility of stock-related social media messages is also underlined in [26]. These findings currently represent the first large-scale, empirical evidence of widespread financial spam in online social networks.

Currently, no system exists that is specifically designed for detecting online financial spam and financial manipulation campaigns. In fact, the more generic problem of detecting online information manipulation is already very challenging, with few existing solutions that demonstrated decent performance. As such, at the time of writing, protection against online financial disinformation must necessarily rely on techniques for defending against generic information manipulation. Successful disinformation campaigns are those that manage to reach and influence a large number of users. To achieve this goal, perpetrators typically leverage large numbers of automated (i.e., bot) or paid (i.e., troll) accounts, in order to reshare and broadcast their malicious messages [14]. Based on this consideration, a first line of defense against information-based market manipulation revolves around the application of bot and troll detection techniques. A recent survey on the topic highlighted that, among the plethora of existing approaches for detecting malicious accounts, those that are based on unsupervised approaches for the analysis of suspicious behavioral similarities are the ones that manage to obtain the best detection performance [14]. Examples of this kind are [12,15,33,38,39]. This is in contrast to earlier approaches based on the application of supervised classifiers that analyze each account individually. The survey in [14] also underlined the importance of accounting for adversaries, motivated in evading detection systems, by design. This can be obtained by designing detection systems that leverage recent advances in adversarial machine learning, such as in [55], or anyway by adopting adversarial approaches to the study and detection of malicious accounts, as done in [18,19]. Another emerging and promising direction of research is aiming to detect so-called coordinated inauthentic behavior (CIB). Also, in this line of research, the focus is posed on coordinated accounts. However, when studying CIB the nature of individual accounts (e.g., whether they are human- or software-operated accounts, bots, trolls, etc.) is not of interest anymore and the only dimensions that are deemed meaningful are coordination and authenticity of the online personas and of the content they share [46,48]. Finally, yet other approaches to contrast online information manipulation are related to the computational detection of fake news and propaganda at scale [20,58].

Trade-Based Manipulation. In contrast to information-based manipulation, trade-based manipulation attempts are exclusively based on buying and selling shares, without requiring to share false or misleading information. These types of market manipulation are as old as the markets themselves. However, they recently regained widespread attention as a consequence of the rise of new technologies. In fact, while the vast majority of long-established stock markets enforce strict regulations for avoiding trade-based manipulations, some of the newest and less regulated exchanges provide fertile ground for such nefarious practices to proliferate once again. Among the newest and less regulated exchanges are cryptocurrency exchanges [47]. In addition to the widespread adoption of, and demand for, cryptocurrencies, also other relatively new technologies facilitated the furious comeback of trade-based market manipulations. As in the case of disinformation campaigns, also trade-based manipulations necessitate large numbers of (aware or unaware) participants to be involved, in order to achieve substantial results. As such, online social networking platforms – characterized by the sheer number of users and by the large support for anonymity – again represent a profitable avenue for manipulators. This is the reason why several scholars recently devoted significant efforts towards the study of online cryptocurrency manipulations [47].

Among the most widespread and potentially detrimental trade-based market frauds, are pump-and-dump schemes and Ponzi schemes. Specifically, pump-and-dump involves the artificial inflation of the price of an owned stock, with the goal of selling it at a higher price. The perpetrators of this fraud typically buy low-value coins way before the scheme takes place. Then, they lure other willing participants and unaware investors into buying the stock, thus causing a surge in price. In turn, this surge inevitably attracts other investors thus raising the price even more. When the price reaches a given target value, the initial participants simultaneously sell. Shortly after, the other aware participants sell as well, thus starting a price collapse. In a matter of minutes the prices plummets, reaching values that are way lower than the initial ones. As a result, a few organizers and early participants manage to obtain large gains, while the vast majority of other aware and unaware investors suffer severe losses. When planning pump-and-dump schemes, orchestrators typically target small, thinly-traded coins, since it is easier to manipulate princes when there is little or no independent information available about the security, or little activity anyway. Based on the above description, attracting many investors is instrumental for successfully orchestrating a pump-and-dump scheme. Traditionally, unaware participants were lured by using spam e-mails, fake press releases and via telemarketing from "boiler room" brokerage houses. However, in more recent times, online financial discussion boards, social networks and messaging apps are the media of choice for attracting participants.

Given the pivotal role of social media in trade-based frauds, a growing number of studies focus on characterizing online social media discussions about cryptocurrencies with the aim to uncover possible manipulations. Among such studies is [29], which investigated Reddit discussions about the Bitcoin, Ethereum, and Monero coins. Authors found that Monero, in particular, is often used for shady or illicit activities. Interestingly, they also measured longer and wider information cascades for Monero, with respect to those of the other coins, showing that many of the users interested in cryptocurrencies are actually interested in coin manipulations [29]. Instead of focusing on a specific platform or set of coins, the work in [47] adopts the first large-scale and context-agnostic approach to investigate online cryptocurrency manipulations. In detail, authors collected a large multi-platform dataset including conversations about a multitude of coins from Twitter, Telegram and Discord, including both genuine cryptocurrency discussions as well as those about cryptocurrency frauds. The large-scale analysis managed to uncover a large number of previously unknown Telegram channels and groups, some of which were invite-only, specifically dedicated to organizing and coordinating pump-and-dump schemes. Contrarily, Discord appeared as a relatively safe platform, for what concerns cryptocurrencies. The study in [47] also allowed to detect hundreds of automated Twitter accounts that are used for advertising ongoing pump-and-dump operations, thus luring unaware investors into the fraud. In addition to the previous studies, a few other works specifically focused on an online platform or coin. As an example, the work in [56] focused on Telegram pump-and-dump schemes, by providing a detailed account of how such frauds unfold on the platform. As a by-product of their analysis, the authors also developed a simple machine learning classifier for predicting the likelihood of a coin being the target for manipulation. Then, they tested a simple trading strategy that invests in coins with a high likelihood of being pumped in the near future. Notably, their results showed that the simple trading strategy allowed to obtain a return as high as 60% over the course of two and a half months. Adding to the observational studies previously summarized, the work in [42] proposed a first inferential analysis. In particular, authors built and leveraged a Telegram pump-and-dump dataset to train machine learning models for solving a number of tasks. The first task that they experimented with aimed at detecting pump-and-dump scams as they unfold, based on the sequence of messages shared in a Telegram group/channel. Then, they also developed a model for estimating the likelihood of a given pump-and-dump attempt to succeed. Within this context, a pump-and-dump is considered successful if the pumped coin manages to reach the target price set by the organizers. As a final result, they also investigated the presence and role of Twitter bots in cryptocurrency-related discussions. Their results confirm earlier findings in [47], showing a large prevalence of bots during coin pumping operations.

Among the other forms of trade-based market manipulation, also Ponzi schemes received scholarly attention. Ponzi schemes – named after the infamous swindler that orchestrated the first of these scams – are investment plans that promise extremely high rates of return in very limited time. In reality, however, participants' money is not invested, but instead it is used to provide returns for earlier backers. Similar to other pyramid investment schemes, in order to be sustainable, also this scheme necessitates a constantly growing inflow of money, to be obtained from an equally growing number of participants. As such, Ponzi schemes eventually bottom out and unravel when the flow of new investors isn't enough to sustain the scam. Based on the aforementioned functioning of this manipulation, perpetrators typically devote all of their efforts to attracting new participants. As in the case of pump-and-dump schemes, social media allow scaling the recruitment of new participants to Ponzi schemes to a whole new level. The study in [47] investigated the presence of Ponzi schemes in Twitter, Telegram and Discord discussions. Authors found no evidence of users involved in Ponzi schemes on Discord. However, they found tens of Telegram channels and groups specifically devoted to these scams. A peculiarity of these channels and groups was that they all pointed towards one another. In fact, every of such channels contained links for joining channels and groups related to other Ponzi schemes. While, on the one hand, this makes it easier for the orchestrators to recruit new investors via mutual advertisement, it also allows to trace back and identify the majority of channels involved in this manipulative practice, with relative ease [47]. Ponzi schemes have also been investigated within the Bitcointalk online discussion board [53]. Authors leveraged techniques for survival analysis with the goal of identifying the key factors that determine the success of Ponzi schemes. Others also proposed a machine learning classifier for detecting such schemes, by analyzing features derived from the Bitcoin blockchain [4].

3.2   Double-Edged Technologies

One fundamental dimension of technological advancement in fintech is undoubt-edly represented by *speed*. Today, market transactions are issued and resolved in a matter of microseconds and at unprecedented volumes, thanks to High-Frequency Trading (HFT) and Automatic Trading (AT). AT identifies trading systems that leverage software algorithms to automatically determine orders to issue, modify or withdraw, with limited or no human intervention. HFT rep-resents a specialization of AT that also introduces dedicated infrastructures to minimize network and computation latencies by leveraging specific facilities such as co-location, proximity hosting, high-speed direct electronic access and high-performance computing [43]. By exploiting these advanced technological means, HFT is capable of monitoring prices and transactions across many dif-ferent global markets at the same time. In addition, it also allows to establish and liquidate positions in very short time-frames, based on such aforementioned real-time market conditions. HFT is thus regarded as an advanced technology capable of opening up new trading possibilities for its adopters, by benefiting from lightning-fast analyses and transactions with respect to the slower tradi-tional traders. These unprecedented capabilities result in the possibility to take advantage even from minor price differences. As a result, high-frequency traders frequently benefit more from a large number of minor transactions than from a few particularly significant ones, as manual traders do [43].

The Role of HFT Under "Stable" and "Critical" Market Conditions.
In light of the disruptive changes introduced by HFT and its sometimes shady uses (e.g., arbitrage, front-running), a large body of work investigated the role and effects of AT and HFT on stock markets. One notable finding emerging from the analysis of the existing literature is that the vast majority of existing studies reported overall positive market effects for the adoption of HFT in stable mar-kets (i.e., when markets are not undergoing a crisis or crash). In detail, it has been documented that HFT contributes to the reduction of information asym-metry between buyers and sellers. Some studies also empirically verified that HFT contributes to market liquidity and to shrink intraday price volatility [21]. Other examples also provided evidence that HFT may contribute to stabilize markets [32], to improve market quality by reducing the bid-ask gap [31], and to reduce trading costs [40]. In summary, all these results hint at the possibility that HFT plays a relevant beneficial and stabilizing role for markets, when these oper-ate in stable conditions. In turn, this finding suggests that regulatory measures designed for hampering the activities of high-frequency traders could in fact lead to negative market consequences, especially in terms of market liquidity [43].

The previous positive results are all related to the adoption of HFT in mar-kets that operate under "normal" conditions. However, opposite results were obtained when analyzing markets during distressed times, as for example in the case of flash crashes. Starting from the infamous 2010 Flash Crash, several studies documented a negative role of HFT in initiating and amplifying mar-ket crashes [13]. To this end, some authors found evidence that HFT tends to exacerbate transient price impacts that are unrelated to fundamentals – a situation that is typically observed during a flash market crash [5]. The key message emerging from the still-growing body of work that examined the role of HFT in distressed markets, is that it acts as a catalyst for existing market dynamics, including bubbles and crashes. The growing interdependencies between disparate financial instruments are likely to lead to even more frequent and complex market crashes in the future. In this rapidly evolving scenario, the technological arms race that is peculiar of AT and HFT could favor the emergence of catastrophic market crashes [51].

Technological Bias and Monopoly. In the previous sections, we highlighted the role played by HFT in generating market crashes. We also addressed the powerful connection between HFT and its underlying technologies, which determines its unprecedented speed and performance. Worryingly, the combination of HFT technology and flash crash opens up new scenarios that give state actors the possibility to carry out market manipulation to strengthen their economy or weaken enemy nations. If the best performing and faster technologies are widely available and almost evenly distributed across all actors in a financial market, no single agent could hold a significant advantage over the others. Nevertheless, a specific entity could obtain a substantial and illegitimate advantage if it succeeds in developing or acquiring a much more efficient technology than those owned by the opponents. The main open problem regarding the possible weaponization of HFT for information warfare is thus related to technological bias and monopoly. Technological bias can be defined as the asymmetry or imbalance in the technology that is available to different economic actors operating within a system. The technology level has never been perfectly balanced between the various players in the stock market. However, if the technological capabilities are too unbalanced, the repercussions on the financial markets can quickly become critical. If the technological asymmetry widens to the point of leading to a technical monopoly, the involved entity could even find itself able to lead the market.

To the best of our knowledge, up to now, nobody has exploited the technological bias in HFT to put on attacks against the national economies and assets. Furthermore, although despite the importance it holds and continues to gain, technological bias failed to attract the interest of the academic world. However, it managed to draw attention from other stakeholders, often directly exposed to the dynamics of the market, including market traders and the state decision-makers. To give an example, the so-called "slow traders" have been avoiding markets that are polluted by high-frequency traders, since they would be overwhelmed. To help slow traders to avoid HFT, numerous finance professionals are continuously debating about changing the structure of the market. As a result, some famous firms are currently basing their business on providing this kind of information, for instance, by developing big data and deep learning platforms that provide daily estimates of aggressive high-frequency traders across different markets.

In addition to HFT, other areas of fintech reported the negative effects of technological bias. For example, we already covered the noteworthy case of ASIC hardware for cryptocurrency mining in Sect. 2.1. In addition, also the improvements that Artificial Intelligence and, more specifically, Deep Learning are bringing to the market forecasting are often considered as another potential factor for technological bias. The application of these powerful techniques may also create several challenges for the efficiency of the market, together with information asymmetry and irrationality of decision-making. The technological division that is thus taking shape can be leveraged by skilled traders for netting excess returns, at the expense of traders who are used to adopting more traditional technologies [28]. In the same paper, the author reports the results for Forex tradings, in contrast with the efficient-market hypothesis. According to the study, the progressive enhancement in computational software and methods will improve the trading strategies of the individual, with the obvious consequence that some traders will be more successful than others, contradicting the classical definition of a market with perfect competition. Nonetheless, it adheres to the adaptive-market hypothesis [37] that sees the market as fiercely competitive ecosystems rather than efficient ones. Given the changes the market undergoes over time, numerous adaptation mistakes can occur, mostly consequence of the different degrees of adaptation of the participants. As a result, more significant returns are obtained by some of them when compared with the others. In this scenario, technological innovation represents a primary driver for change in the ecology of the market [28].

The considerations above apply for direct harms – e.g., immediate financial loss due to both automatic and high-frequency trading, but indirect consequences, for example the diminished confidence in financial markets, are also raising a lot of attention, potentially having a bigger (and worse) impact. Other than changing those who can be harmed by trading, high-frequency trading changed how they might be harmed, and the scale of the harm [22]. Accordingly, the loss of confidence derived from failures and systemic crashes may curtail the investors' appetite for risk, thus resulting in slower (or worse, stalling) economic growth [22]. To support this hypothesis, the authors took into account the Knight Capital Group case. The firm lost $440 million in less than 30 min on August 1st, 2012, because of its new automatic trading software. This software flooded the market with orders thus forcing the temporary closing of the New York Stock Exchange. The harm caused to both the firm itself and its shareholders was tragic and almost led to bankruptcy, other than having a huge indirect impact on both the investing public's confidence and in the structure of financial markets.

Possible countermeasures to the previous issues are still under discussion, and existing proposals are coming primarily from the regulatory and ethics communities. Both computer scientists and engineers seem not to work on possible countermeasures, thus motivating the fact that technical papers discussing security issues of high-frequency trading are lacking. Taking into account regulations, some of the proposed solutions have the goal of de-powering high-frequency trading by changing the way markets evade pending orders. Some have argued that the priority rules determining the sequence of execution of the orders that have been submitted are designed to give priority to speed. However, the regulatory conundrum is whether the time-price priority disproportionately rewards high-frequency traders and leads to risky over-investments in the technology arms race [3]. The main benefit of the currently adopted priority rules is the fair treatment of every order. Nonetheless, other priority rules have been proposed. To make an example, a rule allows every order at a price to get a partial execution, regardless of the time [36]. Others have proposed to replace the continuous trading model with periodic auctions, which can be devised to both minimize the speed advantage and mitigate other negative outcomes coming from continuous trading (e.g., manipulative strategies) [10]. As the primary benefit, the adoption of periodic auctions would allow to reduce the trading speed and to eliminate the arms race for speed. Several markets may already boast auctions at the open and close times, and are considering the introduction of midday auctions, besides the continuous trading segment [36].

Apart from the previous countermeasures, some politicians hinted at the opportunity to introduce other initiatives. To make an example, Hillary Clinton suggested introducing a small tax on the cancellation orders, with the aim of trying to crush the practice of spoofing[3]. The introduction of taxes to financial transactions, however, would face enormous difficulties, also due to the undesirable consequences and the potential risks that such an action may cause [30]. Conversely, specific taxes aiming at thwarting high-frequency trading are seen as a more sensible and desirable possibility, although being difficult to implement [36].

3.3 Threatening Availability

Stock markets prove to be determining players in the modern economy panorama, allowing easy accesses and allocations of capital to the citizens and supporting the stabilization of security prices. A multitude of financial services is offered by stock markets, which can be seen as their hub. For this reason, denying or even only limiting access to these services may have dreadful impacts on the national economy. Even individual citizens, in case of interruption of the service, are immediately affected. An example is given by the widespread panic reaction caused by the suggestion of the possibility of a market holiday in the United States, as well as by the suspended trading in other countries. As with cryptocurrencies, the physical to the virtual transition of the stock market is also critical and introduces a series of security challenges that need to be addressed. Being the stock market fully-online, the first concern that comes into mind is related to its availability.

Denial of Service (DoS) attacks are among the most common types of cyberattacks that aim at limiting the availability of a resource to users. These attacks

---

[3] https://www.cnbc.com/2016/07/22/hillary-clintons-financial-transaction-tax-why-it-may-not-work.html.

are carried out by malicious actors by overwhelming the target resource with fictitious requests, thus preventing some (or worse, all) legitimate requests to be satisfied. When the Denial of Service attack is carried out in a distributed fashion (i.e., the incoming traffic flooding the victim is originated by many sources), it takes the name of Distributed Denial of Service (DDoS). With respect to DoS attacks, DDoS attacks are more difficult to defend against, since there is a multitude of machines to defend against, rather than a single one.

Denial of Service. Denial of Service, as well as Distributed Denial of Service attacks, are usually perpetrated for profit (i.e., ransom to get the service availability back), for obtaining advantage on a competitor, or for ideological reasons. However, there have been cases in which state actors are involved in DDoS attacks for both political and economic reasons. An example is given by the DDoS attack on Estonia in 2007, targeting government services, financial institutions, and media outlets. The impact was devastating, since Estonia was an early adopter of e-government and was almost paperless at the time, enough to have needed to hold the national elections online. For many, this attack is considered to be the first case of cyber warfare in response to the political conflicts between Russia and Estonia, with the former suspected to be the perpetrator[4]. A more recent example involves the 2019 Hong Kong protests against China. During the conflict, the notorious instant messaging app Telegram suffered a large scale DDoS attack, with the aim of preventing protesters from coordinating their efforts. Detailed investigations by Telegram made it possible to understand the origin of the attack, that seems to be carried out by a State-sized actor via IP addresses originating from China[5].

The aforementioned examples show how state actors have the opportunity to weaponize cyber attacks with the aim of satisfying their economic and political goals. Although, until now, no records of state-driven attacks against national stock markets exist, partly due to their physical component, with the gradual dehumanization of stock markets this scenario might promptly change. Considering the sensitivity of the markets to uncertainty, the trading interruption, even for a limited period of time, could cause a sharp fall in stock prices. The online components of stock markets, as well as the ones of other financial institutions (e.g., online banks), among other things, are not new to attacks aimed at undermining their availability, carried out both by hackers and fraudsters.

In 2013, the International Organization of Securities Commissions (IOSCO) published a report with a survey of 46 stock exchanges [45], detailing that more than half of them had already been victims of Denial of Service cyberattacks that year. Most of the attacks considered did not have effects on the functioning of the market itself and caused only less than $1 million costs for the targeted market. A couple of attacks that are worth mentioning are the one against the NASDAQ, NYSE, and BATS stock exchanges in the United States and the one against the

---

[4] https://www.cloudflare.com/learning/ddos/famous-ddos-attacks/.

[5] https://www.pcmag.com/news/chinese-ddos-attack-hits-telegram-during-hong-ko-ng-protests.

Hong Kong Stock Exchange, which overwhelmed its website and heavily affected its ability to both publish filings and display prices. Furthermore, an attacker may have the opportunity to preemptively buy (or sell) shares on a market with the aim of increasing (lowering) the value of the manipulated shares, thus obtaining an immediate biased profit from its move. This is possible to achieve by either targeting a specific company, thus shaping the price of its stocks, or by targeting a specific market, thus causing a flash crash, with potentially nefarious repercussions on whole national stock markets.

4   Conclusion

Economy is among the most important dimensions affected by information warfare, since nations and other state-actors are increasingly interested in exploiting economic leverages to pursue their strategic goals. In this work, we discussed and surveyed the scientific frontier of economic information warfare, specifically focusing on two fundamental technologies – cryptocurrencies and stock markets – that are particularly affected by emerging security threats. Each of the cited topic currently represents a salient along the vast scientific frontier of economic information warfare. For each technology, we highlighted the current state-of-the-art concerning existing and future attacks as well as the possible countermeasures to contrast them. In detail, we discussed threats to cryptocurrencies both with respect to their mathematical and technological foundations (e.g., attempts at breaking elliptic-curve cryptography) as well as their underlying IT infrastructure (e.g., software vulnerabilities and network hijacking). For what concerns stock markets, we discussed the main tools for market manipulation, either information- or trade-based. In addition, we also investigated the new threats introduced by the rise of high-frequency trading (HFT) and by remote stock markets. Finally, we also highlighted some promising directions that can contribute to safeguarding our critical economic systems from the growing threats of information warfare.

References

1. Ali, I.M., Caprolu, M., Di Pietro, R.: Foundations, properties, and security applications of puzzles: a survey. ACM Comput. Surv. (CSUR) **53**(4), 1–38 (2020)
2. Atkins, A., Niranjan, M., Gerding, E.: Financial news predicts stock market volatility better than close price. J. Fin. Data Sci. **4**(2), 120–137 (2018)
3. Baron, M., Brogaard, J., Hagströmer, B., Kirilenko, A.: Risk and return in high-frequency trading. J. Fin. Quant. Anal. **54**(3), 993–1024 (2019)
4. Bartoletti, M., Pes, B., Serusi, S.: Data mining for detecting bitcoin Ponzi schemes. In: The 1st Crypto Valley Conference on Blockchain Technology (CVCBT 2018), pp. 75–84. IEEE (2018)
5. Bellia, M., Christensen, K., Kolokolov, A., Pelizzon, L., Renò, R.: High-frequency trading during flash crashes: walk of fame or hall of shame? SAFE Working Paper (2020)

6. Bendiksen, C., Gibbons, S.: The bitcoin mining network - trends, composition, average creation cost, electricity consumption & sources. CoinShares Research, Whitepaper, December 2019
7. Bollen, J., Mao, H., Zeng, X.: Twitter mood predicts the stock market. J. Comput. Sci. **2**(1), 1–8 (2011)
8. Brown, D.R.: Generic groups, collision resistance, and ECDSA. Des. Codes Crypt. **35**(1), 119–152 (2005)
9. Brumley, B.B., Tuveri, N.: Remote timing attacks are still practical. In: Atluri, V., Diaz, C. (eds.) ESORICS 2011. LNCS, vol. 6879, pp. 355–371. Springer, Heidelberg (2011). https://doi.org/10.1007/978-3-642-23822-2_20
10. Budish, E., Cramton, P., Shim, J.: The high-frequency trading arms race: frequent batch auctions as a market design response. Q. J. Econ. **130**(4), 1547–1621 (2015)
11. Bujari, A., Furini, M., Laina, N.: On using cashtags to predict companies stock trends. In: Proceedings of the 14th IEEE Annual Consumer Communications & Networking Conference (CCNC 2017), pp. 25–28. IEEE (2017)
12. Chavoshi, N., Hamooni, H., Mueen, A.: DeBot: Twitter bot detection via warped correlation. In: The 16th International Conference on Data Mining (ICDM 2016), pp. 817–822. IEEE (2016)
13. Chesterman, S.: 'Move fast and break things': law, technology, and the problem of speed. NUS Law Working Paper (2020)
14. Cresci, S.: A decade of social bot detection. Commun. ACM **63**(10), 72–83 (2020)
15. Cresci, S., Di Pietro, R., Petrocchi, M., Spognardi, A., Tesconi, M.: Social finger-printing: detection of spambot groups through DNA-inspired behavioral modeling. IEEE Trans. Dependable Secure Comput. **15**(4), 561–576 (2017)
16. Cresci, S., Lillo, F., Regoli, D., Tardelli, S., Tesconi, M.: $FAKE: evidence of spam and bot activity in stock microblogs on Twitter. In: The 12th International AAAI Conference on Web and Social Media (ICWSM 2018), pp. 580–583. AAAI (2018)
17. Cresci, S., Lillo, F., Regoli, D., Tardelli, S., Tesconi, M.: Cashtag piggybacking: uncovering spam and bot activity in stock microblogs on twitter. ACM Trans. Web (TWEB) **13**(2), 1–27 (2019)
18. Cresci, S., Petrocchi, M., Spognardi, A., Tognazzi, S.: From reaction to proaction: Unexplored ways to the detection of evolving spambots. In: Companion Proceedings of the Web Conference 2018 (WWW 2018), pp. 1469–1470 (2018)
19. Cresci, S., Petrocchi, M., Spognardi, A., Tognazzi, S.: Better safe than sorry: an adversarial approach to improve social bot detection. In: The 11th ACM Conference on Web Science (WebSci 2019), pp. 47–56 (2019)
20. Da San Martino, G., Cresci, S., Barrón-Cedeño, A., Yu, S., Di Pietro, R., Nakov, P.: A survey on computational propaganda detection. In: The 29th International Joint Conference on Artificial Intelligence (IJCAI 2020), pp. 4826–4832 (2020)
21. Das, S.R.: The future of fintech. Financ. Manage. **48**(4), 981–1007 (2019)
22. Davis, M., Kumiega, A., Van Vliet, B.: Ethics, finance, and automation: a preliminary survey of problems in high frequency trading. Sci. Eng. Ethics **19**(3), 851–874 (2013)
23. Di Pietro, R., Caprolu, M., Raponi, S.: Next generation information warfare: rationales, scenarios, threats, and open issues. In: Mori, P., Furnell, S., Camp, O. (eds.) ICISSP 2019. CCIS, vol. 1221, pp. 24–47. Springer, Cham (2020). https://doi.org/10.1007/978-3-030-49443-8_2
24. Di Pietro, R., Raponi, S., Caprolu, M., Cresci, S.: New Dimensions of Information Warfare, pp. 1–4. Springer, Cham (2021). https://doi.org/10.1007/978-3-030-60618-3_1

25. Ding, X., Zhang, Y., Liu, T., Duan, J.: Deep learning for event-driven stock prediction. In: The 24th International Joint Conference on Artificial Intelligence (IJCAI 2015) (2015)
26. Evans, L., Owda, M., Crockett, K., Vilas, A.F.: Credibility assessment of financial stock tweets. Expert Syst. Appl. **168**, 114351 (2020)
27. Ferrara, E.: Manipulation and abuse on social media. ACM SIGWEB Newsl. (Spring), 1–9 (2015)
28. Galeshchuk, S.: Technological bias at the exchange rate market. Intell. Syst. Account. Fin. Manage. **24**(2–3), 80–86 (2017)
29. Glenski, M., Saldanha, E., Volkova, S.: Characterizing speed and scale of cryptocurrency discussion spread on reddit. In: The 28th International Conference on World Wide Web (WWW 2019), pp. 560–570 (2019)
30. Grahl, J., Lysandrou, P.: The European commission's proposal for a financial transactions tax: a critical assessment. JCMS J. Common Market Stud. **52**(2), 234–249 (2014)
31. Hasbrouck, J., Saar, G.: Low-latency trading. J. Financial Mark. **16**(4), 646–679 (2013)
32. Hendershott, T., Riordan, R.: Algorithmic trading and the market for liquidity. J. Financial Quant. Anal. **48**(4), 1001–1024 (2013)
33. Jiang, M., Cui, P., Beutel, A., Faloutsos, C., Yang, S.: Inferring lockstep behavior from connectivity pattern in large graphs. Knowl. Inf. Syst. **48**(2), 399–428 (2016)
34. Kharratzadeh, M., Coates, M.: Weblog analysis for predicting correlations in stock price evolutions. In: The 6th International Conference on Web and Social Media (ICWSM 2012). AAAI (2012)
35. Kushner, D.: Sony vs. the hackers. IEEE Spectr. **48**(5), 16 (2011)
36. Linton, O., Mahmoodzadeh, S.: Implications of high-frequency trading for security markets. Ann. Rev. Econ. **10**, 237–259 (2018)
37. Lo, A.W.: The adaptive markets hypothesis. J. Portfolio Manage. **30**(5), 15–29 (2004)
38. Mazza, M., Cresci, S., Avvenuti, M., Quattrociocchi, W., Tesconi, M.: RTbust: exploiting temporal patterns for botnet detection on twitter. In: The 11th International Conference on Web Science (WebSci 2019), pp. 183–192. ACM (2019)
39. Mendoza, M., Tesconi, M., Cresci, S.: Bots in social and interaction networks: detection and impact estimation. ACM Trans. Inf. Syst. (TOIS) **39**(1), 1–32 (2020)
40. Menkveld, A.J.: High frequency trading and the new market makers. J. Financial Mark. **16**(4), 712–740 (2013)
41. Michaelis, K., Meyer, C., Schwenk, J.: Randomly failed! the state of randomness in current java implementations. In: Dawson, E. (ed.) CT-RSA 2013. LNCS, vol. 7779, pp. 129–144. Springer, Heidelberg (2013). https://doi.org/10.1007/978-3-642-36095-4_9
42. Mirtaheri, M., Abu-El-Haija, S., Morstatter, F., Steeg, G.V., Galstyan, A.: Identifying and analyzing cryptocurrency manipulations in social media. arXiv preprint arXiv:1902.03110 (2019)
43. Monaco, E.: What FinTech can learn from high-frequency trading: economic consequences, open issues and future of corporate disclosure. In: Lynn, T., Mooney, J.G., Rosati, P., Cummins, M. (eds.) Disrupting Finance. PSDBET, pp. 51–70. Springer, Cham (2019). https://doi.org/10.1007/978-3-030-02330-0_4
44. Nassirtoussi, A.K., Aghabozorgi, S., Wah, T.Y., Ngo, D.C.L.: Text mining for market prediction: a systematic review. Expert Syst. Appl. **41**(16), 7653–7670 (2014)
45. Neyret, A.: Stock market cybercrime. Technical report, Autorité des Marchés Financiers (AMF) (2020)

46. Nizzoli, L., Tardelli, S., Avvenuti, M., Cresci, S., Tesconi, M.: Coordinated behavior on social media in 2019 UK general election. arXiv preprint arXiv:2008.08370 (2020)
47. Nizzoli, L., Tardelli, S., Avvenuti, M., Cresci, S., Tesconi, M., Ferrara, E.: Charting the landscape of online cryptocurrency manipulation. IEEE Access **8**, 113230–113245 (2020)
48. Pacheco, D., Hui, P.M., Torres-Lugo, C., Truong, B.T., Flammini, A., Menczer, F.: Uncovering coordinated networks on social media. arXiv preprint arXiv:2001.05658 (2020)
49. Rajesh, N., Gandy, L.: CashTagNN: using sentiment of tweets with CashTags to predict stock market prices. In: The 11th International Conference on Intelligent Systems: Theories and Applications (SITA 2016), pp. 1–4. IEEE (2016)
50. Schumaker, R.P., Chen, H.: Textual analysis of stock market prediction using breaking financial news: the AZFin text system. ACM Trans. Inf. Syst. (TOIS) **27**(2), 1–19 (2009)
51. Sornette, D., von der Becke, S.: Crashes and high frequency trading: an evaluation of risks posed by high-speed algorithmic trading. The Future of Computer Trading in Financial Markets (2011)
52. Tardelli, S., Avvenuti, M., Tesconi, M., Cresci, S.: Characterizing social bots spreading financial disinformation. In: Meiselwitz, G. (ed.) HCII 2020. LNCS, vol. 12194, pp. 376–392. Springer, Cham (2020). https://doi.org/10.1007/978-3-030-49570-1_26
53. Vasek, M., Moore, T.: Analyzing the Bitcoin Ponzi scheme ecosystem. In: Zohar, A., et al. (eds.) FC 2018. LNCS, vol. 10958, pp. 101–112. Springer, Heidelberg (2019). https://doi.org/10.1007/978-3-662-58820-8_8
54. Voukelatou, V., et al.: Measuring objective and subjective well-being: dimensions and data sources. Int. J. Data Sci. Anal. 1–31 (2020)
55. Wu, B., Liu, L., Yang, Y., Zheng, K., Wang, X.: Using improved conditional generative adversarial networks to detect social bots on twitter. IEEE Access **8**, 36664–36680 (2020)
56. Xu, J., Livshits, B.: The anatomy of a cryptocurrency pump-and-dump scheme. In: The 28th USENIX Security Symposium (SEC 2019), pp. 1609–1625 (2019)
57. Zaborovskaya, A., Zaborovskiy, V., Pletnev, K.: Possibilities of preventing manipulative transactions on the stock market in the conditions of new industrialization. In: The 2nd International Scientific Conference on New Industrialization: Global, National, Regional Dimension (SICNI 2018), pp. 154–160. Atlantis Press (2019)
58. Zhou, X., Zafarani, R.: A survey of fake news: fundamental theories, detection methods, and opportunities. ACM Comput. Surv. (CSUR) **53**(5), 1–40 (2020)

Vulnerabilities, Attacks and Intrusion Detection

Measuring and Modeling Software Vulnerability Security Advisory Platforms

Lucas Miranda[1], Daniel Vieira[1], Mateus Nogueira[1], Leonardo Ventura[1], Miguel Bicudo[1], Matheus Martins[1,2], Lucas Senos[1], Leandro P. de Aguiar[2], Enrico Lovat[2], and Daniel Menasche[1(✉)]

[1] Federal University of Rio de Janeiro, Rio de Janeiro, Brazil
sadoc@dcc.ufrj.br
[2] Siemens Corporate Research, Princeton, NJ, USA

Abstract. In this paper, we report results on a large scale measurement campaign to collect temporal information about events associated with software vulnerabilities. The data is curated so as to extract dates from each of the analyzed security advisories. The resulting time series are our object of study. From our measurements we were able to identify which role was assumed by different platforms (such as websites and forums) in the security landscape, including sources and aggregators of information about vulnerabilities. Then, we propose an analytical model to express the flow of information through security advisories across multiple platforms. The model is based on a queueing network, where each platform corresponds to a queue which adds a delay in the information propagation. Such delays, in turn, have an impact on the visibility of the information at different platforms. Leveraging the proposed model and the collected data, we assess how different system parameters, such as the delays incurred by each platform to propagate its messages, impact the overall flow of information across platforms.

1 Introduction

Background. Software vulnerabilities which threaten modern computer systems are disclosed in a daily basis. Platforms such as the National Vulnerability Database (NVD) and vendor websites are responsible for informing users about such vulnerabilities, through security advisories. Each vulnerability, identified through its Common Vulnerabilities and Exposures identifier (CVE id), is typically associated with many security advisories, which reflect, for instance, the availability of exploits and patches [13].

Timely information about early disclosure of vulnerabilities is key. Accurate information about the impact of vulnerabilities and about which systems are exposed helps to guide decisions, e.g., related to risk aware patch management [19]. Although security platforms play a fundamental role in the security landscape, the flow of information among them is still poorly understood. *In this paper, our goal is to report measurements, and present models and methods to provide insight into how information about vulnerabilities flows across security platforms.*

© Springer Nature Switzerland AG 2021
J. Garcia-Alfaro et al. (Eds.): CRiSIS 2020, LNCS 12528, pp. 31–48, 2021.
https://doi.org/10.1007/978-3-030-68887-5_2

Challenges. There are several challenges pertaining a characterization of the flow of information across security platforms. First, each security platform uses its own format to disseminate data about vulnerabilities. The information retrieved from those platforms must be curated, e.g., to extract publication dates by the sources. Second, there are no models to capture the dynamics of how information flows in the ecosystem. Such models can be instrumental to assess what would occur to the security landscape given events such as important platforms being attacked, e.g., by a DDoS attack, or two platforms merging together. As an example, relevant platforms, such as Security Focus and Security Tracker, have not been recently updated, and the impact is still unclear. Third, some security advisories may be shared in private platforms or in black hat forums, making them unreachable to the general public.

Gaps in Prior Art. The quality and timeliness of security advisories have been considered, for instance, in the context of threat information feeds [12]. However, most of those results are derived from data collected under restrictive non-disclosure agreements, and may not be reproducible in a non-industrial setting. One of our goals is to analyze security advisories made available through public platforms, referred by NVD as authoritative sources for information about vulnerabilities. In addition, there are works considering the flow of vulnerabilities across *software modules* [8]. Nonetheless, we are not aware of previous work on measurements and models of flow of advisories across *software platforms*.

Methods. To tackle the above challenges, we report results on a large scale measurement campaign to collect temporal information about events associated with software vulnerabilities. The data is curated so as to extract dates from each of the analyzed security advisories. The resulting time series of security advisories associated with vulnerabilities are our objects of study. From our measurements we are able to identify which role was assumed by different platforms (such as websites and forums) in the security landscape, including sources and aggregators of information about vulnerabilities. Then, we propose an analytical model to express the flow of information through security advisories across multiple platforms. The model is based on a network of queues, where each platform corresponds to a queue which adds a delay in the information propagation.

Contributions. In summary, our contributions are threefold.

Measurement Campaign and Insights: we retrieved security advisories from the top platforms referred to by NVD. By analyzing the time series of events associated with each vulnerability, we identified and quantified the extent at which platforms are used either as the ultimate sources of information about CVEs or as aggregators to forward advisories from its sources to other platforms.

Analytical Model: we propose and parametrize a queueing network comprised of $M/G/\infty$ queues to express the flow of information through security advisories across multiple platforms. The model is inspired by Sankey diagrams, which are derived from the collected data.

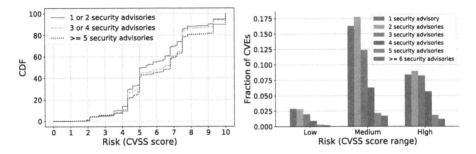

Fig. 1. CDF of risk given number of vulnerability advisories (left) and fraction of CVEs with given number of advisories (right): more advisories correlate with higher risk.

Model-Based Analysis: in light of the proposed analytical model, we extract additional insights about the security advisory ecosystem. Our model allows us to study how different system parameters, such as the order at which platforms issue advisories and the delays incurred by each platform to propagate its advisories, impact the mean number of days it takes for an authority such as NVD to report an advisory.

Paper Organization. The following section sets the ground in the realm of risk aware patch management and reports related work. Measurements and the analytical model are introduced in Sects. 3 and 4. The proposed model is evaluated using the collected measurements at Sect. 5 and Sect. 6 concludes.

2 Risk Aware Patch Management and Related Work

Patch management is key for product developers and asset owners. Patches imply outages explaining why industrial control systems (ICS) patches are typically deferred by 2–3 months [19]. Many enterprises help asset owners to manage risks associated to vulnerabilities, and risk aware vulnerability management products are available in the market; Siemens has the Industrial Vulnerability Manager (IVM) for ICS; Tenable has a complementary product for enterprise IT; the open source community has similar initiatives, e.g., the Exploit Prediction Scoring System (EPSS), a data-driven framework for assessing vulnerability threat.

Risk aware patch management (RAPM) involves tracking risk, e.g., CVSS or EPSS, ranging between 0 and 10, over time. It relies on data made available at security advisory platforms, e.g., to parameterize the temporal components of CVSS or EPSS. We illustrate the applicability of the results reported in the remainder of this paper through two examples in the realm of RAPM.

Assess Impact of Sources on Delays. The measurements and model in this paper support RAPM: if one plans patches based on information from a subset of platforms, how late may patches occur?

Estimate Confidence Levels of Risk. The proposed model supports what-if analysis for RAPM: what are the biases incurred when predicting risk? What is the confidence interval (CI) of risk estimates? How is CI expected to change?

Answering the above questions requires knowledge on how the number of data points associated with vulnerabilities varies over time, which is the main theme of this work. To illustrate that point, Fig. 1, obtained from our measurements (Sect. 3), shows the CDF of risk (CVSS) for three classes of vulnerabilities, varying according to the number of data points associated to each CVE. Vulnerabilities with 1 or 2 advisories tend to have lower risk when compared against vulnerabilities with 5 or more advisories, which attract more visibility. Figure 1(right) further supports that point, showing that vulnerabilities with high risk tend to have more advisories. Advisories are issued by multiple platforms, and confidence levels on risk build up during the period at which the advisories are made public. One of our aims is to measure and model the flow of advisories so as to understand how such confidence builds up across the lifecycle of vulnerabilities.

The lifecycle of vulnerabilities has been considered in previous works, accounting for weaponization and exploitation events [3,18], patching practices [19] and the role of CVSS [10,17] and TI feeds [12]. Our work considers the vulnerability lifecycle from a novel angle, accounting for platforms delays and leveraging Sankey diagrams and networks of queues. Whereas most works focus on predicting weaponization and exploitation, we focus on the flow of advisories across platforms, which is key for RAPM.

We rely on NVD as our reference to select the analyzed security platforms. Previous studies relied on NVD to cluster vulnerabilities [9] and to predict software vulnerabilities and corresponding risks [21]. None of these works leveraged the list of hyperlinks provided by NVD with advisories about each vulnerability, as considered in this paper.

Most of the literature on vulnerability disclosures tracks how vulnerabilities evolve within a software product [11] or across software modules [8]. In this paper, we take a different approach towards the evolution of software vulnerabilities, focusing on evolution across platforms. We believe that those approaches are complementary. In particular, one of the platforms considered in our study, Github [2,7,15], has within itself a rich history of software patches and upgrades whose timelines complement the time series considered in this paper.

3   Measurement Setup and Measurement Insights

Next, we describe our measurement setup, indicating how we selected the multiple sources of data and how we extracted temporal information from those. Then, we report insights obtained from the measurements.

Terminology. We begin by introducing some basic terminology.

CVE id is the Common Vulnerabilities and Exposures (CVE) identifier, which is a unique id used to refer to vulnerabilities.

CVE authority, also known as CVE numbering authority (CNA), is any entity that can issue CVE ids.

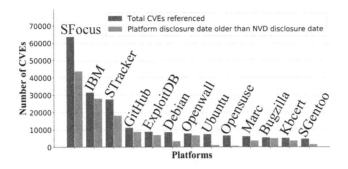

Fig. 2. CVEs per platform.

NVD CVE published date is the date at which the CVE was disclosed at the National Vulnerability Database (NVD). Both CVE and NVD are sponsored by the U.S. Department of Homeland Security (DHS). All vulnerabilities granted a CVE are eventually published by NVD [16].

Security advisory is any piece of information published about a given CVE, including patches, exploits and notes. *We encompass NVD disclosures as security advisories, whose publication dates equal NVD CVE published dates.*

Security advisory platform is a platform that issues security advisories. Examples include NVD and Security Focus.

Security advisory hyperlink is a hyperlink to a security advisory published at a given platform.

Security advisory date is the date at which the material contained in the security advisory was published by its author.

Platform CVE disclosure date is the earliest security advisory date for a given CVE among the collected advisories from a given platform. In particular, the NVD CVE disclosure date coincides with the NVD CVE published date.

CVE disclosure date is the earliest security advisory date for a given CVE among all collected advisories.

In the remainder of this paper, we contrast security advisory dates among platforms and against NVD CVE published dates.

Measurement Setup. We take NVD as our reference platform of security advisories. For each vulnerability, NVD provides its CVE, its NVD CVE published date, and hyperlinks to security advisories by other platforms. We select the top 13 platforms, in addition to NVD, ranked based on the number of encompassed CVEs (see Fig. 2).

For each vulnerability, NVD reports its CVE id together with a list of hyperlinks to security advisories. We download the content of those hyperlinks, and process the corresponding HTML files as described below. Note that for each of the considered platforms we find at least 1500 unique hyperlinks at NVD, and each advisory typically accounts for up to 2 CVEs.

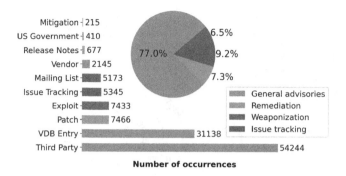

Fig. 3. Security advisory categories.

Accounting for the specifics of the format of the HTML files provided by each platform, we use XPath, the XML Path Language, to extract temporal information from each of those files. Each platform corresponds to a given XPath parametrization to extract the HTML element corresponding to the publication dates of the advisories posted by that platform. After implementing such process, for each security advisory we have its (*i*) publication date, (*ii*) NVD hyperlink, (*iii*) list of CVEs at NVD that contain that hyperlink. We store the elements in a database from which we derive the analysis and insights that follow.[1]

Dataset. Next, we report findings and insights obtained from our measurement campaign. We considered the NVD bundle of vulnerabilities accounting for all vulnerabilities released up to March 26, 2020. This amounts to a total of 576,750 references (hyperlinks) to 336,559 distinct security advisories (unique hyperlinks), from 129,504 CVEs. Then, we crawled the security advisory platforms of interest between March 27, 2020 and March 30, 2020, with March 25, 2020 being the latest CVE publication date at our database. *In the analysis that follows we account for 232,873 references to more than 108,889 distinct advisories released by 13 platforms referred by NVD, targeting 98,407 CVEs.*

Flow of Information Across Security Advisory Platforms. We begin by considering the nature of the security advisories exchanged in the considered platforms. To that aim, Fig. 3 indicates the distribution of the categories of the security advisories, as reported by NVD. Note that some advisories pertain to multiple categories and others have not been classified. The security advisories are distributed across remediation, weaponization, issue tracking and general advisories. In particular, information about exploitation of vulnerabilities in the wild is not captured through those advisories.

The flow of advisories across platforms can be captured through Sankey diagrams, as illustrated in Fig. 4. To produce Fig. 4, we consider for each vulnerability the sequence of platforms that published advisories about the corresponding CVE, ordered by their security advisory dates. The longest sequence in our

---

[1] The data and scripts to produce the reported results are available by contacting the authors.

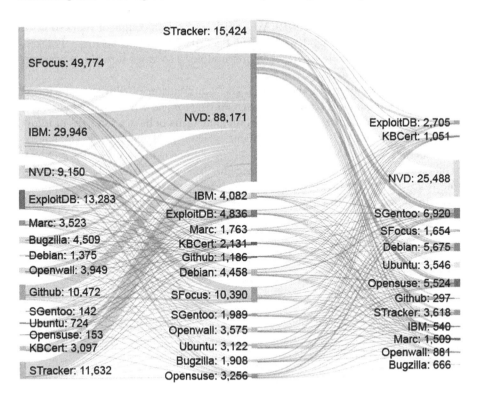

Fig. 4. Flow of information across security advisory platforms

dataset corresponds to CVE-2009-3555, and consists of 13 platforms. Heartbleed (CVE-2014-0196), Shellshock (CVE-2014-6271) and Meltdown (CVE-2017-5754) are vulnerabilities whose sequences comprise at least 6 platforms.

Given the sequences of platforms associated to each CVE, we extract the ordered pairs of consecutive platforms appearing in those sequences. Let $\mathcal{P}$ be the multiset of obtained ordered pairs. If two platforms A and B produce advisories for a given CVE at the same day, no entry is added to $\mathcal{P}$. If they are followed by C at an upcoming day, we add both (A, C) and (B, C) into $\mathcal{P}$. The Sankey diagram in Fig. 4 is generated from $\mathcal{P}$. The width of lines is proportional to the *CVE flow* between pairs of platforms, i.e., the width of the line between (A, B) is proportional to the frequency of ordered pair (A, B) in $\mathcal{P}$. The lines between layers 1 and 2 correspond to ordered pairs (A, B) wherein platform A is the first to publish an advisory about the corresponding CVE. The lines between layers 2 and 3 account for the additional ordered pairs. The analysis in this section accounts for CVEs published by NVD and by at least one additional platform, at a distinct day, noting that those correspond to more than 90% of the vulnerabilities in our dataset.

Figure 4 indicates that Security Focus and Security Tracker platforms play a relevant role in the security advisory ecosystem. Interestingly, they have not been updated since the end of 2019. We envision that in a couple of years some of the platforms shown in Fig. 4 will replace Security Focus and Security Tracker, and one of our purposes is to present a methodology to track how the ecosystem of security advisories evolves over time.

Figure 4 allows us to further assess the contribution of different platforms with respect to the flow of information, accounting for the ordering at which advisories for CVEs flow across platforms. Some platforms behave as sources of information, while others as aggregators. Security Focus, for instance, is the source of advisories for 80% (49774/(10390 + 49774 + 1654)) of its CVE flows. NVD, in contrast, is the aggregator of advisories for 92% ((88171 + 25488)/(88171 + 9150 + 25488)) of its CVE flows in Fig. 4. Other platforms are more symmetric in the flow of CVEs. For example, KBCert is source of advisories for 49% (3097/(3097 + 2131 + 1051)) of its CVE flows.

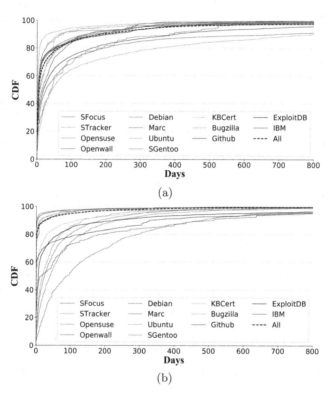

Fig. 5. NVD delay against platforms: (a) accounting for CVEs whose disclosure at platforms other than NVD occurred first and (b) accounting for CVEs whose disclosure at NVD occurred first.

NVD, as an aggregator, typically publishes CVEs after advisories have been announced at other platforms (see Fig. 2). Nonetheless, note that even though NVD is typically not the first platform to report information about vulnerabilities, in many instances it is the second to do so. As we move from the second to the third layer, the height of the NVD bar decreases, indicating its diminishing relevance for advisories already published by more than one platform.

Figure 4 shows that security advisory platforms complement each other with respect to the timing at which they share information. It provides a birds eye of view of the flow of information across platforms, which we detail, analyze and model in the remainder of this work.

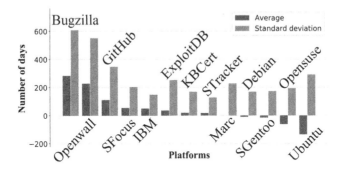

Fig. 6. NVD CVE published date minus source disclosure date.

NVD CVE Published Dates. Next, we aim at contrasting the date at which NVD publishes CVE information, as reported by NVD itself, in its NVD CVE published date field, against the date at which we first found information about the corresponding vulnerabilities in our dataset. Let f be the day at which we first find information about a given vulnerability in a platform other than NVD, and let n be the NVD CVE published date. Figures 5(a) and 5(b) show the cumulative distribution function (CDF) of $n - f$ and $f - n$ for the cases wherein $f \leq n$ and $f > n$, respectively, measured in days. Each solid line corresponds to a different platform. The dashed lines account for data across all platforms, ignoring platform identities to produce the plots.

Figure 5(a) indicates that NVD publishes advisories for up to 60% of the vulnerabilities in less than one month after the disclosure of the corresponding CVE. However, for the other 40% of the vulnerabilities, it may take more than one year for NVD to publish CVE information. The worst case scenario occurs when contrasting NVD against Bugzilla, for which we discover that after two years CVEs were not published at NVD for up to 15% of the vulnerabilities disclosed by Bugzilla.

Figure 5(b) indicates that when NVD is the first to release information about vulnerabilities, at least one of the other platforms quickly catches up. This is represented by the dashed line in Fig. 5(b), with a sharp increase close to zero. The corresponding dashed line in Fig. 5(a), in contrast, indicates that when NVD is not the first to release information, for roughly 20% of the vulnerabilities it may take up to three months for NVD to disclose the corresponding CVE.

Figure 6 provides further insights on how NVD positions against other platforms. Figure 6 shows the mean and standard deviation of NVD CVE published dates minus disclosure dates at other platforms, accounting for vulnerabilities that appeared at the two considered platforms. First, note that Bugzilla

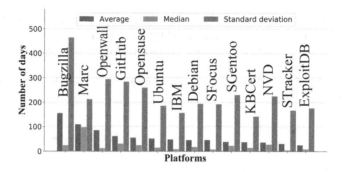

Fig. 7. Disclosure delays between consecutive advisories.

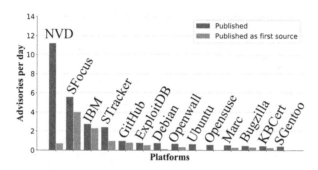

Fig. 8. Rate at which security advisories are published by platforms.

(respectively, Ubuntu) is the platform that provides the most (resp., less) complementary information, concerning timeliness, when contrasted against NVD. Second, note that the standard deviation of the number of days is very large, which might pose challenges for predictive models. Advisories for some vulnerabilities are issued during a long period of time, some of them on the order of years.

Platform Delays. Next, we consider the delays incurred while different security advisories are disclosed at the considered platforms. Figure 7 shows the delays between advisories about a given vulnerability being disclosed in a given platform and the succeeding advisory for the same vulnerability being disclosed by the next platform. The mean delays are much higher than the corresponding medians, indicating that outliers can significantly impact the average. This finding is similar in essence to the observations made on Fig. 6.

Publishing Rates. Figure 8 shows the rate at which security advisories are published by each platform, in units of advisories per day. The corresponding normalized rates, reported in Fig. 9, will be used to validate the model in Sect. 5. As expected, NVD plays a key role in the security advisory ecosystem, publishing and average of 11.2 advisories per day. To account for the order at which information flows across platforms, Fig. 8 also shows the rate at which security

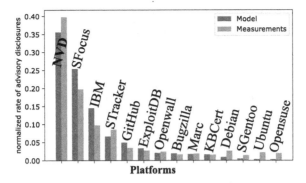

Fig. 9. Normalized rate of security advisory disclosures and model validation.

advisories are first published by each platform. Figure 8, in agreement with the Sankey diagram in Fig. 4, indicates that Security Focus is the platform which most commonly ranks as first to publish security advisories.

4 Analytical Model

Next, we propose and describe an analytical model to assess how local properties of security advisory platforms, such as the probability that an advisory at a platform yields a new advisory at another platform, impact global aspects of the system, such as the mean number of platforms wherein advisories for a given vulnerability are reported. Our model is inspired by the Sankey diagram presented in Fig. 4. While Sankey diagrams are instrumental to provide a visual perspective on the flow of information, the analytical model quantifies the role of each platform by augmenting the Sankey diagrams with temporal information about how many days each platform took to relay advisories to other platforms, as well as probabilistic information about the routing of vulnerabilities across platforms.

Parameters and Metrics of Interest. The model is introduced in Sect. 4.1. Basic output metrics obtained from the model appear in Sect. 4.2. The parameterization of model inputs is described at the end of Sect. 4.2 and the parameterized model is evaluated in Sect. 5.

4.1 Model Description

We model the flow of advisories across platforms through a "network of queues" [6, Chapter 17]. In the simplest setting, each queue corresponds to a security advisory platform. Platforms receive advisories from other platforms in the network or from outside the network of considered platforms, and propagate them after a certain delay. To capture delays, we leverage $M/G/\infty$ queues [6]. We denote by d_i the mean delay incurred between an advisory being published at platform i and at its succeeding platform, measured in days.

In what follows, we refer to an advisory as being relayed or routed from platform i to platform j when platform j publishes an advisory about the vulnerability of interest after i has done so. In particular, after an advisory is relayed from i to j, the advisory at platform j may leverage the advisory published at i. The advisory published by platform j may explicitly refer to previous advisories or may implicitly rely on their content, e.g., to propose a countermeasure.

Key Simplifying Assumption. The key simplifying assumption considered in our model consists of characterizing the flow of information between security platforms inspired by the Sankey diagram in Fig. 4 accounting for two layers while still capturing the fact that information about each CVE may be published by advisories across more than two platforms. Let L be the number of layers in the diagram, with $L = 3$ in Fig. 4. The proposed analytical model requires the estimation of roughly $(L-1)P^2$ parameters corresponding to the routing of advisories between platforms, where P denotes the number of platforms, and the notion of routing is made precise in what follows. As in any modeling exercise, we trade off between simplicity and accuracy, and find that the simplest model with $L = 2$ suffices for our purposes (see Sect. 5). Nonetheless, the model can be easily extended to account for $L > 2$, at the cost of additional complexity.

Routing of Advisories. We consider a set of P security advisory platforms. In addition to those platforms, we introduce a virtual platform, that is always the last platform to publish an advisory about a given vulnerability. The virtual platform, whose sole goal is to simplify model presentation, is denoted as platform ∞, and its index is $P + 1$.

The *routing* of advisories between security advisory platforms is captured through a *routing matrix*. Let R denote the routing matrix. Element r_{ij} denotes the probability that platform i routes an advisory to j, where $\sum_{j=1}^{P+1} r_{ij} = 1$. Note that as the virtual platform $P + 1$ is a sink, $r_{P+1,P+1} = 1$.

The platforms can be grouped into two blocks. The platforms in the first (resp., second) block are transient (resp., absorbing) platforms. Let R_0 (resp., I_u) be the intra-block transition matrix corresponding to elements in the first (resp., second) block, and let R_1 be the inter-block transition matrix. Note that we assume there are u absorbing platforms, and I_u is an $u \times u$ identity matrix. In the simplest case, which constitutes our reference setup, we have a single absorbing platform corresponding to the virtual sink, namely ∞, and $u = 1$. Whenever the dimension of the identity matrix is clear from context, we drop subscript u. Then,

$$R = \begin{pmatrix} R_0 & R_1 \\ \mathbf{0} & I \end{pmatrix}. \tag{1}$$

A published vulnerability is said to be at platform i if platform i was the last platform to publish an advisory about it. Then, the state of the queueing network is given by $(\sigma_1, \ldots, \sigma_P)$ where σ_i is the number of vulnerabilities at platform i. The queueing network state dynamics are given by a continuous time Markov chain, whose infinitesimal generator and steady state probabilities readily follow from the above description and are found in [6].

4.2 Security Advisory Platforms Metrics of Interest

Platform Publishing Rates. Let λ_i be the rate at which advisories for unheard vulnerabilities are first published by platform i, i.e., λ_i is the rate at which platform i discloses advisories whose corresponding CVE disclosure date equals platform i CVE disclosure date. Accordingly, let p_i be the probability that platform i is the first to publish an advisory for a given vulnerability, i.e., p_i is the fraction of vulnerabilities for which advisories are first published by platform i. Then, $\lambda_i = p_i \Lambda$, where Λ is the rate at which new vulnerabilities (and the corresponding security advisories) are reported online.

Let m_{ij} be the mean number of advisories for a given vulnerability, initially published at platform i, to appear at platform j. Matrix M is known as the *fundamental matrix* [6], and is given by

$$M = \sum_{k=0}^{\infty} R_0^k = (I - R_0)^{-1} \qquad (2)$$

where I is the identity matrix and R_0 is the routing matrix R with the row and column corresponding to ∞ being removed as described above. In what follows, we indicate how the fundamental matrix yields our metrics of interest.

Let γ_i be the rate at which advisories are published by platform i. Vector γ is the vector of publishing rates,

$$\gamma = \lambda M = \lambda (I - R_0)^{-1}. \qquad (3)$$

Note that whereas λ is the vector of rates at which advisories for unheard vulnerabilities are published by each platform, vector γ accounts for all advisories.

Platform Hitting and Absorption Probabilities. Next, we consider the problem of quantifying the relative freshness of advisories published across a set of platforms. To that aim, consider a set of S competing platforms. Let b_{ij} be the probability that a given platform $j \in S$ is the first, among the platforms in S, to publish about a vulnerability originally issued by platform $i \notin S$. To compute b_{ij}, we include all platforms in S into a group of absorbing platforms, together with the virtual platform ∞. Following the terminology introduced in Sect. 4.2, let R_1 be a $(P - |S|) \times (|S| + 1)$ matrix, whose elements characterize the routing probabilities between platforms outside S to platforms in S. Similarly, M is the fundamental matrix accounting for platforms outside S. Then, b_{ij} is given by element (i, j) in matrix B

$$B = MR_1. \qquad (4)$$

The derivation of the above equation can be found in [6]. In Sect. 5 we evaluate the above expression to assess how early four of the most popular platforms publish their advisories, when contrasted against the others.

Mean Time Between Platforms. Next, we consider the mean time between platforms, in days. Let column vector $t^{(i)}$ characterize the mean time for a vulnerability to be forwarded by each platform, except i, i.e., $\boldsymbol{t}^{(i)}$ equals $\boldsymbol{d}$, after excluding the i-th element from the latter. Then, the mean time to reach either platform i or the virtual platform ∞, whichever occurs first, is given by

$$\boldsymbol{T}^{(i)} = \left(I - R_0^{(i)}\right)^{-1} \boldsymbol{t}^{(i)} \tag{5}$$

where $R_0^{(i)}$ is obtained from R_0 after removing the column and row corresponding to platform i. Note that if $\boldsymbol{t}^{(i)}$ is a column vector with all its elements equal to 1, the resulting vector obtained from the above equation is the mean number of advisories issued until reaching either platform i or the virtual platform ∞, whichever occurs first.

To obtain matrix T, whose element $t_{i,j}$ corresponds to the mean time to reach platforms j or ∞, given that an advisory is first published at i, it suffices to concatenate column vectors $\tilde{\boldsymbol{T}}^{(i)}$, $i = 1, \ldots, P$, where $\tilde{\boldsymbol{T}}^{(i)}$ is obtained from $\boldsymbol{T}^{(i)}$ adding an entry equal to zero at the i-th position, to capture the fact that the mean time to reach platform i starting from i is zero [6]. In Sect. 5 we evaluate the above expression to assess the time it takes for advisories to flow across platforms.

How to Parametrize Model from Data. The model is parametrized through three sets of parameters: the arrival rates of advisories for new vulnerabilities from outside the considered network of platforms, the delays and the routing matrix.

Let n_i be the number of advisories published by platform i, as observed in the measurements. Similarly, let f_i be the number of advisories published by i, when no other advisory for the corresponding vulnerability has been issued, $f_i \leq n_i$. Also, let τ be the measurement duration, i.e., the time between the publication of the first and last advisories present in the dataset. We denote by $\hat{\lambda}_i$ and $\hat{p}_i$ the estimators of λ_i and p_i, respectively. Then, $\hat{\lambda}_i = f_i/\tau$ and $\hat{p}_i = f_i \big/ \sum_{k=1}^{P} f_k$. We also have $\hat{\Lambda} = \sum_{k=1}^{P} \hat{\lambda}_k$. To parametrize the delays and the routing matrix, we begin by generating the multiset $\mathcal{P}$ of ordered pairs of platforms, as described in Sect. 3. Each ordered pair $(i, j) \in \mathcal{P}$ corresponds to an instance wherein platform j published an advisory about a given vulnerability after an advisory for the same vulnerability appeared at i. Let $\tilde{r}_{ij}$ be the number of times that the ordered pair (i, j) appears at $\mathcal{P}$. Then, denoting by $\hat{r}_{ij}$ the estimator of r_{ij},

$$\hat{r}_{ij} = \tilde{r}_{ij} \bigg/ \sum_{k=1}^{P+1} \tilde{r}_{ik}. \tag{6}$$

To determine $\hat{d}_i$, the estimator of d_i, we also rely on $\mathcal{P}$. To each element $(i, j) \in \mathcal{P}$ we associate its corresponding delay in days, d, and denote the resulting triple by (i, j, d). The mean delay estimate $\hat{d}_i$ is given by the average of the third component of the triples wherein the first component equals i and the second component is different from ∞.

Model Extensions. The proposed model can be easily extended to account for additional layers, i.e., $L > 2$, providing more accurate estimates of the quantities of interest at the expense of a more complex model, involving more parameters to be estimated. Consider, for instance, the Sankey diagram presented in Fig. 4, wherein $L = 3$. To account for $L = 3$, we associate to each node in the first $L - 1$ layers in Fig. 4 its corresponding queue. The resulting queueing network comprises $(L - 1)P^2$ routing probabilities across queues.

5 Evaluation

Next, we evaluate our model leveraging data collected from our measurement campaign. Our goals are to (a) validate the theory using real data, indicating that the estimated metrics of interest are accurate even when the assumptions of the model do not hold and (b) numerically analyze the metrics derived from the model.

The model is parameterized using the methodology described in Sect. 4.2. The routing matrix estimator, $\hat{R}$, is given by (6), the vector of delays, $\hat{d}$, is obtained from Fig. 7, and the vector of disclosure rates of advisories for unheard CVEs, $\hat{\lambda}$, is obtained from Fig. 8 ("published as first source" bars).

Model Validation. Next, we validate our model against measurements. In particular, we aim at verifying if the key simplifying assumption discussed in Sect. 4.1, according to which the flow of advisories across platforms can be approximated through a two layer model, with $L = 2$, already leads to accurate estimates.

To validate our model against measurements, we compare the normalized rate at which platforms disclose security advisories obtained from the model against measurements. We choose the normalized rate as our reference metric for validation purposes as most of the other quantities can be derived from it. Similar results hold for those other metrics (omitted due to space constraints).

According to the model (resp., measurements), the normalized disclosure rate is obtained from (3) (resp., Fig. 8), normalizing the resulting vector so that the sum of rates equals one. Figure 9 indicates that our model estimates are accurate when compared against measurements, with the largest absolute error being less than 0.05. If smaller errors are required, one can trade off between model complexity and accuracy, and parametrize an extended version of the proposed model (see Sect. 4.2).

Assessing Distances Between Platforms. From the routing matrix, we compute our metrics of interest. Figure 10 shows the mean time between platforms, measured in days. It corresponds to matrix T, whose derivation is described in Sect. 4.2 (see Eq. (5)). Each entry (i, j) in the matrix in Fig. 10 corresponds to the mean number of days to route an advisory from platform i to either platform j or to the virtual platform ∞, whatever occurs first. Figure 10 shows that all vulnerabilities take, on average, more than one month to reach a target.

Figure 10 shows that from some platforms, such as Bugzilla and Openwall, it takes a long time to reach all other platforms. This can be explained from

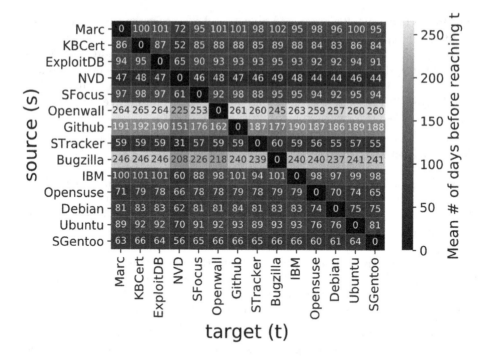

Fig. 10. Mean time between platforms in days.

Figs. 6 and 7. Figure 6 shows that Bugzilla and Openwall are the top two platforms ranked based on the delay until reaching NVD. As NVD is an important hub in the system to relay advisories across platforms, the advisories published on those two platforms tend to take longer to reach any other platform. Recall from Sect. 4.2 that we parametrize delays through the number of days between succeeding advisories are published at consecutive platforms, which for measurements is given by Fig. 7. Bugzilla and Openwall appear as the first and third elements in Fig. 7. This, in turn, indicates that the mean number of days to route an advisory from one of those two platforms to the virtual platform ∞ is the largest among all platforms.

Figure 11 shows the percentage of vulnerabilities for which an advisory first published at platform s will eventually reach platform t, before reaching the virtual absorbing platform ∞ or any other platform in the considered set of targets, comprising Security Tracker, Security Focus and NVD. The figure is obtained using Eq. (4) and the methodology described in Sect. 4.2, and complements Fig. 10. In particular, it indicates that with high probability the advisories initially posted in most of the platforms will reach NVD before absorption. Returning to the Bugzilla and Openwall platforms, this observation, together with the fact that the time to reach NVD from those platforms is large, explains why vulnerabilities initially generated at those platforms take longer to reach either one of the other platforms in the system or be absorbed.

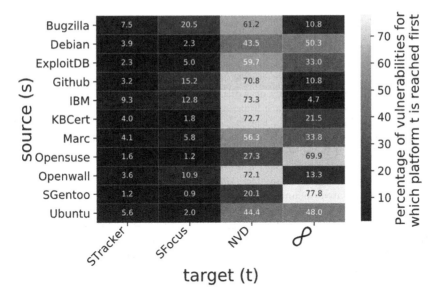

Fig. 11. Percentage of vulnerabilities issued from s for which t is reached first, considering Security Tracker, Security Focus and NVD as targets.

6 Conclusion

In the realm of security, information is the oxygen and security advisory platforms, the trees. Understanding how information flows across platforms is a key step in the full characterization of vulnerability lifecycles. After conducting a large scale measurement campaign, we use those measurements to parametrize a queueing model which allows us to estimate the impact of different parameters, such as the rate at which platforms relay information, on the mean time that vulnerability advisories take to reach a given platform.

Understanding the flow of information across platforms is instrumental for real world operations, such as data-driven risk aware patch management [19] and cybersecurity insurance [4,14,20]. In both cases, the confidence level on the estimates of risk is a function of the quality and the number of security advisories. While assessing how CVSS and EPSS evolve over time, the number of issued advisories serves to parameterize confidence intervals either in retrospect using measurements (Sect. 3) or in hindsight using the proposed model (Sect. 4).

Admins increasingly rely on automated data-driven approaches for decision-making, being utterly bound by the quality and freshness of the ingested information. This work is a step towards characterizing the latter, opening up a number of interesting avenues for research, accounting for advisories maturity and the modeling of topics and their evolution across security advisory platforms [1,5].

Acknowledgments. This project was partially sponsored by CAPES, CNPq and FAPERJ, through grants E-26/203.215/2017 and E-26/211.144/2019, as well as scholarships from Siemens Corporate Research.

References

1. de Boer, M.H., Bakker, B.J., et al.: Text mining in cybersecurity. Multimodal Technol. Interact. **3**(3), 62 (2019)
2. Decan, A., Mens, T., Constantinou, E.: On the impact of security vulnerabilities in the NPM package dependency network. In: Proceedings of the 15th International Conference on Mining Software Repositories, pp. 181–191 (2018)
3. Frei, S., May, M., Fiedler, U., Plattner, B.: Large-scale vulnerability analysis. In: SIGCOMM Workshop on Large-Scale Attack Defense, pp. 131–138 (2006)
4. Gai, K., et al.: A novel secure big data cyber incident analytics framework for cybersecurity insurance. In: Big Data Security on Cloud, pp. 171–176. IEEE (2016)
5. Georgescu, T.M.: Natural language processing model for automatic analysis of cybersecurity-related documents. Symmetry **12**(3), 354 (2020)
6. Harchol-Balter, M.: Performance Modeling and Design of Computer Systems: Queueing Theory in Action. Cambridge University Press, Cambridge (2013)
7. Horawalavithana, S., Bhattacharjee, A., et al.: Mentions of security vulnerabilities on Reddit, Twitter and Github. In: International Conference on Web Intelligence, pp. 200–207 (2019)
8. Hu, W., Wang, Y., Liu, X., Sun, J., Gao, Q., Huang, Y.: Open source software vulnerability propagation analysis algorithm based on knowledge graph. In: IEEE International Conference on Smart Cloud, pp. 121–127. IEEE (2019)
9. Huang, S., Tang, H., et al.: Text clustering on national vulnerability database. In: Computer Engineering and Applications, vol. 2, pp. 295–299. IEEE (2010)
10. Joh, H., Malaiya, Y.K.: A framework for software security risk evaluation using the vulnerability lifecycle and CVSS metrics. In: Proceedings of International Workshop on Risk and Trust in Extended Enterprises, pp. 430–434 (2010)
11. Johnson, P., Gorton, D., Lagerström, R., Ekstedt, M.: Time between vulnerability disclosures. Comput. Secur. **62**, 278–295 (2016)
12. Li, V.G., Dunn, M., Pearce, P., et al.: Reading the tea leaves: a comparative analysis of threat intelligence. In: USENIX Security 2019, pp. 851–867 (2019)
13. MITRE: Common vulnerabilities and exposures (2020). https://cve.mitre.org/
14. Rassam, M.A., Maarof, M., Zainal, A., et al.: Big data analytics adoption for cybersecurity. J. Inf. Assur. Secur. **12**(4) (2017)
15. Rosen, C., Shihab, E.: What are mobile developers asking about? A large scale study using stack overflow. Empirical Softw. Eng. **21**(3), 1192–1223 (2016)
16. Ruohonen, J.: A look at the time delays in CVSS vulnerability scoring. Appl. Comput. Inf. **15**(2), 129–135 (2019)
17. Ruohonen, J., Hyrynsalmi, S., Leppänen, V.: Modeling the delivery of security advisories and CVEs. Comput. Sci. Inf. Syst. **14**(2), 537–555 (2017)
18. Shahzad, M., Shafiq, M.Z., Liu, A.X.: A large scale exploratory analysis of software vulnerability life cycles. In: International Conference on Software Engineering, pp. 771–781 (2012)
19. Wang, B., Li, X., de Aguiar, L.P., Menasche, D.S., Shafiq, Z.: Characterizing and modeling patching practices of industrial control systems. Proc. ACM Meas. Anal. Comput. Syst. **1**(1), 1–23 (2017)
20. Woods, D., Moore, T.: Does insurance have a future in governing cybersecurity? IEEE Secur. Privacy Mag. **18**(1), 21–27 (2019)
21. Zhang, S., Ou, X., Caragea, D.: Predicting cyber risks through national vulnerability database. Inf. Secur. J. **24**(4–6), 194–206 (2015)

Frequency Hopping Spread Spectrum to Counter Relay Attacks in PKESs

Karim Lounis$^{(\boxtimes)}$ and Mohammad Zulkernine

Queen's Reliable Software Technology Lab,
School of Computing Queen's University, Kingston, ON, Canada
{lounis,mzulker}@cs.queensu.ca

Abstract. Passive keyless entry and start systems (PKESs) have been widely deployed in modern cars. These systems have brought many advantages over their predecessors and are considered more secure. However, they are subject to a new type of attack, known as relay attack. Due to this attack, hundreds of cars have been stolen in many countries. Since then, car manufacturers as well as insurance companies have been experiencing an endless nightmare. Researchers have also been working into proposing solutions, mainly based on distance-bounding protocols and sensing technologies, to counter relay attacks but none of the solutions came out with a fundamental mitigation. In this paper, we apply FHSS (Frequency Hopping Spread Spectrum) transmission technique as a physical-layer countermeasure to mitigate relay attacks. By hopping from one frequency to another, within a wide bandwidth, and following a per-session secret-shared frequency hopping sequence, the communication between the car and its associated keyfob can be hidden from the attackers as long as the latter are not aware of the hopping sequence.

Keywords: RFID security · Relay attacks · FHSS · Vehicle security

1 Introduction

To prevent car theft, cars have been traditionally equipped with an authorization system that allows a driver to unlock/lock a car and start/stop its engine. The system relied on a metallic or alloy key (viz., Fig. 1 (a)) that the driver had to physically insert into the door lock to unlock/lock the car and to start/stop the car engine by turning the key clockwise/anticlockwise. Such a system was vulnerable to key copying attacks. The attacker needed to obtain a key for a short time to make a copy at a locksmith. Certain car models used to have the same lock for the car doors as well as for the petrol tank cover. An attacker just had to take the cover and get the lock structure. Later, some car models started using a key that was embedded with an immobilizer chip (viz., Fig. 1 (b)) to prevent key copying as well as physical lock bypassing[1]. In early eighties, car

---

[1] Breaching car security is not limited to stealing the car itself but also includes breaking into the car to grab anything valuable inside, placing a remote controllable ODB (On-board diagnostics) adapter on the car's ODB port, or taking off any part needed by the thief, such as car's doors, bonnet, or any expensive engine's part.

© Springer Nature Switzerland AG 2021
J. Garcia-Alfaro et al. (Eds.): CRiSIS 2020, LNCS 12528, pp. 49–66, 2021.
https://doi.org/10.1007/978-3-030-68887-5_3

manufacturers started thinking about creating a more convenient technology that allows easy access to cars and prevents known classical auto theft attacks. This led to the emergence of keyless entry systems, where the classical metallic key is augmented with a remote controller. Drivers just have to push a button on the remote controller to unlock/lock the car's locking system. Certain remote controllers have the ability to pop up the trunk, whereas others can get the car's engine remotely started (viz., Fig. 2 (a)).

Fig. 1. Car key models: (a) Classical metallic or alloy key, (b) Car key with immobilizer.

Nowadays, keyless entry systems are being widely deployed on most, if not all, car models. The current generation of such systems allow drivers to automatically unlock their cars by just standing few feet away from the car and by carrying an RFID (Radio Frequency IDentification) keyfob in their pockets (viz., Fig. 2 (b)).

(a)   (b)

Fig. 2. Car key models: (a) RF remote controller key, (b) RFID keyfob.

The car gets locked as soon as the driver walks away from the car with the keyfob[2] or after pressing a button on the door handle (viz., Fig. 3 (left)). In addition, drivers can start/stop their car's engines by pushing a "Start Engine" button (viz., Fig. 3 (center)) and having the keyfob present anywhere near the steering wheel. Such systems are commonly known as Passive Keyless Entry and Start systems, or PKES systems for short. They are deployed on most high-end car models. However, this considerable advancement in keyless entry systems has given birth to more advanced auto theft techniques. Among these techniques, applying relay attack for auto theft has been a recent and serious matter of concern for many car manufacturers, insurance companies, and car owners. In a relay attack, attackers collaborate to relay the signals between a car and its associated keyfob by boosting the signals while the car and the keyfob are not in close proximity. In this way, the attackers fool the car into believing that the keyfob is in its proximity and gets unlocked and started.

Due to relay attacks, hundreds of cars, equipped with PKES systems, were stolen. Tracker (a UK vehicle tracking company) reported that 4/5 of all vehicles stolen and recovered by the firm in 2017 were stolen without using the owner's keys. CCTV footages in the UK showed how prestigious cars (Land Rover, Tesla, Mercedes-Benz, BMW, Audi, and Jeep) were stolen from driveways using relay attacks in less than a minute [1]. In December 2019, CBC News (Canadian

---

[2] For security purpose, certain car models get automatically locked after some seconds, if the driver walks away without locking the car.

Fig. 3. RFID push button on door handle (left), the "Start Engine" button (center), and the car door-keypad used on certain American car makes such as Ford, Cadillac, Lincoln, Mercury, and Chevrolet, since the early eighties (right).

Broadcasting Corporation) reported that hundreds of high-end vehicles[3] across Ottawa region (Canada) were stolen since April 2019 [2]. Furthermore, a German automobile club (ADAC) tested relay attack on 237 car models from 30 different manufacturers[4]. They found that only 7 cars could not be either unlocked or started. Interestingly, the use of relay attacks for auto theft has been studied and investigated in the literature and its feasibility has been demonstrated as well. In 2011, researchers [3] managed to unlock and start the engine of ten car models from eight manufacturers using relay attacks. In 2017, a security research team, called UnicornTream, developed a cheap hardware (around $22) to realize a relay attack. The team has demonstrated the feasibility of a relay attack from 300 m [4]. Moreover, RFID location-based attacks (which include relay attacks [5–9]) were discussed in the literature since early nineties [10–12]. A review of these attacks can be found in [13].

Thus far, there is no fundamental countermeasure to completely mitigate relay attacks. Existing countermeasures are either mechanical or technological. Mechanical countermeasures are not practical, not flexible, sometimes not feasible, and not automatic. Technological countermeasures however, are of a great concern in research. Among the technological solutions, round-trip time-based solution (applied in distance-bounding protocols [14]) is being adopted and recommended as the unique physical-layer countermeasure for relay-attacks. It consists of checking the time domain of the car and the keyfob. It verifies whether the communication happens within a predefined and estimated time (a.k.a., delay). Nevertheless, this solution has the following concerns: (1) Most keyless entry systems do not implement a distance-bounding algorithm and (2) If they do, an overestimation of the fixed delay would make the keyless entry system vulnerable to some variants of relay-attacks.

In this paper, we apply FHSS (Frequency Hopping Spread Spectrum) transmission technique on passive keyless entry systems as a physical-layer countermeasure to mitigate relay attacks. The intuition behind using FHSS to mitigate relay attacks is to move and switch the radio domain of the communication between the car and its keyfob over time with respect to the attacker. In fact, for a successful relay attack, the following assumptions must hold: (i) The car-keyfob and the

---

[3] Toyota 4Runners, Highlanders, Tacoma pickup trucks and Lexus GX460.
[4] See ADAC: https://www.youtube.com/watch?v=0AHSDy6AiV0.

attacker's time domain must be the same, which means the attacker needs to be relaying the signals at the same time when the communication between the car and its keyfob takes place (no delays). (ii) The car-keyfob and the attacker's location domain must be the same, which means the attacker has to be physically near the car and keyfob when the car-keyfob communication happens. (iii) The car-keyfob and the attacker's radio domain must be the same, which means the attacker should be tuned on the same frequency over which the car and its keyfob operate. Therefore, we apply FHSS to enforce the communication (including the authentication protocol) between the car and the keyfob to occur on multiple channels (radio domain). At a given time, the car and the keyfob are tuned over a frequency for a very short time before hopping to another frequency following a previously shared secret pseudo-random sequence of frequencies. In this way, an attacker who tries to conduct a relay attack needs to know on which frequency the car and the key are communicating in order to boost the signals. As the attacker does not know the sequence of frequencies, it will be able to boost only some signals. If the car and the keyfob are not in proximity, failing to boost a single signal at a given time would result in a disconnection, which brakes the relay attack. Thus, as long as the sequence of frequencies is kept secret, an attacker will not be able to tune its hardware to receive the signals and amplify them so that the relay attack succeeds. Finally, we believe that as relay attack is a physical-layer attack, proposing a fundamental mitigation solution would only be possible through a physical-layer countermeasure.

The rest of the paper is organized as follows. In Sect. 2, we present the different mechanisms for car keyless entry systems and their related attacks. We also discuss the existing countermeasures. Section 3 studies the possibility of applying FHSS for mitigating relay attacks. We provide recommendations that PKES system's manufacturers can follow to implement PKES systems that are resilient to relay attacks as well as jamming attacks. We discuss the related work in Sect. 4 and conclude the paper in Sect. 5.

2   Cars Keyless Entry Systems Hacking

In this section, we discuss the state of the art in car theft through hacking into their keyless entry systems. Vehicles in general and cars in particular have been equipped with keyless entry technology since early eighties. These systems have evolved from typing a PIN code on a door-keypad (first time used in the 1980 Ford Thunderbird, viz., Fig. 3 (right)), into remotely pressing a button on a remote controller (first time used in the 1982 Renault Fuego), and nowadays, by standing in the car's proximity and carrying a wireless keyfob (first time used in the 1993 Chevrolet Corvette). Each of these mechanisms has brought advantages over its predecessor in terms of security, reliability, and flexibility. At the same time, each mechanism is vulnerable to a certain type of attacks. In the next paragraphs, we present each car's entry mechanism and discuss its germane attacks and possible countermeasures.

Static Remote Controller Keys.
This mechanism consists of remotely
(max 20–35 away from the car) pressing a button on a remote controller
(viz., Fig. 1 (b) and Fig. 1 (c)) to send
a signal that carries a factory fixed-
code to the car over the UHF radio
frequency 315 MHz or 433.92 MHz[5].
The car receives and interprets the
signal to execute the requested command, e.g., unlock car, after verifying
the correctness of the code as illustrated by the MSC[6] of Fig. 4. This
mechanism is vulnerable to interception and replay attacks. An attacker
can intercept the signal using a ded-

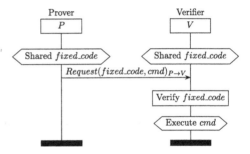

Fig. 4. Fixed code-based authentication for
car remote entry systems. The notation
$M_{P \rightarrow V}$ indicates a message M sent from the
prover, denoted as P, to the verifier, denoted
as V. The cmd denotes the command to execute, e.g., unlock doors.

icated hardware (e.g., HackRF One[7]) when the driver is unlocking the car and
then replay the signal later on to unlock it.

**Dynamic Remote Controller
Keys.** The next generation of
remote controller keys focused on
essentially mitigating replay attacks.
Remote controller keys started
adopting the rolling code (hopping
code) approach where the remote
controller sends a different code
sequence each time a command,
e.g., unlock doors, is sent to the
car. The car and the remote controller are somehow synchronized
over a sequence of codes in the
sense where the next codes (in case
the car has missed some transmitted keypresses) to be used is
known by both car and remote controller (viz., MSC (See footnote 6)
of Fig. 5). This will mainly prevent
replay attacks that are successful on

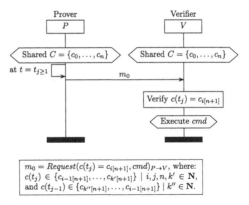

Fig. 5. Rolling code-based authentication for
cars remote entry systems. The notation
$M_{P \rightarrow V}$ indicates a message M that is sent
from the prover, denoted as P, to the verifier, denoted as V. Also, the notation $c(t_j)$
indicates the code $c_{i[n+1]}$ that is sent at time
instant $t = t_j$, and cmd denotes the command, e.g., unlock car's door.

---

[5] Certain car manufacturers, such as Ford and Lincoln, have started adopting the UHF
frequency band between 902.375 MHz and 903.425 MHz.

[6] MSC (Message Sequence Chart) is a graphical language for the description of the
interaction between different components of a system. This language is standardized
by the ITU (International Telecommunication Union).

[7] HackRF One is a transmit and receive capable SDR. It has a 10 MHz to 6 GHz
operating range and up to 20 MHz of bandwidth. It costs around $300.

static controllers. However, the rolling code has been demonstrated to be vulnerable to rolljaming [15] where the attacker prevents the car driver from unlocking its car by jamming the signal at each attempt. The attacker records the rolling code signals (i.e., records the codes) sent each time while performing jamming. The attacker then unlocks the car using the first rolling code signal making the driver think that it has unlocked the car by keypressing. The attacker uses the next rolling codes to unlock the car later on. Also, it has been recently demonstrated that by replaying previously captured codes, certain car models tend to behave in an incorrect way where their keyfob gets disabled locking out their drivers[8]. In addition to disabling the keyfob, in some car models, e.g., 2019 Ford Expedition, the rolling code is reset to zero which would allow the attacker to replay the previously captured codes to unclock and lock the car as long as those codes are replayed in their correct order.

The fixed-code as well as the rolling-code mechanism are both vulnerable to signal blocking attack (a.k.a., remote interference). In this attack, the attacker jams the signal that is transmitted by the car's remote controller when locking the car's doors. The car remains unlocked if the driver does not physically check whether the car is locked or not. Drivers in a hurry tend not to check their cars. The attacker gets into the car once the driver is away and may grab something valuable or plug any adapter into the OBD-II (On-Board Diagnostics II) port for car remote control, car tracking, or key reprogramming [16].

For a better illustration of this attack, we have used a 2010 Dodge Caravan remote control and a garage door remote controller, both operating at the same frequency (around 433.90 MHz). The car's locking-signal is sent at the frequency of 433.92 MHz as illustrated in Fig. 6 (left). By holding the lock button on the garage door remote controller while trying to lock the car, the car's locking-signal gets completely jammed as illustrated in Fig. 6 (right). As a consequence, the car remains unlocked. The same experiment has been conducted on a 2010 Kia Sedona, viz., Fig. 7, using a 315 MHz garage door remote controller.

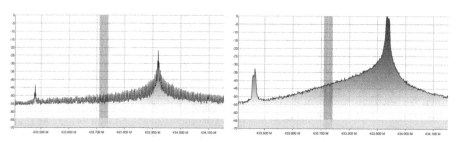

Fig. 6. The locking-signal sent from a Dodge Caravan's remote controller at 433.92 MHz (left) and the jammed signal at the same frequency (right).

Nevertheless, this attack targets only car models that are not equipped with RFID keyless system, which we present in the next paragraph. In fact, the newest car keyless entry systems have not literally replaced their predecessor systems

---

[8] See Hack5: https://www.youtube.com/watch?v=k8rNQ3mBZQ4&ab_channel=Hak5.

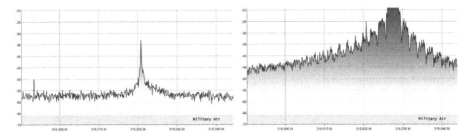

Fig. 7. The locking-signal sent from a Kia Sedona's remote controller at 315.02 MHz (left) and the jammed signal at near frequency (right).

but rather augmented them with a newer technology providing a higher availability. For example, if a car that uses RFID keyless system has been subject to jamming, the car would automatically get locked as soon as the driver walks away. Also, if a thief tries to lock out the driver from unlocking its car through jamming, the driver would be able to unlock its car by just approaching it and touching the door handle or by pressing a button on the door handle as long as the used RFID frequency is different from the one used for jamming.

RFID Keyfobs. To add more security and convenience, hands-free keys appeared in early nineties and started to become more popular in early 2000. In this generation, car keys are transformed into (or augmented with) an RFID-tag (becoming a keyfob, viz., Fig. 2 (b)). The car and the keyfob communicate over LF (Low Frequency) RFID radio frequency band which operates between 125 kHz and 137 kHz[9]. In this system, the keyfob plays the role of a semi-passive RFID-tag, whereas the car plays the role of an RFID-reader. Thus, when the keyfob is approached to the car[10] ($\leq$30 cm around the car), the keyfob circuit gets power-supplied by the car through induction-coupling (or electromagnetic coupling on higher frequencies) phenomenon and an optional lightweight authentication protocol is executed[11]. The car verifies that it is communicating with the correct keyfob and gets unlocked. This is also known as passive keyless entry system as the driver does not get explicitly involved. This has brought many advantages to drivers with respect to their convenience and car security.

Nonetheless, researchers [3,4] demonstrated through relay attacks that it is possible to fool a car into believing that its associated keyfob is located in its proximity so that it gets foolishly unlocked although the keyfob is located

---

[9] In some keyless entry systems, the RFID communication is asymmetric. The communication from the car to the keyfob is performed over LF 125 kHz band (shorter range), whereas the communication from the keyfob to the car is over UHF band with a frequency of 315 MHz, 433.92 MHz, 868 MHz, or 915 MHz for a longer range.

[10] In some car models, the driver has to either press a button or touch a motion sensor on the door handle which lets the car know that the keyfob is around. The car starts broadcasting the signal that supplies power to the keyfob.

[11] The mechanism that a passive RFID-tag uses to respond to an RFID-reader by using the reader's carrier as a power-supplying source is called backscattering.

far away from the car. This happens as the adopted RFID protocol automatically assumes that a keyfob is in close proximity to the car if the car can communicate with the correct keyfob. This has led to the development of RFID distance-bounding protocols [14]. These protocols are authentication protocols that in addition to proving the identity of a given party to another, e.g., keyfob to a car, the protocol also verifies the distance that separates both authenticating parties, by measuring the challenge-response time, which is also known as the round-trip time (RTT) (viz., MSC (See footnote 6) of Fig. 8). If the estimated distance is d and the round-trip time is Δt, then it must hold that $d \leq \frac{1}{2}\Delta t \cdot c$, where c is the speed of light. This type of protocols have mitigated a certain type of relay attacks. Notwithstanding, most cars keyless entry systems used nowadays, implement the authentication protocol in a way where relay attacks are still possible. In present-days, attackers employ signal-amplification relay attack to steal cars [1]. In this type of attack, attackers relay signals from the keyfob to the car and vice-versa by simply amplifying them (viz., MSC (See footnote 6) of Fig. 9).

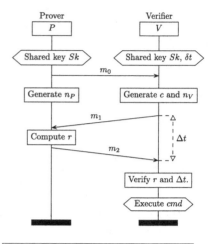

$m_0 = Request(cmd)_{P \rightarrow V}$,
$m_1 = Authentication\_Request(c, n_V)_{V \rightarrow P}$,
$m_2 = Authentication\_Response(r, n_P)_{P \rightarrow V}$,
where: $r = \mathcal{E}_{Sk}(c \parallel n_P \parallel n_V)$ and $|\Delta t - \delta t| < \epsilon$.

Fig. 8. A distance bounding-based authentication for car passive entry systems. The notation $M_{P \rightarrow V}$ indicates a message M that is sent from the prover P to the verifier V. The symbols n_V and n_P denote nonces. The symbol Sk denotes a shared secret between P and V, where $\mathcal{E}$ denotes the encryption function (hash function), and δt the empirical challenge-response turnaround time. Δt is the RTT.

3 Mitigating Relay Attacks

In this section, we propose the use of frequency hopping spread spectrum (FHSS) transmission technique on passive keyless entry and start systems (PKESs) as a physical-layer security to mitigate relay attacks. To that end, we first need to understand in which circumstances an attacker can succeed a relay attack on a PKES system and manage to steal a car. Then, we need to determine in which conditions FHSS can be applied on a PKES system as a mitigation for relay attack. This would help us identify the characteristics that need to be present on future PKES. As many car keyless entry systems do not implement a secure distance-bounding protocol, the relay attack would be feasible, which allows attackers to steal cars. Also, due to the incorrect implementation of such protocols, e.g., overestimation of the delay δt (viz., MSC (See footnote 6) of Fig. 8

and Fig. 9), the use of amplifiers will not be detected and the PKES system's security can be bypassed allowing attackers to steal cars.

Irrespective of whether a PKES is implementing a distance-bounding protocol or not, performing a passive relay attack requires from the attackers the amplification of the signals that are sent from the car to the keyfob and optionally[12] the ones sent from the keyfob to the car. This subsequently implies that attackers need to know the car-keyfob link operational frequency. Also, those amplifiers have some hardware characteristics, such as the operational frequencies, the acquisition bandwidth, the gain, the sensitivity, the related-delay, the physical size, and the price. Essentially, the hardware has to be operational on the car-keyfob frequency, has a wide acquisition bandwidth to capture the signals on a wide band, a high gain and good sensitivity to minimize the noises, and finally be portable and cheap. We note that these

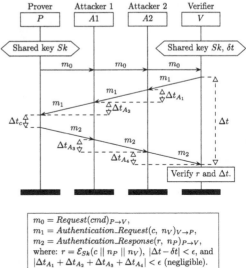

$m_0 = Request(cmd)_{P \rightarrow V}$,
$m_1 = Authentication\_Request(c, n_V)_{V \rightarrow P}$,
$m_2 = Authentication\_Response(r, n_P)_{P \rightarrow V}$,
where: $r = \mathcal{E}_{Sk}(c \parallel n_P \parallel n_V)$, $|\Delta t - \delta t| < \epsilon$, and
$|\Delta t_{A_1} + \Delta t_{A_2} + \Delta t_{A_3} + \Delta t_{A_4}| < \epsilon$ (negligible).

Fig. 9. A relay attack on a passive keyless entry system. $m_i = M_{P \rightarrow V}$ indicates that a message m_i is sent from the prover, denoted as P, to the verifier, denoted as V. The symbols n_V and n_P denote nonces. The symbol Sk denotes a shared secret between P and V, where $\mathcal{E}$ denotes the encryption function (hash function), and δt the empirical challenge-response travel time. The computed round trip time is denoted by Δt.

amplifiers are available on the black market and generally expensive, but not compared to the price of a high-end car.

From a mitigation point of view, if it is possible for the car and keyfob to somehow hide from the attacker the frequency/frequencies that is/are being used during a communication, the attacker will not succeed in boosting all the signals but only the ones that are over the frequencies that its hardware is tuned on. In the telecommunication filed, there exists a way of hiding a transmission from eavesdroppers by rapidly and secretly changing the transmission channel from time to time. This is performed through the use of FHSS technique which we present in the next subsection.

---

[12] In certain relay attacks, attackers relay the LF signals that are sent from the car to the keyfob (short range signal) and leave the UHF signals that are sent from the keyfob to the car (long range signal $\approx$100 m) [3].

3.1 Frequency-Hopping Spread Spectrum

Frequency-Hopping Spread Spectrum (FHSS) is a technique for transmitting radio signals by rapidly varying the frequency (channel) of the carrier following a predetermined pseudo-random sequence of frequencies in a given radio band. In this case, the transmitter as well as the receiver will have to synchronize over the sequence of frequencies to be able to know on which frequency they should be tuned on to send and correctly receive the signals. This technique avoids interference and jamming attacks. It also provides a physical-layer encryption to

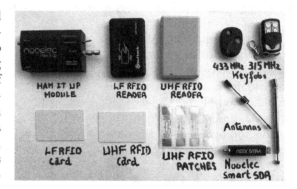

Fig. 10. Set of hardware materials used for the experiments (from left to right, from top to bottom): The NooElec Ham it up module (the black rectangle module), an LF RFID reader (125 kHz), a UHF RFID reader (865 MHz–928 MHz), a 433 MHz keyfob, a 315 MHz keyfob, an LF RFID tags (card), UHF RFID tag (card), UHF RFID tag (patches), NooElec smart SDR, and two antennas compatible with the SDR.

eavesdroppers as long as the sequence of frequencies is kept secret between the transmitter and the receiver. In FHSS, the available frequency band is divided into channels. The transmitter as well as the receiver hop from one channel to another at a predefined hopping-rate.

3.2 Frequency-Hopping Spread Spectrum in RFID

Many RFID standards including EPC[13] Gen2 have incorporated FHSS as part of their standards [17,18], essentially to prevent two UHF RFID-readers from interfering on each other. The standard EPC Gen2 (passive UHF RFID) specifies the operational frequency for the tags to be between 860 MHz and 960 MHz. Usually, depending on the radio regulatory agency of each country, a smaller frequency range between 860 MHz and 960 MHz is used. For example, the allocated frequency range (bandwidth) for UHF-RFID is 902.0 MHz to 928.0 MHz in the US (865.6 MHz to 867.6 MHz in Europe) [19]. Thus the use of FHSS should only be within the regulated radio bandwidth. Notably, the use of FHSS by UHF-tags makes sense as the available bandwidth is large enough [19].

Current PKES systems commonly operate at a lower frequency (LF RFID from 125 kHz to 137 kHz). The available bandwidth is not that wide making it not suitable for FHSS application. In fact, the RF-hardware that an attacker

---

[13] EPCGlobal industry association defines four classes of UHF RFID tags. Class 1 is for passive tags, Class 2 enriches Class 1 with more memory and add cryptography, Class 3 is semi-passive tags, and Class 4 is for active tags.

uses may have an acquisition bandwidth which is larger than the hopping bandwidth. For example, the HackRF One SDR tool has an acquisition bandwidth of 20 MHz. RFID signals sent by hopping within a 12 kHz-bandwidth (|137 kHz–125 kHz|) will be certainly intercepted by the attacker's hardware. Moreover, when a low frequency f_0 is used, its harmonics, i.e., $2 \cdot f_0$, $3 \cdot f_0$, ..., $n \cdot f_0$ are very close to each other with respect to an interception hardware with a wide acquisition bandwidth. This allows an attacker to detect the signal even though its RF-hardware filter is not sharply tuned on the frequency f_0. To demonstrate that, we have used an LF-RFID reader (viz., Fig. 10) that operates on the 125 kHz low frequency band and have observed the

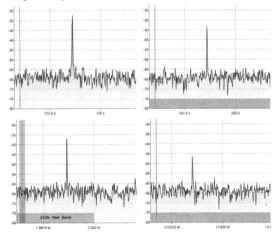

signal spectrum using the NooElec smart SDR along with Ham it up module (viz., Fig. 10) and the SDR♯ software.

Fig. 11. From top to bottom and from left to right: The main harmonic at 123.67 kHz, the 2nd harmonic at 248.65 kHz, the 16th harmonic at 1.998 MHz, and the 110th harmonic at 13.625 MHz, of the 125 kHz RFID-reader signal (carrier).

Figure 11 (top left) shows the RFID-reader's signal broadcasted at $f_0 = 123.67$ kHz (main harmonic). Interestingly, we have also observed the other harmonics at $2 \cdot f_0 = 248.65$ kHz (top right), $3 \cdot f_0, 4 \cdot f_0, 5 \cdot f_0, \ldots$, and also at 1.998 MHz (bottom left) and 13.625 MHz (bottom right). Having a wide acquisition bandwidth makes it difficult to find a narrow band signal on the spectrum if the frequency is too small and unknown. However, this does not guarantee that an eavesdropper cannot capture the signal.

Considering the results in Fig. 11, using FHSS in RFID systems should be on higher-frequency bands. This implies that if we plan to use FHSS on car passive keyless entry and start systems, future keyfobs would be embedded with a UHF RFID-tag instead of an LF RFID-tag, which should not be an issue with respect to the cost. Nonetheless, moving to the UHF-RFID band which has a wider bandwidth than LF band, will not entirely solve the problem of using FHSS in PKES. In fact, each country radio regulatory agency defines the bandwidth to be used in its country. In Europe, the total UHF-RFID bandwidth is 2 MHz divided into 10 channels of 200 kHz-wide each, whereas in the US, the total bandwidth is 26 MHz divided into 50 channels of 500 kHz-wide each. Furthermore, it is important to note that existing RFID-readers that support frequency hopping, only apply FHSS in order to prevent interference with other RFID-readers. In fact, as soon as an RFID-tag is approached to the reader, the frequency is fixed and the communication occurs over the current frequency.

To illustrate that, we have used a UHF-RFID reader/writer that supports FHSS (viz., Fig. 10). We have configured the reader in such a way so that it hops over four channels after each second ($ch_1 = 913.80$ MHz, $ch_2 = 914.20$ MHz, $ch_3 = 914.60$ MHz, and $ch_4 = 915.00$ MHz). We have observed the carrier moving within the spectrum as shown in Fig. 12 and Fig. 13. In Fig. 12, the image on the top shows the reader's carrier intercepted on channel 913.80 MHz, whereas the image on the bottom shows the reader's carrier when it moved to channel 914.20 MHz. Also, in Fig. 13, the image on the top shows the reader's carrier on channel 914.60 MHz, and finally, the image on the bottom shows the reader's carrier on channel 915.00 MHz. At a given time, we have approached the UHF RFID-tag (viz., patch-tag in Fig. 10) to the reader and have observed that the reader's carrier has stopped on the current channel and the communication has taken place. Then, we have moved away the tag from the reader and have

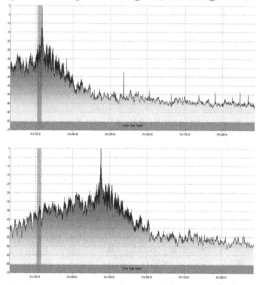

Fig. 12. UHF RFID-reader carrier during frequency hopping over channel $ch_1 = 913.80$ MHz and channel $ch_2 = 914.20$ MHz.

observed that the reader's carrier has moved forward as if it has continued hopping during the tag-reading operation. It is obvious that hopping over four channels is not a perfect way of applying FHSS. A simple hardware with only 1.20 MHz of acquisition bandwidth can intercept all the signals over all four channels. Notwithstanding, we have used only four channels for the sake of explaining the scenario.

Based on the previous results, the RFID-system has to be implemented in such a way so that the data to be exchanged between the reader and the tag should sent over different frequencies separately. Moreover, hopping over 50 UHF channels (902.60 MHz to $928.0, 0$ MHz) seems to be fine to skip eavesdroppers when the latter is using a narrow acquisition bandwidth receptor. In fact, we have configured the RFID-reader to hop over all 50 channels sequentially. Then using the NooElec smart SDR (with Ham it up module) and the SDR♯ software tool, we have tried to intercept the carrier. The NooElec smart SDR hardware has only 2.4 MHz of acquisition bandwidth. Thus, we have only managed to intercept the carrier on four channels. However, if the hopping sequence is randomly generated, the chance of intercepting the carrier will be considerably reduced. Indeed, if we denote the eavesdropper acquisition bandwidth by w^e (where $w^e = |f^e_{max} - f^e_{min}|$) and the system's bandwidth by w^s

(where $w^s = |f^s_{max} - f^s_{min}|$), the probability of the eavesdropper to successfully intercept a signal on a given channel is expressed as $P^e = w^e/w^s$, such that $\lim_{w^s \to \infty} P^e = 0$. From an attacker viewpoint, the success probability P^e of the attacker could also converge to 1 when $|w^e - w^s| < \epsilon$. In fact, nowadays fabricating a UHF transceiver with 26 MHz of acquisition bandwidth is not an impossible project. The current market actually provides public access to devices with such acquisition bandwidth. For instance, the Hack RF One (See footnote 7), is a transceiver that has 20 MHz of acquisition bandwidth and is commonly used for hacking. Such a device can be used to capture the signals that are exchanged within the UHF RFID-band, which is defined by the FCC[14]. Therefore, relying on the currently defined UHF RFID band to apply FHSS for PKES is not a prominent mitigation for relay attack. We need to augment the operational frequency to obtain a wider bandwidth and thus a larger hopping set. This would make the fabrication task of a wide acquisition

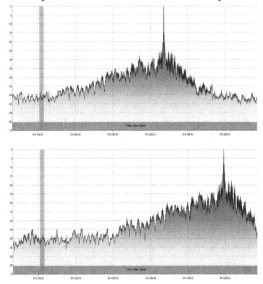

Fig. 13. UHF RFID-reader carrier during frequency hopping over channel 914.60 MHz and channel 915.00 MHz.

bandwidth transceiver very hard and expensive for the attacker. Moreover, amplifying an entire wide band involves the amplification of both signals and noises. The attacker needs to perform additional signal processing to make the right signal reaches its destination in such a way so that it can be correctly interpreted by the car and/or keyfob.

3.3   Applying FHSS on PKESs

Based on the observations and conclusions from the previous sections, in this section we provide solutions that can be followed to implement future PKES systems which will be resilient against relay attacks through the use of FHSS:

- The operational frequency has to be high enough to provide the system with a wide hopping bandwidth. If the EHF/SHF (Extremely/Super High Frequencies) can be adopted, it will be a perfect frequency band to operate on. A wide bandwidth makes the task very hard for the attacker as the latter will have to amplify a wide band which includes other signals as well as many noises.

---

[14] FCC (Federal Communications Commission) is the radio frequency regulation agency in the United-States of America.

Nonetheless, the selected frequency band has to be internationally accepted. Otherwise, interoperability issues may arise. For example, a car locking system (i.e., PKES) manufactured in the US will not be able to operate legally with respect to the frequency regulations in another country.

- The IEEE V-band (40 GHz–75 GHz) is a very suitable frequency band to be adopted in car PKES systems. In fact, within this band, certain frequencies, such as the 24 GHz and 60 GHz, have a higher atmospheric absorption, in particular from humidity (H_2O) and oxygen in the air (O_2). This makes them not suitable for wireless communications, but suitable for securing very short-range communications (≤ 1 m) such as in car PKES systems. Attackers need extremely high power to amplify signals on that band and relay them to a longer distance. Furthermore, the V-band provides a very wide bandwidth, which makes it a perfect band to apply FHSS. For example, if we simply consider a bandwidth of 2 GHz with $f_0 = 60$ GHz being the central frequency of the band and consider radio channels of 500 kHz width, we would have a total of 4000 channels to hop in, which is perfect for applying FHSS and changing the radio domain.

- The hopping sequence has to be shared between the keyfob and the car. It can be provided as a per-car unique list of possible hopping frequencies (shared secret key). Each entry of the list is identified by an Id. The Id is exchanged between the car and its keyfob to agree about the hopping sequence to be used in a given session. Also, the hopping sequences have to be generated in such as way so that designing an RF-hardware with multiple receptors and antennas with wider acquisition bandwidth will be unpractical (very hard) and very expensive to predict the sequences.

- The information that needs to be exchanged between the RFID-reader (car) and the RFID-tag (keyfob) has to be organized in such a way so that it can be transmitted over different channels. That is to say, we do not want the data rate to be very high so that the entire communication (e.g., the execution of the authentication protocol) happens on a single frequency. However, we do want the system to hop from one channel to another at a very high rate.

3.4   PKES Design

Let us consider a passive keyless entry and start system (PKES) implementing a distance-bounding protocol following the Brands and Chaum's distance-bounding protocol model [14]. In such a protocol, the authentication occurs over three phases. The first or the initial phase, which is also known as the setup phase or the slow phase, allows the car (verifier) and its associated keyfob (prover) to share the nonces and agree on the security parameters. The second phase, called the critical or the timed phase, consists of multiple rounds in which the car sends a challenge to the keyfob which replies back with a corresponding response. Thus for k−rounds, there would be k exchanged challenge and response tuples. During this phase, the car measures the RTTs (Round Trip Times) induced by each round execution. Finally, the last phase, which is also known as the authentication phase, allows the car (verifier) to conclude on a decision of whether to unlock the car or not by checking the computed RTTs as well as the responses that the keyfob provided during the second phase. In the positive scenario, the car unlocks the doors. Also, for the same execution of the protocol, it will eventually start the car engine after the driver pushes on the "Start Engine" button. Therefore, to make this system resilient against relay attacks, we augment the protocol with FHSS transmission technique. We can consider changing the operational frequency at each phase as well as at each round during the critical phase (i.e., second phase). The resulting protocol would look like the one illustrated in Fig. 14. In this

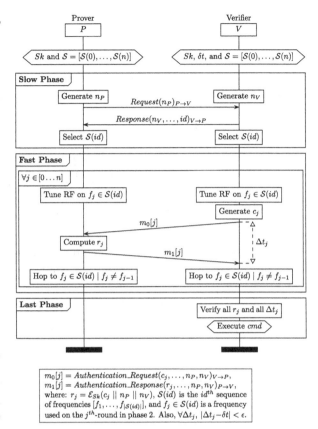

Fig. 14. A distance-bounding protocol adopting FHSS for relay attack mitigation. During the fast phase, the car (verifier) and the keyfob (prover) hop from one frequency f_j to another at each round j. The number of rounds is a security parameter mutually fixed during the first phase.

protocol, and during the first phase, the car and the keyfob exchange nonces and agree on an $id \in [0 \dots n]$ to select a sequence of frequencies $\mathcal{S}(id)$ among a shared list to be used during the second phase. During the fast phase, at each round $j \in [0 \dots n']$, a frequency $f_j \in \mathcal{S}(id)$ is fixed for the entire round. The hoping rate is in this case assumed to be equal to the time of one round. In the extreme case, if an eavesdropper misses to intercept (relay) one single round, the whole protocol execution fails. Otherwise, in the general scenario, if we tolerate the success of $\alpha-$rounds out of $n' + 1$ rounds to unlock the car, the attacker needs to relay at least $k-$rounds ($k \geq \alpha$) to bypass the mechanism. This can be made hard by increasing the value of the parameter α and using a wider hopping bandwidth w^s as we have discussed earlier.

4   Related Work

With respect to mitigating relay attacks for auto theft, the existing solutions can either be mechanical or technical. Mechanical solutions include keeping the keyfob inside a metallic box, freezer, or microwave, covering the keyfob with a foldable-aluminum sleeve (a.k.a., Faraday cage), keeping the keyfob away from the car, disabling the keyfob, parking the car inside a garage, or parking a worthless old car next to the expensive one in such a way so that the old car blocks the new one from moving. These solutions are clearly neither practical nor flexible. Technical solutions include the use of sensing technologies such as measuring the temperature, sound, GPS-position, radio-environment (e.g., Wi-Fi and Bluetooth), signal strength, i.e., RSSI (Received Signal Strength Indicator), light brightness, and motion detection [20]. These solutions tend to make the entry system costly as additional sensors are needed. In addition, sensing-based solutions are not always reliable [21–25]. For example, in a temperature-based solution, the temperature around a keyfob that is inside the driver's pocket is totally different from the temperature that is measured by the car. Also, radio-signals, such as the ones used for GPS-positioning, are not always available (e.g., in underground parking). Moreover, most sensing capabilities can easily be bypassed. The GPS-signal for instance can be spoofed using some SDR-hardware (Software Defined Radio-hardware) allowing attackers to generate fake location signals in the neighborhood and hence fooling any receiver trying to geolocalize itself. Other solutions are based on combining sensing features along with distance estimation or involving other technologies [24–27].

The idea of changing the frequency during a communication to counter relay attacks was proposed through a patent by the Texas Instruments Inc. [28]. Their idea consists of using different frequencies during a challenge-response protocol execution between the car and its keyfob. The idea was very generic irrespective of the frequency band on which it will be used and on which technology it will be adopted. In contrary, we have demonstrated that applying frequency hopping within the frequency band that is currently used by car PKES systems is not that useful. Also, we have shown that applying FHSS is worthwhile on certain frequency bands only, hence can only be adopted by some contactless applications. Another patent [29] has proposed to reduce the transmission power of the keyfob in asymmetric RFID keyless entry system (See footnote 9). The idea consists of reducing the range of the signal that is sent from the keyfob to the car (i.e., UHF-signal) that does not need to be amplified by the thieves. However, this does not entirely mitigate the attack, as it will fail to mitigate the attack if the thief with an amplifier is within that reduced range, which will allow the thief to boost the keyfob signal to the other thief which is beside the car.

5   Conclusion

Car passive keyless entry and start systems (PKESs) are being more and more deployed on modern cars. They provide a better flexibility and security with respect to their predecessor car locking and ignition systems. Nevertheless, they are prone to relay attacks. In a relay attack, attackers relay signals from a car to its keyfob and vice-versa by amplifying the signals to unlock the car doors, start its engine, and drive the car away. Currently, there is no fundamental countermeasure to mitigate relay attacks. Hundreds of high-end cars were stolen during the past three years using relay attacks.

In this paper, we have proposed the use of FHSS (Frequency Hopping Spread Spectrum) as a physical-layer security mechanism to mitigate relay attacks. The intuition behind using this spread spectrum technique is to hide the frequency on which a car and its keyfob communicate. In fact, a successful relay attack requires the attacker to have the initial knowledge of the car-keyfob operational frequency so that the attacker can correctly tune its amplifier. We have started by discussing the state of the art on car passive keyless entry and start systems (PKESs). We have presented each system as well as its related auto-theft attacks and countermeasures. Then, we have studied the application of FHSS on RFID systems, in general, and on PKES systems, in particular, and have proposed recommendations for future PKES implementations. We claim that by following the provided guidelines, future PKES systems would be more resilient not only to relay attacks but also to jamming attacks. Also, designing hardware to bypass the proposed solution would be very hard and expensive for attackers, if not impossible. Finally, we plan to implement the proposed solution and experimentally evaluate it with respect to security and performance.

References

1. Lounis, K.: Stealing High-end Cars Using Relay Attacks, related-articles collected from different sources (2020). https://www.docdroid.net/AUPx0XU/ar-pdf
2. CBC News: Toyota, Lexus Owners Warned About Thefts That Use Relay Attacks (2019). https://www.cbc.ca/news/canada/ottawa/toyota-lexus-relay-attack-1.5380947
3. Francillon, A., Danev, B., Capkun, S.: Relay Attacks on Passive Keyless Entry and Start Systems in Modern Cars. IACR Cryptology ePrint Archive **2010**(332), 1–15 (2010)
4. Zeng, Y., Yang, Q., Li, J.: Chasing cars: keyless entry system attacks. HITBSecConf Amsterdam (2017)
5. Hancke, G.P., Mayes, K., Markantonakis, K.: Confidence in smart token proximity: relay attacks revisited. Comput. Secur. **28**(7), 615–627 (2009)
6. Drimer, S., Murdoch, S.J.: Keep your enemies close: distance bounding against smartcard relay attacks. In :Proceedings of 16th USENIX Security Symposium, USENIX Association (2007)
7. Hu, Y.-C., Perrig, A., Johnson, D.B.: Wormhole attacks in wireless networks. IEEE J. Sel. Areas Commun. **24**(2), 370–380 (2006)
8. Hancke, G.: Practical attacks on proximity identification systems. In: Proceedings of the 27th IEEE Symposium on Security and Privacy (2006)
9. Kfir, Z., Wool, A.: Picking virtual pockets using relay attacks on contactless smartcard. In: the 1st International Conference on Security and Privacy for Emerging Areas in Communications Networks, pp. 47–58 (2005)

10. Desmedt, Y., Goutier, C., Bengio, S.: Special uses and abuses of the fiat-shamir passport protocol. In: Advances in Cryptology 1987, A Conference on the Theory and Applications of Cryptographic Techniques, pp. 21–39 (1987)
11. Desmedt, Y.: Major security problems with unforgeable(ferge)-fiat-shamir proofs of identity and how to overcome them. In: Worldwide Congress on Computer and Communications Security and Protection, pp. 15–17 (1988)
12. Carluccio, D., Lemke, K., Paar, C.: Electromagnetic side channel analysis of a contactless smart card: first results. In: ECryptWorkshop on RFID and Lightweight Crypto (2005)
13. Lounis, K., Zulkernine, M.: Attacks and defenses in short-range wireless technologies for IoT. IEEE Access **8**, 88892–88932 (2020)
14. Brands, S., Chaum, D.: Distance-Bounding Protocols. In: Helleseth, T. (ed.) EUROCRYPT 1993. LNCS, vol. 765, pp. 344–359. Springer, Heidelberg (1994). https://doi.org/10.1007/3-540-48285-7_30
15. Kamkar, S.: Drive It Like You Hacked It: New Attacks and Tools to Wirelessly Steal Cars. DEF CON 23 (2015)
16. Collins, D.: How to Program a Car Key (2019). https://www.carbibles.com/how-to-program-a-car-key/, CarBible
17. EPCGlobal: EPC Radio-Frequency Identity Protocols Class-1 Generation-2 UHF RFID Protocol for Communication at 860 MHz-960 MHz Version 1.2.0 (2008)
18. EPCGlobal: EPC Radio-Frequency Identity Protocols Generation-2, UHF RFID Specification for RFID Air Interface Protocol for Communication at 860 MHz-960 MHz Version 2.0.0 Ratified (2013)
19. Banks, J., Pachano, M., Thompson, L., Hanny, D.: RFID Applied. Wiley, New York (2017)
20. Valko, A.: Relay attack resistant passive keyless entry: securing PKE systems with immobility detection," B.Sc. thesis, TRITA-ITM-EX 2020:48, KTH, School of Industrial Engineering and Management, pp. 1–90 (2020)
21. Choi, S.K., Kim, S.S., Kim, G.H.: Method for preventing relay-attack on smart key system. Patent No. US9210188B2, p. 12 (2015)
22. Wang, J., Lounis, K., Zulkernine, M.: Security features for proximity verification. In: 2019 IEEE 43rd Annual Computer Software and Applications Conference (COMPSAC), pp. 592–597 (2019)
23. Aanjhan, R., Capkun, S.: Are we really close? Verifying proximity in wireless systems. IEEE Secur, Priv. **15**(3), 52–58 (2017)
24. Choi, W., Seo, M., Lee, D.H.: Sound-proximity: 2-factor authentication against relay attack on passive keyless entry and start systems. J. Adv. Transp. article 1935974 (2018)
25. Kumar, S.S., Pandharipande, A.: Secure indoor positioning: relay attacks and mitigation using presence sensing systems. In: IEEE 13th International Conference on Industrial Informatics (INDIN), Cambridge, pp. 82–87 (2015)
26. Frank Stajano, F.-L.W., Christianson, B.: Multichannel protocols to prevent relay attacks. In: Financial Cryptography (2010)
27. Wang, J., Lounis, K., Zulkernine, M.: CSKES: a context-based secure keyless entry system. In: 2019 IEEE 43rd Annual Computer Software and Applications Conference (COMPSAC), pp. 817–822 (2019)
28. Kim, H., Dabak, A.G., Ren, J., Goel, M.: Relay Attack Countermeasure System. Patent No. US2015/0222658A1, pp. 1–11 (2015)
29. Mutti, C.S., Spedaliere, D.: Solutions for relay attacks on passive keyless entry and go. Patent No. WO2013050409A1, p. 4 (2013)

A Deeper Analysis of Adversarial Examples in Intrusion Detection

Mohamed Amine Merzouk[1,2]([✉]), Frédéric Cuppens[3], Nora Boulahia-Cuppens[3], and Reda Yaich[4]

[1] Ecole Nationale Supérieure d'Informatique, Algiers, Algeria
`fm_merzouk@esi.dz`
[2] IMT Atlantique, Rennes, France
`mohamed-amine.merzouk@imt-atlantique.fr`
[3] Polytechnique Montréal, Montréal, Canada
`{frederic.cuppens,nora.boulahia-cuppens}@polymtl.ca`
[4] IRT SystemX, Plaiseau, France
`reda.yaich@irt-systemx.fr`

Abstract. During the last decade, machine learning algorithms have massively integrated the defense arsenal made available to security professionals, especially for intrusion detection. However, and despite the progress made in this area, machine learning models have been found to be vulnerable to slightly modified data samples called adversarial examples. Thereby, a small and well-computed perturbation may allow adversaries to evade intrusion detection systems. Numerous works have already successfully applied adversarial examples to network intrusion detection datasets. Yet little attention was given so far to the practicality of these examples in the implementation of end-to-end network attacks. In this paper, we study the applicability of network attacks based on adversarial examples in real networks. We minutely analyze adversarial examples generated with state-of-the-art algorithms to evaluate their consistency based on several criteria. Our results show a large proportion of invalid examples that are unlikely to lead to real attacks.

Keywords: Adversarial machine learning · Adversarial examples · Intrusion detection · Evasion attacks

1 Introduction

The importance of Artificial Intelligence (AI) and particularly Machine Learning (ML) in cybersecurity cannot be overstated. The synergistic integration of the two disciplines is considered by most specialists as one of the most profitable advances in cybersecurity [30]. Indeed, a description of the current threats landscape is sufficient to understand the interest of cybersecurity professionals from industry and academia in AI and ML. However, it is still relatively simple to deliberately mislead ML models, by means of what is commonly called Adversarial Machine Learning (AdvML) attacks.

© Springer Nature Switzerland AG 2021
J. Garcia-Alfaro et al. (Eds.): CRiSIS 2020, LNCS 12528, pp. 67–84, 2021.
https://doi.org/10.1007/978-3-030-68887-5_4

AdvML research community has been very active in the last few years to illustrate the fragility of ML models with regards to Adversarial Examples (AEs) [19]. AEs are data samples to which a small and deliberate perturbation is added to maliciously influence the output of an ML model towards erroneous predictions. For instance, applied to intrusion detection models, an attacker could transform an instance, that was originally classified as an attack, to be misleadingly classified as a benign entry. Thus allowing adversaries to evade intrusion detection systems.

Contribution: This article tries to answer the question: *Do we really need to worry about AEs in intrusion detection?* In order to do so, we investigate the practicality of AEs generated by state-of-the-art approaches in the execution of end-to-end cyberattacks on computer networks. We provide a comprehensive literature review of research initiatives addressing the vulnerability of intrusion detection systems to AEs. We also design and train an intrusion detection model on the well-known NSL-KDD dataset [33] and generate AEs against it with the most prominent methods. Furthermore, we evaluate their impact on the model and their distance from the original examples. Through an in-depth analysis of the network features of these examples, we identify several criteria that invalidate these attacks. In practice, the outcomes of our work are three-fold:

- An automated environment to train an intrusion detection model and analyse the impact and the consistency of AEs generated against it. The environment is available through a public repository[1] to stimulate further investigations.
- An implementation of Carlini and Wagner [6] L_0-*attack* that is made available to the community through the well-established open-source library Adversarial Robustness Toolbox [23].
- A description of validity criteria that can be used to discard unpractical AEs (cf. Sect. 6).

Paper Organization: Section 2 defines some basic background about artificial neural networks, adversarial machine learning, and the algorithms we use to generate AEs. In Sect. 3 we propose a literature review of research initiatives applying AdvML to intrusion detection. Section 4 details the experimental methodology we followed. In Sect. 5 we present and discuss the results of our experiments and analyze the generated AEs. Section 6 introduces the list of validity criteria for practical AEs. Finally, concluding remarks and future works are detailed in Sect. 7.

2   Background

In this section, we present some background knowledge on artificial neural networks, adversarial machine learning and adversarial examples.

---

[1] https://github.com/mamerzouk/adversarial_analysis.

2.1   Artificial Neural Networks

An Artificial Neural Network (ANN) is a machine learning model represented as a function $f(\cdot)$ that takes a data sample $x \in \mathcal{R}^n$ as an input and outputs a prediction l. ANNs are made of interconnected layers of neurons (perceptrons): small units that compute the sum of their inputs, weighted by the model parameters θ, and pass it through a non-linear activation function to produce an output (activation); this output is then propagated to be the input the neurons of the next layer.

The parameters of a neural network are randomly initialized and optimized through training. The loss function $J_\theta(x, l)$ estimates the error of the model by computing the difference between its output and the correct label. The gradient of the loss function with respect to the parameters $\nabla J_\theta(x, l)$ is then used by algorithms like Stochastic Gradient Descent or Adam to optimize the parameters in order to minimize the loss.

2.2   Adversarial Machine Learning

Adversarial Machine Learning (AdvML) is a recent research discipline that aims to evaluate and improve the robustness of machine learning models against malicious manipulations. The extensive literature in this field reports a wide variety of attacks that fall into four categories [5]:

- *Poisoning attacks* are achieved before the training phase by introducing perturbations among the training data to generate a corrupted model [4].
- *Evasion attacks* happen after the model is trained. They are used to manipulate the input data of a model to provoke erroneous predictions [3].
- *Extraction attacks* try to steal the parameters of a remote model in order to reproduce its behavior or rob confidential information [13].
- *Inversion attacks* abuse a model to extort sensitive information learned from the training data [9].

In our work, we focus on evasion attacks; there are two main types of them: *Untargeted attacks* that aim to cause the model to make erroneous predictions regardless of the output result and *Targeted attacks* that are much complex as they intend to orient the erroneous outcome towards a specific result. The two approaches are equivalent in binary classification (between two classes).

2.3   Adversarial Examples

Adversarial Examples (AEs) are inputs deliberately crafted to fool machine learning models. An AE x' is generally based on a clean example x to which a well-computed and minimal perturbation η is added. This perturbation must be sufficiently important to misclassify the sample in the false class l' instead of the correct class l, while limiting changes to maintain malicious functionality and minimize effort [34]. These changes are communally measured with distance metrics like L_p norms. We described below the three most used L_p norms.

- L_0 measures the number of perturbed features i such as $x_i \neq x'_i$.
- L_2 measures the Euclidean distance between two samples $\sqrt{\sum_{i=1}^{n}(x_i - x'_i)^2}$.
- L_∞ measures the maximum perturbation applied to any data feature.

The problem of finding AEs with minimal perturbation regarding an L_p norm is formulated in Eq. 1. In targeted attacks, l' is known in advance, while in untargeted attacks, l' can be any class other than the correct class l. We also assume that the features must stay in a limited interval we refer to as I.

$$\text{minimize } \|x - x'\|_p \text{ such that } f(x') = l', f(x) \neq l', x' \in I^n \tag{1}$$

This problem being too complex to solve, Szegedy et al. [32] reformulated it in Eq. 2, where c is a positive constant minimized by line-search. They then used the box-constrained L-BFGS optimization method to solve it.

$$\text{minimize } c \cdot \|x - x'\|_2 + J_\theta(x', l') \text{ such that } x' \in I^n \tag{2}$$

2.4 Adversarial Examples Generation Methods

We present some of the ground-breaking methods for the generation of AEs. These methods will later be used in our experiments. Readers interested in a detailed survey on AEs can refer to Yuan et al. [38].

Fast Gradient Sign Method (FGSM) was introduced by Goodfellow et al. [11] to allow the generation of AEs much faster than L-BFGS. It uses the concept of backpropagation but updates the inputs instead of the parameters. Thus, the sign of the gradient of the loss function with respect to the inputs is used to guide the perturbation ϵ (positive or negative), as shown in Eq. 3.

$$x' = x + \epsilon \cdot \text{sign}(\nabla J_\theta(x, l)) \tag{3}$$

Basic Iterative Method (BIM) was introduced by Kurakin et al. [16] and consists of applying FGSM in many iterations with a small perturbation magnitude. The advantage of BIM is that it adapts the perturbation to each iteration, the more iterations it does, the finer the perturbation is. In addition, BIM applies a clipping method, shown in Eq. 4, for every iteration to avoid getting feature values out of the interval I (considered $[0, 1]$ in the equation).

$$\text{Clip}_{x,\xi}\{x'\} = \min\{1, x + \xi, \max\{0, x - \epsilon, x'\}\} \tag{4}$$

DeepFool was introduced by Moosavi-Dezfooli et al. [21]. This method looks for the closest distance from a normal example to the classification boundary it must cross to be misclassified. This distance is the perturbation applied to the example. Since it only looks for the closest distance to a different class, no matter which class, this attack is untargeted. This method originally optimizes the L_2 norm since it uses the Euclidean distance. The author overcame the obstacle of non-linearity in high dimensionality by using an iterative attack with linear approximation. In the case of binary differentiable classifiers, the perturbation is approximated attractively by considering f linear around x_i. The minimal perturbation is then computed by Eq. 5. Despite its efficiency, DeepFool provides only a coarse approximation of the optimal perturbation vectors.

$$\text{argmin}_{\eta_i} \|\eta_i\|_2 \text{ such that } f(x_i) + \nabla f(x_i)^T \cdot \eta_i = 0 \tag{5}$$

Jacobian-based Saliency Map Attack (JSMA) was introduced by Papernot *et al.* [24]. Unlike previous methods, this method tries to minimize the number of perturbed features in order to create AEs with minimal L_0 norm. It starts with an empty set of features and chooses a new feature to perturb in each iteration. It iterates and adds perturbation until the example becomes adversarial or until it reaches another stop criterion. JSMA starts by computing the Jacobian matrix shown in Eq. 6. It is the matrix of the derivatives of each output logit with respect to each feature.

$$J_F(x) = \frac{\partial F(x)}{\partial x} = \left[\frac{\partial F_j(x)}{\partial x_i} \right]_{i \times j} \tag{6}$$

The Jacobian matrix estimates the contribution of each feature to each class. In order to prioritize the most salient attributes, a saliency map is built on the basis of the Jacobian matrix. The attribute with the highest saliency value for the targeted class is chosen to be perturbed in the current iteration.

Carlini&Wagner's attack (C&W) was introduced in Carlini and Wagner [6] as an efficient method to defeat existing defense techniques. The authors first reformulated Eq. 1 as an appropriate optimization instance.

$$\text{minimize } \|\eta\|_p + c \cdot g(x + \eta) \text{ such that } x + \eta \in I^n \tag{7}$$

In Eq. 7, g is an objective function such that $f(x + \eta) = l'$ if and only if $g(x + \eta) \leq 0$. Thus, the two constraints become a single term to minimize. A positive constant c is chosen by binary search to scale the minimization problem. In [6] three methods are introduced for the optimization of each of the L_0, L_2 and L_∞ distance norms:

- L_2-*attack* optimizes Eq. 7 with $p = 2$ using an optimization function to find AEs. It is the main method of the Carlini&Wagner attack, the other methods are based on this one.
- L_∞-*attacks* is an iterative attack, because the L_∞ distance norm is not fully differentiable, and thus optimization algorithms are not efficient. The first term of Eq. 7 is replaced by a new penalty that estimates the L_∞ norm.
- L_0-*attacks* is also iterative since the L_0 norm is not differentiable. In each iteration it applies the L_2-*attack*, it identifies the feature that contributes the least to the AEs using the gradient of the objective function and it fixes its value. The algorithm stops when the remaining subset of features is insufficient to construct AEs.

3 Literature Review

While often chiefly presented as a challenge for AI, AdvML has rapidly attracted the attention of the security research community. This is particularly evident when we analyze the extensive literature devoted to attacking techniques used to evade ML-based intrusion detection and malware detection models [19]. In this section, we review the research initiatives applying pioneer approaches to network intrusion detection.

Rigaki and Elragal [28] first explored the applicability of AEs on deep learning based intrusion detection models and their transferability to other machine learning models. Their experiments were performed using FGSM [11] and JSMA [24]. Wang [35] extended their work by testing DeepFool [21] and the three C&W attacks [6]. The author also discussed the contribution of each feature to the AEs and gave some guidelines on how these features could be manipulated by an adversary. Warzyński and Kołaczek [36] has also used FGSM [11] and successfully misclassified all attack samples as normal traffic. However, the attack parameters and the distance norms have not been reported.

Unlike previous works, Yang et al. [37] assumed a black-box attack scenario where the adversary only knows the output of the model (label or confidence). Three different black-box algorithms were evaluated: Transferring AEs generated on a substitute model using C&W [6], Zeroth Order Optimization (ZOO) [7] and Generative Adversarial Nets (GANs) [10]. Lin et al. [17] introduced IDSGAN, a framework based on GANs to generate AEs that can deceive a black-box intrusion detection system.

It is worth noticing that the experiments of all the previously mentioned works used a Multi-Layer Perceptron (MLP) neural network trained on the NSL-KDD dataset [33].

Martin et al. [18] applied the main attack methods to six different classifiers. They used NSL-KDD [33] and CICIDS2017 [31], a more recent dataset. They showed the robustness of different models before and after re-training them with AEs. Peng et al. [26] proposed an improved boundary-based method to craft AEs for DoS attacks, they also used CICIDS2017 [31].

Ibitoye et al. [12] compared the performance of Self-normalizing Neural Networks (SNNs) [14] with traditional Feed-forward Neural Networks (FNNs) for intrusion detection on the BoT-IoT dataset [15]. Their results show that FNNs outperform SNNs based on multiple performance metrics, while SNNs demonstrate better resilience against AEs. AbouKhamis et al. [1] used a min-max (or saddle-point) approach to train a model against AEs generated using variants of FGSM on the NSW-NB 15 dataset [22]. Principal Component Analysis (PCA) was applied to the dataset to evaluate its impact on the robustness of the model. Clements et al. [8] were able to efficiently fool an intrusion detection model by modifying 1.38 features on average. Alhajjar et al. [2] explored the use of evolutionary computation and GANs to generate AEs against network intrusion detection models. Piplai et al. [27] showed that even intrusion detection models trained with AEs can still be fooled.

Moisejevs [20] proposed a survey on adversarial attacks and defenses in intrusion detection, and Martins *et al.* [19] provided a systematic review on adversarial machine learning applied to intrusion and malware scenarios.

Despite the large number of works addressing adversarial attacks against intrusion detection, little attention was paid to the consistency of the generated AEs. In fact, even if these attacks can fool detection models, they do not represent a real threat if they cannot be implemented. The work reported in this article tries to provide a deeper analysis of the AEs to evaluate whether they can practically lead to the implementation of end-to-end network attacks. As far as we know, no other research initiative presents a such deep analysis to derive comprehensive validity criteria for adversarial attacks (cf. Sect. 6).

4 Experimentation Approach and Settings

In order to evaluate the impact of different adversarial attacks and the consistency of the generated AEs in intrusion detection, we set up a methodical experimentation approach. In this section, we describe our approach, starting from the choice of the dataset and the pre-processing techniques applied to it. Then we present the target ML model, discuss its design and its training. We finally introduce the AEs generation methods and their parameters.

4.1 Dataset and Pre-processing

With all the attention paid to intrusion detection in recent years, several interesting datasets have emerged. Ring *et al.* [29] presented a detailed survey of network intrusion detection datasets, they evaluated 34 datasets based on 15 properties they identified. In order to allow proper comparison with related works, all our experiments are performed using the NSL-KDD dataset [33]. Indeed, despite some drawbacks like its age, NSL-KDD remains the most widely used dataset in the intrusion detection literature.

In terms of pre-processing, we use One-Hot-Encoding to transform categorical features into a vector of binary features. For instance, in NSL-KDD, the `Protocol-type` feature can take three values: `TCP`, `UDP` and `ICMP`. When applying One-Hot-Encoding, this feature is represented by three different binary features and its values can be : $(1, 0, 0)$, $(0, 1, 0)$ or $(0, 0, 1)$. Only one binary feature can hold the value 1 since the instance belongs to a single category. One-Hot-Encoding pre-processing is paramount, particularly for neural network models, as they require numerical features. By applying it, the features count of our dataset rose from 41 to 120.

In addition, we removed the 20th feature `Num-out-bound-cmds` that only held the value 0. Min-Max normalization was also used to scale the values in the range [0, 1] to prevent features with large value ranges from influencing the classification.

Since the main concern of our study is evasion attacks against intrusion detection (classifying attacks as normal traffic), for our experiments, we only consider the attack samples in the test set of NSL-KDD. Also, the dataset has been processed in order to regroup all the attack types into a single label. The classification will only be between two classes: normal and malicious (binary classification problem), which makes the targeted and untargeted attacks equivalent in our scenario.

4.2 Target Model Design and Training

Similarly to most of the previous works, the target model used in our experiments is a Multi-Layer Perceptron (MLP). It has 2 hidden layers of 256 neurons and a Softmax output layer with 2 neurons (Since we have a binary classification problem). The neurons of the hidden layers use the Rectified Linear Unit activation function (ReLU). The loss is computed using the Cross-Entropy Loss function. The model is trained for 1000 epochs using the Adam optimizer to adjust the parameters with a learning rate of 0.001. The model is made as simple and as close as possible to the models used in similar work in order to allow realistic comparisons. Thus, no regularization has been applied to avoid introducing any bias. Neural networks in our experiments are implemented using the open-source machine learning library Pytorch [25] on the programming platform Google Colaboratory.

4.3 Adversarial Attacks Models

In our experiments, the attacks are implemented using the open-source library Adversarial Robustness Toolbox (ART) [23]. The L_0-*attack* of Carlini&Wagner was not available, so we undertook its implementation to enrich ART. The parameters used for each attack are described below. Default parameters are preferred and no clipping was applied, since only few studies specify the parameters used in their experiments. The complete implementation of our experiments can be found on: https://github.com/mamerzouk/adversarial_analysis.

Fast Gradient Sign Method. For our experiments, we apply FGSM as defined in [11]. The gradient of the loss, with respect to the original class, is added to the examples, which makes it untargeted. The perturbation is applied in one single step (no iterations). The maximum perturbation magnitude ϵ is set to 0.1 and the batch size is set to 128.

Basic Iterative Method. For our experiments, we apply BIM with the same parameters as FGSM. We do not specify a target, the attack is thus untargeted. We set the number of iterations to 100 and the magnitude of the perturbation for each iteration to 0.001. This way, the maximum magnitude of the perturbation cannot exceed 0.1. We also set the batch size to 128.

DeepFool: In our experiment, we use DeepFool with a magnitude of 10^{-6} over 100 iterations and a batch size of 128. DeepFool is untargeted by definition and optimizes the L_2 norm.

Carlini&Wagner: The C&W attacks were applied in an untargeted way and with no minimum confidence imposed. The learning rate for the optimization algorithm was set to 0.01, and the batch size was set to 128. The rest of the parameters are kept in the ART default values. Since ART did not contain an implementation of Carlini&Wagner L_0-*attack*, we implemented this attack and made the code available in the experiment notebook.

Jacobian-Based Saliency Map Attack: We allow JSMA to perturb 100% of the features. We apply a perturbation of 0.1 in each iteration. The batch size is set to 128. Since JSMA is a targeted attack, if no target is specified, the implementation of ART randomly chooses a target from the false classes.

5   Evaluation of the Perturbation Potential

In this section, we present the results of our experiments and evaluate the generated AEs. Table 1 shows the accuracy of the model on the AEs generated by each method, along with the mean and maximum of each distance metric.

Table 1. Detection rate and distance metrics of different methods.

Methods	Detection	L_0 norm		L_2 norm		L_∞ norm	
		Mean	Max	Mean	Max	Mean	Max
Clean	75.1188%	0	0	0	0	0	0
FGSM	24.8811%	121	121	1.2099	1.2099	0.1	0.1
BIM	24.8811%	120.9543	121	0.9936	1.1578	0.1	0.1
DeepFool	25.1305%	120.9979	121	0.0177	0.1792	0.0469	0.1772
C&W L_2	22.7382%	13.8185	22	1.1977	7.2848	0.5078	1.4739
C&W L_∞	28.1306%	13.0478	43	0.5832	3.0571	0.2138	0.3
C&W L_0	24.1175%	3.7126	21	2.5272	22.1609	0.9099	2.4803
JSMA	24.8811%	2.0804	4	0.075	0.5	0.1729	0.5

We observe in Table 1 that before perturbing the data, the trained model achieved 75.11% detection rate on attack samples. These results are consistent with state-of-the-art performance on NSL-KDD. More details on the performance of the model can be found in the publicly available notebook.

Table 1 also shows that all the attacks had an impact on the detection rate of the model. Almost all of them considerably decreased the accuracy to around 24%, which represents a 68% decrease.

The similarity in the degradation caused by different methods allows an unbiased evaluation since the differences in the distance metrics are highlighted. These metrics demonstrate the various behavior of each method concerning the perturbation. Thus, we can understand how the attacks perturb the data differently to achieve, approximately, the same result. In the following subsections, we

Table 2. Samples of feature values from AEs of different methods.

Methods	IRC	Telnet	Logged-in	Same-srv-rate
FGSM	−0.1	0.1	−0.1	1.1
BIM	0.1	−0.1	−0.1	1.1
DeepFool	−0.0172	−0.0051	−0.0034	−0.0007
C&W L_2	0	1.4425	1.8378	2.3132
C&W L_∞	1.28	0	0.7274	1.3
C&W L_0	0	1.8155	0.8127	2.0155
JSMA	0.5	1	0	0

analyze the results of each method, and we examine the consistency of generated adversarial examples.

5.1 Fast Gradient Sign Method

We observe in Table 1 that FGSM has an important impact on the detection rate of the model, it decreases the detection rate to 24.88%. Among all the experimented algorithms, FGSM was the fastest. It has the lowest maximum L_∞ distance, which is the same as the mean L_∞ distance. This absence of variance is due to the fact that FGSM perturbs with the same amount all the features of all the examples. The objective is to spread the perturbation on the whole feature space with minimal perturbation magnitude (slightly perturb all the features instead of heavily perturb few features).

However, this method leads to indiscriminate perturbation of all the features. The mean and maximum of the L_0 norm, which refers to the number of perturbed features, is equal to the total number of features. This is consistent with the results of the Fig. 1, a heat map of the percentage of AEs perturbing each feature, that shows that all the features are perturbed in 100% of the AEs generated by FGSM.

This property of FGSM might be problematic for binary features: Since the perturbation applied is always equal to 0.1, it cannot change the value of a binary feature from one state to the other. For example, Table 2 shows an adversarial example generated by FGSM that puts the value of the binary feature Telnet to 0.1. This value invalidates the data sample, making it not practically possible to implement. This observation is valid for 100% of the AEs generated by FGSM, as shown in the Table 3.

Categorical features are also impacted by FGSM: Using One-Hot-Encoding transformed every categorical feature into multiple binary features. Only one of the binary features generated from the same categorical feature can hold the value 1, all the others must hold the value 0. However, FGSM perturbs all these binary features, which consequently activates multiple categories at the same time. We can see in Table 2 that the features IRC and Telnet which are derived from the category Service are both perturbed by FGSM. Since an instance cannot belong to multiple categories, this perturbation invalidates the data sample. Table 3 shows that this observation is also valid for all the AEs generated by FGSM.

FGSM perturbs all the data samples following the sign of the gradient. This perturbation does not consider the definition domain of the feature. Thus, without a clipping function, the perturbation might put the value of a feature below its minimum or above its maximum. The example shown in Table 2 puts the value of `Same-srv-rate`, which is the proportion of connection to the same service among the connection aggregated in `count`, to 1.1. This value is not possible since the maximum proportion is 1. We can also see that `Logged-in` has a negative value −0.1. This value has no interpretation in a real network, so this adversarial example cannot be implemented. As well as all the other examples generated by FGSM according to Table 3.

FGSM was designed to generate AEs very quickly. It uses the simple idea of propagating the gradient of the loss all the way back to the inputs. This method is useful for adversarial training [11] since it allows the fast generation of AEs to re-train the model. However, it spreads the perturbation on all the features to minimise the L_∞ norm. This might be useful for unstructured data like images where features (pixels) do not hold a semantic value. But in the case of heavily structured data like network records, FGSM generates inconsistent values and breaks the semantic links between the features.

5.2 Basic Iterative Method (BIM)

As shown in Table 1, BIM has the same impact as FGSM with slightly better mean distance norms. The maximums are the same, except the L_2 norm which has a smaller maximum for BIM. The difference between the two can be explained by the finer optimization method of BIM that applies small FGSM steps in each iteration. This leads to smaller norm distances.

However, BIM perturbs the features the same way FGSM does. It also inherits all its disadvantages. Table 2 shows that AEs generated by BIM share the same properties as FGSM. Without clipping, the values of the features get out of their definition domain, as `Telnet`, it puts non-binary values on binary features like `Logged-in` and it activates multiple categories of `Service`. These criteria are present in 100% of the AEs generated by BIM, as shown in Table 3, and are sufficient to invalidate them.

5.3 DeepFool

Table 1 shows that DeepFool performs almost as well as the other methods. Since the objective of DeepFool is to optimize the L_2 norm, it has the smallest mean Euclidean distance. It is also noteworthy that DeepFool shows the best mean L_∞ norm and a slightly larger maximum L_∞ than FGSM and BIM.

Just like FGSM or BIM, the mean L_0 norm is almost equal to the total number of features. This demonstrates that DeepFool perturbs all the features of practically all instances. Figure 1 supports the results of the L_0 norm. It shows

Table 3. Proportion of invalidation criteria in AEs of different methods.

Methods	Out-of-range values	Non-binary values	Multiple categories
Clean	0%	0%	0%
FGSM	100%	100%	100%
BIM	100%	100%	100%
DeepFool	100%	100%	100%
C&W L_2	94.7089%	99.9688%	0%
C&W L_∞	80.5345%	90.0802%	0.8493%
C&W L_0	63.5393%	54.0559%	0.1636%
JSMA	0.0155%	67.2952%	67.2796%

indeed that the vast majority of features are perturbed on more than 99% of instances.

Despite its good results, DeepFool stays a method that only focuses on the Euclidean distance. It does not optimize the number of perturbed features; rather, it perturbs a large number of features in practically all the instances to minimize the L_2 norm.

Table 2 shows examples where DeepFool generates non-binary values on binary features like `Logged-in`. It activates multiple categories of `Service` as `IRC` and `Telnet`. It also generates out-of-range values, as for `Same-server-rate`, which is a proportion and cannot be negative. These properties are found in 100% of generated AEs, according to Table 3. Besides, the simultaneous perturbation of all the features may damage the semantic links between them. In the case of network data, this leads to inconsistent samples that cannot be implemented.

5.4   Carlini and Wagner

L_2-**Attack:** As shown in Table 1, Carlini&Wagner L_2-*attack* reduces the detection rate of the model to 22.73%, which is the lowest detection rate recorded. Though it is supposed to optimize the L_2 norm, it has one of the highest mean and maximum Euclidean distance. The L_∞ norm is also high compared to previous methods. However, the L_2-*attack* of Carlini&Wagner does not perturb all the features, the L_0 norm has a mean of 13.81 features and a maximum of 22 features.

From the samples shown in Table 2, we can see how the L_2-*attack* introduces non-binary values like 1.8378 for `Logged-in`. Because of the large magnitude of the perturbation, some features are pushed out of their definition range. For example `Same-server-rate` is pushed to 2.3132 when it should not exceed 1. However, unlike other methods, Carlini&Wagner does not activate multiple categories of the same categorical feature on any data sample. Despite this interesting result, the two first properties make the AEs generated by the L_2-*attack* not applicable to real-world network traffic.

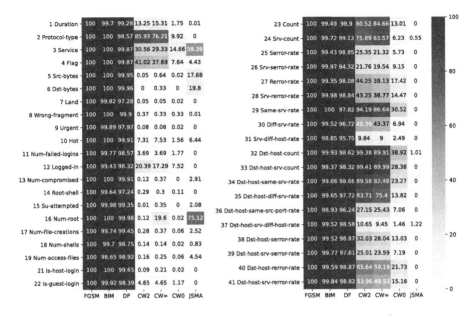

Fig. 1. Heat map of the proportion of AEs perturbing each feature

L_{∞}-**Attack:** Our results show that Carlini&Wagner L_{∞}-*attack*, with the used parameters, was the less efficient method on NSL-KDD. It decreased the accuracy to 28.13%. Even though this method is supposed to optimize the L_{∞} norm, its mean and maximum perturbation values are larger than FGSM, BIM or DeepFool. However, the AEs generated by this method showed relatively small L_0 norm values. Only 12.71 features were perturbed in average with a maximum of 43 perturbed features.

Despite all this, the L_{∞}-*Attack* of Carlini&Wagner presents insufficiency that prevents its use in network data. First, its lower impact on the accuracy reduces the number of feasible adversarial attacks. Even if the perturbation is not spread on a large number of features, Table 2 shows that this attack perturbs some binary features with a non-binary value, it is the case for `Logged-in`. It also puts out-of-range values on features like `Same-server-rate`. But it does not activate multiple categories on more then 0.8% of its AEs.

L_0-**Attack:** As shown in Table 1, the L_0-*attack* of Carlini&Wagner had strong impact on the detection rate by only perturbing 3.7 features on average and a maximum of 21 features. However, these results are explained by the L_2 and L_{∞} norms that are excessively large, by far the highest among all the methods. The Euclidean distance reached 22.16, and the maximum perturbation was up to 2.48 and 0.9 on average. These metrics are extremely high and make the L_0-*attack* of Carlini&Wagner unsuited for network data.

We can see in Table 2 that even if it only perturbs a few features, there is still inconsistency in the data. Binary features like `Logged-in` hold non-binary values.

Also, some features reach very large values, like `Telnet` that was set to 1.81 when its maximum should be 1. However, our results showed that Carlini&Wagner L_0-*attack*, just like other Carlini&Wagner attacks, almost never perturbs multiple categories of the same categorical feature. It focuses its perturbation on the actual category of the instance. This result holds true for the three categorical features `Protocol-type`, `Service` and `Flag`.

5.5   Jacobian-Based Saliency Map Attack

The Jacobian-based Saliency Map Attacks decreased the accuracy to 24.88%, which is the same score as FGSM and BIM. This finding was observed in several executions.

JSMA showed the best L_0, it only perturbed 2.08 features on average and a maximum of 4 features. The average Euclidean distance was around 0.07, and the maximum was 0.5. These are the second-best L_2 norms after DeepFool. The mean L_∞ norm was better than all Carlini&Wagner attacks but the maximum L_∞ reached 0.5, the third-highest after C&W L_0-*attack* and C&W L_2-*attack*.

JSMA certainly shows the most interesting results for a network data application. Unfortunately, Table 2 shows that even AEs generated by JSMA have inconsistency problems. Binary features like `Telnet` are perturbed with non-binary values. Multiple categories of the same categorical feature are activated, is the case for `IRC` and `Telnet`. These two criteria were found in, respectively, 67.29% and 67.27% of the AEs generated by JSMA. Thus, many examples may be disqualified. However, only 0.01% of the examples have out-of-range values, it can be explained by Fig. 1 that shows that JSMA focuses its perturbation on features like `Num-root` or `Src-bytes` and `Dst-bytes` that can reach high values.

6   Criteria for Valid End-To-End Adversarial Attacks

The results presented previously demonstrate the high perturbation potential of adversarial examples on ML-based intrusion detection systems. However, when we perform an in-depth analysis of the data samples generated by the different methods, one can legitimately question the practicality of these samples when it comes to performing real end-to-end cyberattacks. Our results showed that a large portion of the perturbation that was applied to network traffic features invalidate the original network session, making the derived attack hard, if not impossible, to execute in real environments. We summarize below the main invalidation criteria we have identified in our research. This is a non-exhaustive list that can be extended with other criteria.

Non-binary Values: Binary features indicate the presence or the absence of a property in the data, they can only hold the values 0 or 1. Since these features are often important to identify intrusion, AEs generation methods focus on perturbing them. Thus introducing a value between 0 and 1. These values are inconsistent for binary features and cannot be implemented in real network traffic. We have seen examples where the binary feature `Logged-in` was set to 0.72.

Multiple Categories Membership: Categorical features have been converted into binary features to make it possible to use them as inputs for neural networks. One-Hot-Encoding was used to create a binary feature for each instance of the categorical feature. Thus, only one instance can hold the value 1, while all the others must be set to 0. Generation methods often perturb these features by activating multiple categories. Which, even if it is recognized as an attack by the neural network, cannot be implemented in real network traffic. We gave as an example the feature `Service` which cannot be `IRC` and `Telnet` at the same time.

Out-of-Range Values: Every attribute of the network traffic has a limited range of values it can take. But since generation methods apply the perturbation until they reach the adversarial boundary, some features might be pushed out of their definition interval, which generates inconsistent values that cannot be

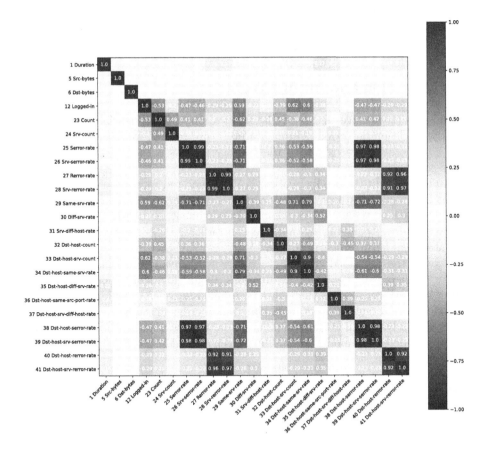

Fig. 2. Heat map of the correlation matrix of NSL-KDD numerical features. (Color figure online)

implemented. As we saw in Table 2, `Same-server-rate` was set to 2.31 by C&W L_2-*attack* when it is a proportion that should not exceed 1. In Table 3, we consider the minimum and maximum values found in the testing set to compute the proportion of AEs containing out-of-range values.

Semantic Links: In contrast to unstructured data like images, network data hold semantic links between features. These links create dependencies that must be kept to ensure the consistency of the traffic. The generation methods do not consider these semantic links and apply an arbitrary perturbation that often breaks them and generates incoherent samples. Unlike other invalidation criteria that are present in Table 3, semantic links are hard to identify. This is due to the fact that there are no explicit rules to express these links. To better illustrate our findings, we computed the heat map of the correlation matrix between the numerical attributes of NSL-KDD illustrated in Fig. 2. The intensity of shades of blue (resp. red) indicates the level of positive (resp. negative) pairwise correlation between the attributes. For example, we can notice a strong positive correlation between `Dst-host-rerror-rate` and `Dst-host-srv-rerror-rate`, or between `Srv-serror-rate` and `Rerror-rate`.

7   Conclusion and Future Work

In this paper, we have discussed the applicability of adversarial examples in network intrusion detection. Through a literature review, we have noticed that little consideration was given to the validity of AEs with respect to network traffic structure and constraints.

We have filled that gap by analyzing AEs generated by state-of-the-art algorithms and identifying key criteria that invalidate them. These criteria include values outpacing the definition domain, assignment of non-binary values to binary features, belonging to multiple contradictory categories, and breaking semantic links between features.

Though the described criteria are sufficient to invalidate AEs, they do not guarantee their validity. Thus, future work should focus on a formal description of network constraints that must be fulfilled in order to validate an attack example. More recent datasets should be used in order to study the perturbation potential of adversarial attacks on different data types. Finally, the vulnerability of intrusion detection models should be proven on real networks with end-to-end attack scenarios.

Acknowledgment. This research was partly funded by the European Union's Horizon 2020 research and innovation program under the Secure Collaborative Intelligent Industrial Automation (SeCoIIA) project, grant agreement No 871967 and IRT SystemX projects (Exploratory research and PFS).

References

1. Abou Khamis, R., Shafiq, O., Matrawy, A.: Investigating resistance of deep learning-based IDS against adversaries using min-max optimization. arXiv preprint:1910.14107 (2019)
2. Alhajjar, E., Maxwell, P., Bastian, N.D.: Adversarial machine learning in network intrusion detection systems. arXiv preprint:2004.11898 (2020)
3. Biggio, B., et al.: Evasion attacks against machine learning at test time. In: Blockeel, H., Kersting, K., Nijssen, S., Železný, F. (eds.) ECML PKDD 2013. LNCS (LNAI), vol. 8190, pp. 387–402. Springer, Heidelberg (2013). https://doi.org/10.1007/978-3-642-40994-3_25
4. Biggio, B., Nelson, B., Laskov, P.: Poisoning attacks against support vector machines. arXiv preprint:1206.6389 (2012)
5. Biggio, B., Roli, F.: Wild patterns: Ten years after the rise of adversarial machine learning. Pattern Recognition (2018)
6. Carlini, N., Wagner, D.: Towards evaluating the robustness of neural networks. In: 2017 IEEE Symposium on Security and Privacy. IEEE (2017)
7. Chen, P.Y., Zhang, H., Sharma, Y., Yi, J., Hsieh, C.J.: Zoo: zeroth order optimization based black-box attacks to deep neural networks without training substitute models. In: 10th ACM Workshop on Artificial Intelligence and Security (2017)
8. Clements, J., Yang, Y., Sharma, A., Hu, H., Lao, Y.: Rallying adversarial techniques against deep learning for network security. arXiv preprint:1903.11688 (2019)
9. Fredrikson, M., Jha, S., Ristenpart, T.: Model inversion attacks that exploit confidence information and basic countermeasures. In: Proceedings of the 22nd ACM SIGSAC Conference on Computer and Communications Security (2015)
10. Goodfellow, I., et al.: Generative adversarial nets. In: Advances in Neural Information Processing Systems (2014)
11. Goodfellow, I.J., Shlens, J., Szegedy, C.: Explaining and harnessing adversarial examples. arXiv preprint:1412.6572 (2014)
12. Ibitoye, O., Shafiq, O., Matrawy, A.: Analyzing adversarial attacks against deep learning for intrusion detection in IoT networks. In: IEEE Global Communications Conference (GLOBECOM) (2019)
13. Jagielski, M., Carlini, N., Berthelot, D., Kurakin, A., Papernot, N.: High accuracy and high fidelity extraction of neural networks. In: 29th USENIX Security Symposium (2020)
14. Klambauer, G., Unterthiner, T., Mayr, A., Hochreiter, S.: Self-normalizing neural networks. In: Advances in Neural Information Processing Systems (2017)
15. Koroniotis, N., Moustafa, N., Sitnikova, E., Turnbull, B.: Towards the development of realistic botnet dataset in the internet of things for network forensic analytics: Bot-IoT dataset. arXiv preprint:1811.00701 (2018)
16. Kurakin, A., Goodfellow, I., Bengio, S.: Adversarial machine learning at scale. arXiv preprint:1611.01236 (2016)
17. Lin, Z., Shi, Y., Xue, Z.: IDSGAN: generative adversarial networks for attack generation against intrusion detection. arXiv preprint:1809.02077 (2018)
18. Martins, N., Cruz, J.M., Cruz, T., Abreu, P.H.: Analyzing the footprint of classifiers in adversarial denial of service contexts. In: EPIA Conference on Artificial Intelligence (2019)
19. Martins, N., Cruz, J.M., Cruz, T., Abreu, P.H.: Adversarial machine learning applied to intrusion and malware scenarios: a systematic review. IEEE Access 8, 35403–35419 (2020)

20. Moisejevs, I.: Adversarial attacks and defenses in intrusion detection systems: A survey. Int. J. Artif. Intell. Expert Syst. (IJAE) **8**(3), 44–62 (2019)

21. Moosavi-Dezfooli, S.M., Fawzi, A., Frossard, P.: DeepFool: a simple and accurate method to fool deep neural networks. In: Proceedings of the IEEE Conference on Computer Vision and Pattern Recognition (2016)

22. Moustafa, N., Slay, J.: UNSW-NB15: a comprehensive data set for network intrusion detection systems (UNSW-NB15 network data set). In: Military Communications and Information Systems Conference (MilCIS) (2015)

23. Nicolae, M.I., et al.: Adversarial robustness toolbox v1.2.0. arXiv preprint:1807.01069 (2018)

24. Papernot, N., McDaniel, P., Jha, S., Fredrikson, M., Celik, Z.B., Swami, A.: The limitations of deep learning in adversarial settings. In: IEEE European Symposium on Security and Privacy (EuroS&P) (2016)

25. Paszke, A., et al.: Pytorch: an imperative style, high-performance deep learning library. In: Advances in Neural Information Processing Systems (2019)

26. Peng, X., Huang, W., Shi, Z.: Adversarial attack against dos intrusion detection: an improved boundary-based method. In: IEEE 31st International Conference on Tools with Artificial Intelligence (ICTAI) (2019)

27. Piplai, A., Chukkapalli, S.S.L., Joshi, A.: Nattack! adversarial attacks to bypass a gan based classifier trained to detect network intrusion. arXiv preprint:2002.08527 (2020)

28. Rigaki, M., Elragal, A.: Adversarial deep learning against intrusion detection classifiers. In: NATO IST-152 Workshop on Intelligent Autonomous Agents for Cyber Defence and Resilience (2017)

29. Ring, M., Wunderlich, S., Scheuring, D., Landes, D., Hotho, A.: A survey of network-based intrusion detection data sets. Comput. Secur. **86**, 147–167 (2019)

30. Rosenberg, I., Shabtai, A., Elovici, Y., Rokach, L.: Adversarial learning in the cyber security domain. arXiv preprint:2007.02407 (2020)

31. Sharafaldin, I., Lashkari, A.H., Ghorbani, A.A.: Toward generating a new intrusion detection dataset and intrusion traffic characterization. In: 4th International Conference on Information Systems Security and Privacy (2018)

32. Szegedy, C., et al.: Intriguing properties of neural networks. arXiv preprint:1312.6199 (2013)

33. Tavallaee, M., Bagheri, E., Lu, W., Ghorbani, A.A.: A detailed analysis of the KDD cup 99 data set. In: IEEE Symposium on Computational Intelligence for Security and Defense Applications (2009)

34. Vorobeychik, Y., Kantarcioglu, M.: Adversarial machine learning. Synthesis Lectures on Artificial Intelligence and Machine Learning (2018)

35. Wang, Z.: Deep learning-based intrusion detection with adversaries. IEEE Access (2018)

36. Warzyński, A., Kołaczek, G.: Intrusion detection systems vulnerability on adversarial examples. In: Innovations in Intelligent Systems and Applications (2018)

37. Yang, K., Liu, J., Zhang, C., Fang, Y.: Adversarial examples against the deep learning based network intrusion detection systems. In: IEEE Military Communications Conference (MILCOM) (2018)

38. Yuan, X., He, P., Zhu, Q., Li, X.: Adversarial examples: attacks and defenses for deep learning. IEEE Trans. Neural Netw. Learn. Syst. **30**, 2805–2824 (2019)

TLS, Openness and Security Control

Implementation Flaws in TLS Stacks: Lessons Learned and Study of TLS 1.3 Benefits

Olivier Levillain[✉]

Télécom SudParis, Institut Polytechnique de Paris, Palaiseau, France
olivier.levillain@telecom-sudparis.eu

Abstract. In the years leading to the definition of TLS 1.3, many vulnerabilities have been published on the TLS protocol, including numerous implementation flaws affecting a wide range of independent stacks. The infamous Heartbleed bug, was estimated to affect more than 20% of the most popular HTTPS servers. We propose a structured review of these implementation flaws. By considering their consequences but also their root causes, we present some lessons learned or yet to be learned. We also assess the impact of TLS 1.3, the latest version of the protocol, on the security of SSL/TLS implementations.

SSL (Secure Sockets Layer) is a cryptographic protocol published by Netscape in 1995 to protect the confidentiality and integrity of HTTP connections, mainly to secure online commercial or financial operations. Since 1999, the protocol has been maintained by the IETF (Internet Engineering Task Force) and has been renamed TLS (Transport Layer Security). In this article, when referring to the protocol in general, we will use the SSL/TLS denomination.

SSL/TLS has now become an essential part of Internet security. The most recent version of the protocol is TLS 1.3 [24], which was published after more than 5 years of discussion within the IETF TLS Working Group.

In this paper, we do not address the question of the theoretical security of the protocol and of its underlying cryptographic mechanisms, but the actual security of the implementations. Indeed, because of bugs or more subtle quirks, there may be unexpected vulnerabilities whose consequences may go beyond the security of the considered transaction or service. We thus studied in depth many known implementation flaws in SSL/TLS stacks to understand their root causes and to propose ways to improve the situation. Indeed some mistakes keep being repeated and affect independent software stacks; this led us to question whether blaming the developers for ignoring the "state of the art" was the right answer.

First, we look at simple, classical programming errors such as buffer overflows or logic errors in Sect. 1. The second category, in Sect. 2, is about parsing bugs, which are sometimes the result of the complexity of the structures to interpret. Next, we look at cryptography-related vulnerabilities in Sect. 3, which are sometimes presented as mistakes from the developers, whereas we strongly believe that obsolete cryptographic primitives are the underlying cause in many cases, leaving the developers who must choose between code modularity and security in a difficult position. The last category, described in Sect. 4, is about issues in SSL/TLS state machines. It is indeed sometimes

© Springer Nature Switzerland AG 2021
J. Garcia-Alfaro et al. (Eds.): CRiSIS 2020, LNCS 12528, pp. 87–104, 2021.
https://doi.org/10.1007/978-3-030-68887-5_5

possible to get an implementation into an invalid state, where it would accept unsolicited or meaningless messages, which can lead to catastrophic consequences for the security of the communications. Each section ends with a decription of the lessons we can learn from the presented problems, as well as a discussion about what TLS 1.3 has brought to improve the situation on the subject.

1 Common Programming Errors

1.1 CVE-2014-1266: Apple's `goto fail`

In February 2014, Apple released a security advisory, indicating that an attacker could bypass the server authentication mechanism on the client side in its operating systems. In the vulnerable function (see listing in Appendix A), a `goto fail` instruction was wrongly duplicated, which means that the actual verification of the server signature (the `sslRawVerify` call) was skipped. So, when the client took that code path (as soon as a Diffie-Hellman ciphersuite was negotiated), the server signature over the parameters was *not* checked and the server was automatically authenticated.

An attacker could thus simply impersonate a TLS server by forcing the use of a vulnerable suite in the `ServerHello` message, then present the legitimate certificates, and finally send an arbitrary `ServerKeyExchange` message, since its authenticity would not be checked: from the client's point of view, the server certificate was however correctly validated, leading to an authentication bypass.

The problem was quickly and easily fixed, but it showed that the corresponding code had not been sufficiently tested or checked using static analysis, since such a trivial case of dead code should have been detected. Such dead code can indeed be detected with modern compilers such as `clang` with `-Wunreachable-code`[1].

After this bug, people started to advocate for better compilers, analysis tools, or even for the use of safer alternative languages instead of the C language. Several commentators explained that this bug would have been avoided, had the developers used curly brackets for their `if` statements. Yet, without tools enforcing such practice, we would still have no guarantee; and if we were using tools, it would be safer to have them identify the root cause (dead code).

1.2 CVE-2014-0092: GnuTLS' `goto fail`

A few days after Apple's `goto fail`, GnuTLS released another advisory concerning a vulnerability in the code checking signatures. The issue was (a little) subtler, about the `check_if_ca` function checking whether a certificate was from a certification authority (CA), and the `_gnutls_verify_certificate2` function checking the signature. Even though the documentation stated these functions returned a boolean value (that is 0 or 1), they could actually also return a negative value in some parsing error cases.

So, when critical functions, such as `gnutls_x509_crt_check_issuer`, called those functions treating the result as a boolean, they would reject certificates with invalid signature, accept valid certificates, but also *accept ill-formed certificates*. Listings in Appendix B contain the relevant code excerpts.

---

[1] However, `gcc` has been silently ignoring this option since version 4.5.

GnuTLS developers fixed the corresponding logic in a defensive way, on the one hand by insuring the called functions indeed returned only 0 or 1, and on the other hand by having the calling functions check the result in a stricter way.

It is worth noting that a similar bug had already been found six years earlier in OpenSSL (CVE-2008-5077) (except that the bug was triggered by the code parsing the signature block, not the certificate). There again, the question of the used tools and languages was raised.

1.3   CVE-2002-0862 and CVE-2011-0228: `BasicConstraints` Checks

To distinguish a CA certificate from a server certificate, the X.509 standard requires relying parties to check the `BasicConstraints` extension. This X.509 extension contains a boolean, `cA`, which should only be true when the certificate belongs to a certification authority. Valid X.509 stacks must in particular check this information when checking a certificate chain. The impact of this boolean is critical, since a certificate with a true `cA` boolean allow, in the common cases, its owner to issue arbitrary certificates for arbitrary domain names.

In 2002, Marlinspike showed that Internet Explorer did not actually check this boolean [19], allowing an attacker to reuse any certificate she possesses (even a simple SSL server one) to sign new arbitrary certificates. This was a trivial yet critical bug. What is more interesting is that the same bug reappeared in 2011 in Apple's TLS stack [21], a different, independent, TLS stack. In both cases, one can at least question the test process.

1.4   CVE-2014-0160: Heartbleed

In April 2014, a devastating vulnerability in OpenSSL was presented – a "common" buffer overrun in the Heartbeat implementation.

Heartbeat is a TLS extension. When it has been negotiated, the client or the server can, at any time, send a Heartbeat record containing data, and the recipient has to echo those data back. Such a mechanism can theoretically be used for two purposes: Path MTU (i.e. maximal packet size) Discovery and a secure Keep Alive mechanism. In practice, both goals are mostly relevant to DTLS, the datagram version of TLS, which can be used over UDP. Yet the Heartbeat extension was integrated into OpenSSL for both DTLS *and* TLS on December 31st 2011[2], and activated by default.

When a vulnerable version of OpenSSL received a Heartbeat request advertising a content longer than the sent payload, it filled the response with the received content and whatever was present afterwards in memory. All kinds of heap-allocated data could be endangered: contents of communications between *other clients* and the server, authentication cookies, user passwords, and even the server's private key. In practice, Durumeric et al. estimated that 24 to 55% of the most popular HTTPS sites were affected by Heartbleed [13].

Fixing the code was trivial, but not handling all the possible consequences. It is hard to say whether or not this vulnerability was known and exploited, but the precautionary principle advocated e.g. for revocation of millions of vulnerable server certificates.

---

[2] The first OpenSSL version with the Heartbeat extension was 1.0.1, published in March 2012.

1.5   CVE-2014-6321: WinShock

In November 2014, Microsoft published a security advisory, MS14-066, with multiple vulnerabilities. One of them, dubbed WinShock, was about a buffer overflow in SChannel, Microsoft's TLS stack.

The flaw was in the `DecodeSigAndReverse` function, which parses ECDSA signatures in the context of client certificate authentication. When handling a client certificate using elliptic-curve cryptography, the certificate, present in the `Certificate` message, is first parsed. The server extracts the public key the elliptic curve used for the signature, either using well known identifiers (several curves can be identified by ASN.1 Object Identifiers) or in an explicit manner (the description then contains the underlying finite field and the curve equation). In both cases, the public key sets the coordinate size. In a second phase, the signature is read from the `CertificateVerify` message, which contains two scalars whose size is given by the curve.

In SChannel, the vulnerable code allocated memory regions for the signature, based on the curve description from the certificate, then read the data from the signature, using this time the encoded ASN.1 length of the signature, *without checking the consistency between both lengths*. It was thus possible to trigger a buffer overflow using long coordinates within a crafted signature in the `CertificateVerify` message. Smashing data in the heap using this vulnerability was proven exploitable in IIS servers: proofs of concept could even lead to remote code execution on vulnerable systems.

In a typical configuration, client certificates are rarely used. However, even unsolicited `Certificate` and `CertificateVerify` were parsed by SChannel, which means an attacker could trigger the vulnerability in any SChannel deployment. So this is a second bug affecting the state machine (more on similar bugs in Sect. 4).

1.6   Lessons Learned

When one look at these vulnerabilities, one might be tempted to blame the developers for making so many mistakes, and for repeating them over and over.

At the same time, it seems the languages or tools used for the development could and should have been more helpful, e.g. by offering a *real* boolean type[3] or by warning for trivial errors such as having obvious dead code in a function.

One way for hardening the code is to configure the tools to be as strict as possible. For example, in C, one can require additional checks using `-Wall -Wextra -Werror` and other similar options at all times.

Some programming languages are better than others to avoid whole classes of bugs, but there is no silver bullets, and it is essential to always understand exactly what you are trading in exchange for what. For example, languages with garbage collector eradicate memory management error such as use-after-free and double-free. Yet having no fine-grain control on memory management means that you cannot easily ensure that secrets (private keys, passwords) are erased as soon as possible from the memory, and actually, they could even be copied at multiple memory locations several times by the garbage collector during their lifetime.

---

[3] The C99 standard introduced such a type, but it seems almost no one makes use of it.

Once developers understand languages constructions and their behavior, they can adopt more robust structures, e.g. always err on the safe side as this was done by GnuTLS developers to fix the `goto fail` bug, by only considering 1 as the valid case, instead of *everything that is not* 0. Another example is the use of bound-checking arrays, where each read or write access is checked at runtime to stay within the array boundaries (as in Java, OCaml or Rust). Even if this kind of mechanisms induces a small overhead, it is a good way to avoid buffer overflows. Yet, developers should be aware that some constructions may evade these safety mechanisms and stay away from unsafe features. Ensuring that third-party libraries behave correctly is also recommended.

All in all, mastering programming languages, choosing adequate compilers and tools and correctly using them can help improve code quality and avoid several classes of software bugs.

A Word About Tests. Another best practice is *negative* testing: when security is involved, it is not sufficient to check that what should work works, it is crucial to also check that what should not work does actually not. Checking that a Handshake fails as expected when a signature is invalid would have prevented Apple's `goto fail` vulnerability.

Moreover, since programmers seem to make the same mistakes time and again in different code bases, it might be useful to build a collection of *negative* and non-regression tests to share between implementations. In this domain, the situation has slightly improved, with tools such as tlsfuzzer[4] and TLS-Attacker[5].

TLS 1.3 Benefits. With regards to languages and tools, TLS 1.3 does not bring anything, since the RFC is a specification. Moreover, the IETF always insisted on letting developers be free to make implementation choices.

2 Parsing Bugs

In the previous section, we studied classical simple errors such as memory management issues. Such bugs can also arise in the parser code. Beyond these somewhat common bugs, parsers trigger another class of vulnerabilities, when the parsed content does not correspond to its intended value. Such bugs can result from a confusion in the specification or a lack of precision in the parsing code.

2.1 CVE-2009-2408: Null Characters in Distinguished Names

In 2009, Marlinspike presented several bugs in TLS stacks leading to authentication bypass [20]. In particular, he presented a difference of behavior between several X.509 implementations in the presence of null characters.

ASN.1 specifications are clear on the subject: the length of a string is explicitly set by a separate field, and most ASN.1 string types do not allow for null characters. Yet,

---

[4] https://github.com/tomato42/tlsfuzzer.
[5] https://github.com/RUB-NDS/TLS-Attacker.

several browsers, e.g. Firefox, actually accepted and interpreted null characters as the end of the string, leading to an alternate interpretation.

Let's consider an attacker, who controls the `evil.com` domain, requesting a certificate for the `www.mybank.com\0.evil.com` domain, where `\0` is the null character. Moreover, we assume the contacted CA simply extracts the top-level domain `evil.com` and sends a validation email to `postmaster@evil.com`. Under these assumptions, the attacker can get their certificate. The provided certificate could then be used against vulnerable browsers to impersonate `www.mybank.com`.

Beyond the obvious misinterpretation from browsers, which should not rely on null characters to end ASN.1 DER strings, there is another bug: the CA should not have accepted ill-formed data as part of a fully-qualified domain name in the first place. This example shows that, as soon as two implementations do not agree on the interpretation of a given element, there is a gap that an attacker can (and will) exploit.

2.2   CVE-2014-3511: OpenSSL Downgrade Attack

TLS allows records from the same type to be split and merged in a very liberal way. What is allowed and forbidden is not always clear in the specification. Yet, splitting records is required in some cases, since Handshake messages can be 16 MB long whereas TLS records are limited to 16 KB.

In July 2014, Benjamin and Langley showed that OpenSSL exhibited a strange behavior when it receives a `ClientHello` message split in very small records. When parsing the first `ClientHello` fragment, an implementation needs at least 6 bytes in the record payload to identify the proposed protocol version. In the absence of this information, OpenSSL was not able to extract the proper version and systematically used TLS 1.0 instead of waiting for the rest of the `ClientHello` message. Moreover, since only the *aggregated content* of the records are integrity-protected, the exact way Handshake messages are split can easily be changed by an attacker without detection.

To fix this bug, OpenSSL developers chose to reject tiny `ClientHello` fragments. This is an incorrect behavior with respect to the specification, but the alternative was deemed too complex to implement. We find that the decision is actually relevant, and that the specification should probably contain some constraints to allow for reasonable expectations from the developers.

This attack shows that the complexity of TLS, combined with the need to support several protocol versions, can lead to subtle implementation difficulties. A similar example is given by Bhargavan et al. [7], with the Alert attack, where an attacker can misalign the boundaries of alert messages (which are 2 bytes long) with the records encapsulating them. It is then possible to send one byte in an unprotected alert record that may be interpreted later as an authenticated piece of alert.

2.3   CVE-2014-1568: NSS/CyaSSL/PolarSSL Signature Forgery

In September 2014, another vulnerability allowing to bypass server authentication on several TLS clients was published. The vulnerability affected NSS, the Firefox cryptographic library, as well as CyaSSL and PolarSSL. It takes its root in the code parsing

DER-encoded RSA signature. DER is a concrete representation of ASN.1 enforcing normal forms: there should be one and only one correct representation for each abstract value.

It is actually a variant of an attack presented in 2006 by Bleichenbacher. The original vulnerability relied on broken RSA implementations that did not check the absence of data beyond the `DigestInfo` block [9]. In the case of a small public exponent (such as 3), it is easy to forge a signature for such a message, that would be accepted by fuzzy implementations.

The vulnerability presented in September 2014 is another universal, relying on three elements to be exploitable: the attacker needs to find an RSA key with a public exponent equal to 3 (this exponent can be anywhere in the certificate chain she is trying to spoof); the ASN.1 DER parser must be too liberal, i.e. accept non-canonically encoded values; DER length computation can silently overflow.

The obvious fix here is to use a strict DER parser. However, it is even possible to avoid the parsing step altogether by re reversing the comparison process while checking a signature: instead of computing $m = s^e$ from the signature s, then *parse* m and finally compare the encompassed hash value inside m, a robust implementation should produce the message $m^\star$ containing the expected `DigestInfo`, then compute $m = s^e$ and compare m to $m^\star$.

By comparing concrete representations instead of abstract ones, we skip the parsing step and the only operations manipulating attacker-controlled data are the s^e computation and the trivial binary comparison. Moreover, since DER is a canonical representation of the abstract value, $m^\star$ is unambiguously defined[6].

2.4   Lessons Learned

Despite the important number of implementations affected by the parsing issues described in this section, it would not be fair to conclude that all these bugs were only the result of poor programming practices. Developers obviously bear their share of responsibility, but several errors were also the result of complex or ill-specified protocols and formats.

In particular, parsing attacker-controlled data is an error-prone process that should never be overlooked. As soon as parsing is not straightforward and can lead to ambiguities, security vulnerabilities may arise, either because of different actors interpreting the same messages differently, or because it allows an attacker to tamper with the expected execution path. We must insist that the so-called robustness principle (*Be liberal in what you accept, conservative in what you send*) is a terribly wrong advice regarding security: it should be replaced by another, simpler, statement: be conservative, always (and report bugs in confusing specifications).

Recipes to improve security would include writing strict parsers, avoid exposing them when possible (e.g. by comparing concrete representations instead of abstract,

---

[6] This is actually an approximation, since some implementations still produce ill-formed `DigestInfo` where the algorithm parameters is omitted, instead of being a DER NULL element. To accommodate such pervasive deviations, a robust implementation should thus produce two versions of $m^\star$.

parsed ones), stress-test the parsers in corner cases. Yet, the real long-term advice is to simplify the specification and to express them using a more formal language, to reduce the possibilities of bugs and ambiguities in the resulting code.

TLS 1.3 Benefits. From the message parsing point of view, RFC 8446 is similar to the previous TLS specifications, but some problematic cases have been described, to disambiguate corner cases such as the Alert attack discussed earlier (Sect. 5.1 of the RFC 8446 is crystal clear on the encapsulation of alerts within records). However, one might still feel uneasy with Handshake messages or extensions whose exact content depends on the context, which adds unnecessary complexity in the parsers.

3 The Real Impact of Obsolete Cryptography on Security

SSL/TLS is a rather old protocol, dating back 1995. The cryptography community has since learned a lot about algorithms, schemes and protocols. This knowledge has not always been taken into account in recent versions of the protocol, mostly for compatibility reasons: TLS 1.2 still (partly) relies on PKCS#1 v1.5 encryption, the CBC mode, and the MAC-then-Encrypt paradigm. In this section, we present the implications on implementations of using obsolete cryptography.

3.1 CVE-2013-0169: The Dangers of MAC-then-Encrypt

Since its inception, SSL/TLS has been supporting the MAC-then-CBC paradigm to protect its records. This led to Lucky13, an attack using a timing information leak during TLS record decryption as a padding oracle [3]. Even if one may think this flaw is *only* an implementation issue (writing constant-time code to decrypt and check the integrity of a record), we believe the problem runs deeper.

Indeed, when one looks at the complex corresponding patch in OpenSSL [18], one is forced to note that it is a vast amount of complex and intricate calls to hash compression functions and decryption primitives. We have traded a simple and intuitive decrypt/unpad/MAC-check sequence with low-level instructions. Moreover, the portability of the OpenSSL fix is debatable, since Langley had to trick the compiler to avoid low-level optimization related to modular reductions on small integers[7].

This is the reason why researchers (and the TLS 1.3 standard) promote higher-level and secure-by-design constructions, such as AEAD ciphers, to obtain strong guarantees on both the confidentiality and the integrity of the protected data.

A simpler path was even presented in 2001 by Krawczyk [15]: Encrypt-then-MAC, which can be proven to be safer. So, despite the Record Protocol protection was known to be flawed in 2001, it was only partially fixed in 2008 with TLS 1.2 and the introduction of AEAD constructions. Only TLS 1.3 completely deprecates the flawed CBC mode (and the biased RC4 algorithm), by forcing the use of AEAD algorithms.

---

[7] In a nutshell, the DIV instruction takes a variable amount of time depending on its argument on Intel CPUs, which could be observable.

The impact on TLS stacks is a difficult choice between straightforward and modular, but flawed, code on the one side, and a complex, hard-to-follow and error-prone, but theoretically sound implementation on the other side.

Considering the difficulty to fix this issue, it is worth discussing the case of s2n, a TLS implementation released by Amazon [17]. Despite including countermeasures against Lucky13, Albrecht et al. showed that the library was nevertheless vulnerable to a weaker, yet still exploitable, form of padding oracle [2]. To avoid writing too low-level code, s2n decryption code execution time was indeed not exactly constant.

3.2 CVE-2016-0270: Issues with GCM Nonce Generation

Another way symmetric cryptography can fail is when you do not fulfill the expected assumption. In general, blockcipher modes of operation require the use of parameters, such as IVs (Initial Values) or Nonces, which are required to be unpredictable or unique, depending on the schemes.

In 2016, Böck et al. showed that several HTTPS servers at large reused nonce values, or generated them in a non-optimal way [11]. Indeed, GCM requires the 64-bit nonce used in TLS to be unique. Reusing a value twice fully breaks the authenticity of connections. It is interesting to notice that drawing random values leads to collisions (hence nonce reuse) faster than a simple counter. The correct fix here is to use such a counter

In other schemes, what is important is not uniqueness, but unpredictability, as is the case with the CBC mode, where leaking the next IV to use can lead to real-world attacks such as BEAST [12].

One way to solve the problem is to force the developer to make the right decision. This is why TLS 1.3 mandates how to generate the nonce in a deterministic way: the value is derived by each participant using authenticated information sent on the wire and a shared secret.

3.3 CVE-2014-0411 and Others: PKCS#1 v1.5 and Bleichenbacher

A valid PKCS#1 v1.5 message is produced by formatting the plaintext and then encrypting it using the raw RSA operation. The expected format for an encrypted message is the following: a null byte, followed by a block type byte (here, 2), then at least 8 random padding bytes, a null character and finally the message to encrypt.

It thus means that every correctly padded plaintext starts with 00 02, which corresponds to a big integer between $2 \times 2^{n-16}$ and $3 \times 2^{n-16}$ (with an n-bit modulus). If an attacker wishes to recover the plaintext P associated to a given ciphertext C, she can multiply C by X^e and submit the new ciphertext to a decryption oracle: the padding will be correct as soon as $P \times X$ is between the expected bounds. By iterating such attempts, it is possible to aggregate information about the original plaintext P and recover it, as was shown by Bleichenbacher in 1998 [8] in his so-called Million Message Attack.

The attack is applicable to RSA encryption key exchange in TLS. As described in RFC 3218, there are three classical countermeasures:

- group all possible errors so they lead to a unique signal, where the padding errors are indistinguishable from other errors;

- where possible, ignore all errors silently and replace the decrypted message by a random string (this is what is recommended for RSA encryption key exchange in TLS since version 1.0);
- use PKCS#1 v2.1 encryption (OAEP).

Even if the Million Message Attack has been known since 1998, it is still a problem in recent TLS implementations. The Bleichenbacher attack resurfaced in the JSSE (Java Secure Socket Extension) SSL/TLS implementation [23]: by reusing standard cryptographic libraries, the JSSE implementation has to rely on them to handle padding errors, which generated a timing difference due to the use of exception. This example shows again a dilemma between code reuse and security: it is impossible to safely reuse standard PKCS#1 v1.5 libraries that throw exceptions. Actually, the attack keeps on resurfacing, with two recent publications exploiting Bleichenbacher oracles and targeting TLS: ROBOT (Return Of Bleichenbacher's Oracle Threats [10]), relying on new signals from vulnerable state machines, and CAT (Cache-like ATtacks [25]).

It is thus clear that PKCS#1 v1.5 is inherently flawed, and, as with the MAC-then-CBC scheme described earlier, developers will get it wrong, time and again, until this obsolete mechanism is removed from the specification. In the mean time, it is crucial to avoid reusing the same RSA key in different contexts (decryption and signature, PKCS#1 v1.5 and v2.1), since a vulnerability in one context may indirectly be used to attack the other (e.g. the DROWN attack [4]).

3.4 Lessons Learned

We can expect three properties from applications involving cryptographic mechanisms: security with regards to known attacks, compatibility with the existing ecosystem, and code modularity (i.e. the ability to reuse and combine existing high-level primitives). In practice, until old versions of TLS have disappeared, it seems difficult or even impossible to have all the properties at once. A developer must pick at most two of them:

- modularity and compatibility, which corresponds to using standard primitives without specific countermeasures, leading to attacks such as Lucky 13;
- security and compatibility, which consists in rewriting large chunks of low-level cryptographic code to add complex countermeasures. The resulting code is error-prone and hard to maintain;
- security and modularity can be obtained by using only up-to-date robust cryptographic constructions (e.g. AEAD modes), at the expense of a compatibility loss.

As history showed with Bleichenbacher attacks and CBC padding oracles, attacks only get better over time: attacks originally considered as impractical later become exploitable. As the very purpose of cryptographic protocols is security, it seems to us that the sensible approach is the third one, to only use sound algorithms and schemes to help developers do their job without having to jump through improbable hoops: a good cryptographic design should be easy to implement, in a modular and portable way, while not allowing for dangerous combinations.

Hopefully, we are now in a situation where HTTP software can rely on modern endpoints supporting at least TLS 1.2. Let us hope this situation expands to other TLS ecosystems (we can cite the use of TLS in SMTP as an area where a huge progression is still needed).

Protocol specification committees should thus listen to cryptographer's advices, and ban flawed algorithms or constructions as soon as possible. The problem with most cryptographic flaws is not *whether* they are exploitable but *when* they will be.

TLS 1.3 Benefits. TLS 1.3 was designed with the best intentions, and no broken or obsolete primitive has survived in the new version of the protocol.

On the symmetric front, the CBC mode and RC4 have disappeared, and only the more modern AEAD constructions have been kept. Moreover, the nonce derivation is completely deterministic, which removes the possibility for error in this area. Finally, after years of using ad-hoc key derivation functions, TLS now uses HKDF, a clean and well-studied scheme proposed by Krawczyk in 2010 [16].

Regarding asymmetric primitives, RSA encryption is no longer used (which removes the possibility of RSA-EXPORT-related attacks such as FREAK); only signed ephemeral Diffie-Hellman key exchange is possible with TLS 1.3. Moreover, the new version of the protocol uses named groups with acceptable sizes (removing other small key attacks such as LogJam [1]). Also, RSA signatures in TLS 1.3 use the Probabilistic Signature Scheme, from the most recent version of the RSA standard (PKCS#1 v2.1).

TLS 1.3 only proposes up-to-date, robust cryptographic algorithms, which should remove some worries from the developers' mind. Strictly speaking, there is still one area where legacy cryptography can be found in TLS 1.3: X.509 certificate management (ECDSA certificates are still rare, while the vast majority of RSA certificates still use the PKCS#1 v1.5 signature scheme). We can only hope that progress is made on this front, which is not directly specified by TLS.

4   The Consequences of Complex State Machines

Since 2014, several attacks concerning flaws in TLS state machine implementations were published. Their impact can be catastrophic, either by skipping essential steps of the protocol or by exposing rarely used parts of code. Such attacks demonstrate how specification complexity can lead to security issues in implementations.

4.1   CVE-2014-0224: *EarlyCCS*

In June 2014, Kikushi showed that the OpenSSL state machine is vulnerable to a subtle attack: a man-in-the-middle between an OpenSSL client and an OpenSSL server, *both* vulnerable, could forge early `ChangeCipherSpec` messages and force the parties to use weak keys, relying only on public data [14].

The main idea behind this attack is to exploit the OpenSSL state machine that, both as a client and a server, accepts an early `ChangeCipherSpec` message, instead of discarding it and/or ending the negotiation. The real `ChangeCipherSpec`, which is still required, will be ignored in practice. At reception time, since no shared secret is defined yet, session keys are derived from a null secret and public random values. Next, the attacker has to keep both connections in a consistent state, encrypting messages with the weak keys and keeping track of record numbers to compute correct MAC values.

In the end, for the handshake to terminate successfully, the attacker has to send correct Finished messages to the client and to the server. Since this message must contain a hash value covering, among other things, the shared secret that was eventually agreed upon, the attacker needs both the client and the server to be vulnerable to complete the handshake.

Actually, as stated in the author's blog post, the corresponding code had already been fixed several times to handle wrongly-ordered ChangeCipherSpec messages: CVE-2004-0079 fixed a null-pointer assignment arising when the message was received before the ciphersuite was specified, CVE-2009-1386 fixed a similar problem in DTLS. Yet, only the direct consequence (a segmentation fault) was investigated in both cases, leaving aside the bigger picture. The genuine flaw was ignored, as well as its security consequences.

It is worth noting that ChangeCipherSpec is *not* a Handshake message, and as such it is *not* hashed in the transcript covered by the Finished message. Thus, adding or removing a ChangeCipherSpec cannot be detected by cryptographic means. Yet, after being removed from the standard, the ChangeCipherSpec were reintroduced as dummy messages in the late drafts of TLS 1.3, to accommodate so-called middleboxes. Even though these messages are not supposed to have any meaning at all, this kind of unnecessary redundancy might again lead to new issues in the years to come.

4.2   SMACK: State Machine AttaCKs

In January 2015, several vulnerabilities were published about various TLS implementations. Using FlexTLS, a flexible TLS stack, researchers tested the state machines of many different TLS stacks [6]. The results were especially worrying since they affected in practice all the known TLS stacks, to various degrees.

CVE-2014-6593: Early Finished (Server Impersonation).   In the first attack, the attacker answers a vulnerable client with the following messages: ServerHello, Certificate (with the identity of the server to impersonate) and Finished, and *skips* the rest of the negotiation (including the ChangeCipherSpec message. Faced with such a shortened handshake, JSSE (Java) and CyaSSL TLS implementations consider the server authenticated and start sending cleartext ApplicationData messages!

Skip Verify **(Client Impersonation).**   In the case of a mutually authenticated connection, the server requests the client to present a certificate (using a Certificate message) and to sign the Handshake transcript with his private key (CertificateVerify). Both these messages are required to properly authenticate the client. However, several implementations accept the Certificate message alone, where the client announces its identity, without the corresponding proof of identity: the Mono implementation indeed considers the second message as optional, but nevertheless authenticates the client; with CyaSSL, the attacker also needs to skip the client ChangeCipherSpec message; finally, with OpenSSL, the flaw is more subtle, since the attack only works when the client presents a certificate containing a static Diffie-Hellman public key.

CVE-2015-0204: FREAK (Factoring RSA Export Keys). The last attack described in the article is FREAK, which got some media coverage. As for the previous attacks, FREAK relies on an active network attacker able to modify the messages on the fly.

The attack consists in forcing a client to use the RSA-EXPORT key exchange method, which was designed to comply with cryptographic restrictions. In a nutshell, with RSA-EXPORT, the server is authenticated using a strong RSA key, but the actual key exchange is done using RSA encryption with a shorter RSA key (at most 512-bit long), to respect the rules limiting the size of encryption keys.

Initially flagged as not critical for OpenSSL (which is rarely used as TLS client stack on desktop computers), FREAK was discovered in practice to affect many different TLS clients beyond OpenSSL: BoringSSL, LibreSSL, Apple SecureTransport, Microsoft SChannel, the Mono TLS stack and Oracle JSSE.

4.3 Black-Box Fuzzing to Evaluate TLS State Machines

In 2015, de Ruiter et al. described another approach to evaluate state machines in TLS stacks [26]. They use state machine learning techniques to analyze different implementations as black boxes. To this aim, they choose an alphabet of abstract TLS messages (typical Handshake messages, application data and Heartbeat messages). Thanks to a software layer translating this abstract alphabet into concrete messages (the so-called test harness), they could build the observable state automata of different implementations.

The expected automata should be a straightforward "happy flow", showing the different steps of a successful TLS session, which should typically consist in 5 states, and one more state to handle all the error cases. This is the observed behavior for the RSA BSAFE Java library. The other studied libraries show more complex state machines. Examples of inferred automata are reproduced from the article in the Appendix C.

It is worth noting that, by studying the deviations of the implementations with regards to the expected simple automata, the researchers have been able to find vulnerabilities, including the Early Finished flaw described earlier. They also uncovered another security bug in GnuTLS 3.3.8, where sending a Heartbeat message would reset the buffer containing the handshake messages; this flaw could allow an attacker to mangle a handshake between a vulnerable client and a vulnerable server.

4.4 Lessons Learned

As shown with these examples, all major TLS implementations did not correctly keep track of the current *state* a session is in, since they all accepted illegal messages in at least one configuration. Ideally, the TLS state machine should be driven by its current state only, not by the incoming messages: at each step, a client or a server should exactly know which messages are valid, and every other messages should trigger an `UnexpectedMessage` fatal alert. The best way to achieve this is to write simple and crystal clear specifications in a formal language (instead of a natural one).

TLS 1.3 Benefits. When we study the state machines for TLS 1.3, the first remark we have to make is that they are not formally defined in the RFC. Indeed, as stated earlier, the IETF insists in letting the developers make their implementation choices, even if this leads to them making avoidable mistakes. We strongly believe that sometimes, there is a good way to implement a protocol, and more formal state machines could and should have been provided in the specification.

That being said, if we consider vanilla TLS (that is TLS without 0 RTT nor Post-Handshake Client Authentication), TLS 1.3 state machines are somewhat simpler that the previous ones. This is obviously true for the automaton handling post handshake traffic, since the only messages to handle are `NewSessionTicket` and `KeyUpdate` messages (which are very simple Handshake messages), and `ApplicationData` records.

For the first (and only) negotiation, a lot of the complexity has disappeared with the removal of several features (renegotiation, the original mechanism to resume sessions). However, during the last months of the review process, several fields and messages were brought back to the specification, to accommodate so-called middleboxes. Indeed, some network devices were shown to be intolerant to TLS 1.3, so the TLS working group proposed to make TLS 1.3 look more like TLS 1.2, by adding useless fields in the `ServerHello` message (compression methods, session identifiers) and by bringing back the cursed `ChangeCipherSpec` message. We would obviously advocate to remove this useless, unauthenticated and dangerous message, which already led to several flaws in real stacks.

Another source of concern are the 0 RTT mode, which allow for an even more efficient protocol, at the expense of weaker security properties (e.g. regarding anti-replay protection), and Post-Handshake Client Authentication, a feature allowing the server to ask for client certificate authentication after the initial handshake has been completed. Both mechanisms introduce an added complexity to the specification.

Overall, it is hard to tell what the exact track record of TLS 1.3 is with regards to specification simplicity and clarity. If we restrict the protocol to what we called vanilla TLS without `ChangeCipherSpec`, the net profit is rather clear to us. Yet, a lot of actors will be tempted to use 0 RTT or compatibility messages to accommodate middleboxes, making the profit less obvious.

5   Related Work

Meyer et al. have proposed a thorough presentation of SSL/TLS flaws in 2013 [22], which describes many security vulnerabilities affecting TLS, not only implementation ones. At that time, the work on TLS 1.3 had not yet begun.

It is also worth mentionning the work of Bernstein et al. on developing a new cryptographic library with a safe API [5]. We indeed believe complex specifications should include implementation constraints to avoid known (and dangerous) traps.

Regarding test suites and tools, the situation has improved over the recent years, with the publication of tools such as tlsfuzzer (see footnote 4) and TLS-Attacker (see footnote 5).

6 Conclusion

Development, network protocols, and cryptography are complex subjects. Implementing TLS combines all those, which can lead to numerous flaws with critical security consequences. There are classes of security flaws that rely on recurring trivial bugs such as memory management errors or integer overflows. To overcome them, there already exists type-safe programming languages or static analysis tools to avoid introducing several kinds of bugs in the first place. The TLS ecosystem also initially lacked an extensive, shared set of security tests, since multiple flaws were discovered, several years apart, in independent implementations of the protocol. Finally, several vulnerabilities result from the complexity and the ambiguities of the TLS specifications.

Overall, the situation has improved with TLS 1.3. From the cryptographic point of view, TLS 1.3 removes many cryptographic algorithms (RC4, MD5 and SHA-1), modes (CBC, PKCS#1 v1.5) and parameters (arbitrary finite field group were replaced by properly sized named groups in DH key exchange). Regarding the protocol specification, the negotiation has been simplified, is more efficient, and has been proven secure... unless we consider complex features such as 0 RTT.

Acknowledgments. This work was supported in part by the French ANR GASP project (ANR-19-CE39-0001).

A Apple's goto fail Vulnerable Code

The following excerpt shows the vulnerable code, with the duplicated goto statement.

```
SSLVerifySignedServerKeyExchange( ... ) {
    OSStatus        err;
    ...
    if ((err = SSLHashSHA1.update(&hashCtx, &serverRandom)) != 0)
    goto fail;
    if ((err = SSLHashSHA1.update(&hashCtx, &signedParams)) != 0)
        goto fail;
        goto fail;
    if ((err = SSLHashSHA1.final(&hashCtx, &hashOut)) != 0)
        goto fail;
    err = sslRawVerify(ctx, ctx->peerPubKey, dataToSign, signature);
    ...
fail:
    SSLFreeBuffer(&signedHashes);
    SSLFreeBuffer(&hashCtx);
    return err;
}
```

B GnuTLS' goto fail Vulnerable Code

The following listing is an extract from the vulnerable function in GnuTLS which returns -1 in case _gnutls_x509_get_signed_data fails while parsing the data. It is interesting to notice that this contradicts to the comments on top of the function.

```
/*
 * Returns only 0 or 1. If 1 it means that the certificate
 * was successfully verified. [...]
 */
static int _gnutls_verify_certificate2( ... ) {
    ...
    result = _gnutls_x509_get_signed_data( ... );
    if (result < 0) {
        gnutls_assert();
        goto cleanup;
    }
    ...
cleanup:
    if (result >= 0 && func)
        func(cert, issuer, NULL, out);
    _gnutls_free_datum(&cert_signed_data);
    _gnutls_free_datum(&cert_signature);

    return result;
}
```

And here is typical site call of the vulnerable function, where only the ret == 0 condition (corresponding to an invalid signature) would lead to reject the certificate, letting negative results be interpreted as good certificates.

```
ret = _gnutls_verify_certificate2( ... );
if (ret == 0) {
    /* if the last certificate in the certificate list is
     * invalid, then the certificate is not trusted.   */
    gnutls_assert();
    status |= output;
    status |= GNUTLS_CERT_INVALID;
    return status;
}
```

C   Examples of Automata Inferred from TLS Implementations

Figure 1 and 2 respectively describe the automata for two flawed implementations.

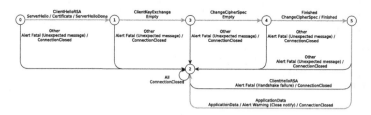

Fig. 1. Observable state automata of the RSA BSAFE JAVA stack (version 6.1.1). 5 states clearly form the expected "happy flow", while the 2 state is the error state, where all invalid sessions eventually end. Source: [26].

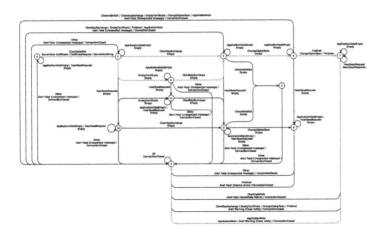

Fig. 2. Observable state automata of GNU TLS 3.3.8. This time, the automata contains 12 states. In particular, states 8 to 10 form a shadow flow, where a Heartbeat message has led to a buffer reset. Source: [26].

References

1. Adrian, D., et al.: Imperfect forward secrecy: how Diffie-Hellman fails in practice. In: Proceedings of the 22nd ACM SIGSAC Conference on Computer and Communications Security, Denver, CO, USA, 12–16 October 2015, pp. 5–17, October 2015
2. Albrecht, M.R., Paterson, K.G.: Lucky microseconds: a timing attack on Amazon's s2n implementation of TLS. IACR Cryptology ePrint Archive (2015). http://eprint.iacr.org/2015/1129
3. AlFardan, N.J., Paterson, K.G.: Lucky thirteen: breaking the TLS and DTLS record protocols. In: 2013 IEEE Symposium on Security and Privacy, SP 2013, Berkeley, CA, USA, pp. 526–540, May 2013
4. Aviram, N., et al.: DROWN: breaking TLS with SSLv2. In: 25th USENIX Security Symposium, Austin, Texas, USA, August 2016
5. Bernstein, D.J., Lange, T., Schwabe, P.: The security impact of a new cryptographic library. In: Hevia, A., Neven, G. (eds.) LATINCRYPT 2012. LNCS, vol. 7533, pp. 159–176. Springer, Heidelberg (2012). https://doi.org/10.1007/978-3-642-33481-8_9
6. Beurdouche, B., et al.: A messy state of the union: taming the composite state machines of TLS. In: 2015 IEEE Symposium on Security and Privacy, SP 2015, San Jose, CA, USA, pp. 535–552, May 2015
7. Bhargavan, K., Fournet, C., Kohlweiss, M., Pironti, A., Strub, P.: Implementing TLS with verified cryptographic security. In: 2013 IEEE Symposium on Security and Privacy, SP 2013, Berkeley, CA, USA, pp. 445–459, May 2013
8. Bleichenbacher, D.: Chosen ciphertext attacks against protocols based on the RSA encryption standard PKCS #1. In: Krawczyk, H. (ed.) CRYPTO 1998. LNCS, vol. 1462, pp. 1–12. Springer, Heidelberg (1998). https://doi.org/10.1007/BFb0055716
9. Bleichenbacher, D.: Rump session at CRYPTO 2006: forging some RSA signatures with pencil and paper. Transposed by Hal Finney on the IETF Web mailing list, August 2006. https://www.ietf.org/mail-archive/web/openpgp/current/msg00999.html

10. Böck, H., Somorovsky, J., Young, C.: Return of bleichenbacher's oracle threat (ROBOT). In: 27th USENIX Security Symposium, USENIX Security 2018, Baltimore, MD, USA, 15–17 August 2018, pp. 817–849, August 2018
11. Böck, H., Zauner, A., Devlin, S., Somorovsky, J., Jovanovic, P.: Nonce-disrespecting adversaries: practical forgery attacks on GCM in TLS. In: 10th USENIX Workshop on Offensive Technologies, WOOT 2016, Austin, USA, August 2016
12. Duong, T., Rizzo, J.: Here come the XOR ninjas. In: Ekoparty Security Conference, September 2011
13. Durumeric, Z., et al.: The matter of heartbleed. In: Proceedings of the 2014 Internet Measurement Conference, IMC 2014, Vancouver, BC, Canada, 5–7 November 2014, pp. 475–488, November 2014
14. Kikuchi, M.: How I discovered CCS injection vulnerability (CVE-2014-0224), June 2014. http://ccsinjection.lepidum.co.jp/blog/2014-06-05/CCS-Injection-en/index.html
15. Krawczyk, H.: The order of encryption and authentication for protecting communications (or: how secure is SSL?). In: Kilian, J. (ed.) CRYPTO 2001. LNCS, vol. 2139, pp. 310–331. Springer, Heidelberg (2001). https://doi.org/10.1007/3-540-44647-8_19
16. Krawczyk, H.: Cryptographic extraction and key derivation: the HKDF scheme. In: Rabin, T. (ed.) CRYPTO 2010. LNCS, vol. 6223, pp. 631–648. Springer, Heidelberg (2010). https://doi.org/10.1007/978-3-642-14623-7_34
17. Amazon Web Services Labs: s2n: an implementation of the TLS/SSL protocols (2015). https://github.com/awslabs/s2n
18. Langley, A.: Lucky thirteen attack on TLS CBC, February 2013. https://www.imperialviolet.org/2013/02/04/luckythirteen.html
19. Marlinspike, M.: Internet explorer SSL vulnerability (2002). http://www.thoughtcrime.org/ie-ssl-chain.txt
20. Marlinspike, M.: More tricks for defeating SSL in practice, July 2009. http://www.blackhat.com/presentations/bh-usa-09/MARLINSPIKE/BHUSA09-Marlinspike-DefeatSSL-SLIDES.pdf
21. Marlinspike, M.: BasicConstraints Back Then, July 2011. http://www.thoughtcrime.org/blog/sslsniff-anniversary-edition/
22. Meyer, C., Schwenk, J.: SoK: lessons learned from SSL/TLS attacks. In: Kim, Y., Lee, H., Perrig, A. (eds.) WISA 2013. LNCS, vol. 8267, pp. 189–209. Springer, Cham (2014). https://doi.org/10.1007/978-3-319-05149-9_12
23. Meyer, C., Somorovsky, J., Weiss, E., Schwenk, J., Schinzel, S., Tews, E.: Revisiting SSL/TLS implementations: new bleichenbacher side channels and attacks. In: Proceedings of the 23rd USENIX Security Symposium, San Diego, CA, USA, pp. 733–748, August 2014
24. Rescorla, E.: The transport layer security (TLS) protocol version 1.3. RFC 8446 (proposed standard), August 2018. https://doi.org/10.17487/RFC8446. https://www.rfc-editor.org/rfc/rfc8446.txt
25. Ronen, E., Gillham, R., Genkin, D., Shamir, A., Wong, D., Yarom, Y.: The 9 lives of bleichenbacher's CAT: new cache ATtacks on TLS implementations. In: 40th IEEE Symposium on Security and Privacy, SP 2019, San Francisco, CA, USA, May 2019
26. de Ruiter, J., Poll, E.: Protocol state fuzzing of TLS implementations. In: 24th USENIX Security Symposium, Washington, D.C., USA, pp. 193–206, August 2015

Security Through Transparency and Openness in Computer Design

Ivo Emanuilov[✉] ⓘ

KU Leuven Centre for IT and IP Law, Leuven, Belgium
ivo.emanuilov@kuleuven.be
http://www.citip.be/

Abstract. Trust in information technology depends on the level of security promised by the software and hardware stack operating on a platform. Consumers rely on cybersecurity updates of the software and firmware running on their devices to keep their privacy and data protected from malicious use. Businesses and governments procure technology which they expect to run for long periods and be kept in line with the state of the art in security. Presently, however, neither consumer, nor business solutions provide sufficient transparency regarding potential cybersecurity risks stemming from either the software or hardware stack embedded in them. Businesses need transparency in order to plan sustainable long-term operations, while consumers need devices that can be easily maintained and repaired and which offer sufficient information regarding real or perceived safety or security hazards. In the quest for security, transparency is a key sociotechnical requirement which lies at the core of trust in computing. As one of the most important abstractions interfacing the hardware and the lowest level software, the instruction set architecture (ISA) is perhaps the most essential element in the path to trust through transparency. Currently, however, the market is dominated by two proprietary ISAs in a duopolistic configuration, and their implementations are controlled by two major companies. This *status quo* has impacted significantly the integrated circuit supply chain in terms of both diversity and transparency.

This paper argues that open ISAs, such as RISC-V, would bring much-needed democratisation of microprocessor design while enabling higher levels of security through their modular design and extensibility. However, open ISAs are facing certain technical, organisations and legal challenges that require conceptual interdisciplinary thinking and coordinated legislative and regulatory response.

Keywords: Cybersecurity · Embedded systems · Open ISA ·
RISC-V · Open hardware · Transparency · IP rights · Liability

This research is funded by the European Union's Horizon 2020 research and innovation programme under the Secure Collaborative Intelligent Industrial Automation (SeCoIIA) project, grant agreement No. 871967.

J. Garcia-Alfaro et al. (Eds.): CRiSIS 2020, LNCS 12528, pp. 105–116, 2021.
https://doi.org/10.1007/978-3-030-68887-5_6

1 Instruction Set Architectures and Their Role for Security

1.1 Instruction Set Architecture in Computer Design

The term 'computer architecture' usually refers to the instruction set architecture, on one hand, and implementation, on the other. In turn, implementation includes logical design (i.e., organisation) and physical design (i.e., hardware). In modern computer science, computer architecture denotes all three major aspects of computer design, that is, instruction set architecture (ISA), organisation (i.e., microarchitecture) and hardware [6].

There are two classes of ISAs, namely Complex Instruction Set Computer (CISC) and Reduced Instruction Set Computer (RISC). Suffice it to say for the time being that despite the commercial success of the Intel 80 × 86 proprietary CISC ISA, RISC has been long-recognised as the superior and preferred class of ISA, especially for customised embedded systems.

The instruction set architecture is one of the most important abstractions which delineates the "boundary between software and hardware" [6]. ISA is the interface between hardware and lowest-level software which "encompasses all the information necessary to write a machine language program that will run correctly, including instructions, registers, memory access, I/O devices..." [12]. For example, a C++ program is compiled into instruction for the central processing unit (CPU) to execute. How does a compiler know what instructions the CPU understands? It is precisely the ISA that provides this information. Essentially, ISA allows computer designers to consider functions independently from the hardware upon which they are executed [12], much like one can talk about the functions of a washing machine independently from its parts (e.g., tub, drain hose, debris filter etc.). Therefore, it is important to distinguish architecture from the implementation on a particular hardware which "obeys the architecture abstraction" [12].

Historically, the proprietary Intel 80 × 86 architecture established itself as the dominant ISA. Despite its notorious technical flaws [7], the success of this ISA was the product of three main factors [6]. The first was the early market choices made by IBM, i.e. when it selected the 80×86 architecture for the initial IBM PC, making binary compatibility with this ISA much desired. The second was the availability of resources afforded by technological innovation driven by Moore's Law which allowed Intel to translate from complex instruction set computing (CISC) to reduced instruction set computing (RISC). Essentially, this meant executing RISC-like instructions through hardware translation which ensured binary compatibility with the at-the-time fast growing software base while offering RISC-like performance. Finally, the high volumes of production of microprocessors helped Intel compensate for the cost of hardware translation from CISC to RISC.

The 80 × 86 ISA has only meaningfully been challenged on a commercial scale by the rise of the ARM ISA in system-on-chip (SoC) designs in the post-PC era, that is, after the launch of the first iPhone [7]. The trend is set to continue as a growing number of Internet of Things (IoT) devices and embedded systems are being procured and deployed in both industrial and consumer settings. This means that in the near future custom SoC platforms will likely become ubiquitous, as there are hardly any devices nowadays without some form of an embedded on-chip processor.

The fact that practically all dominant ISAs are proprietary in nature has given rise to serious concerns regarding the security of the future IoT ecosystem. For example, contemporary SoCs are well known for reusing multiple existing intellectual property (IP) cores to address complexity [14]. IP cores are the "dominant form of technology delivery in the embedded, personal mobile devices, and relate markets" [12]. An IP core is "designed to be incorporated with other logic (hence, it is the 'core' of a chip), including application-specific processors (such as an video encoders or decoders), I/O interfaces, and memory interfaces, and then fabricated to yield a processor optimised for a particular application" [12]. Thus, for instance, in a modern Snapdragon SoC one would find designs from very many different sources, incl. an ARM-licensed IP, that is, the CPU. The growing complexity of SoCs has generated a corresponding growth in the reuse of IP blocks [14]. Since not all of these IP blocks are widely available for inspection and close scrutiny, this has resulted in the dominance of the 'security through obscurity' paradigm in the embedded systems market. Essentially, what one gets with most commercial ARM licences, for example, is a complete core or other product that can be incorporate in a design. The design itself, however, cannot be changed, unless one has an architectural licence. Presently, only very few and very big companies have such a licence, such as Apple, AMD, Nvidia, Qualcomm and others. This means that in all other cases one gets what everybody else gets with the same licence. Unfortunately, the recent examples of the *Spectre* and *Meltdown* security flaws allowing malicious actors to exploit vulnerabilities in the microarchitecture of some modern processors of the Intel, IBM POWER and ARM family have clearly demonstrated the miserable state of hardware *security through obscurity*.

1.2   Role of the Instruction Set Architecture for Security

The *Spectre* and *Meltdown* vulnerabilities relied on a side-channel attack leading to leakage of protected information. Essentially, the attack involved observation of the time required for a task to complete and "converting information invisible at the ISA level into a timing visible attribute" [7]. The unique feature of the *Spectre* and *Meltdown* security flaws is that they exploit a vulnerability in the hardware implementation. Since the current understanding of what constitutes a 'correct implementation' of an ISA is based on the architectural state of execution visible at the ISA level, it does not consider the performance effects of the execution of an instruction sequence [7]. While, technically speaking, *Spectre* and *Meltdown* were the product of a strive for hardware optimisation that had little to do with the ISA itself, the flawed approach of how we ascertain 'correct implementation' of ISA was at least tangentially instrumental for the *success* of these hardware vulnerabilities.

The dominance of proprietary ISAs developed and controlled by just two major companies has nurtured an ecosystem in which even different implementations are likely to be plagued by the very same flaws. In other words, the rigidity of proprietary CPU designs dominated by two main commercial players increases the impact of vulnerabilities such as *Spectre* and *Meltdown* which have proven difficult to patch, with patches coming at significant performance costs. Simply put, having just two major CPU designs in the market means a hardware vulnerability is likely to have much more significant overall impact than if there were many and different, and even customised, implementations. Against this background, this paper joins a line of research arguing that hardware security is synergistic with open ISAs. Open ISAs are a precondition for open implementations [7,10] verifiable through open security review processes and compliant the (legal) principle of security by design. Increasing the number of people and organisations involved in the design and development of secure architectures has already proven its utility in the context of free and open source software. A similar approach has been advocated by researchers calling for openness and transparency in the IT supply chains [2].

The case for a free and open ISA is built on strong technical and legal reasons as noted in [1]. Four specific reasons stand out among them.

First, companies often have patents on certain innovations in their ISAs which would prevent others from using them without proper licensing. Reportedly, Intel's patents over innovations around the 80 × 86 ISA (mostly extensions to the original ISA, such as Memory Protection Extensions (MPX), Software Guard Extensions (SGX) etc.) have been growing steadily in the past few decades [13]. In other words, the innovation surface is much smaller and the incentives - much less attractive, when innovation around alternative ISA-compatible designs is held off by prohibitive licence fees. Furthermore, free and open ISAs are likely to have positive economic impact by increasing competition in the ISA market currently defined by a duopoly.

Second, even though software ecosystems emerge around ISAs, these former are built by communities outside the immediate reach of the company developing the ISA. Furthermore, the expertise needed to develop an ISA is by no means concentrated in said companies; to the contrary, much of the expertise needed is widely available in open hardware communities, and compatibility with an ISA can be verified by open organisations.

Third, the availability and continued support of proprietary ISAs is heavily dependent on the company's will. In other words, if a company ceases its operations, it is likely that its proprietary ISA will go with it too.

Fourth, open ISAs mean development and availability of shared core designs, that is, more transparency and less likelihood of introducing fatal (security) flaws. Indeed, the principle of open design is part and parcel of the foundational Saltzer and Schroeder's 1975 Design Principles for Secure Systems. In their paper, Saltzer and Schroeder argued that "design should not be secret", "mechanisms should not depend on the ignorance of potential attackers, but rather on the possession of specific, more easily protected, keys or passwords" and that "it is simply not realistic attempt to maintain secrecy for any system which receives wide distribution" [15]. Ultimately, open design would make it much more difficult for State actors to intervene in the design process and introduce security backdoors.

1.3   Open ISAs in Practice: The Case of RISC-V

One recent noteworthy example of an open ISA that has generated a lot of interest in the embedded systems community is RISC-V. RISC-V is a royalty-free ISA developed in 2011 by Patterson and Asanović at Berkeley [1]. The driving force behind RISC-V is the desire for flexible, customisable and modular designs that can be implemented on custom chips at lower costs compared to their proprietary counterparts [4].

The need of creating an equivalent of the Linux kernel in the world of microprocessors is justified by the well-known benefits of opening the development and review process to a wider community. The experience gained in almost four decades of free and open source software development is a clear attestation to the success of this approach based on collaboration and transparency. While free and open source hardware and free and open source software are known to have both fundamental and incidental differences [5], the benefits of creating a virtuous cycle of open source hardware platforms based, among others, on open ISAs, are clear. They improve competition, encourage sustainable growth, and allow customisation, greater flexibility and, ultimately, better security.

Indeed, RISC-V is maintained by a community steered by the RISC-V Foundation, a non-profit organisation. The openness of the RISC-V ISA allows for public collaboration which means the *modus operandi* is based on resolving problems and discussing issues before taking any design decisions [7]. Importantly, the modular design of the RISC-V ISA means that the base of instructions running the full open source software stack is small and the optional extensions allow for customisation and optimisation depending on the needs [7]. The simplicity of the RISC-V ISA means less room for hidden flaws as it is all too well known that in the world of computer security complexity breeds vulnerabilities. Furthermore, open ISAs have a particularly strong case to make in times where state-sponsored backdoors can be (and have been) implemented at increasingly lower levels of abstraction in computer design. Specifically, RISC-V allows a manufacturer to know exactly what is going on at the microprocessor level. It also facilitates enhancement and customisation by allowing users to modify or create designs which are aligned with their security needs. Finally, RISC-V is a particularly attractive ISA for governments as they could benefit from procuring open source ISA implementations known to be free of embedded malware [4].

2   Security Promises of Open ISAs

Open ISAs, such as RISC-V, offer a number of security promises. Some of them have already been outlined in the previous sections. This paper argues that in times when cybersecurity and cyber resilience are increasingly becoming a matter of survival, e.g. in light of the *NotPetya* and *WannaCry* attacks against critical infrastructure, such as hospitals and power grids, the need for transparency at all levels of computer hardware and software has become more prominent than ever. There are a number of advantages, but also some concerns regarding the security promises of open ISAs, as summarised in Table 1.

Table 1. Security benefits and risks of open ISAs

Benefits	Risks
Modular design and extensibility	Ecosystem fragmentation
Transparency	Still chance of vulnerabilities
Long-term security evolution	Lack of interest by the community
Community review	Commercial and governmental support and scalability
Royalty-free use	Legacy compatibility, upfront transition costs

First, the modular design of open ISA, like RISC-V, offer not only the ability to implement customised solutions but also to iterate and enhance them in an open and conducive to dialogue environment, such as the respective community created around the ISA. In turn, this would enable much quicker design and development cycles [7] which allegedly implies that fixing issues and security vulnerabilities should be equally quicker. This aspect of open ISAs is also critical in light of the long-term support and availability of devices implementing this ISA. This is especially beneficial in the context of Internet of Things where many connected devices will need to be supported over a long time span. The modular design of open ISAs, like RISC-V, allows security extensions to be added at ease, while keeping them close, if necessary, since the core IP would be standardised anyway [14]. There is a need, however, to define and perhaps redefine the parameters that go into evaluating what constitutes a 'correct implementation' of the ISA. Indeed, ecosystem fragmentation is one of the major challenges before the uptake of RISC-V and it may have considerable security consequences as well (e.g., concerning verification and independent third-party testing).

Second, open ISAs would also make it possible to build test suites for exhaustive testing by all users and would facilitate the application of formal methods for verification of the trustworthiness of hardware [17]. Transparency "allows users to place justified trust in the hardware being used and enabled comprehensive evolutionary improvements to be made" [17]. With more 'eyeballs' looking at the same specification, community-driven open ISAs clearly have the advantage of open security by peer review over their proprietary counterparts. This is not only an advantage for businesses, but equally for governments. In times of growing calls for 'digital sovereignty', implementations based on open specifications would clearly allow governments greater control over the procurement and supply of embedded systems which may become part of a State's critical infrastructure. Specifically, governments could leverage regulatory processes such as 'reverse cascade' to exert regulatory pressure on distributors under their jurisdiction to sell products compliant with certain open and transparent design and manufacturing standards [9]. However, just because a specification is open does not mean it comes without vulnerabilities. Clearly, the paradigm of security through public peer code review is much preferred to security by obscurity, yet there have been cases where the 'many eyeballs' argument has not been very convincing. For one, the Heartbleed vulnerability in the open source OpenSSL library was a case in point described by some as 'open source's worst hour' [16]. Exaggerated as such qualifications might be, Heartbleed showed one thing clearly: just because the code or specification is free and available for public review does not mean that someone will actually carry out this review or that standard analysis approaches work for detection of such vulnerabilities [18]. Lack of interest by the community in certain software packages has often led to lack of support and maintenance for these packages. Granted, this is not a failure of open source *per se*, but it is a fact that needs to be considered in the context of the community created around an open product, service or specifications thereof.

Third, open ISAs can be particularly useful in environments where embedded systems are deployed for long-term use and must therefore conform to objectives concerning long-term security evolution. In such environments, systems would have to be able to support security evolution as the threat landscape evolves. Indeed, the community created around an open product, service or specifications could remain vibrant and active for many decades. However, there is of course also the risk of potential lack of community support. While this is clearly not the case for promising community projects such as RISC-V, the need for support on a commercial scale is critical for the success of microprocessor implementations based on open ISAs.

Fourth, the potentially huge community that may be created around an open ISA would clearly improve the security review and audits of an open specification. These communities, however, need both institutional and financial support in order to grow. Promoting openness and transparency by legal, regulatory and standardisation measures is critical for the creation of a strong community. It is even more important for creating strong incentives for businesses to build a competitive market for support and maintenance services organised around these communities. In other words, encouraging the creation of strong support and maintenance services around open ISAs is critical not only for the uptake of one specification or another, but also for their long-term security evolution.

Finally, one of the main advantages of open ISAs is that their use is free of royalties and licensing costs, meaning one can start relatively quickly with little resources. However, the transition of the entire infrastructure of business or governmental upstream players to implementations based on open ISAs can still have prohibitive costs. Binary compatibility notwithstanding, large-scale deployments would likely require rebuilding the entire supporting infrastructure. While cutting and bleeding edge players may be up for the challenge, the transition in safety-critical environments, such as manufacturing or healthcare, where legacy operational technology and new information technology systems have to play nicely together, may generate significant upfront costs.

3 Legal and Policy Perils of Open ISAs

Besides the purely technical and economic promises and issues of open ISAs, there are vastly important legal and policy perils whose resolution may prove critical for the success of open architectures.

3.1 Manageability, Collaboration and Competition

The first problem concerns the legal infrastructure needed to ensure manageability of open ISAs and the challenge of preventing Balkanisation of this domain. Indeed, the rigidity of established supply chains in the ISA market characterised by a duopoly often creates risks of lock-ins and may entail high and even prohibitive termination costs should one try to leaves the 'walled garden'. However, open ISAs can also bring more competition in the market, by pulling control away from Intel and ARM [4]. Furthermore, the modularity of open ISAs, like RISC-V, can clearly create new markets for customised solutions, e.g. field programmable gate arrays (FPGA), based on specific needs driven, *inter alia*, by security.

The development of open ISAs, organised as a collaboration within a community, carries the potential to democratise computer design. However, collaboration can also bring about certain perils. For example, the RISC-V Foundation is concerned with the "release of RISC-V to the open community for both standardization and ongoing improvement through open collaboration". Standardisation is therefore critical for the success of open ISAs. Indeed, compliance with standards is critical to prevent the fragmentation that may come with the modularity and extensibility of an open ISA, like RISC-V. Unlike proprietary ISAs controlled by large companies, making it easier to verify compliance of an implementation with the specification, open ISAs will open the market to many more companies. Ensuring compliance of many different implementations with one single specification is therefore a fundamentally different challenge. The work carried out in the framework of the RISC-V Foundation is critical, but it must be supplemented by dedicated efforts at governmental level promoting openness and transparency in the procurement of implementations based on open specifications. These efforts, however, should be balanced against the interests of protecting competition and ensuring that collaboration does not mature into collusion.

The ongoing cooperation between industry players demanding open specifications is critical for the success of open ISAs. The community should also be prepared for attacks from incumbent players, like the notorious anti-RISC V website launched by ARM in 2018 [4]. The legal status of the RISC-V Foundation as a steering force and its immunity to trade curbs is equally important.

It is precisely such fears that forced the RISC-V Foundation to move its head-quarters from Delaware to Switzerland in 2019. In times of global geopolitical rage against the deployment of 'foreign' technologies in public infrastructure, to ensure the continuity of development standardisation efforts of RISC-V in a jurisdiction known for its high legal standards is a legal as much as a policy and political question.

3.2   Intellectual Property Rights

Arguably, one of the main advantages of open ISAs is that one does not need to deal with complex contractual arrangements, pay royalties or handle delicate issues over future research and development licensing requirements. However, as Andrew Katz has recently demonstrated in his empirical study, open processor and, more generally, free and open source hardware licensing is far from clear [8].

Indeed, industrial players admit that "currently available copyleft open hard-ware licences are insufficiently clear in their effect to be safely used" and "poten-tial benefits of copyleft licensing in core designs are not yet sufficiently clear to show an overwhelming need to shift to a copyleft model" [8]. Interestingly, the interviewees in this study pointed out that "the lack of open source or low-cost toolchains was an inhibiting factor in the growth of open hardware communities focusing on cores" [8]. As open source toolchains are a much rarer breed in open hardware communities, compared to open source software, there are legal issues which have yet to be resolved. For example, there are questions concerning the legal status of code incorporated by the toolchain into the output, or whether the bitstream is a computer program in the legal sense and, if so, who is running it upon booting the hardware [8].

The choice of appropriate licence is relevant not only from a commercial per-spective, but it is also important for security purposes. In the notorious example of *Heartbleed*, the OpenSSL project was using a custom license which was not compatible with the commonly accepted by the free and open source community GNU General Public License. Arguably, using a standard free and open source licence would have increased the community's involvement through code contri-butions and review [18]. Eventually, this would have had the effect of strength-ening the project's resilience against vulnerabilities such as *Heartbleed*. This line of thought is equally applicable in the context of open processor and, more gen-erally, open hardware licensing, and it goes to show the important connections between intellectual property rights and cybersecurity.

3.3   Liability

In the wake of the *Spectre* and *Meltdown* vulnerabilities, Intel was challenged in several class actions in US courts where the plaintiffs sought damages from Intel. Chief among these lawsuits is the case of *Intel Corp. CPU Marketing, Sales Practices and Product Liability Litigation, case number 3:18-md-02828, in the U.S. District Court for the District of Oregon* [11].

In this case, the plaintiffs based their claims on three main allegations: (1) failure by Intel to disclose defects in its processors, (2) which create security vulnerabilities that could lead to a breach of confidential data and (3) issuing patches to fix these defects which substantially diminish the speed of Intel's processors. Essentially, the plaintiffs argued that Intel prioritised speed over security, making a user's confidential information susceptible to side-channel attacks (i.e., by taking design decisions to implement branch prediction, speculative execution, out-of-order execution, and an unsecured cache subsystem) by exploiting two main flaws.

In the case, Judge Simon dismissed the plaintiffs' claims on grounds of failing to demonstrate the type of injury required to show standing. He highlighted that none of the plaintiffs have discontinued using or replaced their computers because of the alleged defects. He also noted that the plaintiffs "do not explain how this alleged defect would have affected the market price for Intel's chips in light of the fact that it involved all the chips in the market" [11]. The judge continued that the plaintiffs "have not sufficiently alleged what 'adequate measures' they reasonably expected relating to the alleged security vulnerabilities or what they allege was the parties' bargain that Intel did not meet" [11]. He found that "Plaintiffs also allege that Intel's success largely is based on the speed of its processors [but they] do not allege that they would have sacrificed that processing speed for additional security against theoretical vulnerabilities, most of which had been known in the industry for two decades. Plaintiffs instead assert only general, conclusory allegations about desiring and expecting "adequate" security. The Court finds that Plaintiffs have not sufficiently alleged their reasonable expectations for data security or the absence of the specific alleged security vulnerabilities." [11] Judge Simon distinguished this case from data breach cases which are "more instructive because they explicitly consider whether data security was part of the parties' underlying bargain". He continued that "[i]n data breach cases there already has been a breach of security, and the plaintiffs in those cases contend that a minimum level of reasonable security protection was part of the parties' bargain and expectation. Here, in contrast, there has been no data breach. Further, Plaintiffs' allegations show that for decades it was known in the industry that Intel's designs were vulnerable to various side-channel attacks. Yet no actual security breach occurred over the years, despite these known security vulnerabilities. Even after these and other security vulnerabilities became more publicly known, they were still only theoretical and have been exposed in conceptual form. There are no allegations of any actual data breaches or "hacks" to date as a result of the alleged security vulnerabilities" [11].

While this particular case dealt with a problem inherent in the implementation of the Intel 80×86 ISA and not in the ISA itself, it shows that liability cases may be on the rise as more and more hardware vulnerabilities are reported daily. The notorious complexity of the 80×86 ISA and the ever-growing number of instruction set implementations protected by patents is certainly an argument in favour of open ISAs. However, one cannot but think whether this case would be any different had the 80×86 ISA been open. For example, if the implementation had not been entirely correct according to the specification, would the designer be liable and on what grounds? in cases of collaborative open ISAs, such as RISC-V, whose should be the responsibility to define what a 'correct implementation' is? Another layer of complexity is added by cases of attacks combining software and hardware vulnerabilities, particularly computer architecture vulnerabilities [3]. How would the liability be allocated between the different parties in such a case?

It is beyond the scope and ambition of this paper to enter into a discussion on any of these questions. However, it is important to note that transparency of the entire integrated circuit supply chain is key to resolving many of them. At the same time, one should not think that open ISAs are a panacea. They are merely part of the solution and perhaps one of the most important building blocks towards transparent and truly trustworthy computing.

4   Conclusion and Further Work

Transparency is a key sociotechnical requirement which lies at the core of trust in computing. As one of the most important abstractions interfacing the hardware and the lowest level software, the instruction set architecture is perhaps the most critical element in the path to trust through transparency. Presently, two proprietary ISAs dominate the market in a duopolistic configuration and their implementations are controlled by two major companies. This has had a major impact in terms of diversity and transparency.

This paper argued that open ISAs, such as RISC-V, would enable much-needed democratisation of microprocessor design while enabling higher levels of security through their modular design and extensibility. However, open ISAs have certain technical, organisational, legal and policy challenges that require conceptual thinking and legislative and regulatory action. Furthermore, any such action should account for the global nature of the integrated circuit supply chain, meaning transparency regulation would be only as strong as the legal and political power exerted by the party trying to enforce it.

Transparency regulation and openness are critical for the cybersecurity of the impending embedded systems revolution in the face of IoT. Technical solutions, like open designs, should go hand in hand with a legal framework that balances the objective of transparency for cybersecurity against competing and legitimate interests protected by competition law, intellectual property law or tort law.

References

1. Asanović, K., Patterson, D.A.: Instruction Sets Should Be Free: The Case For RISC-V. Technical Report UCB/EECS-2014-146, Electrical Engineering and Computer Sciences, University of California at Berkeley (2014). https://people.eecs.berkeley.edu/~krste/papers/EECS-2014-146.pdf
2. Chattopadhyay, A., et al.: Quattro S Initiative: Eradicate Faults and Backdoors in Information Technology and Facilitate Innovation. Technical Report Quattro S Initiative (2019)

3. Chen, K., Deng, Q., Hou, Y., Jin, Y., Guo, X.: Hardware and software co-verification from security perspective. In: 2019 20th International Workshop on Microprocessor/SoC Test, Security and Verification (MTV), pp. 50–55 (2019). https://doi.org/10.1109/MTV48867.2019.00018
4. Greengard, S.: Will RISC-V revolutionize computing?. Commun. ACM **63**(5), 30–32 (2020). https://doi.org/10.1145/3386377
5. Gupta, G., Nowatzki, T., Gangadhar, V., Sankaralingam, K.: Open-source Hardware: Opportunities and Challenges. arxiv preprint (2016). http://arxiv.org/abs/1606.01980
6. Hennessy, J.L., Patterson, D.A.: Computer Architecture: A Quantitative Approach, 6th edn. Morgan Kaufmann, Amsterdam (2017)
7. Hennessy, J.L., Patterson, D.A.: A new golden age for computer architecture. Commun. ACM **62**(2), 48–60 (2019). https://doi.org/10.1145/3282307
8. Katz, A.: A survey of open processor core licensing. Int. Free Open Source Softw. Law Rev. **10**(1), 21–46 (2018). https://doi.org/10.5033/ifosslr.v10i1.130, https://jolts.world/index.php/jolts/article/view/130
9. Kim, N., Herr, T., Schneier, B.: The reverse cascade: enforcing security on the global IoT supply chain. Technical Report Atlantic Council Scowcroft Center for Strategy and Security (2020). https://www.atlanticcouncil.org/in-depth-research-reports/report/the-reverse-cascade-enforcing-security-on-the-global-iot-supply-chain/
10. Mühlberg, J.T., Van Bulck, J.: Reflections on post-meltdown trusted computing: a case for open security processors. Login USENIX Mag. 43(3), 1–4 (2018). https://lirias.kuleuven.be/retrieve/516518
11. United States District Court for the District of Oregon; In Re: Intel Corp. CPU Marketing, Sales Practices and Products Liability Litigation, Cqse, 3:18-md-02828 (2020)
12. Patterson, D.A., Hennessy, J.L.: Computer Organization and Design: The Hardware/Software Interface. Morgan Kaufmann Publishers, an imprint of Elsevier, risc-v edition edn. (2018)
13. Rodgers, S., Uhlig, R.A.: Intel's X86: Approaching 40 and Still Going Strong. https://newsroom.intel.com/editorials/x86-approaching-40-still-going-strong/
14. Salmon, L.G.: A Perspective on the Role of Open-Source IP In Government Electronic Systems. In: Presentation, DARPA, RISC-V Workshop (2017)
15. Saltzer, J., Schroeder, M.: The protection of information in computer systems. Proc. IEEE **63**(9), 1278–1308 (1975). https://doi.org/10.1109/PROC.1975.9939
16. Vaughan-Nichols, S.J.: Heartbleed: Open source's worst hour. https://www.zdnet.com/article/heartbleed-open-sources-worst-hour/
17. Weber, A., Reith, S., Kasper, M., Kuhlmann, D., Seifert, J.P., Krauß, C.: Sovereignty in Information Technology. Fraunhofer SIT, Fraunhofer Singapore, RheinMain University of Applied Sciences, TU Berlin/T-Labs, White paper (2018)
18. Wheeler, D.A.: Preventing heartbleed. IEEE. Comput. **47**(8), 80–83 (2014). https://doi.org/10.1109/MC.2014.217

An ML Behavior-Based Security Control for Smart Home Systems

Noureddine Amraoui$^{(\boxtimes)}$ and Belhassen Zouari

Mediatron Laboratory, Higher School of Communications of Tunis, Ariana, Tunisia
houcine1amraoui@gmail.com

Abstract. Smart Home Systems (SHSs) automation platforms are now enabling users to automate the control of their SHS devices by installing autonomous third-party applications (called SmartApps). However, intentional/unintentional issues would make SmartApps deviate from their expected behavior, putting the SHS owner's security at risk. To address this issue, in this paper, we introduce an ML behavior-based approach to prevent malicious control of SHS devices by misbehaved SmartApps. To do so, control commands issued by the SmartApps during regular operation are captured to build a One-Class Support Vector Machine (OCSVM) model as a baseline for each installed SmartApp. Then, anomalous commands (i.e., outlier data points) should be detected and rejected, while normal commands (i.e., inlier data points) are allowed to be executed. Through an experimental evaluation conducted on an adapted SHS automation history, our proposed approach exhibits low false acceptance and rejection rates.

Keywords: Anomaly Detection (AD) · Home Automation · Internet of Things (IoT) · Intrusion detection · Smart Home Systems (SHS) · User and entity behavior analysis (UEBA)

1 Introduction

Recent years have seen a proliferation of the Internet of Things (IoT) devices intended for consumers' homes [7]. Owners are transforming their homes into Smart Home Systems (SHSs) with variant IoT Internet-connected sensors, lights, and appliances that can sense and actuate in the physical environment. Several SHS automation platforms (e.g., SmartThings[1]) are now available in the market. These platforms provide a new level of convenience by enabling consumers to automate the control of their SHS devices by installing and delegating authorization to third-party applications (called IoT apps) [9]. To do so, SmartApps use simple Trigger-Action rules where the control action of a given device is only performed when the triggering event has occurred [3]. For instance, a 'Welcome Home' SmartApp sets the mode to home when the light in the living room is turned on.

While SHS automation is supposed to be executed regularly, intentional/ unintentional issues could make SmartApps deviate from their regular behavior,

---

[1] https://www.smartthings.com.

© Springer Nature Switzerland AG 2021
J. Garcia-Alfaro et al. (Eds.): CRiSIS 2020, LNCS 12528, pp. 117–130, 2021.
https://doi.org/10.1007/978-3-030-68887-5_7

putting the SHS owner's security at risk and create unsafe or damaging conditions. First of all, poor configuration by novice SHS users (e.g., parents and kids) at the installing stage of SmartApps can transition the SHS to unsafe physical states due to the conflicting logic of common SmartApps [11]. For example, if the SHS owner installs a new SmartApp, yet, an already installed SmartApp is listening to the action executed on the device controlled by the new SmartApp. As a consequence, this device will be unexpectedly controlled once the new SmartApp is triggered [3]. Secondly, SmartApps provided by different third-party developers may contain some programming faults leading to a bad, hence an unexpected functioning of the SmartApps. Lastly, the Trigger-Action model of SHS platforms provides flexibility for the attacker to embed their malicious logic into the SmartApps using available triggering events (e.g., home mode changing) [4]. The activation of malicious logic makes the SmartApp deviates from its past regular behavior since it starts to perform unexpected automation actions.

Recent works have proposed the enforcement of policies that describe the security and safety properties that refer to regular operation of the SHS [2,3,8,14]. In particular, the adherence of the SHS automation control is continuously checked to the properties defined by the policy, and the control commands causing the policy violations are blocked. Unfortunately, the pre-definition of the policy is the major problem facing this type of system. First, general-purpose policies (e.g., defined by security experts) are not personalized and may not suit all SHSs automation configurations. Moreover, SHS users often do not know exactly what to expect from the system when acquiring it, thus if the policy definition is left for the user him/herself, security and safety properties may not be well defined. Consequently, there is a growing need for a new security model that is personalized and supports self-learning.

Given that the SmartApps leverage the Trigger-Action automation model for operation, they follow a frequent pattern when they are triggered by the occurred events to control the SHS devices. On one hand, the occurred events are the result of the daily living activities of the home inhabitant (e.g., door opening). And because the inhabitant tends to follow frequent patterns when living and performing variant activities inside the home (e.g., every evening he/she back home from work), triggering events also occur in the same particular patterns. On the other hand, since SHS devices are operated by these events (e.g., door opening triggers the light to turn on), SmartApps also control the devices in such a recurrent pattern. This set of regular patterns can be described by several behavioral features such as the occurrence probability of an event, the probability of the SmartApps to control a given device while being triggered by the occurred event, etc. Thus, any deviation of the SHS automation control from such regular behavior could be detected based on the analysis of the SmartApps behavior.

Tracing then assessing users' and entities' activities of a cyber system is better known as User Entity Behavior Analysis (UEBA) [13]. UEBA is a self-learning approach that leverages Anomaly Detection (AD) algorithms. The basic idea is to first build a baseline model over the regular conduct of users and entities.

Then, deviations from this baseline could be further analyzed accordingly. In this paper, we leverage UEBA and AD to devise a framework for securing SHS automation control based on the behavior analysis of the SmartApps. Such an approach has been already leveraged in our prior work to authenticate SHS users and prevent devices from unauthorized control [1]. However, in this work, the SHS user is not included in the behavior analysis and the only monitored entity is the SmartApp. Our proposed framework ensures the three following properties:

- Personalization and self-learning: the framework automatically build an ML One-class Support Vector Machine (OCSVM) for each installed SmartApp in the SHS without any intervention of its owner.
- Continuity: based on a set of behavioral scores that can be calculated and assessed, the behavior of an IoT app is evaluated during its entire lifecycle.
- Trust-based Verification: a confidence score of each installed SmartApps is calculated and evaluated to ban the ones showing steady anomalous behavior.

This paper makes the following contributions:

- First to apply behavior-based anomaly detection to secure SHS automation control.
- Extraction of new Behavioral Scores to monitor and evaluate the SmartApp-based automation control of SHS devices.
- We are the first to adapt the history data of manual control of appliances and objects by inhabitants inside a home environment to be used as the history automation app-based control of SHS IoT devices, to remedy the lack of such data in public repositories.
- Experimental results validate that such a user behavior-based approach is a promising security scheme to be integrated into existing commercial SHS platforms.

The rest of the paper is organized as follows. In Sects. 2, we discuss some of the related works. The design of our proposed framework will be explained in Sect. 3. Section 4 presents the experimental evaluation of the Anomaly Analyzer one of the core modules of the framework. Finally, Sect. 5 concludes this paper and underlines some future directions.

2   Related Work

As summarized in Table 1, several works have been proposed recently to secure SHS automation control from malicious control by the enforcement of policies that describe the security and safety preferences of the SHS owner [2,3,8,14].

Tian et al. proposed SmartAuth, an authorization policy-based system that learns about the SmartApps actual functionality by analyzing their source code and the description provided by developers [14]. Then, the discrepancies between the SmartApps description and their programmed logic are pointed out and displayed to the user through an automatically generated interface.

Table 1. Summary of related work

Ref.	Policy type	Policy definition	Enforcement technique
[7]	General purpose	Derived from security standard recommendations	Boolean satisfiability problem (SAT)
[5]	Personalized	User-defined assisted by information extracted from SmartApps description and their programmed logic	Not specified
[6]	General purpose	Extracted from SmartApps and trigger-action platforms rules	Model Checking
[2]	General purpose	Extracted from SmartApps and trigger-action platforms rules	Reachability Analysis

After that, SmartAuth retrieves the user's explanation and approval for the extracted discrepancies using natural-language-generation techniques. Once a user sets his/her policy settings through the user interface, SmartAuth enforces the policy by blocking unauthorized commands. Celik et al. proposed Soteria, a model checking based-system to verify whether installed SmartApps adhere to security and safety properties. The enforced properties are a set of systematically developed policies that represent the physical behavioral specifications of users' expectations about the safe and secure behavior of an SHS [2]. IoTGuard another policy-based authorization system retrieves SmartApps information (e.g., events and actions) at runtime and stores them in a dynamic model that consists of transitions and states [3]. The dynamic model represents the runtime execution behavior of the SmartApp. Using the reachability analysis technique, this model is then evaluated against the same policies used by Soteria [2]. Recently, Ibrahim et al. proposed an automated technique to derive actionable security rules from security standard recommendations (e.g., OWASP IoT Security Guidance) [8]. The extracted policy is then translated into a formal language to detect policy violation using formal techniques such as the Boolean satisfiability problem (SAT).

Although the proposed systems consider additional design and security features beyond the existing authorization models in current SHS automation (e.g., SmartThings Permission Model), they suffer from a major problem related to the pre-definition of the security policy. Indeed, general-purpose policies as proposed by [2,3], and [8] are not personalized and may not suit all SHSs automation configurations. Moreover, as leveraged by SmartAuth [14], users may not be able to accurately explain their specific security preferences.

To overcome these issues, we propose to build a self-learning Machine Learning (ML) models that summarize the automation behavior of SmartApps by learning their pattern of triggering events and controlled devices. The historical

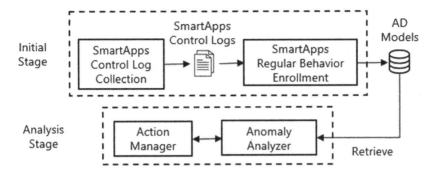

Fig. 1. Operation stages of proposed framework

regular behavior of SmartApps is then used to analyze future automation commands and discriminate their legitimacy or maliciousness. Such an approach is personalized for each SHS and offloads the manual definition of security policy from the user since minor intervention is needed.

3   Proposed Framework

In this section, we first provide an overview of the operation of our proposed framework and present the SHS platform which we consider as a use case. Then, we explain the operation of the framework in detail.

3.1   Overview

Figure 1 shows the operational architecture of our proposed framework including two stages. Before the framework starts securing SHS devices from unexpected SmartApps automation control, an initiation stage is first performed on the historical control of the SmartApps including two processes viz., SmartApps Control Log Collection, and SmartApps Regular Behavior Enrollment. The result of the initial stage is the AD models summarizing the regular behavioral patterns of the SmartApps seen in the SmartApps Control Log. Once AD models are built, the framework starts analyzing the control commands issued by SmartApps. This stage includes two modules viz., Anomaly Analyzer and Action Manager.

To show the concrete operation of our proposed framework, we consider the SmartThings platform as a use case in this paper which has the largest number of supported SmartApps among all the SHS platforms. SmartThings is a cloud-backed SHS platform that allows third-party developers to publish their automation apps (called SmartApps) [4]. An SHS owner can install and delegate authorization to these apps to autonomously monitor and control his/her home devices.

As depicted in Fig. 2, SmartThings uses a cloud backend to abstracts physical SHS devices into device handler instances. These software wrappers handle

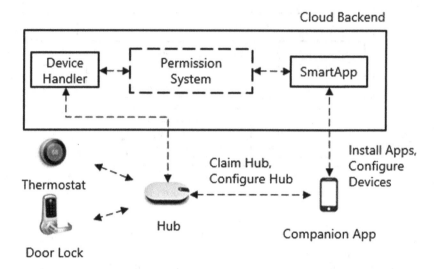

Fig. 2. SmartThings architecture

the real underlying communication between the cloud and the physical devices. SmartApps can subscribe to the events fired by a set of instances of device handlers and issue commands to control the devices handlers.

SmartThings also provide a smartphone companion app for users so they can install SmartApps published in the store, and configure and delegate authorization to the SmartApps that support the capabilities provided by their devices. The permission model is the security architecture that governs the access of a SmartApp to the commands and attributes provided by the devices handlers. Commands represent ways in which a device can be controlled or actuated (e.g., turn on/turn off). Attributes represent the state information of a device (e.g., on/off) [5]. When a user installs a SmartApp, an enumeration process is triggered that scans all the physical devices currently paired with the user's hub, and that supports the commands and attributes claimed by the SmartApp. Once the user chooses one of the suggested devices, the SmartApp is authorized to control the selected device.

Figure 3 shows the distribution of the framework modules on the architecture of SmartThings. In the following, we discuss the operation of each module for both stages.

3.2   Initial Stage

The initial stage is the first process the framework has to perform after being deployed to be ready for the analysis stage.

SmartApps Log Collection. The first step towards the building of regular SmartApps behavioral patterns is the collection of their historical automation

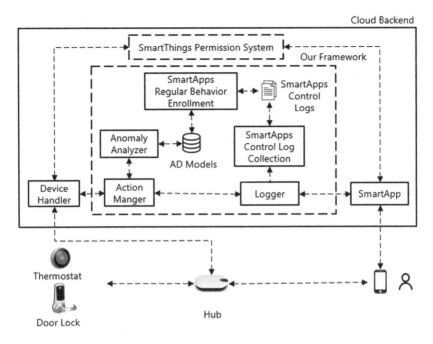

Fig. 3. Distribution of our framework modules on SmartThings platform

traces. To accomplish this task we add the Logger, a module that intercepts the automation control commands issued by the SmartApps towards the devices handlers and sends them to be saved in the SmartApps Control Log file. The information extracted from a control command includes: SmartApp ID, triggering event, controlled device, control action, and timestamp.

SmartApps Regular Behavior Enrollment. Once the SmartApps Control Log is collected, the baseline models summarizing the behavioral patterns of each one of the installed SmartApps are built. This process is called Enrollment and its output is a set of AD models that are saved to be retrieved in the analysis stage. As described in Fig. 4, the Enrollment process includes four sub-processes. The subsequent sections explain each sub-process in detail.

(a) SmartApps Control Log Segmentation: before being used in the construction of Probabilistic Models and the training of AD models, the collected SmartApps Control Log needs first to be prepared. This task allows the extraction of more information about the SmartApps patterns. Given that the behavior of an SHS inhabitant through the 24 h of the day is generally segmented into a set of frequent periods wherein the user has some specific behavioral routines (e.g., waking up and going to work in the morning). And because the SmartApps behavior is related to the SHS owner behavior (i.e., triggering event occurs due to SHS inhabitant physical activities), the log

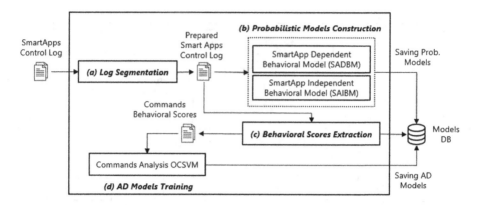

Fig. 4. Process of SmartApps regular behavior enrollment

segmentation consists of adding the corresponding time interval of the day (i.e., period) to each record in the SmartApps Control Log.

(b) Probabilistic Models Construction: a Probabilistic Model is of a set of vectors and matrices containing different probabilities that describe the SmartApps behavioral patterns seen in the prepared SmartApps Control Log. In particular, we distinguish two types of models. The SmartApps Dependent Behavioral Model (SADBM) contains the behavioral probabilities related to the SmartApp itself. Whereas, the SmartApps Independent Behavioral Model (SAIBM) contains the behavioral probabilities related to the set of occurred events and installed SmartApps. Table 2 describes the parameter of each model.

(c) Behavioral Scores Extraction: we call the Behavioral Scores, the data on which the AD Models are trained. Extracting these scores consists of calculating a tuple of numeric values for each command seen in the SmartApps Control Log using the constructed Probabilistic Models (i.e., SADBM and SAISBM) (cf. Fig. 4). Hence, a Trigger-Action command issued by a SmartApps is described by the six following behavioral scores:

- Event Occurrence: probability of the SmartApps to be triggered by the occurred event.
- Device Control Given Event: probability of the SmartApps to control the given device while being triggered by the occurred event.
- SmartApp Transition: probability of the given SmartApp to be triggered after the previous one has been triggered.
- SmartApp Transition Latency: time interval between the triggering of the given SmartApp and the triggering of the previous one.
- Events Transition: probability of the SmartApp to be triggered by the occurred event after being triggered by the previous one.
- Events Transition Latencies: time interval between the occurrence of the given event and the previous one.

(d) AD Models Training: training AD models on the set of extracted Behavioral Scores is the fruit of all the previous Enrollment sub-processes. Since our objective is to discriminate legitimate control commands from anomalous ones, we are dealing with a binary classification problem in terms of Machine Learning. However, as only regular Behavioral Scores are available during the Enrollment stage, One-Class Classification (OCC) should be used in such a situation. In this work, we use the One-Class Support Vector Machines (OCSVM) [12] as it has shown high performances in detecting anomalies in many other application domains compared to other AD algorithms [6].

Table 2. Probabilistic models description

Model	Parameter	Type	Description
SADBM	App Related Event	Vector	Probability values of the set of installed SmartApps to be triggered by related event(s)
	App Controlled Devices	Vector	Probability values of the set of installed SmartApps to control related device(s) given the occurrence of related event(s)
SAIBM	Apps Transitions	Matrix	Probability values of transition between every two SmartApps for all the set of installed SmartApps
	Apps Transitions Latencies	Matrix	Time interval between the triggering between every two SmartApps for all the set of installed SmartApps
	Events Transitions	Matrix	Probability values of transition between everytwo events for all the set of occurred events
	Events Transitions Latencies	Matrix	Time interval between the occurrence of every two events for all the set of occurred events

3.3 Analysis Stage

To prevent unwanted devices operation resulted from SmartApps behaving against their expected behaviors, the Action Manager (AM) intercepts the commands issued by SmartApps to analyze their legitimacy/anomaly via the Anomaly Analyzer (AA). Then, it takes security actions accordingly.

Anomaly Analyzer. As shown in Fig. 5, upon receiving a control command from the AM, the anomaly analysis sub-process is triggered. In particular, AA first calculates the Behavioral Scores (BSs) from different parameters of the command (e.g., event, controlled device, etc.). Then, it retrieves the trained OCSVM model and applies it to the calculated scores. The application of the OCSVM outputs an Anomaly Score (AS) that varies in the range of $[-1,+1]$.

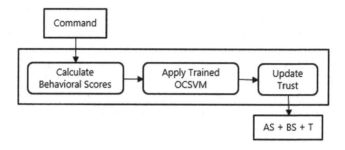

Fig. 5. Anomaly analyzer process

Moreover, AA updates the SmartApps trust (T) using the resulted AS (explained in the following). Finally, it sends the three obtained parameters i.e., AS, BSs, and T back to AM.

Action Manager. Figure 6 depicts the process of the Action Manager (AM). Once a command is issued by a SmartApp, AM sends it to AA which sends back three parameters i.e., AS, BSs, and T, as explained before. After that, AM starts by testing the legitimacy of the issued command from the obtained AS. In particular, if AS is above a predefined Anomaly Threshold (AT), AM sends the command to the device handler to be executed. However, if AS is below AT, AM prompts the user to confirm whether the command (i.e., occurred event and the

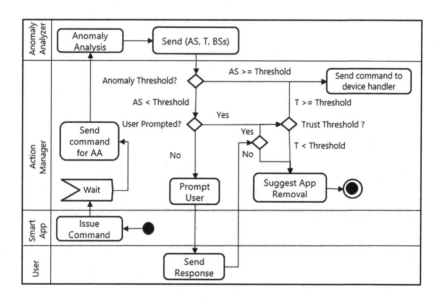

Fig. 6. Action manager process

action on the device) is suspicious or not. If the user confirms that command is suspicious, the AM suggests the SmartApp removal to the user.

However, if the user confirms that the command is not suspicious, or if he/she is already prompted for the given SmartApp, a trust-based verification is employed. In particular, AM updates a confidence score for each requested command to evaluate the trust towards the SmartApp. To do so, a trust (T) value is calculated from AS outputted by AA. If this value is still below the allowed level of trust called Lockout Threshold (LT), the SmartApp is allowed to operate and its commands are sent to be executed. However, once the T value drops below the LT, the SmartApp must be stopped and its removal is suggested to the user. The formula that we adopt to calculate the change in SmartApp trust is the one described in [10] (cf. Eq. 1), where the parameter AT represents the predefined Anomaly Threshold. Parameter B is the value of AS in which the maximum value of penalty/reward is given, whereas the parameters C and D are the upper bound value of the reward and the penalty, respectively.

$$\Delta_{Trust}(AS_i) = min(\frac{D(1 + \frac{1}{C})}{\frac{1}{C} + exp(-\frac{AS_i - AT}{B})} - D, C) \tag{1}$$

4   Experimental Evaluation

In this section, we evaluate the ability of the Anomaly Analyzer in detecting anomalous automation commands issued from misbehaved SmartApps on datasets that involve different SHSs.

4.1   Evaluation Dataset

To remedy the lack of SmartApps-based automation control history in public repositories, we propose to use the history data of manual control of appliances and objects by inhabitants in real-world home environments. We assume that the devices controlled by inhabitants are controlled by the automation SmartApps. The data we will be using for this purpose is the one collected in the MIT House Consortium [15]. For two weeks, sensors were installed in everyday objects such as drawers and refrigerators to record opening-closing events in two single-person apartments as the inhabitants carried out everyday activities. The recorded inhabitant's activities (e.g., eating) are grouped into a set of categories (e.g., personal needs). Since SHS devices' automation control is based on the Trigger-Action model, we came up with the idea to assume that the SmartApps IDs are the activities categories, the triggering events are the activities themselves, whereas, the controlled devices with the particular control actions and timestamps are extracted as they are. Thus, the obtained SmartApps Control Log includes necessary information as needed viz., SmartApp ID, event, device, action, timestamp. The description of the obtained Control Logs for both SHSs is given in Table 3.

Table 3. Evaluation dataset description

	SHS 1	SHS 2
# of installed apps	6	6
# of controlled devices	75	70
# of control commands	5977	4479

4.2 Evaluation Methodology

Our evaluation dataset contains the automation control history of two SHSs, where six SmartApps are installed in each. Consequently, six SmartApp baselines (i.e., Probabilistic Models, control commands Behavioral Scores, and OCSVM models) are built for each SHS over the extracted control logs of each SmartApp. To evaluate the ability of the Anomaly Analyzer in discriminating misbehaved SmartApps from regular ones, we follow a primary-vs-adversary strategy. In particular, we first search for common installed SmartApps from the two SHSs. Then, we evaluate each SmartApp OCSVM model of the chosen primary's SHS against the behavioral scores of the corresponding SmartApp from the adversary's SHS, and vice versa. To make sure that the results will not be biased or coincidental, a 5-fold cross-validation is employed. In particular, the behavioral scores for each SmartApp are split into two parts (80% and 20%). The 80% part is used to train the OCSVM of each SmartApp. Then, the remaining 20% part is combined with adversarial Behavioral Scores of the corresponding adversary SmartApp to construct the final testing Behavioral Scores.

4.3 Results and Discussion

Since the goal of Anomaly Analyzer is to identify malicious control commands without incorrectly rejecting the legitimate ones, we calculate the fraction of testing control commands that have been incorrectly accepted, better known as False Acceptance Rate (FAR). Whereas, to measure the user convenience level, we calculate the fraction of benign control commands that have been incorrectly rejected, better known as False Rejection Rate (FRR).

Unfortunately, since the two rates cannot be simultaneously reduced, we should prioritize the reduction of one of them over the increase of the other. We recall that the Action Manager (AM) uses an Anomaly Threshold (AT) to discriminate the legitimacy/anomaly of a control command from the outputted Anomaly Score (AS) that varies in the range of $[-1,+1]$. If a SmartApp issues a malicious control command for the first time, the user is prompted by the AM to confirm the legitimacy/anomaly of this command. However, prompting the user too often cannot satisfy the real-time SHS automation (e.g., users need to be awake to respond). This case implies that the frequency of prompts must be reduced as low as possible and our proposed framework should be more user-friendly than secure. To guarantee such a feature, the FRR should be reduced and prioritized over the FAR, hence the AT value must be chosen as low near to the negative end of the AS range.

Table 4. Obtained results of FAR and FRR for Subject1 vs Subject2

	Subject 1 (Primary)							
	SmartApp 0		SmartApp 1		SmartApp 2		SmartApp 3	
	FAR	FRR	FAR	FRR	FAR	FRR	FAR	FRR
Subject 2 (Adversary)								
SmartApp 0	0.0801	0.0172						
SmartApp 1			0.0680	0.0130				
SmartApp 2					0.0435	0.0110		
SmartApp 3							0.0473	0.0324

By choosing such an AT value, Table 4 gives the obtained values for the FAR and FRR rates for one of the testing scenarios i.e., SHS 1 as the primary vs SHS 2 as the adversary (4 common SmartApps have been found among the two SHSs). We can see that the FRR reach in the worst cases a value of 2.5%. This low rate ensures that benign control commands are rarely rejected. Hence, a better experience is provided for the user since he/she is not falsely prompted very often. On the other hand, we can see that the FAR reach 7.22% in the worst cases. Such an acceptable rate ensures that malicious control commands are rarely accepted. Hence, the removal suggestion of malicious SmartApps to the user happens as quickly as possible and these SmartApps were not able to issue many control commands.

5 Conclusion

In this paper, we investigated the feasibility of building Anomaly detection (AD) models on the regular behavior of a Smart Home Systems (SHS) automation SmartApps when controlling the SHS devices. The AD models were the basis of our proposed security framework to continuously confirm or reject automation control commands issued by the SmartApps according to their deviation from this AD baseline. In particular, a One-Class Support Vector Machines (OCSVM) was trained on regular behavioral scores which have been extracted from the control logs of the SmartApps. In the future, we plan to investigate how the trained OCSVM models should be updated to cope with the change of SmartApps regular behavior using the Incremental version of OCSVM.

References

1. Amraoui, N., Besrour, A., Ksantini, R., Zouari, B.: Implicit and continuous authentication of smart home users. In: Barolli, L., Takizawa, M., Xhafa, F., Enokido, T. (eds.) AINA 2019. AISC, vol. 926, pp. 1228–1239. Springer, Cham (2020). https://doi.org/10.1007/978-3-030-15032-7_103
2. Celik, Z.B., McDaniel, P., Tan, G.: Soteria: automated IoT safety and security analysis. In: 2018 USENIX Annual Technical Conference (USENIXATC 2018) (2018)

3. Celik, Z.B., Tan, G., McDaniel, P.D.: IoTGuard: Dynamic Enforcement of Security and Safety Policy in Commodity IoT. NDSS (2019)
4. Chi, H., et al.: Cross-App Interference Threats in Smart Homes: Categorization, Detection and Handling. arXiv preprint arXiv:1808.02125 (2018)
5. Fernandes, E., Jung, J., Prakash, A.: Security analysis of emerging smart home applications. In: 2016 IEEE Symposium on Security and Privacy (SP), IEEE (2016)
6. Garcia-Font, V., Garrigues, C., Rifa-Pous, H.: A comparative study of anomaly detection techniques for smart city wireless sensor networks. Sensors J. **16**, 868 (2016)
7. He, W., et al.: Rethinking access control and authentication for the home internet of things (IoT). In: 27th USENIX Security Symposium (USENIX Security 2018) (2018)
8. Ibrahim, K.E., et al.: Poster: Defining Actionable Rules for Verifying IoT Security (2020)
9. Kafle, K., et al.: A Study of data store-based home automation. In: Proceedings of the Ninth ACM Conference on Data and Application Security and Privacy (2019)
10. Mondal, S., Bours, P.: A continuous combination of security & forensics for mobile devices. J. Inf. Secur. Appl. **40**, 63–77 (2018)
11. Nguyen, D.T., et al.: IoTSan: fortifying the safety of IoT systems. In: Proceedings of the 14th International Conference on emerging Networking EXperiments and Technologies (2018)
12. Schölkopf, B., Platt, J., Taylor, J.S., et al.: Estimating the support of a high-dimensional distribution. Neural Comput. J. **13**, 1443–1471 (2001)
13. Shashanka, M., Shen, M.Y., Wang, J.: User and entity behavior analytics for enterprise security. In: 2016 IEEE International Conference on Big Data (Big Data), IEEE (2016)
14. Tian, Y., et al.: SmartAuth: User-centered authorization for the internet of things. In: 26th USENIX Security Symposium (USENIX Security 2017) (2017)
15. Tapia, E.M., Intille, S.S., Larson, K.: Activity recognition in the home using simple and ubiquitous sensors. In: Ferscha, A., Mattern, F. (eds.) Pervasive 2004. LNCS, vol. 3001, pp. 158–175. Springer, Heidelberg (2004). https://doi.org/10.1007/978-3-540-24646-6_10

Access Control, Risk Assessment and Security Knowledge

A Posteriori Analysis of Policy Temporal Compliance

Farah Dernaika[1,2(✉)], Nora Cuppens-Boulahia[3], Frédéric Cuppens[3], and Olivier Raynaud[2]

[1] IMT Atlantique, Rennes, France
farah.dernaika@imt-atlantique.fr
[2] Be-ys Research, Geneva, Switzerland
[3] Polytechnique Montreal, Montreal, Canada

Abstract. The a posteriori access control is being more and more deployed especially in environments where more flexibility is needed when requesting access to information resources. To check if the security rules are being respected; this kind of access control relies on a monitoring process based on logs. It is thus fundamental to have a comprehensive analysis to take fair decisions and apply sanctions if needed. However, understanding what is happening in the logs is challenging, and the correlation between logged events and the security policy is arduous. Moreover, the security attributes and their values may evolve over time. Therefore, we propose a verification mechanism of policy temporal compliance, based on SWRL and Event Calculus, to check if the required attributes were respected at the appropriate time.

Keywords: Access control · Event Calculus · Log Semantic Enrichment

1 Introduction

In traditional access control mechanisms, user privileges are known in advance, and rules are set up according to a well-defined security policy. In consequence, access to information resources is only granted to authorized users. However, in certain environments, it is important to assure the continuity of daily activity services, where sensitive fields are involved, as in the healthcare domain. As a matter of fact, a lot of errors and unanticipated emergencies may occur, where a more flexible access control model should be adopted [22].

In the a posteriori access control model, access to information is given based on a trust level offered to the user. Its prime concerns are auditability and accountability in order to detect potential violations of the security policy and prevent future misuse of privileges. This monitoring process starts by analyzing logs since they trace and record all the executed actions in the information system. Thus, logs are the central part of auditing in the a posteriori access control, that is reviewed for action legitimacy checking and accountability purposes.

[7] addressed the question of which information should be included in logs for meaningful a posteriori compliance control. However this is rarely respected,

© Springer Nature Switzerland AG 2021
J. Garcia-Alfaro et al. (Eds.): CRiSIS 2020, LNCS 12528, pp. 133–148, 2021.
https://doi.org/10.1007/978-3-030-68887-5_8

and useful information can be found somewhere else than logs. In consequence, a valid explanation of policy conformity should exist, and the validity of this explanation relies on the availability of the necessary information for assessing policy compliance.

On one side, security policies are often expressed according to access control models such as Role-Based Access Control (RBAC) [16], Attribute-Based Access Control (ABAC) [19], Organization-Based Access Control (OrBAC) [14], etc. These models assign permissions indirectly to the users through their attributes, and sometimes object attributes and contextual constraints as well. On the other side, logs do not trace this kind of information in general. In consequence, establishing links between the explicitly defined attributes in the security policy, and the logged data is not that evident. This leads to the need to semantically enrich logged data with complementary information, in such a way log analysis is accurate enough to make fair decisions when violations are committed.

Conversely, when performing an a priori access control, access attributes values are checked at the time of the access request. As a consequence, the system guarantees the respect of the security rules when granting access to the user. However, in the a posteriori access control, a lot of changes in the security attributes can take place between the time of access and the time of investigation (change of role, role delegation, change of status, etc.), and contextual conditions evolve between accesses (e.g. emergencies) [9]. Therefore, it is important to verify that the access attributes values and conditions were the same as those defined in the security policy *at the time* when the information resource was accessed. This is similar to the case of forensics for criminal investigations, where the importance does not reside in where the suspect is now, but in where he/she was when the crime was committed. For this purpose, the Event Calculus (EC), that is a formal language for representing and reasoning about dynamic systems, was used in access control to handle time-constrained permissions [4].

In this paper, we present a novel approach that leverages the a posteriori access control to include temporal verification. To accomplish that, we use the Event Calculus (EC), which we express in SWRL, and that we integrate in a multi-agent system to gather the different attributes defined in the security policy. Our main contributions are (1) improving the a posteriori access control by adding the temporal aspect to policy compliance, (2) modeling log events and the security policy in the Event Calculus to realize this temporal verification, and (3) proposing a multi-agent system architecture to contextualize log events in the case of an expressive security policy.

To the best of our knowledge, this temporal aspect of the a posteriori access control was never treated in the literature.

The rest of this paper is organized as follows: Sect. 2 exposes some needed fundamentals, Sect. 3 presents our a posteriori access control framework, Sect. 4 illustrates our multi-agent system and how policy temporal compliance is done using the Event Calculus, Sect. 5 illustrates an example, Sect. 6 evaluates our approach, Sect. 7 discusses related work, and Sect. 8 gets into the conclusion.

2 Fundamentals

In this section, we provide some background on the Event Calculus, and the Semantic Web technologies, based on which we built our policy temporal compliance framework.

2.1 Event Calculus

The Event Calculus is a logical language for representing and reasoning about events and their effects. The authors in [29], described it as "a logical mechanism that infers what's true when given what happens when and what actions do".

In addition, the language of the Event Calculus consists of: (1) a set of event types or actions (2) a set of fluents, that is a set of properties which values can change over time (and can be true or false) (3) a set of time points. These three elements are essential to feed the basic predicates that constitute the language, and that are represented in Table 1.

Table 1. Event calculus basic predicates

Predicate	Meaning
$Initiates(e,f,t)$	If event e is executed at time t, fluent f is true after t
$Terminates(e,f,t)$	If event e is executed at time t, fluent f is false after t
$Happens(e,\ t)$	Event e occurs at time t
$HoldsAt(f,t)$	Fluent f holds at time t
$Clipped(t1,f,t2)$	Fluent f is terminated between times $t1$ and $t2$

Furthermore, relating the various predicates together can form domain-independent axioms that formalize the correct evolution of a fluent. In this section, we provide this set of axioms:

$$HoldsAt(f,t) \leftarrow Happens(e,t_1) \wedge Initiates(e,f,t_1) \wedge (t_1 < t) \wedge \neg Clipped(t_1,f,t) \tag{1}$$

$$Clipped(t_1,f,t_2) \longleftrightarrow \exists e,t \ [Happens(e,t) \wedge (t_1 \leq t < t_2) \wedge Terminates(e,f,t)] \tag{2}$$

Expression (1) indicates that a fluent is true at time t if and only if it has been made true in the past and has not been made false in the meantime. The predicate $Initiates$ introduces the event, that activates the fluent, at the time of its execution. For instance, assigning the role Doctor to a user, leads to the user having the role Doctor. This can be expressed using $Initiates$ as $Initiates(setRole(user,Doctor),role(user,Doctor),t)$. Similarly, $Terminates(removeRole(user,Doctor),role(user,Doctor),t)$, indicates that removing the role Doctor of a user terminates the fact of that user being a Doctor.

Moreover, the *Clipped* predicate presented in (2), states that an event's occurrence terminates a fluent during an interval of time.

In contrast, a fluent's value may remain the same over time. Thus, we introduce the predicate *Always(f)*, to express that a fluent f is always true if and only if it holds at any time t, as follows:

$$Always(f) \longleftrightarrow \forall\ t,\ HoldsAt(f,t) \tag{3}$$

That being said, if a fluent holds at time t, and at time t, the fact of being true always causes another fluent to be true, then this latter is also true at time t:

$$\forall\ t,\ HoldsAt(f \rightarrow g,t)\ \wedge\ HoldsAt(f,t)\ \rightarrow\ HoldsAt(g,t) \tag{4}$$

In addition, saying that the conjunction of two fluents is true, is equivalent to saying that each fluent is true:

$$\forall\ t,\ HoldsAt(f \wedge g,t)\ \longleftrightarrow\ HoldsAt(f,t)\ \wedge\ HoldsAt(g,t) \tag{5}$$

It is worth mentioning that the events in EC can be natural events like lightning or accidental crash of a hard disk. Since we are dealing with access control, we shall consider, in the following, events that are caused by the execution of an action by a subject on an object.

2.2   OWL and SWRL

The Web Ontology Language OWL [23] is a family of knowledge representation languages based on Description Logic (DL) [2] with a representation in RDF. It forms an ontology by defining real-world concepts and their relationships in vocabularies. The concepts in an OWL ontology are named as classes, and relationships as properties. Moreover, OWL ontologies include axioms that assert constraints over their concepts and individuals. These axioms can be expressed as ground assertions or as derivation rules.

The Semantic Web Rule Language (SWRL) [18] is used to express rules as well as logic, that was proposed for the Semantic Web. Its syntax is of the form: *antecedent* $\rightarrow$ *consequent*, where both antecedent and consequent are conjunctions of atoms written $a_1 \wedge ... \wedge a_n$. Each atom can be formed from unary predicates (classes), binary predicates (properties), equalities or inequalities, and variables are prefixed with a question mark (e.g. ?x).

Moreover, SWRL was extended with some built-in libraries to facilitate some tasks, such as, directly creating new individuals in a rule. For instance, the built-in *swrlx:makeOWLThing(?x,?y)* will cause an individual to be created and bound to ?x for every value of variable ?y matched in a rule.

We also distinguish a sub-language of SWRL, that is SQWRL (Semantic Query-Enhanced Web Rule Language), which provides SQL-like operators for extracting information from OWL ontologies (e.g. *owl:Thing(?i)* $\rightarrow$ *sqwrl:select(?i)*). SQWRL querying helps in achieving axioms that could not be expressed directly in SWRL because of the lack of existential quantification support in the language.

2.3   Modeling Event Calculus in SWRL

The authors in [24] developed an ontology for a simplified version of the Event Calculus that deals with discrete time points, that is the Discrete Event Calculus (DEC). In this ontology, each of the *Fluent, Event*, as well as the Event Calculus predicates *HoldsAt, Happens, Initiates, Terminates*, and *Clipped*, are represented as Classes, and they are related with the properties *hasEvent, hasFluent*, and *hasTime*. Moreover, they expressed some DEC axioms, according to SWRL. Thus, we adapted their proposal so that it suits our case of the a posteriori access control.

Modelling the EC predicates as classes is justified by the fact that SWRL predicates do not support having more than two attributes, while some of the formers require more.

To explain this modelization, we recall the *"reification"* or *"objectification"* approach that permits to take advantage of the richer semantics of the entity-relationship model to re-express the semantics of the n-ary relation:

Let $R(a_1, a_2, ..., a_n)$ be a n-ary relation.

Reifying R consists in creating a unary relation $RE(e)$, and n binary relations $RA_1(E, a_1)$, ..., $RA_n(E, a_n)$, which fulfill the following axiom:

$$\forall a_1, \forall a_2, \ldots, \forall a_n, \ R(a_1, a_2, \ldots, a_n) \ \longleftrightarrow \ \exists \ e, \ RE(e) \ \wedge RA_1(e, a_1) \ \wedge RA_2(e, a_2) \ \wedge \ldots \wedge RA_n \ (e, a_n).$$

In the case of the Event Calculus, e will be a created individual of the class representing an EC predicate (*e.g. Happens, Initiates, Terminates, etc.*), a_i will be individuals of the classes representing the components of the EC (*Fluent, Event, and Time*), and RA_i the properties relating e to a_i. For example, the ternary relation *Initiates(e,f,t)* will be represented in SWRL as *Initiates(?initiates) $\wedge$ hasEvent(?initiates, ?event) $\wedge$ hasFluent(?initiates, ?fluent) $\wedge$ hasTime(?initiates, ?time)*.

It has been also proved that this translation preserves semantics in [11].

Another reason to chose this translation is the lack of support of negation as failure in OWL and SWRL. The only way to express this latter in OWL/SWRL is to use classical negation, by defining the complement of the predicate (e.g. HoldsAt) as an OWL class (e.g. NotHoldsAt).

The interpretation of (1) in SWRL is as follows:

Happens(?happens) $\wedge$ *Event(?e)* $\wedge$ *hasEvent(?happens, ?e)* $\wedge$ *hasTime(?happens, ?t1)* $\wedge$ *Initiates(?initiates)* $\wedge$ *hasEvent(?initiates, ?e)* $\wedge$ *hasFluent(?initiates, ?fluent)* $\wedge$ *hasTime(?initiates, ?t1)* $\wedge$ *NotClipped(?notClipped)* $\wedge$ *hasStartTime(?notClipped, ?t1)* $\wedge$ *hasEndTime(?notClipped, ?t)* $\wedge$ *hasFluent(?notClipped, ?fluent)* $\wedge$ *swrlb:lessThan(?t1, ?t)* $\wedge$ *swrlx:makeOWLThing(?holdsAt, ?t)* $\rightarrow$ *HoldsAt(?holdsAt)* $\wedge$ *hasFluent(?holdsAt, ?fluent)* $\wedge$ *hasTime(?holdsAt, ?t)*

Similarly, we can express (2), (4), and (5) in SWRL.

3   A Posteriori Access Control Framework

The goal of performing this kind of access control is to detect every potential violation of the deployed security policy. It is a mechanism based on log analysis, because logs record all the events that happened in an application domain in a chronological order. Thus, we distinguish two inevitable components of the a posteriori access control that are: *logs* and the *security policy*. We however, add another level to this verification to include *temporal compliance*.

In this perspective, our approach helps in answering the following questions:

(1) For a logged event, do the user and object have the right attributes and values, and is the action executed in the right context?
(2) If they have ever had the right attributes, did they have them at the same time of the access?

Therefore, we can distinguish two approaches. The first one consists in taking all the logs and translating them into SWRL facts. This approach is not satisfactory, since it requires a lot of time to translate, which is costing, in addition to the need of loading all the facts into memory. The second approach, that we adopted, goes through a semantic mediator and a multi-agent approach to get the necessary information as and when it is needed.

In the following, we present our multi-agent system which gathers the needed information and checks temporal compliance.

4   Multi-Agent System Architecture and Functioning

The proposed multi-agent system architecture is depicted in Fig. 1.

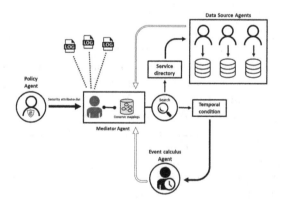

Fig. 1. MAS architecture

Its main job is to gather the needed attributes from different organizational data sources, and to check if the defined temporal conditions are satisfied or not. We distinguish four types of agents, that we present in details in the following subsections:

- **Policy Agent** handles the rules defined in the security policy. It is the one responsible of providing the attributes to be fetched to the mediator agent.
- **Mediator Agent** is the *maestro* of the whole information gathering process. Once it gets the attributes from the policy agent, it orchestrates all the exchanged messages with the agents.
- **Data Source Agent** retrieves information from a specific data source.
- **Event Calculus Agent** verifies the temporal conditions defined in the security policy using the Event Calculus.

4.1   The Policy Agent

The *Policy Agent (Po)* is located on the policy side.

We chose to model the security policy according to ABAC since it allows more flexibility, than any other access control model. It represents a rich and standard policy specification as any number of attributes can be added within the same extensible framework.

In addition, we formalized the ABAC policy using OWL since it has shown very important advantages. First, it is adequately representational to capture distinct activities that are required (obligations), restricted (prohibitions), and authorized but not necessarily expected (permissions), by an entity (subject) on a resource (object) within the system, and the circumstances within which it applies. Next, the power of reasoning helps in determining access decisions and supporting analysis in case of policy conflicts [10].

We got inspired from [17] and [30], where each *Subject, Object,* and *Action* are defined as Classes, and their corresponding *Attributes* are defined as Properties. Moreover, we added a new class *Context* to describe contextual conditions, as well as its corresponding property that has *Action* as domain and *Context* as range.

To express security rules we used SWRL, for its well defined structure, expressivity, and flexibility. Each security rule, can be written in the form of *Condition* → *is-permitted(u,a,o)*, where *a* is an action executed by a user *u* on an object *o*. As an example, we will consider verifying a rule related to the medical field, and applied in an Electronic Health Record (EHR) application, since it appeared to be suitable for applying the a posteriori access control.

A rule example is: ***"A doctor may create a prescription during an office visit"***, and can be expressed in SWRL as:

> *Action(?a) ∧ type(?a,create) ∧ subject(?a, ?u) ∧ role(?u,Doctor) ∧ object (?a,?o) ∧ oType(?o,Prescription) ∧ context(?a,?w) ∧ cType(?w,Office Visit) → isPermitted(?a).*

Therefore, the *Policy Agent (Po)* parses the defined SWRL rules, to construct a list of Subject Attributes, Object Attributes and Contextual Condition to be verified. For each predicate defined in the SWRL rule, the agent gets the domain and range of the predicate and associates the defined values to the corresponding classes.

In the following, we consider that the security rules are static and do not go through changes over time. By static, we mean that the expression of the security policy is defined once and for all, meanwhile its application may vary depending on the context. For every security rule, this hypothesis can be expressed as:

$$Always(Condition \rightarrow is\text{-}permitted(u,a,o)) \tag{6}$$

Therefore, with respect to the rule defining *Always*, when an access is done at time *t*, the required condition should be held at that same time *t*.

4.2   The Mediator Agent

As mentioned earlier, logs are the first source to consult when performing an a posteriori access control.

In a previous work [13], we proposed to use a semantic mediator, that is based on query rewriting to retrieve information from multiple log sources, to extract information from logs. The extracted information is of the form *<Subject, Action, Object, Timestamp>*. Thus, the **Mediator Agent (Med)**, is settled in that semantic mediator.

We represent a log event as $e=(u,a,o)$, that is an action a that was executed by a user u, on an object o, and that happened at a certain time t.

Therefore, every action, representing an event, in the log follows *Happens(e,t)* and can be represented in SWRL as: *Happens(?happens) $\wedge$ Action(?e) $\wedge$ type(?e,?a) $\wedge$ subject(?e,?u) $\wedge$ object(?e,?o) $\wedge$ hasEvent(?happens,?e) $\wedge$ hasTime(?happens,?t)*.

Once the list of attributes is received, **Med** starts the semantic enrichment process. Its main goal is to get these attributes' values and timestamps, relatively to the information extracted from logs, to verify their compliance with the policy.

It is worth mentioning that we consider that the logs contain at least one element, from which we can get the security attributes defined in the security policy. Moreover, to detect the type of the extracted values, for example, if the subject's extracted value corresponds to a UserID, HostName, IP, etc., we used regular expressions and a dictionary-based classifier [26].

Pursuing our example, we consider that we extracted the following event e_1 from the logs:

Subject	Action	Object	Timestamp
9003	CREATE	PRE35876	2019-07-22 14:59:04

In consequence, we obtain: *Happens(happens$_1$) $\wedge$ Action(e$_1$) $\wedge$ type(e$_1$, CREATE) $\wedge$ subject(e$_1$,9003) $\wedge$ object(e$_1$,PRE35876) $\wedge$ hasEvent(happens$_1$,e$_1$) $\wedge$ hasTime(happens$_1$,2019-07-22 14:59:04)*.

4.3   Data Source Agents

In a real organization, not all the information is stored in one place. It can have many databases that can have the same or different type of information. That's why we consider having many data sources, each one represented by a **Data Source Agent (DS)**.

To search for a specific attribute, **Med** searches in a service directory, where each agent registered the information that it provides, and identifies the agent to which it should send a request message to get the corresponding attribute's value and timestamp.

Next, when a **DS** receives a request, it gets the corresponding information. For instance, if the data source is an SQL database, the agent will execute SQL queries, and replies to the mediator agent with an inform message containing the requested information. Moreover, we consider that the **DS** has access to the history logs of the data source, and that it knows the events responsible for assigning and removing an attribute's value. It will search then for these events, that are related to the extracted log elements, and their timestamps, and send them back to **Med**. It must also be pointed out that agents may have different vocabularies. To resolve this heterogeneity, we can establish mappings between the different concepts handled by the different agents (e.g. equivalence between two different entities handled by two different agents) [31].

4.4   Event Calculus Agent

Once **Med** has collected all the attributes values and the time of their assignment/removal, it sends them in an inform message to the **Event Calculus Agent (EC)**, so that it can assess policy temporal compliance.

The main goal is to deduce a violation when a non permitted access is logged (is done); hence, verifying the following:

$$Happens((u,a,o),t) \wedge \neg HoldsAt(is\text{-}permitted(u,a,o),t) \rightarrow violation(u,a,o) \quad (7)$$

Expression (7) can be expressed in SWRL as follows:

> $Happens(?happens) \wedge Action(?e) \wedge type(?e,?a) \wedge subject(?e,?u) \wedge object(?e,?o) \wedge hasEvent(?happens,?e) \wedge hasTime(?happens,t) \wedge NotHoldsAt(?notholdsAt) \wedge isPermitted(?e) \wedge hasFluent(?holdsAt,?e) \wedge hasTime(?holdsAt,?t) \rightarrow Violation(?e)$

However, to check if a permitted action holds at access time, we should verify that the condition (the required attributes) holds at that time as in (6).

In ABAC, the condition consists in having the right subject attributes, object attributes, and environmental attributes (context), with the right values. And since these attributes may evolve over time, we consider each one of them as a fluent. Let m be a function that maps each pair of *attribute-value* to a fluent:

$$m: att * Dom(att) \longrightarrow Fluents$$
$$x.att_i = v_i \longrightarrow f_i$$

where *att* is the set of all attributes, *Dom(att)* is the set of all possible values that an attribute can take, $x \in \{$Subject, Object, Environment$\}$, att_i is the attribute name and v_i its value.

Hence, the conjunction of all the fluents f_i constitutes the final condition to be verified, that is also a fluent. We define the condition fluent as:

$$f_{cond} = \bigwedge_{i=1}^{n} f_i$$

where n is the total number of the required access attributes.

Therefore, to verify if the condition holds at time t, we need to check *HoldsAt(f_{cond},t)* $\equiv$ *HoldsAt(f_1 \wedge f_2 \wedge ... \wedge f_n, t)*, by applying (5).

In our example, the creation of the prescription is permitted, we need to validate that all the attributes defined in the policy (*Role, Type, Context*), had the right values at the time t of the action execution.

In consequence, $f_1 = role(?u,Doctor)$, $f_2 = oType(?o,Prescription)$, and $f_3 = cType(?w,OfficeVisit)$.

To express this conjunction of fluents in SWRL, we considered having two disjoint subclasses, *SuperFluent* and *SubFluent*, of the class *Fluent*, that represent f_{cond} and f_i respectively, and are related with the property *hasSubFluent*. Thus, for each condition fluent, we generate an individual of the class *SuperFluent* that is related to its sub-fluents with *hasSubFluent(?f,?f_i)*.

For instance, *hasSubFluent(f,f_1), hasSubFluent(f,f_2), hasSubFluent(f,f_3)*.

Next, once the sub-fluents are identified, we should check if they hold at access time t according to expression (1). It is worth mentioning that fluents that necessitate two arguments, have the relations *hasDomain* and *hasRange* to refer to their arguments. For example, the fluent *role(?u,Doctor)* is initiated using setRole as follows:

Happens(?happens) $\wedge$ *setRole(?e)* $\wedge$ *hasDomain(?e,?u)* $\wedge$ *hasRange(?e,Doctor)* $\wedge$ *hasEvent(?happens,?e)* $\wedge$ *hasTime(?happens,?t)* $\wedge$ *swrlx:makeOWLThing(?initiates,?e)* $\wedge$ *SubFluent(?fluent)* $\wedge$ *Role(?fluent)* $\wedge$ *hasDomain(?fluent,?u)* $\wedge$ *hasRange(?fluent,Doctor)* $\rightarrow$ *Initiates(?initiates)* $\wedge$ *hasEvent(?initiates,?e)* $\wedge$ *hasFluent(?initiates,?fluent)* $\wedge$ *hasTime(?initiates,?t)*

Moreover, *role(?u,Doctor)* holds at time t if the role Doctor was assigned to the user *?u* before t, and has not been removed in the meantime as in (1). In the same way, we can define the rules for the fluents *oType(?o,Prescription)*, and *cType(?w,OfficeVisit)* to be held, by replacing *setRole*, with the corresponding activating events.

After checking if each sub-fluent holds at t or not, we need to check if the final fluent (the conjunction of all sub-fluents), holds at t. To do so, we used the following SQWRL query:

> $HoldsAt(?holdsAt) \quad \wedge \quad hasFluent(?holdsAt, ?f) \quad \wedge \quad SubFluent(?f) \quad \wedge$
> $sqwrl{:}makeSet(?s,\ ?f) \wedge sqwrl{:}groupBy(?s,\ ?holdsAt) \wedge SuperFluent(?fl) \wedge$
> $hasSubFluent(?fl, ?fs) \wedge sqwrl{:}makeSet(?s2, ?fs) \wedge sqwrl{:}groupBy(?s2, ?fl) \wedge$
> $sqwrl{:}contains(?s, ?s2) \rightarrow sqwrl{:}select(?holdsAt, ?fs)$

This latter, constructs two sets of sub-fluents, one for each generated *holdsAt* individual, and one for each *SuperFluent* defined initially. After that, it compares the two obtained sets. If the set of the initially defined fluents is contained in the generated fluents set, then the query returns a result and a new *HoldsAt* individual is created with the corresponding *SuperFluent* and access *time* associated. If the query result is empty, it means that at least one of the sub-fluents doesn't hold at t, leading to the creation of a *NotHoldsAt* individual associated with the *SuperFluent* and access *time*.

It is known that OWL and SWRL are based on the open-world assumption, where everything is assumed possible unless explicitly stated otherwise.

However, it has been demonstrated in [25] that negation-as-failure can be implemented on top of purely open-world systems using queries. This is where the utility of the above SQWRL query appears to force the creation of a *NotHoldsAt* individual, and thus assuring negation.

Finally, expression (6) can be expressed in SWRL as follows:

> $HoldsAt(?holdsAt) \quad \wedge \quad hasFluent(?holdsAt, ?f) \quad \wedge \quad hasTime(?holdsAt, ?t) \quad \wedge$
> $SuperFluent(?f) \quad \wedge \quad isRelatedTo(?f, ?e) \quad \wedge \quad action(?e, ?a) \quad \wedge \quad subject(?e, ?u)$
> $\wedge \quad object(?e, ?o) \quad \wedge \quad swrlx{:}makeOWLThing(?holdsAt2, ?holdsAt) \quad \rightarrow \quad HoldsAt(?holdsAt2) \quad \wedge \quad isPermitted(?e) \quad \wedge \quad hasFluent(?holdsAt2, ?e) \quad \wedge \quad hasTime(?holdsAt2, ?t)$

The *hasAction*, *hasSubject*, and *hasObject* properties are added to the *SuperFluent* representing the condition, so that we can relate which *action*, that was executed by which *subject*, on which *object*, is permitted.

It is also worth to mention that since the policy compliance is checked a posteriori and not in real time, the verification is done rule by rule, and the decision of whether there is a violation or not is computed once all the attributes and timestamps are gathered.

5 Illustrating the Example

Illustrating the above steps in our example, the list sent from **Po** to **Med** contains the attributes Role of the Subject, Type of the Object, and the Context in which the Action should be done at every time, in addition to their respective values. Moreover, we consider that DS_1 provides the *Role* of a *Medical ID* (9003), and DS_2 provides the *Type* of a *Resource ID* (PRE35876). **Med** sends request messages to these two agents to get the timestamps of the events responsible for assigning and/or removing the Role and Type of 9003 and PRE35876 respectively. These messages have the following forms:

Request(SearchAttributeTime, Med, DS_1, (Role, Doctor, MedicalID, 9003)) and *Request(SearchAttributeTime, Med, DS_2, (Type, Prescription, ResourceID, PRE35876))*.

Continuing, $\boldsymbol{DS_1}$ will search for the timestamps of the events *setRole(9003,Doctor)* and *removeRole(9003,Doctor)*, if any, and replies to **Med** with an inform message as follows: *Inform(DS_1, Med, Happens(setRole(9003,Doctor), 2019-05-16 10:34:21))*. Similarly, $\boldsymbol{DS_2}$ will reply to **Med** with the timestamps of the events concerning the Type of the Object: *Inform(DS_2, Med, Happens(setType(PRE35876, Prescription), 2019-07-22 14:59:04))*.

Moving on to the contextual condition, it can be looked up in a similar way, as our approach is generic. Normally, its activating and deactivating events appear in the application logs, hence, the semantic mediator is used to look for them homogeneously. However, **Med** does not have an a priori knowledge of them. Thus, it will solicit **EC**, where they are defined.

Med sends a request message to **EC** asking it for the initiating and terminating events of an office visit.

Considering that in an EHR application, the *office visit* holds from the time of its creation, till the time it is saved, we suppose that the activating and terminating events of an office visit are *create office visit* and *save office visit* respectively. After that, **Med** queries the logs to get the timestamps of these events as in [13].

At this point, **Med** has collected all the attributes values and the time of their assignment/removal. Now that all the condition inputs are ready, **Med** sends them in an inform message to **EC**, so it can assess policy compliance according to expression (7).

Verifying (7) leads to verifying (6) to see if the logged event is permitted or not at the time it was done. Furthermore, (6) consists in validating if the value of the attribute *Role* of the subject, the value of the attribute *Type* of the object, and the contextual condition *office visit* hold at *2019-07-22 14:59:04* as in (1).

Supposedly that *2019-07-22 15:32:45* and *2019-07-22 16:05:18* are the timestamps at which the user *9003* has created and saved the office visit *OFF91383*, respectively, the contextual condition *office visit* does not hold at *2019-07-22 14:59:04*, since it was started after the creation of the prescription, leading to the detection of a violation.

6   Capabilities Evaluation

In this section, we discuss the capability metrics that are assured by our approach. Normally, the capabilities of an access control policy verification model are described by a set of reference metrics. Therefore, we use some metrics that were provided in [21] to evaluate access control policy verification tools that can be adopted in the a posteriori access control.

To start with, *completeness* is a metric that is frequently examined. This latter assures that each access request should be either accepted or denied by the access control policy. It is evident that the response in our approach is boolean, since it consists in either a violation or not. When checking the compliance of a logged event with a security rule, all the attributes defined in that rule should be respected. If at least one required attribute did not hold at the time of the access, the corresponding rule in the security policy is considered to be violated. In consequence, our proposal is complete.

Furthermore, it is very important to assure *liveness*. Our approach guarantees it as we consider that all the attributes are logged somewhere (which is a security requirement), thus our policy compliance mechanism will neither wait nor repeat the same operation forever to find these attributes.

Besides, our approach is capable of *supporting any access control model*. For instance, ABAC can be replaced with RBAC or any other model, and the policy agent will do the job to inform of which elements should be searched for verification. Therefore, *model-specific properties* are respected, such as *availability*. The use of the Event Calculus allows us to check if a subject, for example, had the required attributes at a specific time. However, we consider the case of a static security policy and we leave the problematic of the evolution of this latter a future work.

Other interesting metrics are *inconsistency* and *redundancy*. In this work, we assume that the policy is free of conflict and redundancy. Thus, it is enough to have the logged event matching at least one rule in the security policy to decide that it is not a violation.

7   Related Work

The problematic of the a posteriori access control was introduced in [15], where a logical framework, based on logs, was proposed to check if the actions executed in a system are authorized or not. In [8] the authors introduced a framework for policy compliance control, where users are audited and asked to justify their actions. Moreover, the a posteriori access control had a success in the healthcare domain. For instance, [12] outlined the needed architecture to apply audit based access control in electronic health record systems, and discussed the advantages and limitations of their proposal. Furthermore, in order to detect policy violations, [1] proposed a framework that transforms IHE-ATNA logs into a compliant format with an access and usage analysis led by an OrBAC policy [14]. The core idea was to structure these logs to bring them close to the security policy by using a reformatting procedure that maps the relevant structures and contents of logs to the concepts of the used policy. Nevertheless, almost none of them treated log analysis in case of an expressive security policy. The best effort was [1], for the ability to converge logging data and policy structural concepts, but it still does not treat the temporal aspect of the conditions. As a good log analysis leads to good decisions for accountability, it is fundamental to enrich the logs with complementary information related to the security policy, while incorporating a mechanism for temporal conditions verification. We thus study topics that are related to temporal access control.

Extending traditional access control models was a main interest of many researches. For instance, in [6], a temporal extension of the role based access control model (TRBAC) was presented. The main features of this extension were the support for periodic enabling/disabling of roles, individual exceptions, and the possibility of specifying temporal dependencies among such actions, expressed by means of role triggers. TRBAC was then improved in [20] to be more generalized, and capable of expressing a wider range of temporal constraints such as duration constraints on roles, user-role, and role-permission assignments.

On the other hand, the Event Calculus has been proved to be powerful when it comes to access control security policies. In this respect, [5] showed how security models concerning the discretionary access control can be represented using the simplified Event Calculus (SEC). [27] described the use of Event Calculus for developing a language that supports specification and analysis of authorization policies for Web service composition. Moreover, in [3], the authors used Event Calculus and abductive reasoning to develop an expressive language to analyze policy-based systems. The language combines authorization, obligation and refrain policies, and the abductive analysis is used to detect modality conflicts and a range of application-specific conflicts. In addition, [4] showed how a range of temporal RBAC (TRBAC) security models can be represented as logic programs incorporating the simplified Event Calculus (SEC), that valorizes time-constrained permissions and roles membership. It also showed how clausal form logic expressing integrity constraints can enforce high-level security requirements.

8   Conclusion and Future Perspectives

Our proposed multi-agent system is very helpful when analyzing logs for an a posteriori access control. It eliminates human tasks by automating the collection of access attributes, and their timestamps, in order to attempt policy temporal compliance. This added value of temporal verification was achieved using the Event Calculus, that we modelled in SWRL.

Nevertheless, taking decisions about the legitimacy of the executed actions in the information system, requires having all the information. In consequence, one limitation of our approach is the unavailability of the needed information. One missing attribute, that can be due to a source breakdown, not functioning agent, or simply not logged information, etc., can disrupt the violation detection mechanism.

[28] proposed an approach for access control under uncertainty, where users can afford the cost of the permission. However, the cost is calculated based on probabilities, which cannot be applicable in case of an a posteriori access control, where decision is binary and applying sanctions is involved. Consequently, it is important to treat this latter drawback in a future work, as well as considering the administration policy, where the rules might also change over time.

Acknowledgments. This research is funded by *Be-ys Research*, Meyrin 123, c/o BDO SA, 1219 Châtelaine, GENEVE, a mark of the group *be-ys* dedicated to research and innovation.

References

1. Azkia, H., Cuppens-Boulahia, N., Cuppens, F., Coatrieux, G.: Reconciling IHE-ATNA profile with a posteriori contextual access and usage control policy in health-care environment. In: 2010 6th International Conference on Information Assurance and Security, IAS 2010, pp. 197–203 (2010). https://doi.org/10.1109/ISIAS.2010.5604060
2. Baader, F., Calvanese, D., McGuinness, D., Patel-Schneider, P., Nardi, D.: The Description Logic Handbook: Theory Implementation and Applications. Cambridge University Press, Cambridge (2003)
3. Bandara, A.K., Lupu, E.C., Russo, A.: Using event calculus to formalise policy specification and analysis. In: Proceedings POLICY 2003. IEEE 4th International Workshop on Policies for Distributed Systems and Networks, pp. 26–39. IEEE (2003)
4. Barker, S.: Data protection by logic programming. In: Lloyd, J. (ed.) CL 2000. LNCS (LNAI), vol. 1861, pp. 1300–1314. Springer, Heidelberg (2000). https://doi.org/10.1007/3-540-44957-4_87
5. Barker, S.: Temporal authorization in the simplified event calculus. In: Atluri, V., Hale, J. (eds.) Research Advances in Database and Information Systems Security. ITIFIP, vol. 43, pp. 271–284. Springer, Boston, MA (2000). https://doi.org/10.1007/978-0-387-35508-5_18
6. Bertino, E., Bonatti, P.A., Ferrari, E.: Trbac: a temporal role-based access control model. ACM Trans. Inf. Syst. Secur. (TISSEC) **4**(3), 191–233 (2001)
7. Butin, D., Chicote, M., Le Métayer, D.: Log design for accountability. In: 2013 IEEE Security and Privacy Workshops, pp. 1–7. IEEE (2013)
8. Cederquist, J.G., Corin, R., Dekker, M.A., Etalle, S., den Hartog, J.I., Lenzini, G.: Audit-based compliance control. Int. J. Inf. Secur. **6**(2–3), 133–151 (2007). https://doi.org/10.1007/s10207-007-0017-y
9. Cuppens, F., Cuppens-Boulahia, N.: Modeling contextual security policies. Int. J. Inf. Secur. **7**(4), 285–305 (2008). https://doi.org/10.1007/s10207-007-0051-9
10. Cuppens, F., Cuppens-Boulahia, N., Ghorbel, M.B.: High level conflict management strategies in advanced access control models. Electron. Notes Theor. Comput. Sci. **186**, 3–26 (2007)
11. Dahchour, M., Pirotte, A.: The semantics of reifying n-ary relationships as classes. In: ICEIS, vol. 2, pp. 580–586 (2002)
12. Dekker, M.A.C., Etalle, S.: Audit-based access control for electronic health records. Electron. Notes Theor. Comput. Sci. **168**, 221–236 (2007)
13. Dernaika, F., Cuppens-Boulahia, N., Cuppens, F., Raynaud, O.: Semantic mediation for a posteriori log analysis. In: Proceedings of the 14th International Conference on Availability, Reliability and Security, p. 88. ACM (2019)
14. El Kalam, A.A., et al.: Or-bac: un modèle de contrôle d'accès basé sur les organisations. Cahiers francophones de la recherche en sécurité de l'information **1**, 30–43 (2003)
15. Etalle, S., Winsborough, W.H.: A posteriori compliance control categories and subject descriptors, pp. 11–20 (2007)

16. Ferraiolo, D., Cugini, J., Kuhn, D.R.: Role-based access control (RBAC): features and motivations. In: Proceedings of 11th Annual Computer Security Application Conference, pp. 241–48 (1995)
17. Finin, T., et al.: R owl bac: representing role based access control in owl. In: Proceedings of the 13th ACM Symposium on Access Control Models and Technologies, pp. 73–82 (2008)
18. Horrocks, I., Patel-Schneider, P.F., Boley, H., Tabet, S., Grosof, B., Dean, M., et al.: SWRL: a semantic web rule language combining OWL and RuleML. W3C Member Submission **21**(79), 1-31 (2004)
19. Hu, V.C., et al.: Guide to attribute based access control (ABAC) definition and considerations (draft). NIST Spec. Publ. **800**(162), (2013)
20. Joshi, J.B., Bertino, E., Latif, U., Ghafoor, A.: A generalized temporal role-based access control model. IEEE Trans. Knowl. Data Eng. **17**(1), 4–23 (2005)
21. Li, A., Li, Q., Hu, V.C., Di, J.: Evaluating the capability and performance of access control policy verification tools. In: MILCOM 2015–2015 IEEE Military Communications Conference, pp. 366–371. IEEE (2015)
22. Longstaff, J.J., Lockyer, M.A., Thick, M.: A model of accountability, confidentiality and override for healthcare and other applications. In: Proceedings of the Fifth ACM Workshop on Role-based Access Control, pp. 71–76. ACM (2000)
23. McGuinness, D.L., Van Harmelen, F., et al.: Owl web ontology language overview. W3C Recommendation **10**(10), 2004 (2004)
24. Mepham, W., Gardner, S.: Implementing discrete event calculus with semantic web technologies. In: 2009 Fifth International Conference on Next Generation Web Services Practices, pp. 90–93. IEEE (2009)
25. Ng, G.: Open vs closed world, rules vs queries: use cases from industry. In: OWLED (2005)
26. Puranik, N.: A Specialist Approach for the Classification of Column Data. University of Maryland, Baltimore County (2012)
27. Rouached, M., Godart, C.: Securing web service compositions: formalizing authorization policies using event calculus. In: Dan, A., Lamersdorf, W. (eds.) ICSOC 2006. LNCS, vol. 4294, pp. 440–446. Springer, Heidelberg (2006). https://doi.org/10.1007/11948148_37
28. Salim, F., Reid, J., Dawson, E., Dulleck, U.: An approach to access control under uncertainty. In: 2011 Sixth International Conference on Availability, Reliability and Security, pp. 1–8. IEEE (2011)
29. Shanahan, M.: The event calculus explained. In: Wooldridge, M.J., Veloso, M. (eds.) Artificial Intelligence Today. LNCS (LNAI), vol. 1600, pp. 409–430. Springer, Heidelberg (1999). https://doi.org/10.1007/3-540-48317-9_17
30. Sharma, N.K., Joshi, A.: Representing attribute based access control policies in owl. In: 2016 IEEE Tenth International Conference on Semantic Computing (ICSC), pp. 333–336. IEEE (2016)
31. Weinstein, P.C., Birmingham, W.P.: Agent communication with differentiated ontologies: eight new measures of description compatibility. Michigan Univ Ann Arbor Dept Of Electrical Engineering And Computer Science, Technical Report (1999)

Asset-Driven Approach for Security Risk Assessment in IoT Systems

Salim Chehida[1][(✉)], Abdelhakim Baouya[1], Diego Fernández Alonso[2],
Paul-Emmanuel Brun[3], Guillemette Massot[3], Marius Bozga[1],
and Saddek Bensalem[1]

[1] University of Grenoble Alpes, CNRS, VERIMAG, 38000 Grenoble, France
`salim.chehida@univ-grenoble-alpes.fr`
[2] EMALCSA, A Coruña, Spain
[3] Airbus CyberSecurity SAS, Elancourt, France

Abstract. The growth of damage caused by security issues in IoT-based systems requires the definition of a rigorous methodology allowing risks assessment and protecting the system against them. In this work, we propose an approach that follows the security standards to identify and analyse the potential risks. Our approach starts by specifying the system assets considering IoT domain model and the potential threats that might compromise them. Starting from the list of threats, we define the security objectives then technical requirements and countermeasures that can cover these objectives. We apply our approach to an IoT system for monitoring and control the management of the urban water cycle.

Keywords: Risk assessment · IoT · Asset · Threat · Security objectives · Security requirements · Countermeasures

1 Introduction

An IoT-based system consists of a collection of devices that collaborate through the Internet to provide numerous services. The capability of these devices is to achieve smart tasks while communicating between them, with users. Computer systems have permitted the integration of IoT in several applications such as (i) smart air conditioning in buildings, (ii) health monitoring for early detection of illnesses, (iii) control and optimization of energy consumption, and (iv) environmental monitoring for detection of emergencies. However, the incorporation of a large number of devices using several communication technologies and protocols leads to many security challenges. Several papers such as [11,14,15,17] have portrayed many vulnerabilities that can be exploited by attackers to circumvent the security measures and to damage IoT systems.

Security Risk Assessment (SRA) is the process that aims to improve confidence and security level by mitigating risks while covering system vulnerabilities. According to [16], SRA methods are classified in three perspectives: *Asset-driven*, *Service-driven*, and *Business-driven*. The asset-driven perspective assesses risks

© Springer Nature Switzerland AG 2021
J. Garcia-Alfaro et al. (Eds.): CRiSIS 2020, LNCS 12528, pp. 149–163, 2021.
https://doi.org/10.1007/978-3-030-68887-5_9

starting from the assets. Business-driven considers risks in the business processes level. The service-driven perspective uses services as an input of risk analysis. Several generic methodologies based on the different perspectives have been proposed. However, the complexity and the dynamic of IoT systems highlights the need for new approaches that allow defining a trust security policy.

In this work, we propose an asset-driven approach adapted for the security risk assessment of IoT systems. Our approach considers existing methodologies and standards for the identification of the threats associated with IoT infrastructures and the security requirements that allow dealing with these threats. Then, a set of defences is deployed to ensure requirements and protect the system against relevant risks. Among the specificities of our method compared to the other methods presented in Sect. 2: (i) It is dedicated to IoT systems and it considers the IoT domain model to identify the assets list, (ii) It follows the relevant security standards to define the security requirements and an iterative analysis approach to manage the complexity and the dynamic of IoT systems.

The rest of this paper is organized as follows. Section 2 briefly explains the main approaches proposed for SRA. Section 3 presents the different steps of our approach, and Sect. 4 applies it to assess the risk of an IoT-based system for water management infrastructure. Finally, we give our conclusions in Sect. 5.

2 State of the Art

The paper [16] presents a survey and taxonomy for SRA methods. In this section, we present the most methods and tools used in practice.

2.1 Aurum

AURUM (Automated Risk and Utility Management) method [5] supports the NIST SP 800-30 risk management standard [18]. It consists of three main steps: (i) identification of potential risks and their impacts,(ii) prioritization and implementation of adequate preventive countermeasures, and (iii) evaluation of the impact of countermeasures and whether they decrease the risks. Among the advantages of AURUM:

- It uses *Bayesian threat likelihood determination* for threat evaluation.
- It allows automated calculation of threat impacts and automated definition of controls for the risks mitigation.
- It provides interactive decision and analysis system to support risk manager investigating possible scenarios and characterizing the problems.

2.2 CORAS

CORAS [3] is a model-based risk assessment methodology. It uses the Unified Modelling Language (UML) [13] for describing the target of assessment at the hight level of abstraction, communication with different stakeholders involved in risk assessment, documenting intermediate results, and presenting the overall conclusions. The CORAS method includes seven main steps:

- Introductory meeting to discuss the overall goals of the analysis.
- High-level analysis and description of threats and vulnerabilities.
- Refinement and approval of documentation by the client.
- Identification of risk and potential unwanted incidents by people with expertise on the target of the analysis.
- Risk estimation by giving likelihood values for identified unwanted incidents.
- Evaluation and correction of identified risks with the client.
- Discussion about risk treatment and countermeasures cost and benefit.

2.3   CRAMM

CRAMM (CCTA Risk Analysis and Management Method) [21] is a tool based on qualitative risk assessment methodology proposed by *UK government's Central Computer and Telecommunications Agency* for demonstrating the need for action and justifying prioritized countermeasures at the managerial level, based on quantifiable results. CRAMM consists of the next steps:

- Initial meetings, interviews and structured questionnaires for data collection and objectives definition.
- Identification and evaluation of different assets such as data, application software and physical assets based on the impacts of breaches of confidentiality, integrity, availability and non-repudiation.
- Threat and vulnerability assessment using predefined tables for threat/asset group and threat/impact combinations.
- Risk management by providing a set of countermeasures for mitigating the identified risks.

2.4   EBIOS

EBIOS method [20] allows the assessment and treatment of risks associated with an Information System (IS) and the implementation of a security policy adapted to the needs of an organization. It groups five steps :

- The first step deals with context establishment and the relationship between the business context and the IS.
- In the second step, security requirements are determined based on feared security events.
- In the third step, a risk study is conducted in order to identify and analyze threat scenarios.
- In the fourth step, information from the previous steps is used to identify risks and describe the necessary and sufficient security goals relating to the risks.
- In the final step, the necessary security controls are determined, and any residual risk is made explicit.

2.5 MEHARI

MEHARI (MEthod for Harmonized Analysis of RIsk) [1] is a method for risk analysis of IS. It involves the following steps [19]:

– Context establishment of the entire organization or particular parts (business activity, type of asset or threat, etc.).
– Stakes analysis and assets classification as primary and secondary, according to ISO/IEC 27005 [9].
– Risk identification by collecting threats and security measures needed to reduce the risks.
– Risk analysis by providing possible risk scenarios associated with the assets and the various threats.
– Risk assessment by the quantification of risk scenarios on 4 levels and the management of the most serious scenarios.

3 BRAIN-IoT Risk Assessment Methodology

BRAIN-IoT project[1] aims to develop a framework for reducing the effort of developing, validating, operating and monitoring IoT-based systems. As part of this project, we propose a risk assessment methodology depicted in Fig. 1.

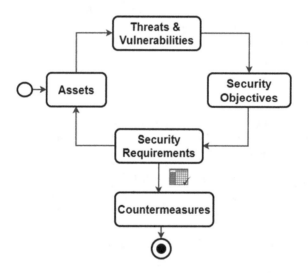

Fig. 1. BRAIN-IoT risk assessment methodology.

This method is appropriate for risk analysis of IoT systems, and it inspires the best practices from existing approaches presented in Sect. 2. Our approach

---
[1] http://www.brain-iot.eu/.

is iterative, and technical requirements could be refined following the refinement of the system assets. It involves the client, and the results of each phase must be checked. After validation of the requirements with the client, countermeasures are provided to protect the system against the identified risks. The next sections will detail the different steps.

3.1 Identification of Assets

The specification of assets is the first phase of our methodology. This phase plays a significant part because it is central to determine the risks. Following the ISO/IEC 27001 definition [7], an asset is *"any tangible or intangible thing or characteristic that has value to an organization"*. Therefore, an asset could be in different forms, tangible or intangible, hardware or software, service or infrastructure, etc. After the identification, the assets can be evaluated using a qualitative or quantitative way. The qualitative way highlights the importance of the assets based on their security level determined by three aspects: confidentiality, integrity, and availability. The quantitative evaluation is based on the actual environment and the value of the assets.

To establish a common definition of IoT systems assets and their relationships, an IoT domain model is required. In this work, we refer to the model proposed by [6] (see Fig. 2) that allows avoiding fuzzy terminologies and helping in the risk analysis of IoT systems. This model has been developed within the IoT-A project[2], and it aims to come to a common understanding. It defines five main concepts.

(a) **User**
    The user represents who interacts with a real-world object. The interaction between User and Physical Entity (PE) is carried out physically or through software interfaces and electronic devices. Users can either be humans or Active Digital Artefacts (ADA), e.g., programs embedded in manufacturing robots.

(b) **Augmented Entity (AE)**
    AE is the combination (composition) of PE together with its digital representation, and it can be considered as "Thing". VE (Virtual Entity) is a kind of digital artefact that represents PE.

(c) **Device**
    The device is hardware with computing capabilities. It can be physically attached to PE, or may also be in its environment. There are three types of devices. *Sensors* that allow PEs monitoring, *Actuators* that can act on PEs, and *Tags* that allow to identify PEs and can be read by sensors.

(d) **Resource**
    Resources are software components that implement certain functionalities, for example: providing information about PE's, allowing the execution of actuation tasks or analysing data provided by multiple sensors. They may be hosted on a device, or they could be located anywhere in the network.

---

[2] http://www.iot-a.eu.

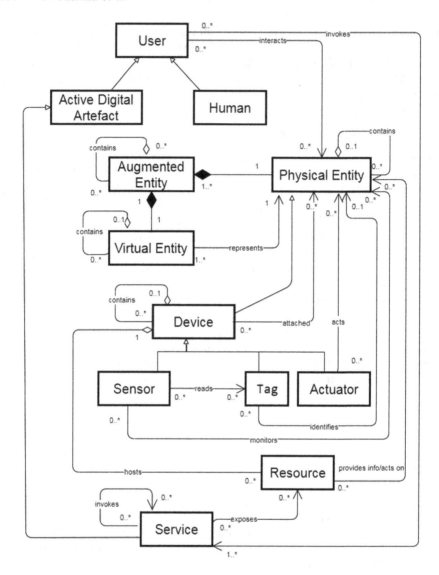

Fig. 2. Domain model for IoT.

(e) **Service**

Service exposes the resources through a common interface and makes them available for users and other services. It may also invoke other services and combine the results.

In our methodology, we rely on the IoT domain model to identify the different assets of IoT systems and to understand the correlation between them. We can also distinguish between *hardware assets*, such as the different types of devices and *software assets*, such as services, resources, and ADA. Assets should be listed in a table. We give *an ID* to the asset, which will be used in the next steps for traceability and also *a description* that provides a quick overview of the asset and its perimeter.

3.2   Threats and Vulnerabilities

According to ISO/IEC 27001 [7], a threat is a *"potential cause of an unwanted incident, which may result in harm to a system or organization"*. In NISP SP800-30 [18], threat is *"a potential, for a particular threat-source, to successfully exercise a particular vulnerability"*. A threat could be the result of an external and non-controllable incident or an attack on the system. Threat-sources can be categorized into environment factors or human factors.

Vulnerability refers to the openness of a system to the threats. According to [7], *"vulnerability refers to the weakness that is related to the organizations' assets, which sometimes could cause an unexpected incident"*. In NISP SP800-30 [18], *"vulnerability means a flaw or weakness of the systems' security flow, design, and implementation that could lead to a security breach or violation of the security policy"*. Vulnerabilities can be divided into two categories. The first type of vulnerabilities affects the asset itself, such as technical issues, system breaches, etc. The second ones are caused by insufficient organization management at a higher level [7].

A list of generic threats is provided by SRA methodologies presented in Sect. 2. In our method, we consider EBIOS database [20], which is compatible with all relevant ISO standards (13335, 15408, 17799, 31000, 27005, and 27001) and provides a complete list of possible threats (42 threats) designed to be exhaustive (see Table 1). EBIOS threat database is widely used in risk assessment. Some works like [22] have used it for risk analysis of IoT systems. In Table 1 taken from the EBIOS knowledge bases, threats are classified into eight main categories. Threat impact in terms of Availability (A), Confidentiality (C), and Integrity (I) is assessed.

In our approach, all potential threats towards the essential assets should be recognized using *threat-asset matrix* that allows the traceability of threats for each asset. The matrix should be completed and validated with the client.

3.3   Security Objectives

Security objectives are derived from threats. They are the main guideline to counter the identified threats and to satisfy the security principles. In our methodology, we consider security objectives from the standard ISO/IEC-27002 [8]. This standard gives general guidance on the commonly accepted goals of information security management. It describes general principles structured around 35 security objectives and 114 controls. The risk managers should specify security objectives that cover the full list of threats for each asset. After the

Table 1. EBIOS threat list.

Type	ID	Description	A	C	I
Physical damage	T-1010	Fire	x		x
	T-1020	Water damage	x		x
	T-1030	Pollution	x		x
	T-1040	Major accident	x		x
	T-1050	Destruction of equipment or media	x		x
Natural events	T-2010	Climatic phenomenon	x		x
	T-2020	Seismic phenomenon	x		x
	T-2030	Volcanic phenomenon	x		x
	T-2040	Meteorological phenomenon	x		x
	T-2050	Flood	x		x
Loss of essential services	T-3010	Failure of air-conditioning	x		
	T-3020	Loss of power supply	x		
	T-3030	Failure of telecommunication equipment	x		
Disturbance due to radiation	T-4010	Electromagnetic radiation	x		x
	T-4020	Thermal radiation	x		x
	T-4030	Electromagnetic pulses	x		x
Compromise of information	T-5010	Interception of compromising interference signals		x	
	T-5020	Remote spying	x	x	x
	T-5030	Eavesdropping		x	
	T-5040	Theft of media or documents		x	
	T-5050	Theft of Equipment	x	x	
	T-5060	Retrieval or recycled or discarded media		x	
	T-5070	Disclosure		x	
	T-5080	Data from untrustworthy sources	x		x
	T-5090	Tampering with hardware		x	
	T-5100	Tampering with software	x	x	x
	T-5110	Position detection		x	
Technical failures	T-6010	Equipment failure	x		
	T-6020	Equipment malfunction	x		
	T-6030	Saturation of the information system	x		
	T-6040	Software malfunction	x		x
	T-6050	Breach of information system maintainability	x		
Unauthorised actions	T-7010	Unauthorised use or equipment	x	x	x
	T-7020	Fraudulent copying of software		x	
	T-7030	Use of counterfeit or copied software	x		
	T-7040	Corruption of data		x	x
	T-7050	Illegal processing of data		x	
Compromise of functions	T-8010	Error in use	x	x	x
	T-8020	Abuse of rights	x	x	x
	T-8030	Forging of rights	x	x	x
	T-8040	Denial of actions			x
	T-8050	Breach of personnel availability	x		

identification of security objectives, a mapping of each security objective should
be done with the threat list. This will help to identify any gaps in the security
objective coverage. The mapping could be done with an *objectives traceability
matrix*.

3.4 Security Requirements and Countermeasures

This phase provides the technical security requirements, which are a set of rules broken down into three main categories: confidentiality, integrity, and availability. Each security objective should lead to the implementation of one or more technical requirements that could be defined in the *requirements table*.

Countermeasures are mechanisms that can be deployed to defend the system, and thwart attacks exploiting its vulnerabilities. They should cover all security requirements. Several recent surveys like [15] and [14] present countermeasures for IoT systems security. They can be secure protocols, secure frameworks, authentication and encryption solutions, hardware security solutions such as TPM (Trusted Platform Module), and more. There are some approaches like [4] that can help risk managers to determinate impactful and adequate countermeasures considering organization defense budget. In [4], the *Attack-Defense Tree* (ADT) [10] is used for modeling the combination between countermeasures and attacks that can exploit the threats and vulnerabilities presented in the second phase of our approach. Then, the *Attack-Defense Strategies Exploration* tool [12] evaluates the impact of the countermeasures on the attack cost and pinpoints defense actions portraying a good balance between defenses and their provided impact on the attack cost regarding the organization's defense budget.

4 Case Study

We apply our methodology on the industrial case study of water infrastructure that manages the urban water cycle in the city of la Coruña in Spain. An IoT system controls a large number of devices dispersed in large and varied geographical sites, with numerous interactions with other elements and services related to human activities.

In our water management system, we have identified 55 assets with their associated threats, security objectives, requirements, and countermeasures. The complete study is given in the excel file at [2]. Table 2 shows examples of 11 assets. For each asset, we can have many of the same model installed in the infrastructure. We classify the assets according to the IoT domain model presented in Sect. 3.1. In Table 2, we distinguish six devices of type sensor and four devices of type actuator. The asset A-1093 is an active digital artefact.

Table 2. Water management system assets.

Asset ID	Asset description	Asset type
A-1050	Submersible probe with vented cable. Probe of hydrostatic level 0,6 BAR 10 m per cable IFM	Sensors : water level
A-1051	Ultrasonic sensor with reaching of 1.300 mm	
A-1053	MEASURING TRANSDUCER SITRANS P, FOR PRESSURE AND ABSOLUTE PRESSURE SERIES Z	Sensors : pressure
A-1054	Pressure sensor with screen (range 0 to 6 bar) PT-006-SEG14-A-ZVG/US/ /W	
A-1056	Flow meter SIEMENS SITRANS F M MAG 5000	Sensors : water flow
A-1057	NUBIS MWN65-NKOP 18337996	
A-1060	Submersible centrifuge electric pump Pedrollo MC 30/50 Series	Actuators : pumps
A-1064	Water pump speroni SCR 25/80–180 NF.0215	
A-1065	Servo control Diamant PILOT. Electric regulatory valve (identification pending)	Actuators : electric valves
A-1066	Servo control Diamant PILOT. Electric regulatory valve 24V-50/60 Hz. UP04420/19	
A-1093	SICA-MEDUSA platform that receives/send information from/to devices	ADA

In Table 3, we present threats from Table 1 related to assets presented in Table 2. Sensors and actuators are generally vulnerable to physical damage that can be caused by external events linked to the natural or industrial environment and person gaining access to equipment and causing its destruction. They are also susceptible to risks of natural events (specific climatic conditions, volcanic and meteorological phenomenons, etc.), failure of telecommunication equipment, tampering attacks, events causing equipment failure or malfunction, error in use and malicious access. There are also other threats that are related to specific devices. The SICA-MEDUSA platform is vulnerable to compromise of information and functions, technical failures, and unauthorized actions. Besides, the software infrastructure is deployed independently of the physical platform, so it is not vulnerable to environmental and physical impedances.

Table 3. Threat-asset matrix.

	A-1050	A-1051	A-1053	A-1054	A-1056	A-1057	A-1060	A-1064	A-1065	A-1066	A-1093
T-1010	X	X	X	X	X	X	X	X	X	X	
T-1020					X	X			X	X	
T-1030					X	X	X	X	X	X	
T-1040	X	X	X	X	X	X	X	X	X	X	
T-1050	X	X	X	X	X	X	X	X	X	X	
T-2010	X	X	X	X	X	X	X	X	X	X	
T-2020		X	X	X	X	X	X	X	X	X	
T-2030	X	X	X	X	X	X	X	X	X	X	
T-2040	X	X	X	X	X	X					
T-2050					X	X		X	X	X	
T-3010							X	X			
T-3020		X	X	X							
T-3030	X	X	X	X	X	X	X	X	X	X	
T-4010		X			X						
T-4020					X						
T-4030		X			X						
T-5010											
T-5020											
T-5030											X
T-5040											X
T-5050					X		X	X	X	X	
T-5060											X
T-5070											X
T-5080											X
T-5090	X	X	X	X	X	X	X	X	X	X	
T-5100					X						X
T-5110											
T-6010	X	X	X	X	X	X	X	X	X	X	
T-6020	X	X	X	X	X	X	X	X	X	X	
T-6030											X
T-6040					X				X		X
T-6050					X						X
T-7010											X
T-7020											X
T-7030											X
T-7040					X						X
T-7050											X
T-8010	X	X	X	X	X	X	X	X	X	X	X
T-8020	X	X	X	X	X						X
T-8030											X
T-8040											X
T-8050											

In Table 4, we provide examples of 9 security objectives, the threats they cover, and their rationale for considering them for the water management system. For instance, *network security management* objective can prevent eavesdropping, tampering attacks, and some unauthorized actions.

Table 4. Security objectives.

ID	Security objective	Security objective description	Threats
O-1020	Back-up	Back-up of data and software from water management platform should be taken and tested regularly	T-10XX T-20XX
O-1030	Network security management	Ensure the protection of the communication between the gateway and internet, the LAN network, the access from the outside, and to the devices	T-5030 T-5090 T-7010 T-7020 T-7040
O-1040	Security of exchanged information	Protect the exchange of information between the devices, as well as the data collected by the sensors and devices connected through the edge nodes	T-5070 T-5080
O-1050	Monitoring	Observe and check the processes, infrastructures and logs from water management platform in order to detect unauthorized information processing	T-5030 T-5040 T-60xx T-70xx T-80xx
O-2010	User access management	Manage the users account information, the users passwords, and the users registration to guarantee and secure access to systems and services	T-7010 T-7020 T-7040 T-8020 T-8030
O-2020	Network access control	Protect data center, network ports, and the equipment in networks and the servers to prevent unauthorized use of networked services	T-6030 T-70xx
O-3010	Correct processing in applications	Check the data input and the data output of water management applications in order to know that they are correct and to prevent errors and unauthorized modification	T-60xx
O-3020	Cryptographic controls	Protect the sensible information in the communication between the devices and the nodes by applying cryptographic techniques	T-8020 T-8030
O-3030	Security of system files	The access to system files should be restricted. The infected system files should be detected	T-8020

Table 5. Security requirements and countermeasures.

SR ID	Security requirements description	Countermeasures
R-1030-0020	The access from the outside must be allowed only to authorized users and machines	VPN and DMZ (demilitarized zone) allow to reach this requirement
R-1030-0030	The communication between the gateway and internet shall be encrypted and authenticated	TLS (Transport Layer Security) allows to perform such kind of encryption and authentication
R-1030-0040	The communication point to point shall be encrypted and authenticated	SMQTT protocol integrates Attribute-Based Encryption (ABE) algorithm to secure IoT networks
R-1030-0050	Unknown devices must be unauthorized to connect to the LAN network	SRAM-PUF protocol allows to check the authenticity of devices by using unclonable device IDs
R-1030-0060	Only the system staff shall be allowed to deploy devices into the network	Authentication technology combined with TLS allow to ensure this requirement. Trust aware RPL routing protocol allows to detect malicious nodes
R-1030-0070	Computers and laptops shall have authentication system for logging	Access control technologies on computer and laptop allow to reach this requirement
R-1030-0080	If there is a file that contains the user's authentication keys this file shall be stored using a secure environment	TPM (Trusted Platform Module) allows a good security level for key protection. LEA-M encryption algorithm allows to mask secret keys Of cryptographic implementations

In Table 5, we give examples of security requirements and countermeasures that can implement *network security management* objective (O-1030). Several requirements are defined to ensure the authentication of the devices and the security of the communication between them. Also, several secure protocols such as TLS, SMQTT, and SRAM-PUF are proposed to implement security requirements. Security requirements and countermeasures implementing the other security objectives from Table 4 are given in [2].

5   Conclusion

We have presented a risk assessment methodology that follows the security standards to prevent possible threats in IoT systems. Our method provides several advantages. We relied on the IoT domain model to identify the assets of the system. We used a complete list of possible threats extracted from standards to identify all the potential risks and the requirements needed to mitigate these risks. We have followed an iterative approach that responds to the need for evolution. If the system incorporates new assets, we identify the threats related to these assets, then the requirements and countermeasures needed to prevent the identified threats.

In this paper, we have also provided the implementation of our methodology on water management infrastructure. In the analysis carried out, several threats related to the target infrastructures not previously considered were discovered in this study. We are planning in the future to apply our method to other IoT systems.

Acknowledgments. The research leading to these results has been supported by the European Union through the BRAIN-IoT project H2020-EU.2.1.1. Grant agreement ID: 780089.

References

1. MEHARI: Method for Harmonized Analysis of Risk (2010). https://en.wikipedia.org/wiki/MEHARI
2. Risk assessment in water management infrastructure (2020). https://github.com/SafetyAnalysis/Asset-driven-Approach-for-Security-Risk-Assessment-in-IoT-Systems/blob/master/EMALCSA-RiskAssessment.xlsx
3. den Braber, F., Hogganvik, I., Lund, M.S., Stølen, K., Vraalsen, F.: Model-based security analysis in seven steps – a guided tour to theCORAS method. BT Technol. J. **25**(1), 101–117 (2007). https://doi.org/10.1007/s10550-007-0013-9, http://link.springer.com/10.1007/s10550-007-0013-9
4. Chehida, S., Baouya, A., Bozga, M., Bensalem, S.: Exploration of impactful countermeasures on IoT attacks. In: 2020 9th Mediterranean Conference on Embedded Computing (MECO) (2020)
5. Ekelhart, A., Fenz, S., Neubauer, T.: AURUM: a framework for information security risk management. In: 2009 42nd Hawaii International Conference on System Sciences, pp. 1–10 (2009)
6. Haller, S., Serbanati, A., Bauer, M., Carrez, F.: A domain model for the internet of things. In: 2013 IEEE International Conference on Green Computing and Communications and IEEE Internet of Things and IEEE Cyber, Physical and Social Computing, pp. 411–417 (2013)

7. ISO/IEC 27001:2013: Information technology – Security techniques – Information security management systems – Requirements (2013). https://www.iso.org/standard/54534.html
8. ISO/IEC 27002:2013: Information technology – Security techniques – Code of practice for information security controls (2013). https://www.iso.org/standard/54533.html
9. ISO/IEC 27005:2011: Information technology – Security techniques – Information security risk management (2011). https://www.iso.org/standard/56742.html
10. Kordy, B., Mauw, S., Radomirović, S., Schweitzer, P.: Foundations of attack–defense trees. In: Degano, P., Etalle, S., Guttman, J. (eds.) FAST 2010. LNCS, vol. 6561, pp. 80–95. Springer, Heidelberg (2011). https://doi.org/10.1007/978-3-642-19751-2_6
11. Lin, J., Yu, W., Zhang, N., Yang, X., Zhang, H., Zhao, W.: A survey on internet of things: architecture, enabling technologies, security and privacy, and applications. IEEE Int. Things J. 4(5), 1125–1142 (2017)
12. Medioni, B.L., Nouri, A., Bozga, M., Legay, A., Bensalem, S.: Mitigating security risks through attack strategies exploration. In: Margaria, T., Steffen, B. (eds.) ISoLA 2018. LNCS, vol. 11245, pp. 392–413. Springer, Cham (2018). https://doi.org/10.1007/978-3-030-03421-4_25
13. Object Management Group: Unified Modeling Language (UML): Superstructure, version 2.0 (2005)
14. Radoglou Grammatikis, P.I., Sarigiannidis, P.G., Moscholios, I.D.: Securing the internet of things: challenges, threats and solutions. Internet Things 5, 41–70 (2019). https://doi.org/10.1016/j.iot.2018.11.003
15. Sengupta, J., Ruj, S., Das Bit, S.: A comprehensive survey on attacks, security issues and blockchain solutions for IoT and IIoT. J. Netw. Comput. Appl. 149, 102481 (2020). https://doi.org/10.1016/j.jnca.2019.102481
16. Shameli-Sendi, A., Aghababaei-Barzegar, R., Cheriet, M.: Taxonomy of information security risk assessment (ISRA). Comput. Secur. 57, 14–30 (2016). https://doi.org/10.1016/j.cose.2015.11.001,https://linkinghub.elsevier.com/retrieve/pii/S0167404815001650
17. Sicari, S., Rizzardi, A., Grieco, L., Coen-Porisini, A.: Security, privacy and trust in internet of things: the road ahead. Comput. Netw. 76, 146–164 (2015). https://doi.org/10.1016/j.comnet.2014.11.008
18. Stoneburner, G., Goguen, A., Feringa, A.: Risk management guide for information technology systems. Nist Spec. Publ. 800(30), 800-830 (2002)
19. The European Union Agency for Cybersecurity: Mehari (2010). https://www.enisa.europa.eu/topics/threat-risk-management/risk-management/current-risk/risk-management-inventory/rm-ra-methods/m_mehari.html
20. The National Cybersecurity Agency of France (ANSSI): EBIOS 2010 - Expression of Needs and Identification of Security objectives. (2010). https://www.ssi.gouv.fr/guide/ebios-2010-expression-des-besoins-et-identification-des-objectifs-de-securite/
21. Yazar, Z.: A qualitative risk analysis and management tool-CRAMM. SANS InfoSec Reading Room White Paper 11, 12–32 (2002)
22. Zahra, B.F., Abdelhamid, B.: Risk analysis in Internet of things using EBIOS. In: 2017 IEEE 7th Annual Computing and Communication Workshop and Conference (CCWC), pp. 1–7. IEEE (2017)

Heterogeneous Security Events Prioritization Using Auto-encoders

Alexandre Dey[1,2,3]($\boxtimes$), Eric Totel[1], and Sylvain Navers[3]

[1] IMT-Atlantique, Nantes, France
eric.totel@imt-atlantique.fr
[2] Inria, Univ. Rennes, IRISA, Rennes, France
[3] Airbus CyberSecurity, Elancourt, France
{alexandre.dey,sylvain.navers}@airbus.com

Abstract. In a large monitored information system, analysts are confronted with a huge number of heterogeneous events or alerts produced by audit mechanisms or Intrusion Detection Systems. Even though they can use SIEM software to collect and analyse these events (In this paper we call events all events or alerts produced by the monitoring processes), detecting previously unknown threats is tedious. Event prioritization tools can help the analyst focus on potentially anomalous events. To compute a measure of priority among events, we propose in this paper to define the notion of an anomaly score for each attribute of the analyzed events and a method for regrouping events in clusters to reduce the number of alerts the analysts have to qualify. The anomaly score is computed using neural networks (i.e., auto-encoders) trained on a normal dataset of events, and then used to provide the analyst with the information of the difference between normal learned events and the events actually produced by the monitoring system. Additionally, the auto-encoders also provide a way to regroup similar events via clustering.

Keywords: Heterogeneous logs · Anomaly detection · Anomaly score · Cybersecurity · Intrusion detection · Machine learning

1 Introduction

Security monitoring of information systems requires to log events happening during the execution of processes at system level, the exchange of data via the network or the application warnings. In addition to event logging, Intrusion Detection Systems can produce alerts that are likely to be the consequence of an attack. Due to the huge number of events produced, even if a monitoring strategy has been clearly defined, it is difficult for the analysts to detect what are important events from the security point view, i.e., what are the events that are symptomatic of an intrusion inside the system.

The current practices consist in collecting all security events in a SIEM (Security Information and Event Management) solution. This solution is able to correlate information included in multiple events in order to recognize known attack

J. Garcia-Alfaro et al. (Eds.): CRiSIS 2020, LNCS 12528, pp. 164–180, 2021.
https://doi.org/10.1007/978-3-030-68887-5_10

patterns. Despite the definition of highly accurate correlation processes [14], this treatment still requires to manually write static correlation rules. Thus, the effectiveness of the detection relies on the ability of the analysts to write a complete set of correct correlation rules for known attacks. Furthermore, this set of rules should be updated continuously to take into account the newly discovered threats. As a consequence this tremendous task is clearly insufficient to emphasize all attack steps, and a lot of anomalous events stay hidden to the analyst.

During the threat hunting process, analysts rely on prioritization tools to highlight the most anomalous events and identify misbehaving entities in the system. If necessary, a more thorough forensic analysis of these entities can be performed. After this analysis, they should be able to produce a set of Indicators of Compromise (IoC) and eventual correlation rules. As a way of prioritizing events, in this paper, we propose an approach which associates an anomaly score to each attribute of an event[1]. These per attribute scores are then combined to provide a global anomaly score to the event. The higher this score is, the lower the probability of it being a consequence of a normal behavior is. This approach relies on the use of Artificial Intelligence mechanisms, more specifically, neural networks auto-encoders. The originality of the approach is that the computation is applied to any type of events (i.e., network, system and application events). While other related methods require complex feature engineering to transform attributes into compliant inputs for the chosen algorithms (e.g., for strings, choice between feature hashing, one-hot encoding, TF-IDF, etc.), our method only requires analysts to identify events attributes as being a numerical, categorical or string variable. This makes it easier to adapt to new category of security event. A major contribution of our approach is the introduction of a way for auto-encoders to provide a cluster identifier to each event. The identifier is used to easily and accurately regroup similar events. This clustering lowers the volume of redundant information presented to analysts which lead to almost three orders of magnitude reduction for our test dataset. The main advantage of our method is the possibility to rapidly adapt it to new security event sources, providing as output a cluster identifier and an anomaly score to the analyzed events. This paper is organized as follows: Sect. 2 presents the state of the art in anomaly detection using Artificial Intelligence techniques. Section 3 explains how the anomaly score is computed. In Sect. 4 we describe how the approach is implemented. Finally Sect. 5 presents the results obtained on a data set produced using an environment of heterogeneous Operating Systems on an internal network.

---

[1] Attributes are the fields of an event. Connection duration, source IP address, number of bytes received are examples of attributes for a network event.

2   State of the Art in AI Applied to Security Monitoring

Our approach permits to categorize attributes of events as being normal or abnormal. A lot of work uses Artificial Intelligence approaches to attain a similar objective (i.e., detecting anomalies), mainly machine learning techniques. Kriegel et al. [3] computes the anomaly score based on the distance with the nearest neighbours, with a high distance to the other points indicating a potential anomaly. Pang et al. [19] proposed a nearest neighbours based method, that scales to larger datasets (several millions of events) by computing the pairwise distance between random samples of point instead of the whole dataset. Ester et al. [9] proposed DBSCAN, an approach that identifies high density of points as clusters and classify points inside low density region as anomalies. However, these approaches are sensible to a high dimensional data (the "curse of dimensionality" described by Bellman et al. [2]). As a consequence Kriegel et al. [13] proposed a work that scales to large number of attributes in data. All the methods mentioned above rely on a notion of distance that needs to be defined specifically for the problem at hand, which can prove difficult, especially for complex data structures (e.g., the distance between two strings, two events with heterogeneous attributes types, etc.)

A variant of Principal Component Analysis has been also used by Pascoal et al. [20] to propose an approach that is robust to noise in the training dataset (e.g., a few attack traces in the normal data). Scholkopf et al. [23] proposed one of the most used algorithm for anomaly detection by training SVM (Support Vector Machines). Data Mining techniques have been used by He et al. [11] to measure the level of anomaly of a transaction. This type of approach have been extended by Akoglu et al. [1] to limit the number of frequent pattern used to compute the anomaly score. Pattern mining algorithm requires categorical data as input, and therefore a suitable transformation of the input data should be found for numerical data.

The use of Bayesian Networks [22] has been tested by Wong et al. [27] to perform anomaly detection. This type of approach permits also to diagnose and explain a detected anomaly. However, Bayesian methods requires to identify the most likely probability distribution for the events, which can be challenging.

The algorithm Isolation Forest proposed by Liu et al. [15] was applied to security by Ding et al. [7]. This permits to classify quickly the abnormal activities. This technique does not require any kind of normalization on numerical variables, but it requires categorical values to be transformed into numerical values and cannot handle text values without specific transformation methods.

Similarly to our approach Hawkins et al. [10] propose a method based on neural networks to compute anomaly score. This approach is called Replicator Neural Networks (RNN). With the rise of Deep Learning and more specifically Deep Neural Networks (DNN), RNN have regain interest in the form of deep auto-encoders and a robust variant of the algorithm has been proposed by Zhou et al. [28]. Mirsky et al. [18] relies on an ensemble of auto-encoder to improve the robustness and accuracy. Due to recent advancements in deep learning, auto-encoders can be adapted to various kind of data (e.g., text, time-series, images, categorical, numerical, etc.). However, such a network is computationally inten-sive to train and is best suited for high volume of training data. Veeramachaneni et al. propose an active learning based approach for large scale security mon-itoring [26]. The authors combine a Principal Component Analysis approach, auto-encoders and a distance-based approach for anomaly detection, but they still require complex feature selection and transformation for each event sources. In [8], a deep learning method is used to spot anomalous patterns inside log files. However, the considered threat model is mainly focused on Denial of Ser-vice and workflow interruption, and the method has therefore not been assessed on broader range of hostile behaviors.

Shen et al. [24] and Liu et al. [16] propose methods that rely on embedding of security-related information, like our method. The former's objective is to model the evolution of exploitation methodology for known vulnerability, and is therefore more related to cyber threat intelligence than security monitoring. The latter aims at detecting complete attack (i.e., not anomalous events) and relies on complex sets of rules to build graphs, which is hard to adapt to new types of security events and threat models.

Our approach draws inspiration from state-of-the art deep learning tech-niques to take as input numerical (e.g., connection duration, file size, etc.), cat-egorical (e.g., port number, user identifier, hostname, etc.) and string (e.g., a command and its arguments) attributes. Doing so permits the use of simple and generic methodology for input transformation. In addition, we exploit the latent representation of the auto-encoder in a novel way to provide clustering capabil-ities. This is used to regroup similar event and lower the volume of information that is presented to the analysts.

3 Computing Anomaly Score on Heterogeneous Events

3.1 Basics on Neural Networks Auto-encoders for Anomaly Detection

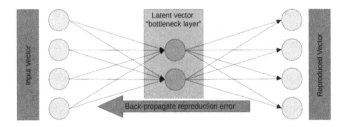

Fig. 1. Overview of an autoencoder

Auto-encoders (Fig. 1) are by definition a particular structure of neural networks that are trained in an unsupervised way (i.e., without the expected output value in the training dataset) and composed of an encoder, which maps input vectors to a low dimension representation (also called latent space), and a decoder which tries to reconstruct the original input vector from the latent space.

The input vectors are vectors containing numerical values (integers, floats or vectors of integers or floats). For anomaly scoring, the auto-encoder is first trained on normal data to compress and decompress the input vectors with as little loss of information as possible (i.e., an approximation of the identity function). Then, an inference phase that takes as inputs events produced during the monitoring process, to which we apply the auto-encoders estimated identity function. As output we obtain a result that can slightly differ from the input. We name this difference "reproduction error", and we use this difference to estimate the deviation of the input from learnt normal known inputs. More specifically, the auto-encoder is biased towards normal events, and therefore, the reproduction error is higher for anomalous events.

During the security monitoring process, an information system produces a huge number of heterogeneous events. These events can be for example extracted from the operating system (e.g., system calls), from network (e.g., connections, protocols, network IDS alerts, etc.), or from specific monitored applications (e.g., web server requests logs). Moreover, different types of operating systems can be used (e.g., Windows and Linux systems), generating different formats of events. Also, an event that is the consequence of a normal behaviour on one system, might be a sign of an intruder in another one. Our objective is to create normal behaviour models from all these heterogeneous events in order to compute, for each event, an anomaly score, and do so with a minimal configuration step.

Due to their ability to handle heterogeneous attributes, we chose to adapt neural network auto-encoders to compute an anomaly score (Sect. 3.5) for security events. We also exploit the latent space of these auto-encoders to provide a cluster identifier to each event, later used to regroup similar events in clusters (Sect. 3.4). In this section, the structure of the auto-encoders is provided (Sect. 3.3), as well as the transformations that are applied on the events before being processed by the auto-encoder (Sect. 3.2).

3.2 Input Transformation

As explained in Subsect. 3.1, the auto-encoder takes as input a vector of numerical values. The goal of the input transformation process is to transform the vector containing the value of the attributes of an event into a vector suitable as input for the auto-encoder. This transformation process is presented in Algorithm 1.

There are three possible types of variables that can be taken as input to our auto-encoders. The first type, like any machine learning algorithm, is numerical variables. The second one, the categorical variables, are variables whose values belong to a finite set and cannot be mathematically ordered (e.g., username 'Bob" is neither superior or inferior to username "Alice"). Finally, raw strings are considered as sequences of categorical values.

Normalizing Numerical Attributes. For numerical variables (integers and floats) taking raw values as input is not the most efficient way of learning the normal distribution of numerical attributes [12]. This paper proposes as a remediation to normalize the numerical values from a set of floats into a reduced

Algorithm 1. Event Attribute Vector Transformation

```
function TRANSFORMCATEGORY(attribute)
    for all pattern in KnownPatterns do
        if MATCHPATTERN(pattern, attribute) then
            attribute ← pattern
            break
        end if
    end for
    if attribute in KnownCategories then
        return value ← KnownCategories[attribute]
    else
        return value ← KnownCategories[DefaultValue]
    end if
    return value
end function
function TRANSFORM(event)
    Vector ← ∅
    for all SelectedAttribute in event do
        switch SelectedAttribute.type do
            case categorical
                Vector[i] ← TRANSFORMCATEGORY(SelectedAttribute)
            case string
                Vector[i] ← STRINGTOINTEGERARRAY(SelectedAttribute)
            case number
                Vector[i] ← SCALEVALUE(SelectedAttribute)
        end for
    return Vector
end function
```

interval (e.g., the set $[0, 1]$). This transformation is produced by the **ScaleValue** function in Algorithm 1.

In the context of anomaly detection, outliers with extreme values can reside in normal data. To limit their impact on the normalization process, we find the 90th percentile Q_{90} inside the training dataset (i.e., 90% of the normal values are below Q_{90}). The transformation then consists in dividing the input by Q_{90}. In case the value of the attribute grows exponentially, as suggested by Kaastra et al. [12], the result of the transformation will be the logarithm of the initial value divided by the logarithm of Q_{90}.

Normalizing Categorical Attributes. To handle categorical variables in the auto-encoder, we draw inspiration from *word2vec* [17]. The goal of this technique is to map each word in a continuous vector space (i.e., vectors of floats) based on its context (other words appearing in the same sentences). This mapping is generally called an embedding. This permits to treat natural language, such as the recognition of semantics of words in sentences. We use the following analogy: an event is a sentence and its attributes are the words composing it.

The neural network will optimize the embedding function based on the other attributes of the given event, that will represent the context of the transformed attribute. This context allows us to determine if a category of an attribute is normal in a given context.

In practice, a categorical embedding layer of a neural network takes as input a category identifier (i.e., an integer) that represents a vector filled with as much

0 as the total number of categories, except for a 1 at the corresponding identifier. When the total number of categories is large, a proportionally large number of parameters needs to be optimized. To reduce the induced computational complexity, we propose the use of regular expressions (regex) to map every string matching the same pattern to the same category identifier. For example, if we consider all HTML files in a web server repository as being of the same category, we can map them to the same identifier using the regular expression *.html. However, as with any security tools relying on regex, the regex should be carefully chosen to prevent an attacker from bypassing them.

For a given value of an attribute, if the category is known (or if it matches a predefined regex), it returns the corresponding identifier. In case the category was never encountered before (frequent in the context of anomaly detection), it returns an integer corresponding to the category "Unknown". This corresponds to the function **TransformCategory** in Algorithm 1.

Normalizing Raw String Attributes. Strings, as found in security events, have their own syntax and semantic. As such, it is possible to apply Natural Language Processing (NLP) techniques to handle them [8]. The approach chosen for our auto-encoders requires that a sentence is represented as a raw array of integers, and this transformation is performed by the function **StringToIntegerArray** in Algorithm 1. In NLP, the interpretation is the following: every character of a string (the UTF-8 code of the character) is a word, and the string is a sentence.

3.3 Neural Network Structure

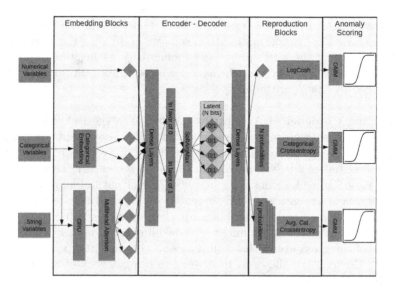

Fig. 2. Our proposed neural network structure

Given the diversity of inputs, each attribute needs to be processed differently by the auto-encoder. For the embedding part, the first layers are organized into independent blocks, one block for each input attribute. The output of each block is then horizontally concatenated before being processed by the shared layers of the encoder. Symmetrically, for the decoding part, the encoder outputs first pass through shared layers, and the last shared layer output is used as input to every reconstruction blocks.

We implemented three types of blocks (Embedding Blocks - Fig. 2), one for each type of variable (i.e., categorical, numerical or strings). For numerical values, the transformation corresponds to a one neuron layer. For categorical values, the input layer is composed of as much neurons as possible categories. The input block for strings is more complex. The structure chosen is inspired by state of the art NLP techniques: a combination of Gated Recurrent Units (GRU) neural networks [4] and multi-head self attention [25]. GRU are designed to learn long term dependencies between steps of a sequence. Attention mechanism highlights the most relevant steps inside a sequence. When combined together, they can compute pertinent low dimension representation of long sequences. However, these techniques have a high computational cost. Therefore, when the number of different strings is limited or when it is possible to find regex that reduces this number, strings should be handle as categorical variables.

3.4   Event Clustering

In the cybersecurity domain, regrouping similar events can ease the analysis process (i.e., analyzing a few groups of events instead of all events one by one). In addition to its interesting properties for anomaly detection, the auto-encoder can also provide a low dimension representation of its inputs thanks to its latent layer. This latent layer can be used for event clustering. Recent work [6] obtained good clustering performance by combining auto-encoders with Gaussian mixture model. In the case of security events, we found that the dominance of categorical variables leads to many clusters with a standard deviation close to 0, which is not an ideal case for Gaussian models (due to the division by the standard deviation in the Gaussian equation). By outputting vectors of bits (either 0 or 1), the approach we propose better fits the discrete nature of the variables found in security events (Fig. 3).

$$f(x_0, x_1) = \frac{e^{\beta x_1}}{e^{\beta x_0} + e^{\beta x_1}} \tag{1}$$

Fig. 3. Soft-ArgMax for binary variables. β controls the steepness

The latent layer is divided into 2 blocks of N components. For each of the component if the value of the first block is higher than the value of the second block, the corresponding component in the latent space will be close to 0. Otherwise, the component value in the latent space will be 1. We need to use the Soft-ArgMax function (Eq. 1) so that the output of the latent layer is either close to 0 or close to 1, while still being able to compute a gradient (required for neural networks). The output of the latent layer is therefore a vector of N bits. These N bits define a cluster identifier, that is later used to regroup the events with equal identifier (Subsect. 5.2) (Fig. 4).

3.5 Anomaly Score Computation

$$f(x, \hat{x}) = logcosh(\hat{x} - x) \quad (2) \qquad f(x, \hat{x}) = -\sum_{i}^{N} x_i * log(\hat{x}_i) \quad (3)$$

Fig. 4. Loss functions: x is the input value and $\hat{x}$ the output one. N is the total number of categories and x_i the probability of being the ith category

Per Attribute Score. Different types of variables also means different ways of computing the reproduction error. For numerical values, we use the logarithm of the hyperbolic cosine (Eq. 2). It behaves like $x^2/2$ for small value of x (i.e., fits more gradually when loss is close to 0) while behaving close to $x - ln(2)$ when x is large, which avoids giving more importance to extreme values. As output for categorical variables, the auto-encoder expresses a probability of being every possible category. As a measure of the error, we use the categorical cross entropy (Eq. 3). Similarly to categorical variables, for each character of a string, the auto-encoder outputs a probability distribution over possible characters. We use the average categorical crossentropy across every character as the error function.

Due to the diversity of attributes and types of attributes, the reproduction error for one attribute is not directly comparable with the reproduction error of another attribute. As an example, if error E_0 for attribute a_0 ranges from 0 to 1 and error E_1 for attribute a_1 ranges from 1 to 1.5, $E_0 < E_1$ is not indicative of anything. To be able to provide hindsight of what attribute might have caused the anomaly, we need to be able to compare anomaly score between attributes (Fig. 5).

$$erf(x) = \frac{2}{\sqrt{\pi}} \int_{O}^{x} e^{-t^2} dt \quad (4) \qquad CDF(x) = \frac{1 + erf\left(\frac{x-\mu}{\sigma\sqrt{2}}\right)}{2} \quad (5)$$

Fig. 5. Cumulative Distribution Function at value x for as Gaussian distribution parametrized by (μ, σ). The error function is denoted erf

During our experiments on multiple datasets and types of security events, we have found that for most attributes, a Gaussian mixture model is an appropriate approximation of the true distribution of the reproduction error on normal data. The Expectation-Maximization algorithm [5] is used to find the parameters (mean μ, standard deviation σ and probability ϕ for each Gaussian). We take the parameters (μ_0, σ_0) of the Gaussian with the highest μ (i.e., the distribution of the least normal events). The anomaly scoring function for a single attribute is defined as the Cumulative Distribution Function (CDF) of the Gaussian distribution parametrized by (μ_0, σ_0), which provide a score between 0 and 1 to each attribute of an input vector. A score close to 0 implies that the value of the attribute is considered normal, and a score close to 1 means that the value is likely anomalous.

Global Anomaly Score. At this point, we have a score between 0 and 1 for each attribute of the events. However, different types of event (e.g., network and system events) may have different number of attributes. As a simple way of providing a final anomaly score for an event, we use the metric (6), which essentially computes the frequency of anomalous attributes inside an event. (Fig. 6)

$$S = \frac{1}{n_e} \sum_{i=1}^{n_e} \begin{cases} 1, & \text{if } a_i > T_i \\ 0, & \text{if } a_i \leq T_i \end{cases} \tag{6}$$

Fig. 6. Anomaly score S for an event with n_e attributes with a score of $(a_1, a_2, ..., a_{n_e})$. $(T_1, T_2, ..., T_{n_e})$ is a threshold vector whose attribute can be configured individually

Finding Suitable Per Attribute Thresholds. In our approach, before computing the anomaly score for an event (Eq. 6), we need to determine a set of thresholds $(T_1, T_2, ..., T_{n_e})$ (with n_e the number of attributes) above which attributes will be considered abnormal. To this end, we link the cluster identifier and the threshold. For a given cluster, we compute the 99th percentile of the score for each attribute on normal data and use it as the threshold. During inference, it is possible to encounter never-before-seen cluster identifier, and in this case the threshold for each attribute will be the global average score of the attribute on normal data (i.e., independent from cluster identifier).

4   Implementation

4.1   Heterogeneous Events

The monitored system produces events by observing different layers: system layer, network layer and application layer. The observation at system layer consists in recorded system calls. These system calls can vary from an operating system to another (e.g., Linux or Windows). The system call level observation consists in executed processes and write access to files. This information is logged using the tool *auditd* for Linux. On Windows machine, we use Sysmon to log the executed commands and created files. At network layer we produce network events by inspecting network flow from OSI layer 2 (link) to Layer 5 (application level protocols). At network level, we use the Zeek tool [21] (the new name of the Bro tool). For application events, HTTP requests in the Apache HTTP server and Squid HTTP proxy logs are collected.

Formally, a logged event is an array of attributes whose values can be either a string, an integer or a float. Strings can be either handled as raw strings (e.g., a command and its arguments) or as categorical variables (e.g., the executable path), and integer as either numerical values (e.g., number of bytes) or categorical values (e.g., port number). Therefore, instead of string, integer or float, we will consider that the type of an attribute of an event can be either categorical, numerical or string. Occasionally, attributes of an event might be missing (e.g., transport error, logging failure, etc.), and in that case, the event will not be analyzed. We will denote a type of event as a set of retained attribute and their corresponding type. For example the zeek DNS log event type can be defined as $\{source.ip : categorical, destination.ip : categorical, dns.query : string, dns.answers : string\}$. We need to create one auto-encoder model per event type. The complete list of event types is given in Subsect. 4.3.

4.2   The Monitored System Architecture

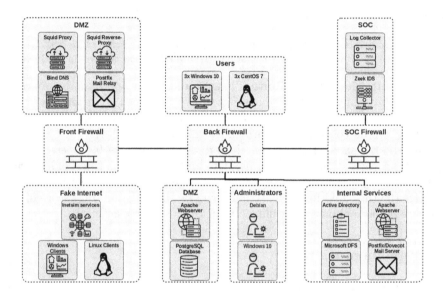

Fig. 7. Overview of the monitored system

For assessing our approach, we used virtual machines to deploy an Information System architecture reproducing the behavior of a small to medium sized company (Fig. 7). The monitored part of the system is composed of 20 machines that are distributed across 6 different VLAN separated by 3 firewalls. The Zeek IDS tool analyzes the Ethernet traffic of each of these VLAN and logs the connection and the DNS requests. Linux machines are based on CentOS 7. The Microsoft machines run on Windows Server 2016 for the servers and Windows 10 for the workstations. To simulate the activity of internal users connecting to the Internet, we use the tool InetSim to mimic a few external services (e.g., web, DNS). Multiple clients are also deployed outside the network and are browsing the company's public website. To generate the attack behaviour, we have intentionally introduced vulnerabilities inside the public website to facilitate exploitation.

4.3   Considered Event Types

There are four different sources of events that are used to monitor the security from the OS (Auditd, Sysmon), network (Zeek) and application (HTTP server and proxy logs) point of view. From each of these point of view, different aspects are considered (e.g., process and file monitoring by the OS) and require different sets of attributes, which we call event types. We organize the collected events into seven different event types and we describe them in the following list.

Auditd (Linux)

- *Executed process*: {command line: str., process working directory: cat., executable: cat., hostname: cat., effective id: cat., effective group id: cat., user id: cat., user group id: cat.}
- *Write access to files*: {hostname: cat., process working directory: cat., executable: cat., outcome: cat., syscall: cat., effective id: cat., effective group id: cat., user id: cat., group id: cat., file path: cat.}

Sysmon (Windows)

- *Executed commands*: {process args: str., process working directory: cat., executable: cat., parent executable: cat., hostname: cat., user id: cat., group id: cat.}
- *File creation*: {hostname: cat., process working directory: cat., executable: cat., file path: cat., user id: cat., group id: cat.}

Zeek

- *DNS*: {source IP: cat., destination IP: cat., dns query: str., dns answers: str.}
- *Network connection*: {source IP: cat., destination IP: cat., destination port: cat., network transport: cat., duration: num., total response bytes: num., total origin bytes: num.}

Apache and Squid Logs

- *HTTP requests*: {hostname: cat., method: cat., status_code: cat., source address: cat., url: str., user agent: str.}

5   Approach Assessment

5.1   Collecting Data

To perform the learning phase of the auto-encoders, we must collect logs corresponding to the normal activity of the monitored system. The recorded activity is composed of users of the company regularly browsing both the internal and the public website of the company (available from the external network). They also exchange emails inside and outside the company. Users create, edit and delete documents and share some of these documents with other users through the company's shared directories. Additionally, administrators regularly perform actions (e.g., configuration changes). Finally, multiple clients from the simulated Internet zone browse the public server. User and client actions have been automated using tools that directly manipulate the user interface so that they effectively generate events that can be seen in system logs. The administrative tasks have been performed manually.

Training Dataset. The generated dataset is composed of 8 738 080 normal events and correspond to a month of activity. 1 017 682 (11.6%) are generated by auditd, 29 992 (0.3%) by Sysmon, 7 013 337 (80.3%) by Zeek and 677 069 (7.7%) are HTTP requets. As these different types of events have different attributes, a model has to be learnt for each of these types, thus, we separate the dataset in 7 sub-datasets. Each of these sub-datasets is randomly divided in 3 parts. 60% of the data is used for training the model. 20% to periodically evaluate the performances of the model on unknown data and stop the training once the performances degrade (early stopping), which help combat over-fitting and reduce the number of false positives. The remaining 20% are used to adapt the different parameters (Sect. 3.5) and finalize the model on never-before-seen data. This separation in three sub-datasets is common for neural network training. We train one model for each of the 7 event types.

Attack dataset. During a business day, the following attack is performed:

1. The attacker crawls the public web server of the company in order to find a potential vulnerability;
2. He exploits a vulnerability on the public web server of the company;
3. Then, he can modify a page restricted to the moderators of the web site;
4. A moderator visits the page from inside the company network, CVE-2018-8495 is exploited and the user unwisely accepts the execution of the script;
5. The script deploys a remote access trojan on the machine and contacts the command and control server;
6. The attacker stealthily scans a few hosts and finds the file server;
7. A file is downloaded from the file server and uploaded to the attacker's server;
8. The attacker erases its tracks and leaves the company's network.

The resulting dataset contains 298 302 events with both normal and abnormal activities. In total, around 1500 events are related to the attack (0.5%).

5.2   Assessing Clustering Capabilities

The proposed auto-encoder provides a cluster identifier for each event. We can use this identifier to regroup events together to lower the total number of alerts an analyst has to investigate. On the attack dataset, we obtain a total of 191 different cluster identifiers. By design, the auto-encoder tends to project unknown data points closer to normal points in the latent space. Therefore, a normal event and an anomaly can share the same cluster identifier. To avoid mixing normal and anomalous events inside a group, events are regrouped if they have the same cluster identifier as well as the same anomaly score (Eq. 6). With these conditions, we regroup the 298 302 events of our attack dataset into 293 groups.

In a typical IT system, a significant change to the system (e.g., new user) can lead to repeated and similar false positives. Inside our attack dataset, we identified approximately 10500 of these false positives and they are regrouped into 84 different clusters (125 events per cluster on average). For our attack scenario, we identified 1500 events related to the attack, and they are regrouped into 28 different clusters (54 events per cluster on average). This confirms that the chosen clustering approach helps reduce the number of false positives to be analyzed without diluting relevant attack information inside large clusters.

5.3   Anomaly Detection Results

The size reduction, detailed in the previous section, allowed us to manually annotate the dataset and we found that the original 0.5% of anomaly in the attack dataset are now distributed in 28 groups (9.56%). From there we can compute metrics relative to the performance of our approach (Fig. 8).

$$P = \frac{TP}{FP + TP} \quad (7) \qquad R = \frac{TP}{FN + TP} \quad (8) \qquad F_1 = 2 \times \frac{P \times R}{P + R} \quad (9)$$

Fig. 8. Precision (P), Recall (R) and F_1 score

Due to the imbalance in class distribution (only 9.56% of positives), we chose to use precision (7) that correspond to the ratio of true positives among all the events classified as anomalies, the recall (8), also known as the true positive rate, and F_1 score (9) metrics, which is the harmonic mean of the recall and the precision. For all these metrics, a value of 1 implies a perfect classifier, and a value of 0 a useless one. In a context of a prioritisation tool, analysts will define a maximum number of alerts that they can handle in a day. For this reason, we provide the recall (i.e., proportion of anomalies accurately identified) when considering the top 100, 50 and 10 groups (with regard to their anomaly score). We provide the results in Table 1. We also found a false positive rate of 0.12% on normal data with the threshold set as the minimum score of attack related events (i.e., 100% true positive rate).

Table 1. F_1 score, precision and recall for the top 10, 50 and 100

Top N groups	F_1	Precision	Recall
10	0.162	0.333	0.107
50	**0.5**	0.342	0.929
100	0.44	0.28	1

More specifically, from a threat hunter perspective, analyzing the top 10 groups of events would be enough to determine that arbitrary code have been executed on the web server and on the infected Windows machine. Analyzing the top 50 events is enough to reconstruct the major steps of the attack and identify the attacker IP address as an Indicator of Compromise (IoC).

6 Conclusion

In this paper, we proposed a method that relies on neural networks auto-encoders to compute anomaly scores for heterogeneous events prioritisation. We propose an original approach to exploit the latent space of the auto-encoders to provide clustering capabilities. This is used to reduce the volume of information that is presented to the analysts by regrouping similar events together.

We drew inspiration from state-of-the-art deep learning techniques to handle the most common attribute types found inside security events (numerical, categorical and string attributes). These techniques simplify the design of the feature extraction and transformation processes that are required by any machine learning-based approach. This allowed us to quickly create a specific model for each event types inside our dataset. While other machine learning methods for anomaly detection have already been proposed, they need specific feature engineering for each new type of events, which requires knowledge in data science that is rarely available among Security Operation Center (SOC) analysts.

Using our method, we regrouped the 298 302 events of our test dataset in 293 groups. When manually analyzing these groups, we found all the attack-related events within the 100 groups with the highest anomaly scores.

The ability to prioritize heterogeneous events is the first step towards behavioural anomaly-based attack detection tools for SOC. Future work will focus on anomaly contextualisation using automated correlation techniques, as well as visualization techniques to further simplify the investigation process for analysts.

References

1. Akoglu, L., Tong, H., Vreeken, J., Faloutsos, C.: Fast and reliable anomaly detection in categorical data. In: Proceedings of the 21st ACM international conference on Information and Knowledge Management, pp. 415–424. ACM (2012)
2. Bellman, R.E., Dreyfus, S.E.: Applied Dynamic Programming. Princeton University Press, Princeton (2015)
3. Breunig, M.M., Kriegel, H.P., Ng, R.T., Sander, J.: Lof: identifying density-based local outliers. In: Proceedings of the 2000 ACM SIGMOD International Conference on Management of Data, pp. 93–104 (2000)
4. Cho, K., et al.: Learning phrase representations using RNN encoder-decoder for statistical machine translation. arXiv preprint arXiv:1406.1078 (2014)
5. Dempster, A.P., Laird, N.M., Rubin, D.B.: Maximum likelihood from incomplete data via the EM algorithm. J. Roy. Stat. Soc.: Ser. B (Methodol.) 39(1), 1–22 (1977)
6. Dilokthanakul, N., et al.: Deep unsupervised clustering with Gaussian mixture variational autoencoders. arXiv preprint arXiv:1611.02648 (2016)
7. Ding, Z., Fei, M.: An anomaly detection approach based on isolation forest algorithm for streaming data using sliding window. IFAC Proc. Volumes 46(20), 12–17 (2013)

8. Du, M., Li, F., Zheng, G., Srikumar, V.: Deeplog: anomaly detection and diagnosis from system logs through deep learning. In: Proceedings of the 2017 ACM SIGSAC Conference on Computer and Communications Security, pp. 1285–1298. ACM (2017)

9. Ester, M., Kriegel, H.P., Sander, J., Xu, X., et al.: A density-based algorithm for discovering clusters in large spatial databases with noise. Kdd **96**, 226–231 (1996)

10. Hawkins, S., He, H., Williams, G., Baxter, R.: Outlier detection using replicator neural networks. In: Kambayashi, Y., Winiwarter, W., Arikawa, M. (eds.) DaWaK 2002. LNCS, vol. 2454, pp. 170–180. Springer, Heidelberg (2002). https://doi.org/10.1007/3-540-46145-0_17

11. He, Z., Xu, X., Huang, J.Z., Deng, S.: A frequent pattern discovery method for outlier detection. In: Li, Q., Wang, G., Feng, L. (eds.) WAIM 2004. LNCS, vol. 3129, pp. 726–732. Springer, Heidelberg (2004). https://doi.org/10.1007/978-3-540-27772-9_80

12. Kaastra, I., Boyd, M.: Designing a neural network for forecasting financial and economic time series. Neurocomputing **10**(3), 215–236 (1996)

13. Kriegel, H.P., S hubert, M., Zimek, A.: Angle-based outlier detection in high-dimensional data. In: Proceeding of the 14th ACM SIGKDD International Conference on Knowledge Discovery and Data Mining - KDD 08, p. 444. ACM Press (2008). https://doi.org/10.1145/1401890.1401946

14. Lanoe, D., Hurfin, M., Totel, E.: A scalable and efficient correlation engine to detect multi-step attacks in distributed systems. In: 2018 IEEE 37th Symposium on Reliable Distributed Systems (SRDS), pp. 31–40, October 2018. https://doi.org/10.1109/SRDS.2018.00014

15. Liu, F.T., Ting, K.M., Zhou, Z.H.: Isolation forest. In: 2008 Eighth IEEE International Conference on Data Mining, pp. 413–422. IEEE (2008)

16. Liu, F., Wen, Y., Zhang, D., Jiang, X., Xing, X., Meng, D.: Log2vec: a heterogeneous graph embedding based approach for detecting cyber threats within enterprise. In: Proceedings of the 2019 ACM SIGSAC Conference on Computer and Communications Security, pp. 1777–1794 (2019)

17. Mikolov, T., Chen, K., Corrado, G.S., Dean, J.: Efficient estimation of word representations in vector space. CoRR abs/1301.3781 (2013)

18. Mirsky, Y., Doitshman, T., Elovici, Y., Shabtai, A.: Kitsune: an ensemble of autoencoders for online network intrusion detection. arXiv preprint arXiv:1802.09089 (2018)

19. Pang, G., Ting, K.M., Albrecht, D.: Lesinn: detecting anomalies by identifying least similar nearest neighbours. In: 2015 IEEE International Conference on Data Mining Workshop (ICDMW), pp. 623–630. IEEE, November 2015. https://doi.org/10.1109/ICDMW.2015.62

20. Pascoal, C., De Oliveira, M.R., Valadas, R., Filzmoser, P., Salvador, P., Pacheco, A.: Robust feature selection and robust pca for internet traffic anomaly detection. In: 2012 Proceedings IEEE Infocom, pp. 1755–1763. IEEE (2012)

21. Paxson, V.: Bro: a system for detecting network intruders in real-time. Comput. Netw. **31**(23–24), 2435–2463 (1999)

22. Pearl, J.: Probabilistic Reasoning in Intelligent Systems: Networks of Plausible Inference. Elsevier, Amsterdam (2014)

23. Schölkopf, B., Williamson, R.C., Smola, A.J., Shawe-Taylor, J., Platt, J.C.: Support vector method for novelty detection. In: Advances in Neural Information Processing Systems, pp. 582–588 (2000)

24. Shen, Y., Stringhini, G.: Attack2vec: leveraging temporal word embeddings to understand the evolution of cyberattacks. In: 28th {USENIX} Security Symposium Security 2019, pp. 905–921 (2019)
25. Vaswani, A., et al.: Attention is all you need. In: Advances in Neural Information Processing Systems, pp. 5998–6008 (2017)
26. Veeramachaneni, K., Arnaldo, I., Korrapati, V., Bassias, C., Li, K.: Aî 2: training a big data machine to defend. In: 2016 IEEE 2nd International Conference on Big Data Security on Cloud (BigDataSecurity), IEEE International Conference on High Performance and Smart Computing (HPSC), and IEEE International Conference on Intelligent Data and Security (IDS), pp. 49–54. IEEE (2016)
27. Wong, W.K., Moore, A.W., Cooper, G.F., Wagner, M.M.: Bayesian network anomaly pattern detection for disease outbreaks. In: Proceedings of the 20th International Conference on Machine Learning (ICML-03), pp. 808–815 (2003)
28. Zhou, C., Paffenroth, R.C.: Anomaly detection with robust deep autoencoders. In: Proceedings of the 23rd ACM SIGKDD International Conference on Knowledge Discovery and Data Mining, pp. 665–674. ACM (2017)

Community Knowledge About Security:
Identification and Classification of User Contributions

Fabien Patrick Viertel[(✉)], Wasja Brunotte, Yannick Evers, and Kurt Schneider

Software Engineering Group, Leibniz Universität Hannover, Hanover, Germany
{fabien.viertel,wasja.brunotte,kurt.schneider}@inf.uni-hannover.de,
yevers@posteo.de

Abstract. Nowadays, confidential data of users and companies are processed by various software applications. Therefore, it is necessary to protect them against security flaws in source code, which could, for example, allow the infringement of privacy. However, developers are usually not equipped with the required expertise to fulfill this task.

To their rescue, there are tools like security code clone detectors to disclose vulnerable methods in source code. They try to find clones of written project code and vulnerable code fragments stored in a reference repository. Existing vulnerability databases, for instance the National Vulnerability Database (NVD), contain data on reported weaknesses, but the availability of example code for their occurrence, patch and exploit is scarce. Developers also use community websites to find help for secure implementations.

In this paper, we propose a semi-automated process to extract security-related code from the Stack Exchange community network, where also the coding community Stack Overflow belongs. We classify the obtained code through artificial intelligence combined with natural language processing into the three security types: vulnerable, patch or exploit. In a twofold evaluation, we compared both parts with the manual activity of security experts. At first, for the search, our approach shows better precision than the experts as well as a moderate recall. Secondly, the results show that the classification of code fragments in security types is not quite easy. The investigated approaches and security experts perform with different strength regarding types of security.

Keywords: Source code · Security · Clone detection · Community knowledge · Artificial intelligence

1 Introduction

Current software applications process a lot of confidential data from users and companies. The infringement of privacy through recent occurring data breaches, enabled by security flaws in source code, increases the importance of secure software. Unfortunately, the security background of developers is deficient [1]. This requires to support when developing secure software. Publicly accessible vulnerability databases like the National Vulnerability Database (NVD)[1] fill these

---

[1] National Vulnerability Database Link: https://nvd.nist.gov/ (01.2020).

© Springer Nature Switzerland AG 2021
J. Garcia-Alfaro et al. (Eds.): CRiSIS 2020, LNCS 12528, pp. 181–197, 2021.
https://doi.org/10.1007/978-3-030-68887-5_11

knowledge gaps. It consists of textual descriptions on reported vulnerabilities. The manual search for required security information to identify vulnerabilities in source code fragments of software projects is a time-consuming and inconvenient task. Developers have to manually check the whole project code for containing software artifacts like imported libraries, classes and concrete methods. However, with a search engine their names can be used to uncover insecurities among them.

For developers' support, tools like Security Code Clone Detectors highlight potential vulnerabilities in source code [14]. Depending on the predefined scope they recognize code clones between multiple methods, classes or files based on their similarity. For disclosing insecure fragments, reference code is needed which depicts the occurrence of vulnerabilities in source code. To find multiple security flaws, references of vulnerable code can be stored in a repository.

Unfortunately, the availability of all types of security-related code is scarce. Some of the NVD entries provide links referring to other reports or repositories that contain partially source code examples for the vulnerability, its patch, or exploit. However, security issues also will be discussed within coding communities, for example Stack Overflow, which is a website of the Stack Exchange community network. Some of the user-posts on these websites provide security-related code fragments and count therefore as a reference for developers to receive feedback for developing secure software. Source code examples of the three types of security content might be helpful to understand how a vulnerability occurs, how it can be patched and which aspects invoke the vulnerability by viewing the code of potential attacks. It is a challenging task to create such a code repository including only security-related code fragments. The terms used in coding communities to identify security-related content are not trivial. Furthermore, the writing style to identify the security-related content differs between posts and communities, which complicates the finding of security-related content in a specific community. This led us to the following research questions (RQ):

- **RQ1: Can we semi-automatically extract security knowledge from code communities?**
  By means of this RQ, we manually analyze the content of Stack Exchange to find indicators referring to security-related knowledge contained within its user posts to automatically extract this information.
- **RQ2: Could artificial intelligence approaches be leveraged in order to classify code fragments into vulnerabilities, patches, and exploits semi-automatically?**
  Within this RQ, we evaluate and compare a set of different machine learning approaches combined with natural language processing for the classification of texts. We investigate their capability to distinguish between the types of security content, described within user contributions on Stack Exchange.

In this work, we analyzed whether it is possible to semi-automatically extract source code of communities like Stack Overflow to create a code repository of the mentioned security code types. Security experts will quickly be overwhelmed by the time-consuming task of examining all the discussions within these communities for their security relevance. Furthermore, it is not trivial to distinguish whether a code snippet represents a vulnerability, a patch or an exploit. To solve this problem, we have developed an approach to semi-automatically export security relevant discussions, categorize them into these three types and extract their containing code snippets into a repository. Our contributions are as follows:

- A process for creating a *security code repository* that is accessible for the security code clone detection, which consisting of code fragments separated into the three named security types: vulnerability, patch and exploit (Sect. 4).
- A summary of *text classification approaches* including artificial intelligence and innovative techniques to distinguish between the types of security content (Sect. 5).
- An evaluation of these different techniques in comparison with the performance of security experts when performing this tasks (Sect. 6).

The importance of *software security knowledge* already have been realized. Stack Overflow has also been used in the past to gain further knowledge for software development. However, previous work does not consider existing source code for creating a security code repository grouped in vulnerable, patched and exploit code fragments to support developers and to enable code clone detection with the goal to detect vulnerabilities. We discussed related work in Sect. 2.

2   Related Work

Software security is the science of implementing software to continuously provide its service even under malicious attacks. It is about security knowledge of common threats and using this knowledge continuously over the software development lifestyle [6]. Previous research already considers the systematical organization and management of software security knowledge. Barnum and McGraw [2] introduces a model representing seven concepts and its relations of software security knowledge. They identified attack pattern, vulnerability, guideline, historical risk, rule, principals and exploit as knowledge elements for their model. In our work, we focusing on vulnerabilities, patches and exploits, which are somehow considered in these models. We achieved security knowledge represented as code fragments and texts from past user contributions on Stack Exchange.

Much of the work focuses on Stack Overflow for extracting source code or related data. Wong et al. [15] introduced a procedure to enhance source code fragments with comments by the text of Stack Overflow posts. They used code clone detection to find clones between the source code of a project and posted on this platform. Whenever a code clone is found, they extract and add a comment out of the related text of the post. Security was not considered for their approach.

There are approaches for analyzing texts and dividing them into different types. Cicero and Maira [3] use deep convolutional neural networks for a sentiment analysis for short texts such as single sentences and twitter messages. As a result of their approach, texts are classified according to whether they are positive or negative. They estimate this task as difficult due to the limited contextual information they usually contain. For training their network, the Stanford Twitter Sentiment Corpus consists of Twitter messages and the Stanford Sentiment Tree-bank containing sentences of movie reviews is used.

In comparison to our approach, the named related works do not consider security at all. Furthermore, from our literature review and our own related knowledge, there is no work that recognizes the distinction of security-related content into vulnerable, patch or exploit information.

Yang et al. [16] analyzed security questions on Stack Overflow to highlight the popularity and difficulty of different topics. They used tags that could be set on this question and answer platform to identify security-related questions. Latent Dirichlet Allocation tuned with Generic Algorithm to cluster meta data was used for their analysis. Thus, they identified that the questions cover a wide range of security topics. Mainly they belong to the five categories: web security, mobile security, cryptography, software security and system security. In contrast to our work, they do not distinct between the three mentioned types of security content. Furthermore, they do not consider answers of Stack Overflow posts.

3   Background

The Stack Exchange question and answer network, consists of about 130 web pages, for example, Stack Overflow, Super User, Information Security and Server Fault. Each main post is a description of a problem, a question or a statement for a discussion. They can be answered by several contributions that could be rated by community members. For every question, single to multiple tags can be assigned, for example, to identify whether a post treats issues for concrete programming languages or even security-related content. The tags for programming languages are useful, but in contrast, the security tag is often not set.

3.1   Data, Information and Knowledge

In the literature there is a disagreement about the definition and relation of the terms *data, information* and *knowledge* [12]. This inconsistency makes its definition important. We agree to the definition of Spek and Spijkervet [11]:

- **Data.** Not yet interpreted symbols.
- **Information.** Data assigned with a meaning.
- **Knowledge.** The ability to assign meaning.

Each content of posts is data, which can be interpreted by contributions of community members with natural language texts to form information that expresses community knowledge. In the case of security, we define *Community Knowledge about Security* as the ability to categorize concrete content as vulnerable, patch or exploit.

3.2   Security Related Information

Within code communities, we can differentiate between two kinds of content: source code and text within natural language. On Stack Overflow the first is primarily represented within code fragments that are usually placed within dedicated areas. In the latter case, texts on this page are generally the major part of the posts. These texts are, for example, the description of a concrete concern of the questioner or responses to it. Within these texts, security-related terms could be mentioned that indicate some security affiliation of the post content.

For this work, we make a distinction between three security types respectively code types. These types are vulnerability, patch and exploit, defined as follows.

- **Vulnerability.** Within the Common Vulnerabilities and Exposures (CVE)[2] database, it is defined as follows: "A 'vulnerability' is a weakness in the computational logic (e.g., code) found in software and some hardware components (e.g., firmware) that, when exploited, results in a negative impact to confidentiality, integrity, OR availability...". When relating this to our classification, a vulnerable post contains source code fragments with - at least - a weakness or names a program such as a software library being vulnerable.
- **Patch.** It removes a potential vulnerability so that it cannot be exploited anymore. A post is classified as a patch if it contains at least one code fragment that removes a potential security flaw or it describes the steps to apply for dealing with it.
- **Exploit.** An exploit can maliciously uses a vulnerability to invoke a negative impact to confidentiality, integrity, or availability of a software system. A post should be classified as exploit if it consists of source code that take advantage of a vulnerability or it describes an attack strategy on how to exploit a concrete security flaw.

4   Approach

Our process for creating a security code repository relies on programming community websites on which such code snippets can be found. To this end, we used Stack Exchange, a well-known question and answer platform for developers that is freely accessible to the public. In the context of this work, the security code repository consists of community knowledge represented by security-related source code fragments. These fragments are example code of vulnerabilities, their exploits or patches. The process for creating this repository is shown in Fig. 1, and contains the steps *Extract, Search & Filter, Classify & Export,* and *Verify.*

Extract. To find security-related code snippets on the Stack Exchange network, adequate terms for the search are needed. One possible step to identify a concrete vulnerability might be its unique CVE identifier (ID), which identifies a concrete product-specific vulnerability stored in the NVD. Using CVE-IDs in the search for security-related content on this platform is insufficient, simply

---

[2] Common Vulnerabilities and Exposures: https://cve.mitre.org/about/ (01.2020).

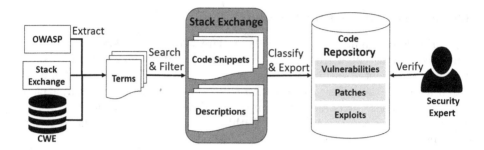

Fig. 1. Approach overview.

because of their absence. Unfortunately, the community almost never mentions concrete CVE-IDs in their contributions. More often they name types of the vulnerabilities. The Common Weakness and Exposure (CWE) add types of vulnerabilities to a list. To obtain suitable terms for the search on Stack Exchange, we manually inspect the CWE-types. To find more valid search terms, we also check the most infamous weaknesses within the internet applications listed by the Open Web Application Security Project (OWASP) top 10[3].

The manual search on Stack Overflow using general terms like security, delivered more security-related terms extracted from posts found this way. Among others, we figured out that the search for attack strategies like Cross-site scripting (XSS) is expedient. The non-enclosed set of search-terms are listed as follows:

– Terms: attack, security weakness, "prone to", vulnerable, security bug, weak security, XSS, insecure hash, sql injection, session fixation, shell injection, exposing sessionid, command injection, "remote code execution", injection attack, weak password hash, cross site scripting, "deserialization attack", request forgery, man in the middle attack, insecure encryption, reflection attack, veracode, CWE.

Search and Filter. For searching security-related posts on Stack Exchange, the pre-extracted terms will be used. To adjust the results of the search to specific programming languages, we defined a filter. Within this work, we exemplary focus on a repository containing Java code fragments to limit the number of results. Therefore, we filtered for Java code within the posts. At first, we checked the tags of posts to find if any of them are set to Java; secondly, we check whether common Java keywords appear in code fragments within posts. For further processing, all resulting code fragments are stored in a file for each post.

Classify. We analyze different text-classification approaches to semi-automatically categorize the results of search in the three classes of security-related content: vulnerabilities, patches and exploits. In this work, we define and restrict these classes according to their occurrence in posts within Sect. 3.

---

[3] OWASP Link: https://www.owasp.org/index.php/Top_10-2017_Top_10 (01.2020).

For the classification of code fragments, its textual description inside of the Stack Exchange posts is used. The investigated text-classification approaches are described in Sect. 5.

Export. The classified findings are stored into a code repository with a SQLite database inside of its root. For all matches its related meta-information provided by Stack Exchange posts is saved. This information is composed of links to the posts, descriptions, consisting security-related terms and - if found - a correlating CVE-ID. Included terms are a subset of previously listed ones that we defined for the search on Stack Exchange.

Verify. As post-processing, the repository content has to be reviewed for excluding code fragments that do not contribute to a vulnerability, patch or exploit but are downloaded and stored like that. For example, if a code fragment on Stack Exchange with at least one weakness in it is found, it often does not mean the whole source code within code blocks is vulnerable. A security expert has to delete the unaffected code parts in these snippets so that only the critical code remains. Furthermore, in the case of wrongly classified findings, they have to assign the right security type. Otherwise, developers using the repository may have difficulties recognizing the vulnerability in code fragments. Also code clone detectors using the repository would mark secure code as potentially vulnerable. The effort of the manual verification of results depends on the number of found code fragments, that are security-related, their correct extraction and classification, which could be derived from the evaluation done in this work. For each extracted and classified code fragment, it must be verified whether all code parts belong to the assigned type. We also have reviewed the resulting security flaws to check their suitability for representing a vulnerable code fragment. For example, non-eligible vulnerabilities can be patched only by importing a more recent library version or by loading them dynamically by a string literal. Code fragments for which weaknesses are spread over multiple methods were partially also ignored. The reason for this is that in the most cases code changes were too small to detect code clones meaningfully by the clone detection. The elements do not apply have to be removed, which takes on Median 36 s.

5 Classification

One subtask to create a valid security code repository is to find security-related content. The results have to be classified into types of security content to be able to differentiate between them. Especially, for the security code clone detection, it is important to distinguish between vulnerabilities, patches and exploits within its reference code repository. Otherwise, the vulnerability detection would detect secure patched code fragments as being vulnerable.

We identified dependencies indicating the security type among the main post, also named question, with its answers. This is attributed to the fact that answers usually appear on the original post. An example is that the questioner sometimes posts vulnerable code and asks the community about the security of it. More often, questioners do not have security in mind and will be pointed to a containing vulnerability inside of posted source code by answers of the community. Therefore, questions will be grouped with each of its answers into pairs for their classification in security types. We created tuples, whose formal definition is as follows: $< Question, Answer_n >, n \in \mathbb{N}$

The n is an index representing a concrete answer responding to a question, where n can be a number from one to the total amount of answers to that question. The problem is, that stack exchange tuples sometimes cannot be assigned to just a single type because they contain data of multiple types. For example, this can be happen if a questioner adds insecure code to a question which is answered by a post identifying the code fragment contained as vulnerable and referencing on securely patched code. In this case, the tuple would be classified as containing vulnerable and patched information, for example source code. In these situations, usually manual rework is required.

We investigated procedures to semi-automatically classify findings on the Stack Exchange platform in the types of security-related content mentioned. The focus is on their ability to distinguish between these three classes. In the following, the approaches will be described briefly.

Keyword-Based. The Keyword-based classifier assigns the class affiliation of a post via leveraging keywords that signalizing the type of security-related content. If a post with its answers includes terms representing the named classes, then it will be automatically assigned to the corresponding class. We obtained these terms by the manual analysis of random findings obtained by the search on Stack Overflow described in Sect. 4. Table 1 shows the keywords and regular expressions assigned to their classes.

Table 1. Terms of the keyword classifier.

Class	Terms
Vulnerability	Vulnerable, issue, you shouldn't, you should not, side note, dangerous, do not use, risk, wrong way, not advised, cause of vulnerability, not safe, is unsafe, vulnerabilit(y | ies), you should (read|inform), is sensitive to, awful, you are not, less vulnerable
Patch	Add this, safer, better, suggest, instead use, instead of, fix, you should (?! not | read | inform), you can use, you also should, less vulnerable, resolve, prevent, right way, patching, better is to, you may (?! not), (?<!(n't) | (not) | nw) use
Exploit	Exploit, (someone | somebody | attacker | user) (could | can), (illustration of | that is | that's) why, demonstrate

Naive Bayes with Bag of Words. A frequently used procedure for text classification is the Naive Bayes classifier [9]. A Bayes classifier relies on the Bayes' theorem. For the Bayes' theorem, the naive assumption is that the probability of every element is independent of the occurrence of other elements within classifiable ones. In our example, this means, that the likelihood of occurrence of a word A is always independent of the presence of a word B. Unfortunately, we see that this assumption is not always true. If the word *security* occurs, then the word *vulnerability* will appear more likely. Nevertheless, the classifier usually produces suitable results despite of this naive assumption.

A well-known model used in *Natural Language Processing (NLP)* to transform text into suitable properties is the so-called *Bag of Words*. The idea is to transform each text before the classification into an unordered set consisting of each word assigned with its number of occurrence. Usually, each word of the training set is placed in such a set, and its occurrence is counted for the texts to be classified. The disadvantage of this NLP procedure is that the order of words is not considered, which has an impact on the semantics of a sentence.

To distinguish between the three classes vulnerable, patch and exploit, a classifier for every class was trained based on data representing these individual classes. Before its training, a pre-processing of the training data is necessary to remove non-alphabetic signs so that only letters remain inside of texts.

Naive Bayes with N-grams. To consider information about the order of words, the naive Bayes classifier could be enriched by *N-grams*. Words will now be grouped to a size of N. The higher N is chosen, the more context information will be considered. The problem is that the word combinations with increasing N occur more and more rarely, which makes them less informative. As an example, we investigated the number of N-grams that performs well for our approach. We identified a number of two and three as a valid value for N.

Support Vector Machines. A further supervised machine learning approach is the SVM [10]. Every object that has to be classified could be represented as a vector in an n-dimensional space. A vector could be represented as the pre-named Bag of Words model included with N-grams. To improve the validity of vectors, frequent words without any special meaning will be removed as so-called stopwords. These are, for example, articles and conjunctions. Furthermore, words with the same semantic will be merged. This procedure is called stemming. Afterward, rarely-occurring words will be removed, so that vectors reduce their size to a fixed amount of elements. We identified 500 attributes as a valid threshold by examining applied classifications with different sizes.

Neural Network with Word2Vec. To consider the word order of sentences, it is possible to use *Recurrent Neural Networks (RNN)* [13]. It has a kind of memory of previously processed data. In this case, the input is single words, which will be added to classify a whole text up to its last word. After each word of a text has been processed, the final output is used for its classification.

Mikolov et al. [7,8] of Google introduced an approach called *Word2Vec* to transform each word into a vector consisting of descriptive attributes. For each word, a vector in an n-dimensional space is created. Similar terms have a smaller distance to each other and thereby also its relations are represented. For our text classification, Word2Vec determines the number of neurons for the input layer of the NN by the size of its generated vector.

For the valid training of such a Word2Vec model, much domain-specific text for the classification is required. The algorithm considers each word as well as its surrounding words and its ordering. Thereby, Word2Vec uses a further NN internally, which is described in detail within the pre-cited work. A pre-trained general valid NN for Word2Vec could be used, with the one disadvantage that domain-specific vocabulary is usually not included and could not be considered for the classification. Alternatively, the training could be applied to specific texts, which suitably represent a concrete domain. Within such a network, also domain-specific vocabulary could be considered within later classifications. We consider two types of NNs that differ regarding the Word2Vec. One is a pre-trained network on Google News contributions delivered by Google. The second is a self-trained network based on security-related posts found on Stack Overflow.

ULMFiT. A new training procedure for a NN is the Universal Language Model Fine-tuning for Text Classification (ULMFiT) by Howard and Ruder [4]. They classified movie reviews of the Internet Movie Database (IMDb) within the classes of positive or negative reviews. Similar to Word2Vec, a language model is trained on Wikipedia texts. In their approach, they consider a further step to enrich the trained language model with domain specific information. After this adaption, the NN still remembers on the pre-learned general language knowledge but will be enhanced by the information of a few available domain-specific texts. The authors mention that in this approach, fewer training data are required for getting suitable results for the text classification. For our work, we adapted the approach regarding the domain specific language model. We exchanged the IMDb domain-specific language model with a model trained on Stack Overflow.

6   Evaluation

We evaluated the suitability of our approach including text classification algorithms to address our research questions. The evaluation is divided into two parts: Firstly, we examine the amount of found results and their relevance. The second deals with the classification of the search results. For both parts we compared the approaches with the manual work of 10 security experts. They belong to the groups of professionals, researchers and graduate students. Practitioners work in an area related to software development or security. All participants had to deal with a security-related topic for six months or a semester, at least. We considered the work with the NVD, cryptography or other security-related topics. Furthermore, the taking of courses in which these security topics will be taught enable it to be a participant for the conducted experiment. Eight of the participants have already worked with CVE-IDs and all of them with Stack Overflow before. Their security expertise varies from six months to 18 years to receive input from different experiences, listed in the following tuples [$years : persons$] within (0.5:1, 1:4, 2–4:4, 18:1).

6.1   RQ1: Can We Semi-automatically Extract Security Knowledge from Code Communities?

Test Setup for the Search. Our tool-based evaluation consists of three iterations (I_n). Each iteration is performed with different settings. The search was limited to the Java programming language in all iterations. **1. Iteration.** All the search terms are used and no filter is applied. Hereby, as many results as possible are found. The tag is set to Java. **2. Iteration.** Very general search terms are excluded as well as negative-rated answers. Limiting attached source code to the Java programming language is done by a Java-filter instead of filtering by tag. Thus, results with missing Java tag are also found. Additionally, results that do not contain code are eliminated by a filter. The goal is to find less irrelevant results. **3. Iteration.** As far as possible, only relevant results should be found during this iteration. General search terms will be excluded, only specific ones are used. If the search terms are only included in the source code, an additional filter ignores these founds. Instead of the Java filter, again the tag is used.

We used *precision* (P) and *recall* (R) to measure the quality of the search results as described by Manning et al. [5]. The weighting of precision and recall can be adjusted by the selection of search terms, tags and filters. Ideally precision and recall are both 100%. Although a high recall usually harms the precision. A recall of 100% indicates that every security-related post could be found. A leak in precision invokes a miss-classification of results. This means that found posts that do not contain any security-relevant topics are recognized as such.

The recall has been very difficult to measure since it requires knowledge of all posts on Stack Exchange that are relevant for the search. Manually inspecting all posts is not possible in practice because of the large number. In response, we compared the search results from the software with the results of the 10 security experts. To limit the time for the search we used the highest time frame the software needed for searching and storing the security information as an upper boundary. The result was 17 min. Afterward, we measured how many relevant posts were found by the security experts within 17 min.

The search was also limited to Stack Overflow. Within this period, the security experts have found a total of 235 results of which we manually identified 95 as security-related. These 95 results provide the basis for our relative recall and correspond to 100%. Thus, the recall for the different iterations is calculated by inspecting how many of the 95 results that were found by the security experts were found during each pass by the tool.

The software returns a large number of results in each iteration (Sect. 6.1). To calculate the precision, it is too time-consuming to check all these results by hand. Thus, we selected 100 random results from each pass.

Analysis of Search Results. The results for the search are summarized in Table 2. Precision and Recall are stated as percentage values. The high value for the elapsed time in iteration 2 can be explained by the fact of the missing Java tag constraint. A lot of posts of other programming languages were downloaded.

Table 2. Search results.

	Security Experts	I_1	I_2	I_3
Elapsed Time [min]	17	7.5	16.5	3.5
Results (Avg/Med)	235 (23,5/20)	7929	4830	3151
True Positives	95	51	68	78
False Positives	140	49	32	22
P Avg(Med) [%]	76 (78)	51	68	78
R [%]	100	53	37	27

and had to be rejected later by the programming language filter. As expected, the amount of results found by the software is much higher than what was found by the security experts. The stronger search constraints that were used in the second and third iteration caused a decrease of the values for results and recall. The precision increased simultaneously. At the first pass, a recall of 53% was calculated, i.e., the software also found about half what was found by the security experts. Assuming that some of the results of the software would not have been found by the security expert may lead to the hypothesis that the recall is might be coequal. To prove that, we had to restrict the task in searching, which would prevent the observation of the natural use of the search on Stack Overflow.

The precision increases with stronger search constraints. In the third iteration, a precision value of 78% is reached. This value comes close to the precision reached by the security expert. Thus, a precision of 78% is probably high enough for most uses, especially since it yields into more findings with a value of 3151. Besides, we prefer a higher precision than a higher recall since we want to get fewer irrelevant results than the mere quantity. Regarding the recall, the software is inferior to humans, but this is maybe attributable to the design decision of evaluation. The security experts always have a perfect recall, because they define the reference for the software. Considering precision, the software is superior to security experts. However, by optimizing of precision only, the software exceeds the precision of the subjects. Furthermore, a more notable amount of data is collected by the software in comparison to the experts during the same time span. Each single security expert found on average 23,5 security-related posts.

Results and Discussion. We manually checked the obtained security-related source code fragments for their security types to get a better understanding of them and to create a set for training and testing the classifiers. We selected the code fragments out of the run of Iteration 2 because of their higher amount of security-related results by keeping a moderate precision. Figure 2 visualizes the distribution of the different security types from 200 randomly picked posts. The majority of information is from type of vulnerability followed by patch. In many cases, a result contains both security types, vulnerability and patch. That is because a possible fix is recommended for a given vulnerability. In contrast, the security type Exploit is less common. Code fragments that are not security related were not assigned to any of these three classes. Therefore, we create the group of *not assigned* code fragments. Its proportion is 10%.

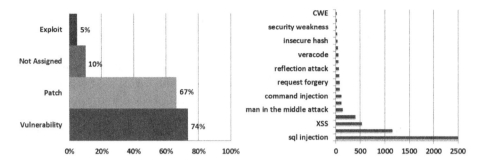

Fig. 2. Results per information types.   **Fig. 3.** Results per search terms.

Furthermore, we checked the number of results for each of the different search terms of Iteration 2. The terms indicate the kind of vulnerabilities retrieved from Stack Exchange. These were expressed by the attack strategies and terms identified by the manual search on Stack Overflow. The results are shown in Fig. 3. A total of 4830 results were found. A result may belong to several search terms. Terms with less than 20 results are ignored for reasons of space.

It should be noted that a large part of the security-related discussions on Stack Exchange deal with *SQL Injection*. The search term "SQL Injection" provides even more results than the general search term "vulnerable". Excluding results with this vulnerability type and the second most frequent type (XSS), only 1815 posts remain for other types. This corresponds with 35% of the results. Almost all results (98%) are from Stack Overflow. The remaining platforms (2%) returned hardly any results. Our approach achieved a well precision of 78% (Iteration 3). That means we receive a better search performance than security experts. Regarding to RQ1, we demonstrated that it is possible to extract security knowledge out of code communities semi-automatically but still manual rework is required because of the false predictions.

6.2 RQ2: Could Artificial Intelligence Approaches Be Leveraged in Order to Classify the Code Fragments into Vulnerabilities, Patches, and Exploits Semi-automatically?

Test Setup for the Classifiers. The performance of the classifiers is evaluated by the metrics precision, recall, F_1-measure (F1) and accuracy (ACC). The F_1-measure is the harmonic mean of precision and recall. An accuracy we understand the proportion of correctly classified posts. The earlier 200 manually-classified results are used as a set for training and testing the classifiers. Since the security information varies in its occurrence, we balanced the set for each information type. Thus, we tried to ensure a better comparability and optimal training. Each set contains as many elements of the same security type as without this type. Therefore, the sizes of sets varies according to the different types.

The resulting sets contain 106 results for vulnerabilities, 132 for patches and only 20 for exploits. We used the *leave-one-out cross validation* to ensure a reliable evaluation. Therefore, we divided the sets into ten parts. Within each of ten steps, one of the parts is used as a test set and the others for training. In this way, after the entire process, the whole set was used for testing while in each iteration 90% of the set could still be used for training. Since neural network classifiers give different results on each pass because the initial seed weights are random, the leave-one-out cross-validation has been performed four times on the neural network and ULMFiT. Finally, the averaged values were adopted.

The results of the classifiers are compared to the performance of security experts for better comparability. Each expert have classified the same set of 33 randomly picked question-answer tuples out of the data set, which always ends in a balanced test set, such that every security type takes place in the same proportion. The security experts assign to each SO question-answer pair one of the security types: vulnerability, patch, exploit, or does not match any of them.

Results and Discussion. The results of the classifier evaluation considering recall, precision and accuracy are summarized in Table 3. Naive Bayes without N-grams delivers the best results for classifying vulnerabilities respecting on recall, F_1-measure and accuracy. In contrast to the results achieved by the security experts, the precision is marginally lower but the overall performance is better. The keyword-based classifier achieves a similar good F_1 value like the Naive Bayes classifier. A classifier which categorizes all findings as vulnerabilities would reach a precision of 50%. For vulnerabilities and patches, almost all the approaches provide a classification precision that is recognizably above a random classification except the NN pre-trained by Google News.

Table 3. Classification results for all information types.

Classifier	Vulnerability				Fix				Exploit			
	P	R	F1	ACC	P	R	F1	ACC	P	R	F1	ACC
Keyword-based	54	98	70	52	59	88	71	63	100	50	67	75
Naive Bayes	69	77	73	72	52	48	50	52	36	40	38	35
Naive Bayes (2/3-grams)	61	70	65	62	55	52	53	55	45	50	47	45
Support vector machine	61	64	62	61	52	44	48	52	0	0	-	30
NN (Stack overflow)	68	65	66	67	61	66	63	62	53	65	57	54
NN (Google news)	57	48	52	53	41	45	43	58	40	60	48	49
ULMFiT	59	65	62	60	60	61	60	60	37	40	38	40
Security experts	78	58	61	68	78	65	70	72	82	68	72	76

For vulnerabilities and patches the security experts received the highest precision. The keyword-based classifier surpasses the humans in recognizing exploits.

In contrast, for the recall the security experts perform best in the case of exploits. But comparing the recall for vulnerabilities, they are only better than the NN trained by Google news, other approaches received a better recall.

For patches and exploits, the security experts have the highest accuracy, but for vulnerabilities the Naive Bayes classifier is better. Regarding precision, Naive Bayes using N-Grams, the Support Vector Machine and the neural network (Google News) deliver results that are partially slightly above in some cases under a random classification for some security types. Regarding the F1-measure the security experts only performs the best for exploits. For the other types the machine surpasses the experts. With a training set of only 20 results, there is not enough data for the training of the exploit classifiers. However, it can be seen that the keyword classifier, which does not use training data, performs best. Since the keywords were selected from previously considered results that could be part of the test set, the result may be biased. Thus, unconsciously information from the test set may have flowed into the classifier.

Our evaluation reveals that classifying Stack Overflow posts into the different security types is also a challenging task for security experts. The correct classification by the security experts in one of the three categories was highly subjective in some special cases. For example, one post on Stack Overflow dealt with a feature extension of a software component. The code fragment that was attached in an answer contained a SQL Injection to implement such a feature. It is a kind of exploit, but the intention of the author was adding a feature.

Neural networks require a large amount of data to train with. Within this evaluation, the amount of data might not be large enough to answer RQ2 conclusively. Generally, a training set consists of more than 10,000 samples. Hence, much more security-related training data would be required. However, our evaluation showed a recognizable tendency that the artificial intelligence approaches used might be suitable for the classification of security-related Stack Exchange posts. Respectively to the security types and approaches, they perform almost the same as the security experts and in some cases better. Depending on the chosen metric for some cases - the experts and others - the algorithms receive better results. On average over all security types, the security experts receive a better precision than the algorithms, but some of them still reach a good performance. If the goal is to obtain only correct results, neither a single security expert nor the approaches could work independently. Results from both have to be revised, or even better, discussed by multiple security experts. For practice, a possible good approach could it be to make a preselection via the automated approaches, followed by a manual check of security experts. A security repository[4] containing Java code fragments is created using the approach described before.

7   Conclusion

In general, developers' security knowledge is deficient. Fortunately, tools such as security code clone detectors exist that support them in writing secure software.

---

[4] Security Repository Link: https://github.com/viertel/SecurityCodeRepository.

Their effectiveness depends on the underlying reference code repository they use. For security checks, these repositories have to consist of source code examples of security flaws. Within this paper, we have introduced an approach to obtain security-related source code from programming community web pages like Stack Overflow. A significant challenge of this work is to distinguish between code examples that represent vulnerabilities, patches, and exploits. Therefore, the textual description of user contributions on these coding community websites is leveraged to ascribe posted code fragments the correct security type. To achieve that, we evaluated text classification approaches for their assignment capability.

Furthermore, a case study with 10 security experts was applied to compare their search and classification ability with the approaches described in this work. The results of the evaluation show that the automatic search of security-related content on Stack Exchange works with a better precision as the individuals. For the classification of posts in the mentioned types, we show that the results of manual classification by security experts and the automatic classification by various approaches are related to the security types. In general, the automatic approaches have a higher recall and the security expert receives a higher or - at least - a similar precision. The conclusion of the automatic search and classification results is a first pre-selection of security-related content of community web pages, but manual rework is still required. If the goal is a perfect precision, the work of single security experts also has to be revised.

Our future research will strive to extend the considered approaches for the search of security-related content with machine learning and natural language processing techniques. We also plan to train the classifiers with more data, to improve the results of the classification hopefully.

References

1. Acar, Y., Stransky, C., Wermke, D., Mazurek, M.L., Fahl, S.: Security developer studies with github users: exploring a convenience sample. In: Symposium on Usable Privacy and Security (SOUPS) (2017)
2. Barnum, S., McGraw, G.: Knowledge for software security. IEEE Secur. Privacy **3**(2), 74–78 (2005)
3. Dos Santos, C., Gatti, M.: Deep convolutional neural networks for sentiment analysis of short texts. In: Proceedings of COLING 2014, the 25th International Conference on Computational Linguistics: Technical Papers, pp. 69–78 (2014)
4. Howard, J., Ruder, S.: Universal Language Model Fine-tuning for Text Classification. arXiv e-prints, January 2018
5. Manning, C., Raghavan, P., Schütze, H.: Introduction to information retrieval. Nat. Lang. Eng. **16**(1), 100–103 (2010)
6. McGraw, G.: Software security. IEEE Secur. Privacy **2**(2), 80–83 (2004)
7. Mikolov, T., Chen, K., Corrado, G., Dean, J.: Efficient Estimation of Word Representations in Vector Space. arXiv e-prints, January 2013
8. Mikolov, T., Sutskever, I., Chen, K., Corrado, G., Dean, J.: Distributed Representations of Words and Phrases and their Compositionality. arXiv e-prints (2013)
9. Raschka, S.: Naive Bayes and Text Classification I - Introduction and Theory. arXiv e-prints, October 2014

10. Silva, C., Ribeiro, B.: Inductive Inference for Large Scale Text Classification: Kernel Approaches and Techniques, vol. 255, January 2010
11. Van der Spek, R., Spijkervet, A.: Knowledge management: Dealing intelligently with Knowledge management and its integrative elements **31**(2)
12. Stenmark, D.: Information vs. knowledge: the role of intranets in knowledge management. In: Proceedings of the 35th Annual Hawaii International Conference on System Sciences, pp. 928–937. IEEE (2002)
13. Svozil, D., Kvasnicka, V., Pospichal, J.: Intro to multi-layer feed-forward neural networks. Chemometr. Intell. Lab. Syst. **39**(1), 43–62 (1997)
14. Viertel, F.P., Brunotte, W., Strüber, D., Schneider, K.: Detecting security vulnerabilities using clone detection and community knowledge. In: Proceedings 31st Conference on Software Engineering and Knowledge Engineering, pp. 245–252 (2019)
15. Wong, E., Yang, J., Tan, L.: Autocomment: mining question and answer sites for automatic comment generation. In: Proceedings of the 28th International Conference on Automated Software Engineering (ASE 2013), pp. 562–567 (2013)
16. Yang, X.-L., Lo, D., Xia, X., Wan, Z.-Y., Sun, J.-L.: What security questions do developers ask? A large-scale study of stack overflow posts. J. Comput. Sci. Technol. **31**(5), 910–924 (2016). https://doi.org/10.1007/s11390-016-1672-0

Risk Analysis, Neural Networks
and Web Protection

Modelling Security Risk Scenarios Using Subjective Attack Trees

Nasser Al-Hadhrami$^{(\boxtimes)}$ ⓘ, Matthew Collinson$^{(\boxtimes)}$ ⓘ, and Nir Oren$^{(\boxtimes)}$ ⓘ

University of Aberdeen, Aberdeen AB24 3UE, UK
{r01nama,matthew.collinson,n.oren}@abdn.ac.uk

Abstract. We propose a novel attack tree model, called a subjective attack tree, aiming to address the limitations of traditional attack trees, which use precise values for likelihoods of security events. In many situations, it is often difficult to elicit accurate probabilities due to lack of knowledge, or insufficient historical data, making the evaluation of risk in existing approaches unreliable. In this paper, we consider the modelling of uncertainty about probabilities, via subjective opinions, resulting in a model taking second-order uncertainty into account. We propose an approach to derive subjective opinions about security events based on two main criteria, namely a vulnerability level and technical difficulty to conduct an attack, using subjective logic. These subjective opinions are then used as input parameters in the proposed model. The propagation method of subjective opinions is also discussed. Our approach is evaluated against traditional attack trees using the Stuxnet self-installation scenario. Our results show that taking uncertainty about probabilities into account during security risk analysis can lead to different outcomes, and therefore different security decisions.

Keywords: Attack trees · Risk analysis · Subjective logic

1 Introduction

Attack trees (ATs) [19] have been widely used in recent years as an effective model to analyze security of systems against potential cyber-attacks. One important parameter in ATs used to analyse security risk is the likelihood of *successful attacks* (in literature, also referred to as security events). However, several probabilistic ATs [2, 5, 12, 16, 17, 20] use precise values for likelihoods using the probabilistic approach. In many situations, it is difficult to elicit accurate probabilities due to lack of knowledge, or insufficient historical data, making the evaluation of risk in existing approaches unreliable.

Furthermore, the determination of likelihoods in ATs is not based on a solid foundation based on specific criteria, but rather on a direct assignment of values to ATs leaves. To address this weakness, Abdo [1] proposed the modelling of additional information about security events, e.g., vulnerability information, and that the successful occurrence of attacks is evaluated according to two criteria,

ⓒ Springer Nature Switzerland AG 2021
J. Garcia-Alfaro et al. (Eds.): CRiSIS 2020, LNCS 12528, pp. 201–218, 2021.
https://doi.org/10.1007/978-3-030-68887-5_12

namely a vulnerability level (i.e., how easy or hard is to exploit a vulnerability) and technical difficulty to conduct an attack, described by two qualitative scales (see Fig. 1) as follows: easy (E), medium (M), and hard (H), for the vulnerability level, and trivial (T), moderate (M), difficult (D), and very difficult (VD), for the technical difficulty (a detailed description of these two scales can be found in [1]). The final output, representing likelihoods of security input events, is then obtained from combining the qualitative expressions of the two criteria in a form of a matrix as depicted in Fig. 1. The work, however, has two major problems. First, it provides only a qualitative evaluation of ATs, and is therefore not suitable for effective decision-making that requires numerical values to make sound decisions. Second, the determination of a vulnerability level and technical difficulty of an attack in a precise manner is often difficult. With continuous emergence of new vulnerabilities— the so called zero-day vulnerabilities— security analysts might be unable to give precise evaluations about their risk levels. In addition, attackers nowadays may have the skills that enable them to conduct cyber-attacks successfully (or discover new attack strategies) even in presence of protected devices and networks with various security technologies. Therefore, it's difficult to precisely evaluate the level of technical difficulty to conduct an attack. Based on such reasons, it is essential to find a way that allows for the modelling of *uncertainty* about the *values* (i.e., the levels) of the two criteria.

In this paper, we address the current limitations of ATs by allowing for *uncertainty* modelling about likelihoods, via *subjective opinions*. In Subjective Logic [9], a subjective opinion represents the probability distribution of a random variable complemented by an *uncertainty* degree about the distribution. Our approach results in a model taking *second-order uncertainty*, i.e., uncertainty about probabilities, into account. We refer to such an AT model as a *Subjective Attack Tree*, abbreviated SAT. We use the evaluation matrix in Fig. 1 as one possible way to derive subjective opinions about security events in absence of knowledge or evidence about the evaluation of the two criteria of a vulnerability level and technical difficulty of an attack. Hence, the SAT model (the abstract model in Sect. 3 and propagation method in Sect. 5) can be used independently from the evaluation methodology we propose in Sect. 4 if security analysts prefer to directly assign opinions to the leaves, or if they wish to consider different evaluation methodologies. In comparison to ATs, the SAT model adds a bit more complexity in that it allows also to propagate uncertainty values so that uncertainty about likelihoods of the top events (i.e., root nodes) is also computed.

Explicitly modelling uncertainty degrees about the input parameters in ATs is important as this may lead to different outcomes, e.g., different attack paths prioritization, different enforced sets of countermeasures, different decisions. Apart from such importance, explicitly taking uncertainty about probabilities into account offers a more flexible approach to decision-making process based on factors such as organisations' financial capabilities (budget), risk attitudes, etc. Suppose for example a security analyst is *completely* uncertain about whether an attacker can successfully conduct an attack. In contrast to guessing single probabilities (in absence of knowledge/evidence), our approach allows, for instance, risk-averse security managers to consider the worst-case scenario (pessimistic view) and make decisions so as to protect the system. Others who are risk-seeking, especially those with limited budget, may consider the best-case scenario (optimistic view), and therefore will not need to spend more to protect systems. Decision-making in traditional probabilistic approach leads always to applying strict single decisions under all circumstances.

This work makes the following major contributions. (1) we develop a new model of ATs, called SAT, that takes second-order uncertainty into account. (2) we propose a methodology to derive opinions about security events based on the two criteria discussed in [1] using Subjective Logic. (3) we conduct an experimental evaluation that compares our approach with traditional ATs, demonstrating that the results differ and would lead to different decisions being made.

The rest of the paper is organised as follows. In Sect. 2, we give an overview of attack trees and discuss some related work. In Sect. 3, we give an overview of Subjective Logic. In Sect. 4, we discuss our SAT model, followed by an approach, in Sect. 5, to evaluate likelihoods of security events using Subjective Logic. In Sect. 6, we discuss the propagation method of subjective opinions in SATs. In Sect. 7, we evaluate our approach against traditional ATs, using the Stuxnet attack tree example. Finally, in Sect. 8, we conclude the paper, discussing prospects for future work.

Likelihood levels	Technical difficulty of an attack			
	T	M	D	VD
Exploitability — E	4	4	3	2
Exploitability — M	4	3	2	1
Exploitability — H	2	2	1	1

Fig. 1. The evaluation matrix of security events as proposed in [1].

2 Attack Trees and Related Work

An attack tree (AT) was first introduced in 1999 by Schneier [19] as a tool to analyse and evaluate all possible attack scenarios against complex systems in a structured, hierarchical way. The general idea of ATs is to identify one or more *attack goals* against a system and then break down each goal into sub-goals (or sub-attacks), which in turn can be further broken down into other sub-goals, until reaching a state where sub-attacks cannot be further refined. These final sub-attacks, representing the leaves of an AT, are the basic security events (or action) an attacker can perform, by exploiting existing vulnerabilities, to achieve their overall goal, i.e., the root node of an AT. A refinement from the root node to the leaves can be either conjunctive (via AND node) or disjunctive (via OR node). With AND node, *all* children nodes must be satisfied to complete an attack, while with OR node, *at least one* of the children nodes has to be satisfied.

The values of nodes in a tree can be of different forms, depending on the security attributes or properties need to be analysed. Such values may represent the probability of success of a given attack, the likelihood that an attacker will try a given attack, the impact of an attack, and so on. Earlier works in this field considered attack trees using only one estimated parameter, such as attack probability, cost or feasibility of the attack, skill level required, etc. [13,14,19]. Opel [15] considered multi-parameter attack trees (attack trees that study several security attributes of interest), but the actual tree computations in their model still use only one input parameter at a time.

An advanced step towards better understanding the attacker's motivation was made in [3]. The authors considered a multi-parameter attack tree where security properties of interest need to be analysed represent, for examples, gain of the attacker, probability of success, probability of getting caught, and expected penalties.

The above models of ATs have a significant drawback when they come to practical application. The input parameters considered to be precise point estimates based on the probabilistic approach. In [10], the authors addressed this point by suggesting the use of interval values to estimate the input parameters rather than single values. Their approach was basically intended to handle the estimation problem in the multi-parameter AT approach of [3]. While interval values may be a useful method to model the uncertainty about some input parameters, e.g., cost, expected penalties, they are still incapable to model ignorance of or complete uncertainty about likelihoods evaluations of attacks. In addition, specifying lower and upper bounds do not resolve the issue on how these values were precisely determined.

A fuzzy logic approach was employed to model uncertainty in ATs [4]. The approach is based on defining a set of qualitative expressions of likelihoods (e.g., very low, low, high) that describe various levels of likelihoods, and then uses fuzzy numbers to represents experts' judgments on them. The fuzzy logic approach is suitable for applications that involve fuzzy sets, and when there is some difficulty in determining the exact set that a given value should belong to. However, the approach does not model well situations when there is, for instance, a complete uncertainty about the evaluations.

A Bayesian network approach for ATs is explored in [8]. The authors proposed a methodology that translates ATs into Bayesian Networks. The proposed approach can deal with different ATs extensions, and allows the quantitative evaluation of combined attacks modelled as a set of ATs. The Bayesian network approach considers the conditional relations between the nodes, and does not say anything about the values of the leaves (i.e., it employs also the probabilistic approach to assign precise values to the security events).

Our approach differs from all above in that it runs under second-order uncertainty (i.e., uncertainty about probability values) using subjective logic. This allows to better model situations when there is high (or even complete) uncertainty about exact values. Furthermore, subjective logic offers a methodology that easily allows to establish opinions from verbal categories because people often find it difficult to express opinions as numerical values— qualitative verbal categories are intuitively easier [9].

3   Subjective Logic

Subjective logic [9] is a formalism for reasoning under uncertainty that extends probabilistic logic by allowing also for uncertainty degrees to be expressed about probability values. While the idea of probabilistic logic is to combine the strengths of probability calculus and logic, the idea of Subjective Logic is to model uncertainty about the probabilities themselves, making itself a useful tool to reason with argument models in presence of uncertain or incomplete evidence.

Subjective Logic is based on Dempster-Shafer (also called evidence) theory [7], and thus operates on a *frame of discernment*, denoted by Θ, representing the set of possible system states, referred to as atomic, or primitive, system states, only one of which represents the actual system state.

In many scenarios, it is often difficult to determine the actual system state, and it thus makes sense to define non-atomic (or non-primitive) states, consisting of the union of a number of primitive states. The powerset of Θ, denoted by 2^{Θ}, consists of all possible unions of primitive states. A non-primitive state may contain other states within it. These are referred to as substates of the state.

Definition 1 *(Belief Mass Assignment). Given a frame of discernment Θ, we can associate a belief mass assignment $m_{\Theta}(x)$ with each substate $x \in 2^{\Theta}$ such that $m_{\Theta}(x) \geq 0$, $m_{\Theta}(\emptyset) = 0$, and $\sum_{x \in 2^{\Theta}} m_{\Theta}(x) = 1$. For a substate x, $m_{\Theta}(x)$ is its* belief mass.

Subjective logic operates on a 3-dimensional metric called *opinion*. Three classes (types) of opinions are defined, namely *binomial* opinions, *multinomial* opinions, and *hyper* opinions. In this paper, we deal only with binomial opinions.

Definition 2 *(Binomial opinion). Let $X = \{x, \bar{x}\}$ be a state space containing x and its complement $\bar{x}$. A binomial opinion about the truth of state x is the tuple $\omega_x = \langle b_x, d_x, u_x, a_x \rangle$, where b_x is the belief mass in support of x being true, d_x is the belief mass in support of x being false, u_x is the amount of uncommitted belief mass, and a_x is the a priori probability, also called the* base rate*, in the absence of committed belief mass. Further, these components must satisfy $b_x + d_x + u_x = 1$ and $b_x, d_x, u_x, a_x \in [0, 1]$.*

A subjective opinion with $u_x = 0$ is called a *dogmatic opinion*, and corresponds to the classic probability distribution. A dogmatic belief for which $b_x(x) = 1$, for some $x \in \mathbb{X}$, is called an *absolute opinion*. An opinion with $u_x = 1$ is called a *vacuous opinion*. For a given binomial opinion ω_X, the corresponding *projected probability distribution* $\mathbf{P}(x) : x \to [0, 1]$ is determined as

$$\mathbf{P}(x) = b_x + a_x \cdot u_x \tag{1}$$

where $\mathbf{P}(x)$ represents the probability estimation of x which varies from the base rate value, in the case of complete ignorance ($u_x = 1$), to the actual probability in case that $u_x = 0$.

Subjective Logic provides a standard set of logical operators. In this paper we need to deal with only three operators. These are the conjunction (also called multiplication), disjunction (also called co-multiplication), and addition operators.

Definition 3 *(Conjunction Operator). Given two opinions* $\omega_x = \langle b_x, d_x, u_x, a_x \rangle$ *and* $\omega_y = \langle b_y, d_y, u_y, a_y \rangle$ *where x and y belong to independent frames of discernment, we compute the conjunction of the two opinions,* $\omega_{x \wedge y}$, *as*

$$b_{x \wedge y} = b_x b_y + \frac{(1 - a_x)a_y b_x u_y + a_x(1 - a_y)u_x b_y}{1 - a_x a_y},$$

$$d_{x \wedge y} = d_x + d_y - d_x d_y,$$

$$u_{x \wedge y} = u_x u_y + \frac{(1 - a_y)b_x u_y + (1 - a_x)u_x b_y}{1 - a_x a_y},$$

$$a_{x \wedge y} = a_x a_y.$$

By using the symbol $(\cdot)$ to denote this operator, multiplication of opinions can be written as $\omega_{x \wedge y} = \omega_x \cdot \omega_y$.

Definition 4 *(Disjunction Operator). Given two opinions* $\omega_x = \langle b_x, d_x, u_x, a_x \rangle$ *and* $\omega_y = \langle b_y, d_y, u_y, a_y \rangle$ *where x and y belong to independent frames of discernment, we compute the disjunction of the two opinions,* $\omega_{x \vee y}$, *as*

$$b_{x \vee y} = b_x + b_y - b_x b_y,$$

$$d_{x \vee y} = d_x d_y + \frac{a_x(1 - a_y)d_x u_y + (1 - a_x)a_y u_x d_y}{a_X + a_y - a_x a_y},$$

$$u_{x \vee y} = u_x u_y + \frac{a_y d_x u_y + a_x u_x d_y}{a_x + a_y - a_x a_y},$$

$$a_{x \vee y} = a_x + a_y - a_x a_y.$$

By using the symbol $(\sqcup)$ to denote this operator, co-multiplication of opinions can be written as $\omega_{x \vee y} = \omega_x \sqcup \omega_y$.

Definition 5 *(Addition Operator). Given two opinions* $\omega_x = \langle b_x, d_x, u_x, a_x \rangle$ *and* $\omega_y = \langle b_y, d_y, u_y, a_y \rangle$ *where x and y be two disjoint subsets of the same frame X, i.e.,* $x \cap y = \emptyset$, *we compute the addition of the two opinions,* $\omega_{x \cap y}$, *as*

$$b_{x \cap y} = b_x + b_y,$$

$$d_{x \cap y} = \frac{a_x(d_x - b_y) + a_y(d_y - b_x)}{a_x + a_y},$$

$$u_{x \cap y} = \frac{a_x u_x + a_y u_y}{a_x + a_y},$$

$$a_{x \cap y} = a_x + a_y.$$

By using the symbol $(+)$ to denote this operator, addition of opinions can be written as $\omega_{x \cap y} = \omega_x + \omega_y$.

4   Subjective Attack Trees

In this section, we discuss our approach to model security risk scenarios under second-order uncertainty, using Subjective Attack Trees (SATs).

In SATs, the tree structure is not different from the one in traditional ATs in that it also allows for the decomposition of the main goal of an attacker into sub-goals either conjunctively or disjunctively, except that the input parameters represent subjective opinions rather than probabilities.

Figure 2 shows an example SAT with three possible paths (ways) an attacker can choose to achieve their main goal (MG). These paths begin by the execution of the following security events: (SE_1 and SE_2), SE_3, and (SE_4 and SE_5). Taking the first path with security events SE_1 and SE_2 as an example, the subjective opinions on them, respectively, are denoted by ω_{SE_1} and ω_{SE_2}. The subjective opinion on sub-goal 1 (ω_{SG_1}) is computed from the *conjunction* of ω_{SE_1} and ω_{SE_2}, and the subjective opinion on the main goal (ω_{MG}) is computed from the *disjunction* of ω_{SG_1} and ω_{SG_2}. The subjective opinion on MG represents the *belief* that an attacker can successfully achieve their main goal, the *disbelief* that an attacker can successfully achieve their main goal, and the *uncertainty* degree about the distribution of these belief and disbelief values.

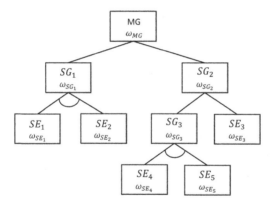

Fig. 2. A Subjective Attack Tree (SAT) model uses subjective opinions as input parameters to capture uncertainty degrees about the events' likelihoods. Here, ω_i is a subjective opinion capturing aspects of the likelihood of event i.

5   Security Events Evaluation Using Subjective Logic

In this section, we propose an approach to derive subjective opinions about security events, using the evaluation and two criteria proposed in [1]. In our approach, uncertainty about likelihoods of security events (as discussed in the introduction) is due to uncertainty about the evaluation of the two criteria. We first need to consider quantitative values describing likelihood levels from combining technical difficulty levels with the vulnerability levels. An example of mapping qualitative scales into corresponding quantitative values is shown in Table 1.

Table 1. Corresponding quantitative values to likelihood qualitative scales.

Rating	Qualitative scales	Quantitative values	Description
1	Very low	[0.1–0.2]	Highly unlikely to occur
2	Low	[0.2–0.4]	Will most likely not occur
3	Moderate	[0.4–0.6]	Possible to occur
4	High	[0.6–0.8]	Likely to occur
5	Very high	[0.8–1.0]	Highly likely to occur

5.1   The Two Criteria Evaluation

We mentioned in the introduction that it is often difficult to precisely determine the level of a vulnerability or technical difficulty of an attack. We propose a novel way to model uncertainty about the evaluation of these two criteria, allowing one to derive subjective opinions about security events, used then as input parameters in SATs.

Since each criterion specifies a number of categories (i.e., levels), where only one category represents the truth value in a given case, these categories thus represent the state space of a given criterion, and accordingly, the two criteria can be thought of as two frames of discernment. The state space of a vulnerability level is $VL = \{e, m, h\}$, and the state space of the technical difficulty is $TD = \{t, m, d, vd\}$. In our approach, security analysts need to assign values from the interval [0, 1] to each category, denoting their *degrees of belief* that each category represents the truth value. In addition, they complement these degrees by an uncertainty mass, provided that the sum of all the beliefs and uncertainty mass must equal to one. Furthermore, they assign a base rate to each category, as prior probability in absence of evidence, where the sum of the base rates must equal to one. Unless specified otherwise, we assume a uniform distribution for the base rates— the base rate of each category in the vulnerability level's frame of discernment is given as $1/3$ (≈ 0.33), and as $1/4$ ($= 0.25$) in the technical difficulty's frame of discernment. Figure 3 shows three examples of belief assignments in a vulnerability level's frame of discernment given different uncertainty masses about beliefs distribution.

b_e	b_m	b_h	u_{VL}
0	0	1	0

(a)

b_e	b_m	b_h	u_{VL}
0	0	0.8	0.2

(b)

b_e	b_m	b_h	u_{VL}
0	0	0	1

(c)

Fig. 3. Examples of belief assignments in a vulnerability level's frame of discernment: (a) the vulnerability level is 'high' with 100% confidence (i.e., 0 uncertainty), (b) the vulnerability level is 'high' with 0.2 uncertainty, and (c) complete uncertainty about the vulnerability level. u_{VL} stands for the uncertainty mass in the frame of discernment.

5.2 Evaluation Rules for Security Events

Because of uncertainty about the values of the two criteria, computing final opinions about security events directly using an evaluation matrix such as of Fig. 1 is too complex. This requires to do multiplication of each likelihood level with the values of the corresponding combination of a Vulnerability level and technical difficulty, meaning that we need to perform twelve calculations. To facilitate the computation of subjective opinions, we propose a simple specification that translates the matrix in Fig. 1 into a form of rules, calling them *evaluation rules*. The specification compacts the matrix information using a simple syntax such as

$$(VL = value_{VL}) \wedge (TD = value_{TD}) \Rightarrow^W SE, \qquad (2)$$

where $VL = value_{VL}$ denotes the level of a vulnerability, $TD = value_{TD}$ denotes the technical difficulty of an attack, SE denotes security events for evaluation, and $\wedge$ is the conjunction symbol (i.e., AND). $VL = value_{VL}$ and $AD = value_{TD}$ are called the *antecedents* of the rule, while SE is the *consequent*. Further, the rule is given some form of weight, represented by W above the implication symbol $\Rightarrow$, denoting the likelihood level of SE occurrence given the values of the antecedents. The rule's weight corresponds to a cell value in a matrix. For example, the evaluation of a security event given that the vulnerability level is *easy E* and technical difficulty is *difficult D* according to the matrix in Fig. 1 can be formulated as (assuming that the quantitative value corresponding to rating 3 is 0.5):

$$(VL = easy) \wedge (TD = difficult) \Rightarrow^{0.5} SE$$

When the same evaluation (i.e., the same unique likelihood level) is given for more than one combination, we use the *union* operator ($\cup$) as follows

$$(VL = value_{VL} \wedge TD = value_{TD})_{comb_1}$$
$$\cup (VL = value_{VL} \wedge TD = value_{TD})_{comb_2} \qquad (3)$$
$$\cup \cdots \cup (VL = value_{VL} \wedge TD = value_{TD})_{comb_n} \Rightarrow^W SE,$$

where $comb_1$ denotes the first combination of vulnerability level and technical difficulty, $comb_2$ denotes the second combination, and so on, and $comb_1 \neq comb_2 \neq \cdots \neq comb_n$.

This rule can be further simplified. We may use the relation symbols of $\leq$ and $\geq$ to express a group of consecutive cells whose combinations are less than or equal (or greater than or equal) a certain level of vulnerability, technical difficulty, or both of them (with the assumption that there is a total order on the values of the two criteria). For example, the combinations of (hard H, trivial T) and (hard H, moderate M) in Fig. 1 can be expressed as $(VL = hard) \wedge (TD \leq moderate)$. $TD \leq moderate$ in this example means that the technical difficulty's values are *moderate* and *trivial*. Accordingly, the evaluation rule is written as (with 0.3 corresponds to rating 2):

$$(VL \leq medium) \wedge (TD \leq moderate) \Rightarrow^{0.3} SE. \tag{4}$$

As in Eq. 3, the union symbol $\cup$ can be also used to link antecedents that involve the relation symbols $\leq$ and $\geq$ in their expressions. For example, in Fig. 1, since the rating 4 (0.7 in our quantitative example) is given for $(VL \leq medium \wedge TD = trivial)$ and for $(VL = easy \wedge AD = moderate)$, we formulate the evaluation's rule as

$$(VL \leq medium \wedge TD = trivial) \cup (VL = easy \wedge TD = moderate) \Rightarrow^{0.7} SE.$$

Based on the above discussion, we generalise Eq. 2, Eq. 3, and Eq. 4 to obtain a more general form of security events evaluation as follows

$$
\begin{aligned}
& (VL \odot value_{VL} \wedge TD \odot value_{TD})_{comb_1} \\
& \cup (VL \odot value_{VL} \wedge TD \odot value_{TD})_{comb_2} \\
& \cup \cdots \cup (VL \odot value_{VL} \wedge TD \odot value_{TD})_{comb_n} \Rightarrow^W SE,
\end{aligned} \tag{5}
$$

where $\odot$ is any relation symbol from the set $\{=, \leq, \geq\}$, $comb_1$ denotes the first combination of likelihood level and technical difficulty, $comb_2$ denotes the second combination, and so on, and $comb_1 \neq comb_2 \neq \cdots \neq comb_n$.

5.3   Computing Final Opinions About Security Events

We use the proposed evaluation rules to derive subjective opinions about security events. We first need to evaluate each single antecedent in a rule (e.g., $VL = hard$ and $TD \geq difficult$) using the belief assignments in the frames of discernment of the two criteria. Next, we evaluate the combined antecedents in a rule (e.g., $(VL = easy \wedge TD \leq moderate) \cup (VL = medium \wedge TD = trivial)$) using the corresponding operators of $\wedge$ and $\cup$ in Subjective Logic. The symbol $(\wedge)$ is used to link two antecedents of different types to express a combination of technical difficulty and vulnerability level. The symbol $(\cup)$ is used to link multiple combinations of the same evaluation.

First, each single antecedent is evaluated by deriving a *binomial* opinion about it since their states can be either true or false. To derive a binomial opinion about an antecedent of the form $CT = value_{CT}$, where $CT \in \{VL, TD\}$ (i.e., the criterion type), and $value_{CT}$ is a category belongs to a given criterion, the

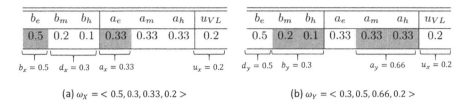

Fig. 4. Deriving binomial opinions about two antecedents (a) $X : VL = easy$, and (b) $Y : VL \geq medium$.

belief mass of the binomial opinion takes exactly the same belief mass associated to the category $value_{CT}$ in the frame of discernment, and the disbelief mass of the binomial opinion is equal to the *sum* of all beliefs assigned to the other categories. The uncertainty of the subjective opinion takes the same uncertainty mass associated to the whole frame of discernment. Further, the base rate of the binomial opinion is exactly the same base rate associated to that category. Figure 4 shows an example beliefs and base rates assignments in a VL's frame of discernment. Suppose we want to derive a subjective opinion about $VL = easy$, this process is demonstrated in Fig. 4 (a).

To derive a binomial opinion about an antecedent of the form $CT \odot value_{CT}$, where $\odot \in \{\leq, \geq\}$, the belief mass of the binomial subjective opinion is the *sum* of all beliefs assigned to the categories starting from $value_{CT}$ and higher than this category in case of $\odot = \{\geq\}$, or the *sum* of all beliefs assigned to the categories starting from $value_{CT}$ and lower than this category in case of $\odot = \{\leq\}$. The disbelief mass of the binomial opinion takes the *sum* of all beliefs assigned to the remaining categories. The uncertainty of the binomial opinion takes exactly the same uncertainty mass associated to the whole frame of discernment. Further, the base rate of the binomial opinion is the *sum* of all base rates assigned to the categories starting from $value_{CT}$ and higher than this category in case of $\odot = \{\geq\}$, or the *sum* of all base rates assigned to the categories starting from $value_{CT}$ and lower than this category in case of $\odot = \{\leq\}$. Figure 4 (b) demonstrates the process of deriving a binomial opinion about $VL \geq medium$.

As a next step, we derive a binomial opinion about the antecedents. In Subjective Logic, the symbol $\wedge$ corresponds to the multiplication (conjunction) operator, and the symbol $\cup$ corresponds to the addition operator. Following this, we derive a final opinion about a security event. This is achieved by multiplying the obtained subjective opinion about the antecedents with the rule's weight. Because of uncertainty about the two criteria values, different evaluations (i.e., different subjective opinions) are obtained for security events, and the number of evaluations is equal to the number of rules.

Let r_i be an evaluation rule, where $1 \leq i \leq n$, and n is the number of evaluation rules, and the rule's strength is denoted by W_{r_i}. Let also SE be a security event for evaluation. According to Eq. 5 and the operators of conjunction ($\cdot$) and addition ($+$), the subjective opinion on the security event SE is computed

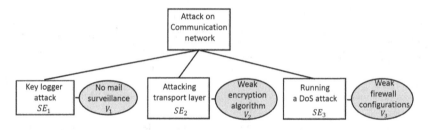

Fig. 5. The security actions and associated vulnerabilities (ovals) in Example 1.

from rule r_i as follows

$$
\begin{aligned}
\omega_{SE_i} =& ((\omega_{VL} \odot value_{VL} \cdot \omega_{TD} \odot value_{TD}) comb_1 \\
&+ (\omega_{VL} \odot value_{VL} \cdot \omega_{TD} \odot value_{TD}) comb_2 \\
&+ \cdots + (\omega_{VL} \odot value_{VL} \cdot \omega_{TD} \odot value_{TD}) comb_n) . W_{r_i}.
\end{aligned}
\tag{6}
$$

To perform multiplication of a subjective opinion (about the antecedents) with a single value (the rule weight), we multiply each of the belief mass and base rate of the subjective opinion with the rule weight while maintaining the same uncertainty degree. This process ensures that the projected probability of the resulting subjective opinion (about a security event) is the same as if we multiply the projected probability of the subjective opinion about the antecedents with the rule weight. Formally, assuming $\omega_x = \langle b_x, d_x, u_x, a_x \rangle$ is the subjective opinion about antecedents in a rule of wight y ($W = y$), then a subjective opinion about a security event SE is computed as $\omega_x = \langle b_x.y, d_x, u_x, a_x.y \rangle$.

Finally, because of different possible outcomes obtained for a security event, we choose only one outcome to represent an input parameter in a SAT. In this paper, we work under the *most expected* risk scenario, by choosing the outcome that represents the most expected likelihood for a security event. For this purpose, we use the projected probability function (see Eq. 1), which provides an estimate for the ground truth value of a variable by capturing the most likely value in presence of base rates.

Example 1 Suppose that in order to disrupt a communication network, the attacker needs to perform any of the following security actions: installing a key logger, attacking the transport layer, or running a DoS attack, via exploiting some existing vulnerabilities as shown in Fig. 5. Suppose also the evaluation of security events is expressed by the following three rules:

$$r_1 : (VL \leq medium \wedge TD \leq moderate) \Rightarrow^{0.8} SE$$
$$r_2 : (VL = easy \wedge TD \geq difficult) \cup (VL = hard \wedge TD \leq moderate) \Rightarrow^{0.5} SE$$
$$r_3 : (VL \geq medium \wedge TD \geq difficult) \Rightarrow^{0.2} SE$$

Further, the beliefs assignments to each category in the frames of discernment of the level of each vulnerability and technical difficulty of each security event is given in Table 2. By deriving binomial opinions about the antecedents of the three rules, and using Eq. 6 to compute subjective opinions about the security events, we obtain three possible subjective opinions for each security event (see Table 3). Having computed the projected probability of these subjective opinions to obtain the most expected value of each security event, we conclude that $\omega_{SE_1} = \langle 0.618, 0.252, 0.130, 0.264 \rangle$, $\omega_{SE_2} = \langle 0.142, 0.569, 0.289, 0.660 \rangle$, and $\omega_{SE_3} = \langle 0.567, 0.287, 0.146, 0.264 \rangle$, and these would represent input parameters in Fig. 5.

Table 2. Beliefs assignments in the frames of discernment of (a) the level of each vulnerability and (b) technical difficulty of each attack in Example 1.

Vulnerability	b_e	b_m	b_h	u_{VL}	Event	b_t	b_m	b_d	b_{vd}	u_{TD}
V_1	0.15	0.60	0.05	0.20	SE_1	0.85	0.05	0.05	0.00	0.05
V_1	0.00	0.15	0.70	0.15	SE_1	0.00	0.00	0.65	0.05	0.30
V_2	0.30	0.50	0.10	0.10	SE_2	0.20	0.60	0.05	0.00	0.15

Table 3. The possible subjective opinions about security events in Example 1.

Security event	Possible subjective opinions	Rule of derivation
SE_1	$\langle 0.618, 0.252, 0.130, 0.264 \rangle$	r_1
	$\langle 0.047, 0.863, 0.090, 0.165 \rangle$	r_2
	$\langle 0.009, 0.952, 0.039, 0.660 \rangle$	r_3
SE_2	$\langle 0.009, 0.912, 0.079, 0.264 \rangle$	r_1
	$\langle 0.053, 0.797, 0.150, 0.165 \rangle$	r_2
	$\langle 0.142, 0.569, 0.289, 0.660 \rangle$	r_3
SE_3	$\langle 0.567, 0.287, 0.146, 0.264 \rangle$	r_1
	$\langle 0.068, 0.865, 0.067, 0.165 \rangle$	r_2
	$\langle 0.011, 0.904, 0.085, 0.660 \rangle$	r_3

6   Propagation of Subjective Opinions in SATs

So far, we have discussed the model of SAT and how to derive subjective opinions about security events as input parameters in the model. In this section, we discuss how these subjective opinions are propagated (through the gates of AND and OR) such that a subjective opinion on the root node can be then obtained.

Subjective opinions are propagated through AND gate using the *conjunction* operator. Let Z be an AND node in a SAT, with X and Y are its children. Let also $\omega_X = \langle b_x, d_x, u_x, a_x \rangle$ and $\omega_y = \langle b_y, d_y, u_y, a_y \rangle$ be the subjective opinions on X and Y, respectively. The subjective opinion on Z, ω_Z, is computed as

$\omega_Z = \omega_x \cdot \omega_y$. Figure 6 (a) shows an example computation of a subjective opinion on event Z via AND gate.

Subjective opinions are propagated through OR gate using the *disjunction* operator. Let Z be an OR node in a SAT, with X and Y are its children. Let also $\omega_X = \langle b_x, d_x, u_x, a_x \rangle$ and $\omega_y = \langle b_y, d_y, u_y, a_y \rangle$ be the subjective opinions on X and Y, respectively. The subjective opinion on Z, ω_Z, is computed as $\omega_Z = \omega_x \sqcup \omega_y$. Figure 6 (b) shows an example computation of a subjective opinion on event Z via OR gate.

The operators of conjunction and disjunction on subjective opinions proved to be commutative and associative [9], and therefore the order of nodes (both AND and OR nodes) in an AT is not important.

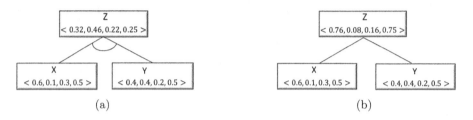

(a)   (b)

Fig. 6. Computing an opinion on event Z via (a) AND gate, and (b) OR gate.

7   Experimental Evaluation

We conduct an experimental evaluation to compare our approach with traditional probabilistic ATs, using the Stuxnet attack tree [1] as an illustrative example. To make the example simple, we consider only the operation of self-installation as demonstrated in Fig. 7. Also, we omit the modelling of the vulnerability information about the security events, assuming their evaluations are obtained according to the two criteria and methodology we proposed in this paper, since the main goal of the section is to demonstrate why uncertainty should be taken into account when conducting risk analysis using models such as ATs.

We conduct three experiments, in each of which, we work with a different set of probabilities to compute the likelihood of the attack. We then start producing uncertainty about these probabilities. Uncertainty about a probability distribution is produced such that it affects a support to its belief mass only, a support to its disbelief mass only, or a support to both its belief and disbelief masses.

For a better study of the impact of uncertainty about the probabilities on the outcomes, we produce different degrees of uncertainty at each time of evaluation. We choose that, at each time, uncertainty about the probabilities is increased by at most %25, and for one time we consider the situation of complete uncertainty about the security events' probabilities. Here, we consider the following uncertainty categories: (1) $u_X \in [0.01, 0.25]$, (2) $u_X \in [0.26, 0.50]$, (3)

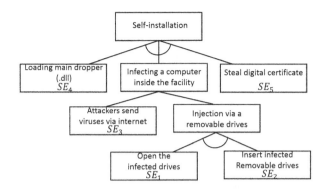

Fig. 7. Attack tree of "Stuxnet self-installation".

$u_X \in [0.51, 0.75]$, (4) $u_X \in [0.76, 1.0]$, and (5) $u_X = 1.0$, where X is any security event in the given AT. Due to space limitation in this paper, we show only the set of probabilities and subjective opinions used in Experiment 1 (see Table 4). The set of probabilities used in the other two experiments are as follows: 0.3, 0.8, 0.6, 0.7, and 0.5 (for experiment 2), and 0.6, 0.9, 0.6, 0.1, and 0.1 (for experiment 3) for the security events SE_1, SE_2, SE_3, SE_4, and SE_5 in order. Uncertainty about these probabilities is produced in the same way as in Experiment 1.

Table 4. Probabilities and subjective opinions used in Experiment 1.

Uncertainty	SE_1	SE_2	SE_3	SE_4	SE_5
$u_x = 0$	0.7	0.86	0.6	0.8	0.9
$u_x \in [0.01, 0.25]$	$\langle 0.60, 0.25, 0.15 \rangle$	$\langle 0.65, 0.10, 0.25 \rangle$	$\langle 0.40, 0.40, 0.20 \rangle$	$\langle 0.65, 0.25, 0.10 \rangle$	$\langle 0.70, 0.08, 0.22 \rangle$
$u_x \in [0.26, 0.50]$	$\langle 0.50, 0.20, 0.30 \rangle$	$\langle 0.55, 0.10, 0.35 \rangle$	$\langle 0.30, 0.25, 0.45 \rangle$	$\langle 0.30, 0.20, 0.50 \rangle$	$\langle 0.60, 0.00, 0.40 \rangle$
$u_x \in [0.51, 0.75]$	$\langle 0.25, 0.05, 0.70 \rangle$	$\langle 0.35, 0.10, 0.55 \rangle$	$\langle 0.17, 0.20, 0.63 \rangle$	$\langle 0.15, 0.10, 0.75 \rangle$	$\langle 0.34, 0.00, 0.66 \rangle$
$u_x \in [0.76, 1.00]$	$\langle 0.20, 0.00, 0.80 \rangle$	$\langle 0.10, 0.05, 0.85 \rangle$	$\langle 0.00, 0.00, 0.10 \rangle$	$\langle 0.05, 0.00, 0.95 \rangle$	$\langle 0.01, 0.00, 0.99 \rangle$
$u_x = 1$	$\langle 0.00, 0.00, 0.10 \rangle$	$\langle 0.00, 0.00, 0.10 \rangle$	$\langle 0.00, 0.00, 0.10 \rangle$	$\langle 0.00, 0.00, 0.10 \rangle$	$\langle 0.00, 0.00, 0.10 \rangle$

In addition to the given AT structure of self-installation, we repeat the same above experiments for a modified structure in which AND gates are replaced with OR gates, and vice versa, the OR gates are replaced with AND gates (although this doesn't offer a real representation of the self-installation scenario, but we do so for demonstration purposes only, and therefore should not be taken as a real representation of the attack). We do swap between the gates in order to also study the outcomes in case that the target node of evaluation is of type OR.

Using the prorogation method of probabilities (discussed in literature) and propagation method of subjective opinions (discussed in this paper), we obtained probabilities for the self-installation attack and subjective opinions on it. To compare the outcomes (likelihoods) from using both approaches, we assumed here the most expected scenarios when dealing with subjective opinions by computing

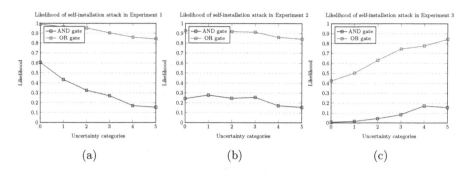

Fig. 8. Likelihood of self-installation attack in the three experiments using AT (denoted by uncertainty category with label 0), and SAT models (denoted by uncertainty categories with labels 1 to 5 as defined in text).

their projected probabilities. Figure 8 shows the likelihoods of self-installation attack in each experiment when there is no uncertainty about the probabilities (AT model) and when there is uncertainty about them (SAT model) based on the five defined uncertainty categories (numbered from 1 to 5), and with different gate type of the root node.

In Experiment 1, and in case of AND gate of the root node, the likelihood of self-installation attack decreases as uncertainty about the probabilities increases, and the decrease is to somewhat sharp in case of total uncertainty about the probabilities, resulting in a reduction from 0.605 to 0.15625 (i.e., the difference in probability is approximately 0.448). Unlike the case of AND gate, the projected probabilities of the subjective opinions given that the root node is of type OR decease very slightly as uncertainty increases, and the difference in the probability when there is no uncertainty and when there is total uncertainty about the probabilities is only 0.147. Here, the effect of uncertainty about probabilities in this particular case is very small. Graph (a) of Fig. 8 demonstrates that taking uncertainty about the probabilities into account when the root node is of type AND leads to very different results than in case of OR gate.

In Experiment 2, whether the root node is of type AND or OR, the results are not considerably different in case of AT or SAT model. The maximum difference in probability using both structures when there is no uncertainty about the probabilities and when working with total uncertainty about them is only 0.084.

In Experiment 3, both structures result in an increase in the likelihood of the attack as uncertainty increases. However, the increase is very high in case of OR gate, nearly 0.42 as probability difference when using the probabilistic approach and when $u_X = 1.0$, while it is slight in case of AND gate (only 0.159). The analysis here is opposite to the one in Experiment 1, where both gates lead to a decrease in the likelihood and such a decrease is sharper in case of AND gate than of OR gate.

Importantly, there are cases such that in the AT approach, the decision is to not protect the system, while it is the reverse in the SAT model. As an example with OR structure in Experiment 3, the security manager would only consider a protection mechanism against the attack if the probability is greater than 0.5. This example, in particular, and the results from Experiment 1, in general, clearly demonstrate the importance of modelling uncertainty about probabilities when conducting security risk analysis—*doing so can lead to completely different security decisions being made.*

8   Conclusions and Future Work

We developed a new model of attack trees, called a subjective attack tree, that takes second-order uncertainty about input parameters into account, via subjective opinions. We proposed an approach to derive subjective opinions security events based on two criteria, a vulnerability level and technical difficulty of an attack. Our approach involved development of evaluation rules using subjective logic. Propagation of subjective opinions has been also discussed. Finally, we evaluated our approach against traditional ATs, showing that SATs lead to different outcomes in contrast to ATs, leading to different decisions being made.

As future work, we will consider other criteria to evaluate likelihoods of security events, such as connectivity of systems, technology and communication protocols used, users' behaviour, etc. Further, the current work has presented the foundation of SATs with only one input parameter, i.e., likelihood. For effective risk and decision analysis, we will need to extend the model by incorporating countermeasures, allowing for additional parameters to be included, such as cost of attack, cost of countermeasure, impact, and so on. We will discuss the impact of uncertainty in selecting the optimal set of countermeasures, comparing the results with existing approaches, e.g., [6,11,18,20].

References

1. Abdo, H.: Dealing with uncertainty in risk analysis: combining safety and security. Ph.D. thesis (2017)
2. Buldas, A., Gadyatskaya, O., Lenin, A., Mauw, S., Trujillo-Rasua, R.: Attribute evaluation on attack trees with incomplete information. Comput. Secur. **88**, 101630 (2020)
3. Buldas, A., Laud, P., Priisalu, J., Saarepera, M., Willemson, J.: Rational choice of security measures via multi-parameter attack trees. In: Lopez, J. (ed.) CRITIS 2006. LNCS, vol. 4347, pp. 235–248. Springer, Heidelberg (2006). https://doi.org/10.1007/11962977_19
4. Buoni, A., Fedrizzi, M., Mezei, J.: A delphi-based approach to fraud detection using attack trees and fuzzy numbers. In: Proceeding of the IASK International Conferences, pp. 21–28 (2010)
5. Edge, K., Raines, R., Grimaila, M., Baldwin, R., Bennington, R., Reuter, C.: The use of attack and protection trees to analyze security for an online banking system. In: 2007 40th Annual Hawaii International Conference on System Sciences (HICSS 2007), p. 144b. IEEE (2007)

6. Edge, K.S., Dalton, G.C., Raines, R.A., Mills, R.F.: Using attack and protection trees to analyze threats and defenses to homeland security. In: MILCOM 2006–2006 IEEE Military Communications Conference, pp. 1–7. IEEE (2006)
7. Gordon, J., Shortliffe, E.H.: The dempster-shafer theory of evidence. Rule-Based Expert Systems: The MYCIN Experiments of the Stanford Heuristic Programming Project **3**, 832–838 (1984)
8. Gribaudo, M., Iacono, M., Marrone, S.: Exploiting bayesian networks for the analysis of combined attack trees (2015)
9. Jøsang, A.: Subjective logic. Springer, Berlin (2016)
10. Jürgenson, A., Willemson, J.: Processing multi-parameter attacktrees with estimated parameter values. In: Miyaji, A., Kikuchi, H., Rannenberg, K. (eds.) IWSEC 2007. LNCS, vol. 4752, pp. 308–319. Springer, Heidelberg (2007). https://doi.org/10.1007/978-3-540-75651-4_21
11. Kordy, B., Mauw, S., Radomirović, S., Schweitzer, P.: Foundations of attack–defense trees. In: Degano, P., Etalle, S., Guttman, J. (eds.) FAST 2010. LNCS, vol. 6561, pp. 80–95. Springer, Heidelberg (2011). https://doi.org/10.1007/978-3-642-19751-2_6
12. Kumar, R., Stoelinga, M.: Quantitative security and safety analysis with attack-fault trees. In: 2017 IEEE 18th International Symposium on High Assurance Systems Engineering (HASE), pp. 25–32. IEEE (2017)
13. Mauw, S., Oostdijk, M.: Foundations of attack trees. In: Won, D.H., Kim, S. (eds.) ICISC 2005. LNCS, vol. 3935, pp. 186–198. Springer, Heidelberg (2006). https://doi.org/10.1007/11734727_17
14. Moore, A.P., Ellison, R.J., Linger, R.C.: Attack modeling for information security and survivability. Carnegie-Mellon Univ Pittsburgh Pa Software Engineering Inst, Tech. rep. (2001)
15. Opel, A.: Design and implementation of a support tool for attack trees. Internship Thesis, Otto-von-Guericke University Magdeburg (2005)
16. Pieters, W., Davarynejad, M.: Calculating adversarial risk from attack trees: control strength and probabilistic attackers. In: Garcia-Alfaro, J., Herrera-Joancomartí, J., Lupu, E., Posegga, J., Aldini, A., Martinelli, F., Suri, N. (eds.) DPM/QASA/SETOP -2014. LNCS, vol. 8872, pp. 201–215. Springer, Cham (2015). https://doi.org/10.1007/978-3-319-17016-9_13
17. Roy, A., Kim, D.S., Trivedi, K.S.: Cyber security analysis using attack countermeasure trees. In: Proceedings of the Sixth Annual Workshop on Cyber Security and Information Intelligence Research, pp. 1–4 (2010)
18. Roy, A., Kim, D.S., Trivedi, K.S.: Attack countermeasure trees (act): towards unifying the constructs of attack and defense trees. Secur. Commun. Netwk. **5**(8), 929–943 (2012)
19. Schneier, B.: Attack trees. Dr. Dobb's journal **24**(12), 21–29 (1999)
20. Wang, P., Lin, W.H., Kuo, P.T., Lin, H.T., Wang, T.C.: Threat risk analysis for cloud security based on attack-defense trees. In: 2012 8th International Conference on Computing Technology and Information Management (NCM and ICNIT), vol. 1, pp. 106–111. IEEE (2012)

Premium Access to Convolutional Neural Networks

Julien Bringer[1], Hervé Chabanne[2,3], and Linda Guiga[2,3(✉)]

[1] Kallistech, Paris, France
[2] Idemia, Paris, France
{herve.chabanne,linda.guiga}@idemia.com
[3] Télécom Paris, Paris, France

Abstract. Neural Networks (NNs) are today used for all our daily tasks; for instance, in mobile phones. We here want to show how to restrict their access to privileged users. Our solution relies on a degraded implementation which can be corrected thanks to a PIN. We explain how to select a few parameters in an NN so as to maximize the gap in the accuracy between the premium and the degraded modes. We report experiments on an implementation of our proposal on a deep NN to prove its practicability.

Keywords: Neural Networks · Software protection · Reverse engineering

1 Introduction

Today, many applications rely on Neural Networks (NNs) to perform different classification tasks. Here, we want to investigate how to restrict their use to a set of privileged users, who have access to a premium mode. The premium mode is carried out by providing each user with an NN specially trained for their personal use.

The first idea behind our solution comes from [19]. [19] describes how, in 2016, mobile RSA's SecurID and Vasco DIGIPASS Software Tokens can be hacked despite relying on different defense mechanisms implemented to thwart reverse engineering processes. Its conclusion is that in such a hostile environment, quoting: "The best defense against the attacks shown in this paper is securing the mobile token with a PIN".

As our protection relies on low-entropy PINs, we cannot let hackers perform brute-force attacks at ease. Rather than implementing simple work/no-work modes for the application, we implement a default degraded classification task for incorrect PINs vs an optimal one for the privileged users. Switching from a degraded mode to the premium optimal one is achieved through the modification of some of the NN's parameters. We consider that the attacker has access to the NN's implementation in a degraded mode. We are well aware that an attacker might perform an exhaustive search on all PINs. However, our goal is to slow each attempt down.

© Springer Nature Switzerland AG 2021
J. Garcia-Alfaro et al. (Eds.): CRiSIS 2020, LNCS 12528, pp. 219–234, 2021.
https://doi.org/10.1007/978-3-030-68887-5_13

A particular emphasis is given to the way we store these critical parameters in the mobile phone. Although our method could also be applied to other contexts, we believe that our method could be applied to mobile phones, as we take storage space into account.

Our second idea relies on some specific layers: the convolutional ones. These are found in Convolutional Neural Networks (CNNs), which are, for instance, the most used NNs for image processing. We select some parameters in a given convolutional layer as the ones enabling us to move from degraded modes to the optimal one.

Going a step further, we exploit the fact that we are dealing with NNs. During a training phase with a dedicated database, the parameters of an NN are optimized. One strategy we introduce uses the fact that an attacker who does not have full access to testing facilities will be unable to find optimal parameters through retraining.

To sum up, each privileged user is provided with an NN trained for him and a PIN enabling him to reach the premium mode of his NN. We end this introduction with a description of some Related Works. In Sect. 2.1, we provide some background about NNs. We describe our proposal to store optimal parameters in Sect. 3. To illustrate its practicability, we detail two examples of parameter selection to show how an unprivileged user would end up with degraded outputs and we report in Sect. 4 our experiments on an NN based on ResNet18 [9] which is typical of deep learning. Section 5 concludes.

1.1 Related Works

Android offers a multi-layer security strategy. [18] describes this security model (see also [1]). Moreover, one may add ad-hoc protections for obfuscating the code making it harder to reverse-engineer [4]. There is an on-going cat-and-mouse game between hackers and developers. However, it seems to us that developers may have a hard time whenever the full access to the code is available to hackers. For instance, for white-box cryptography, where the code for encrypting with DES or AES symmetric algorithms are given to attackers, all academic proposals have been broken so far [8]. Moreover, while complementary to our proposal, anti-reverse engineering techniques tend to inflate the size of the code a lot. For instance, for DES or AES, there may be a multiplication by 16k of the code size, from less than 1KB for an unprotected implementation to more than 16MB. As NNs – such as the one we are considering – are initially large, such an expansion cannot be handled in an embedded environment.

Some papers consider the use of hardware enclaves such as Intel SGX to protect NNs in the cloud setting [11,12,24,25]. However, reverse-engineering and model inversion attacks still remain possible on some protected systems [24,28, 29]. Moreover, even though they provide a – relatively – protected environment for their users, they do not consider giving access to predictions to all users, with a degraded mode for unprivileged users.

There are also various works related to deep learning and NNs on mobile phones: for a secure hardware-based implementation of NNs on mobile devices, see [2]. For a comprehensive study on the deployment of deep learning Android apps, see [30].

Our approach is different. We want to force the hacker to measure the performances of the deployed NN without having the possibility to rely on a dedicated database. Here, we study an example of facial recognition (see [27] for a survey of this domain). We believe it is relevant, as a typical deep learning task.

Previous works have studied the notion of privileged information [16,26]. However, they focus on the training phase of NNs, and study how a Student network could achieve a better accuracy when provided with privileged information while training along a Teacher network. Thus, they differ from our work in the sense that this paper focuses on the end-user and the inference phase.

2 Background

2.1 Convolutional Neural Networks

Today, Convolutional Neural Networks (CNNs) are used for making predictions in various fields of application ranging from image processing [3], to classification [21,22] and segmentation [20].

They are composed of several layers:

- Convolutional layers compute a convolution between one – or several – filter F and the input, as follows:

$$O_{i,j} = \sum_{k=1}^{h} \sum_{l=1}^{w} X_{i+k,j+l} \cdot F_{k,l}$$

where O is the output of the convolution. A convolution can be seen in Fig. 1.

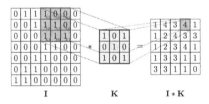

Fig. 1. Convolution between an input I and a filter K

The elements of the filter are the weights of the layer and will be designated either by 'weights' or by 'parameters' in the rest of the paper.
- Other layer types include fully connected layers – through weights – to all the elements from the previous layer.

– A nonlinear function is applied at the end of each layer. The most popular one is the ReLU (Rectified Linear Unit) function defined as the max of a value and zero. It is used to activate – or deactivate – elements of the layer.
– Finally, pooling layers are usually present between other layers in order to reduce the dimensionality of the input.

The input of each layer consists of different channels. For instance, in image processing, the input of the model is usually divided in three channels corresponding to the RGB colors.

The weights – and other parameters – of a CNN are trained over several epochs – i.e. runs on a training data set – so as to reach a value guaranteeing the best possible prediction accuracy. Given their large number of parameters, and the necessity of high accuracy nowadays, some NNs take days – or even months – to train.

Several techniques are added over the years to make training more efficient. One of these consists in adding a Batch Normalization layer to improve the training phase. In 2015, the authors of [14] discovered this type of layer whose purpose is to make training faster, more efficient and more stable. The layer normalizes its input. Thus, given an element $x_{i,j}$ in a batch B of its input, the layer computes:

$$\tilde{x}_{i,j} = \gamma \frac{x_{i,j} - \mu_B}{\mathbb{V}_B} + \beta \tag{1}$$

where γ and β are parameters optimized during the training phase, and $\mathbb{V}_B$ and μ_B are the considered batch's variance and expected value respectively.

2.2 ResNet18

At first glance, one could imagine that the more layers an NN contains, the better its accuracy will be, once fully trained. However, a known problem occurs for deep neural networks during training. In 2016, the authors of [9] discovered ResNet as a way to better train deeper NNs, without having to deal with it. This is achieved thanks to residual blocks corresponding to "identity shortcuts", described in Fig. 2. More generally, the architecture of Residual Neural Networks introduces these skipping connections. The authors argue that thanks to the identity mapping, the training should be similar be it with or without the shortcut layer. This is why large ResNet architectures, containing sometimes up to 1,001 layers [10], are efficiently trained with a high accuracy.

The model we consider here is based on a particular instance of ResNet: ResNet18. The latter is composed of 17 convolutional layers, a fully connected layer, a max pooling layer and a final global average pooling layer.

2.3 Selecting Optimal Parameters

Our selection strategy aims at choosing only a few parameters – called optimal – which have an impact on the accuracy of the NN.

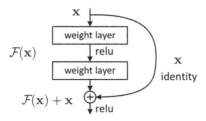

Fig. 2. Residual block in ResNet

Section 4 is devoted to detailing how this works on a particular instance of an NN. We will report how the fulfillment of the first criteria is achieved in this case. We also address the second criteria to penalize an attacker who has a limited access to the training database (see Sect. 4.2).

Minimizing the Number of Parameters. The authors of [23] show that some neurons have a higher impact on the model's prediction than others. Indeed, [23] defines a neuron i's sensitivity given an input x as follows:

$$\Delta(i,x) = argmin_\delta\{|\delta|| f(x) \neq \tilde{f}^i_\delta(x)\}$$

where f is the original model and $\tilde{f}$ is a modified model where noise δ was added to the output of neuron i.

It corresponds to the minimal noise one needs to add to neuron i for the classification to change. The authors of [23] observe that a large number of neurons have a high sensitivity (small Δ).

This result shows that it is possible to select few parameters to protect, and still prevent the attacker from getting a good accuracy.

When the Attacker Does Not Have Access to the Database. [5] operates a distinction between static and dynamic parameters. We will also make such a distinction, but our definition of static parameters is slightly different from theirs. Let us define the following:

1. We say that a parameter w remains unchanged from one training epoch to the next if
   $$|w_{current\_layer} - w_{previous\_layer}| < r \cdot w_{previous\_layer} \text{ where } r = 10^{-2}$$
2. We denote *static parameters* the parameters that have not changed over the last epoch.
3. *Dynamic parameters* are the non-static parameters.

The choice of r in Point 1. comes from the fact that a slight change in a parameter does not lead to a noticeable drop in the accuracy. What interests us when studying the parameter fluctuation is the way the modifications influence the accuracy. Thus, r is tuned so that the resulting evolution curves for the number of static parameters is representative of the evolution of the accuracy. I.e. r is chosen so that when the accuracy changes less, the number of static parameters increases drastically. After trying several values for r, we selected $r = 10^{-2}$, as it enabled us to differentiate between static and dynamic parameters as per the previous explanation.

Static parameters are easier to obtain by the attacker through a shorter training. Moreover, dynamic parameters are the ones that change the accuracy over the last few epochs and bring it to its optimal value. For those two reasons, protecting the dynamic parameters seems to be a viable strategy in order to limit the number of parameters to protect.

2.4   Per User Training

For a same NN architecture, training with different initialization parameters results in different weights for all layers (see [7]). As our privileged users benefit from dedicated training, they do share the same NN architecture, but with different parameters. For our proposal, this means that we have to modify the optimal parameters for each of the privileged users' NN. To the best of our knowledge, given a trained NN, there is no way to deduce the parameters computed through another training with a different initialization of the same NN.

2.5   Finite Fields

Let $\mathbb{F}$ denote a finite field with 2^l elements such that $2^l - 1$ is a prime. For instance, $\mathbb{F} = \mathbb{F}_{2^{521}}$.

Lemma 1. *1. The non-zero elements of $\mathbb{F}$ form a multiplicative group.*
2. This group is cyclic.
3. In this group, all elements are generators except the unity.

Point 2. of the previous lemma means that all non-zero elements can be expressed as powers of a single element called a generator.

For a proof, see [17].

Let us further note that since l is taken to be a prime, all elements of $\mathbb{F}$ are invertible modulo $p = 2^l - 1$.

3   Protecting Optimal Parameters

Here, we suppose we have a set of n optimal parameters $\{o_1, \ldots, o_n\}$ that we want to keep secret. These secrets have to be protected by a PIN, in such a way that for all PIN values, the protection returns legitimate values. An attacker knows the way the parameters are stored and can try all PIN values.

Let $\mathbb{F}$ denote a finite field with 2^l elements such that $2^l - 1$ is a prime. For instance, $\mathbb{F} = \mathbb{F}_{2^{521}}$.

We want to keep l small. This means that we want a small n too. An example of doing that is given in the next section.

Denote $O = *|o_1| \dots |o_n \in \mathbb{F}$ where $|$ stands for the concatenation and $*$ is a bitstring with no particular value which is introduced to fit the length of the finite field $\mathbb{F}$ elements.

Given a PIN value, we then compute

$$g = O^{1/\text{PIN}} \in \mathbb{F} \qquad (2)$$

Let us note that g always satisfies (2) according to Lemma 1.

We store the function $f : \pi \mapsto g^{\pi} \in \mathbb{F}$. We have: $f(\pi) = O$ if and only if $\pi = $ PIN.

Thanks to Point 3. of Lemma 1, g is a generator of the multiplicative group of $\mathbb{F}$ and f(all the values between 1 and $2^l - 1$) $= \mathbb{F} \setminus \{0\}$, which implies that an attacker who tries all possible values of PIN will get all elements of $\mathbb{F}$. This way, she cannot identify which one has been chosen for O.

Note that the implementation of function f does not have to be secured.

4   Example of Application: Facial Recognition

In this section, we consider an adapted version of the ResNet18 [9] model architecture to the task of facial recognition. We think that this is a relevant example, as it demonstrates the feasibility of our concept on an NN structure that is used in different applications, including in a mobile environment. Moreover, relying on facial recognition facilitates experiments on large data sets and comparisons with large scale benchmarks. Our architecture extends ResNet18 and relies on 14 million parameters across 76 layers. Our goal is to extract at most around a hundred parameters.

For facial recognition, the performances are assessed thanks to the accuracy of the recognition. On the one hand, false positives might happen, allowing unauthorized individuals to be recognized. On the other hand, false negatives might be a nuisance to genuine users. More precisely, the error is measured as follows: given a maximal False Acceptance Rate (FAR) – i.e. the probability of a malicious individual being authenticated, assess the False Rejection Rate (FRR) – i.e. the probability of a genuine user being rejected.

The accuracy of our ResNet18-based model on the Labeled Faces in the Wild (LFW) database [13] in our proprietary setting is as follows (3):

- For $FAR = 10^{-4}$, $FRR = 0.24$ %
- For $FAR = 10^{-5}$, $FRR = 0.70$ %

In our case, we reach the best accuracy after 13 training epochs.

4.1   Optimal Parameters for ResNet18

Given the large number of parameters in our NN model, carefully selecting the parameters to protect allows us to limit the size of $\mathbb{F}$ (see Sect. 3). In the following section, we describe two main parameter selection strategies. In the first, we protect parameters from batch normalization layers, either by protecting all the parameters of one layer, or by using the method described in Sect. 2.3. In the second, we describe a strategy to sample elements from a convolutional layer, as a way to limit the number of optimal parameters.

4.2 Batch Normalization

Generating Suboptimal Parameters. When selecting a set of parameters to protect in an NN, the first, most intuitive, strategy would be to protect a layer with few parameters. As explained in Sect. 2, batch normalization layers aim at normalizing the input. For this reason, each of the layer's parameters affect one whole input channel. The said parameters are therefore scarce and impactful. Thus, batch normalization layers are one obvious choice of layer to protect. More specifically, we will focus here on the γ parameters mentioned in (1). We randomize the parameters of a batch normalization layer in the middle of the architecture (38th layer out of 76). The layer contains 128 γ parameters.

Even though the attacker does not have access to trained weights, observing the other batch normalization layers might enable them to spot erroneous settings if the random parameters selected do not reflect the usual distribution of γ parameters. To prevent this, we compute the distribution of the chosen layer's γ parameters and generate values following the same distribution. Figure 3 shows that the γ parameters we generated have, indeed, a distribution similar to that of the original batch normalization γ parameters.

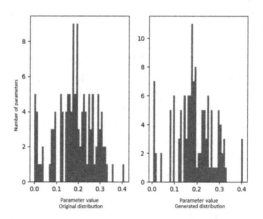

Fig. 3. Distribution of the γ parameters in a batch normalization layer from the ResNet18 network, with the original distribution on the left and the generated distribution on the right

Once we have established the way suboptimal parameters have been generated, we can observe the associated drop in the accuracy and evaluate the security of our process for this strategy.

When we change the selected layer's γ parameters to random ones following the distribution of batch normalization layers, we get the following accuracy:

- For $FAR = 10^{-4}$, $FRR = 0.32$ %
- For $FAR = 10^{-5}$, $FRR = 0.96$ %

Thus, the false rejection rate for $FAR = 10^{-4}$ has increased by 33% and the rate for $FAR = 10^{-5}$ has increased by 37.1% compared to the original model (see (3) for reference). This corresponds to the accuracy of the model after only 8 training epochs. Thus, modifying only one small layer over the 76 ones already results in a critical drop in the accuracy. Protecting the 128 γ parameters of the batch normalization layer would therefore be enough to distinguish between premium and degraded accesses.

The following section describes a second strategy.

Static VS Dynamic. Depending on the layers, the proportion of static parameters – as defined in Sect. 2.3 – varies a lot. While convolutional layers contain mainly dynamic parameters as shown in Fig. 4, the γ parameters in batch normalization layers tend to be mostly static, as can be seen in Fig. 5. Figure 6 shows the distribution of the number of epochs for which the γ parameters have been static. We can see that most γ parameters do not change over the last epoch at least. This explains our definition of static parameters: we seek to select a minimal number of parameters.

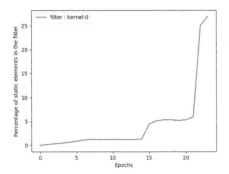

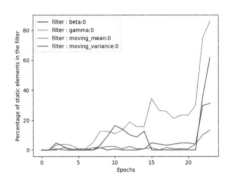

Fig. 4. Percentage of static parameters in a convolutional filter with relation to the epoch.

Fig. 5. Percentage of static parameters for each parameter type in a batch normalization layer with relation to the epoch.

Considering this, the advantages of batch normalization layers are threefold:

- They contain few parameters.
- As stated before, γ parameters in batch normalization layers influence several input elements and can have a noticeable effect on the following layers.

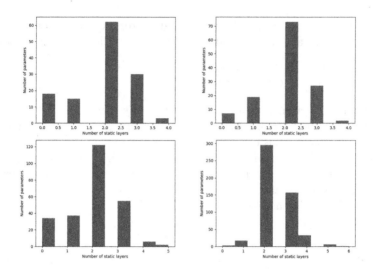

Fig. 6. Number of epochs for which the γ parameters have been static, in four different batch normalization layers

- The large proportion of static parameters means we can protect a few parameters from various batch normalization layers.

Our new strategy is therefore to protect the dynamic parameters from several batch normalization layers.

Since only a few parameters per layer are modified, it is no longer necessary to copy the layer's distribution: making sure the random elements generated are in the range $[0, 0.4]$ is enough to fool a potential attacker who cannot train the model.

Selecting the static parameters from the four batch normalization layers whose histograms are displayed in Fig. 6 results in protecting 62 parameters (18 in the first layer, 7 in the second, 34 in the fourth and 3 in the last). We replace the selected γ parameters by uniformly generated ones in the range $[0, 0.4]$. This leads to the following accuracy:

- For $FAR = 10^{-4}$, $FRR = 0.28$ %
- For $FAR = 10^{-5}$, $FRR = 0.86$ %

Even though the drop in the accuracy is less drastic than in the previous experiment on a batch normalizations layer, the FRR for $FAR = 10^{-5}$ still corresponds to the accuracy at the end of the 8th training epoch.

Thus, this new method enables us to halve the number of parameters to protect while significantly dropping the accuracy (the accuracies obtained are summarized in Table 1).

The question that remains is whether defining static parameters as parameters that have not changed over the last 2 (or more) epochs would lead to an improved security.

Taking now into account the last 2 epochs, and considering 3 batch normalization layers, we have to protect 124 γ parameters. This leads to an accuracy of:

– For $FAR = 10^{-4}$, $FRR = 0.34$ %
– For $FAR = 10^{-5}$, $FRR = 0.99$ %

Since this new accuracy corresponds to the accuracy at the beginning of the 8th training epoch, we consider that the increased drop in the accuracy does not outweigh the increase in the number of parameters to protect. This confirms our choice of one epoch for the definition of static parameters.

4.3 Convolutional Layer

In this section, we explain how to further drop the accuracy of the degraded modes, while keeping around the same number of protected parameters.

Figure 1 shows how a convolutional layer computes the next layer's neurons. A convolutional filter is usually much smaller than the layer's input. Indeed, filters are usually 3×3 or 5×5 windows. On the other hand, when dealing with the Labeled Faces in the Wild (LFW) [13] data set, the model's input is commonly 250×250 images. Thus, each of the few parameters in a given filter impacts a large number of parameters. With the values considered, one filter value modification changes the value of $248 \times 248 = 61,504$ neurons from the following layer.

Therefore, even though convolutional layers have more parameters than batch normalization ones, we can still further limit the number of selected optimal parameters in the convolutional case.

Another element we need to take into account, however, is that the number of filters in a convolutional layer is usually high. For instance, if there are 3 input channels and 64 output channels, the layer stores $64 \times 3 = 192$ filters. Observing any drop in the accuracy requires a change in several such filters. For instance, feeding degraded values to all the parameters of only two filters among the 192 results in almost no drop in the accuracy. Given the explanation in the previous paragraph, the approach we consider is to randomly select one element among each set of *input_channels_number* filters. Thus, in the previous example, each output channel requires three filters. For each output channel, we randomly select one parameter among the three filters as an optimal parameter.

Furthermore, the depth of the selected convolutional layer matters. Indeed, if the said layer is among the first architecture layers, we can take advantage of the chain reaction. In a convolutional layer, each input neuron impacts several neurons in the following layer due to the way convolutions are computed. Each degraded filter parameter in the considered layer will change the value of a large number of neurons from the following layer, which, in turn, will impact several neurons in the layer after that, and so on. Given that our model is a convolutional neural network, most layers are convolutional ones. This explains why limiting ourselves to few parameters in one convolutional layer at the very beginning of the architecture can lead to a large drop in the accuracy.

Selecting a layer early in the architecture yields three other advantages:

1. the number of input channels is lower in the first layers (and only 3 in the first convolutional layer).
2. the number of output channels is lower in the first layers.
3. the input and output sizes are larger.

Points (1) and (2) ensure a minimal overall number of filter parameters for the considered convolutional layer. Point (3) results in a higher impact for every degraded filter parameter.

Finally, let us note that, given the fact we only consider one parameter per filter, we do not need to take into account the filter's parameters distribution: if the degraded parameters are in the range of possible values, the attacker cannot detect the degradation.

To summarize, the strategy to select the optimal parameters is as follows:

– Consider the model's first convolutional layer.
– For each output channel, select one element among the three filters for that channel.

In order to check that the first convolution has a higher impact on the predictions than batch normalization layers, we compare the sensitivity (as explained in Sect. 2.3) of the two strategies on a ResNet18 architecture trained on the CIFAR10 dataset [15]. Thus, we select one image (the second image from the CIFAR10 testing set for instance), and plot, on the one hand, the minimum δ one needs to add to all the γ parameters of each batch normalization layer in order to change the model's prediction (Fig. 7), and, on the other hand, the minimum δ to add to 64 parameters from the first convolutional layer, randomly selected according to our strategy (Fig. 8). Figure 8 shows that the peak sensitivity (over the various sets of parameters) for the convolutional layer considered is slightly lower than 0.1. On the other hand, changing all parameters from the various batch normalization layers shows that, for most layers, the sensitivity is higher than 1 (see Fig. 7). Since we are interested in a low sensitivity – meaning that a slight change in the protected parameters would lead to a significant change in the accuracy –, Fig. 7 and 8 confirm that the first convolutional parameters, selected according to our strategy, are more sensitive to small noise than batch normalization ones.

For our model, this strategy results in 64 selected parameters. As before, we can encode each parameter on 8 bits, thus leading to all the parameters being encoded on 512 bits overall. When we change 64 parameters from the model's first convolutional layer – selected as described previously – to random ones, we get the following accuracy:

– For $FAR = 10^{-4}$, $FRR = 0.34$ %
– For $FAR = 10^{-5}$, $FRR = 0.97$ %

Thus, with only half the parameters, we reach almost the same accuracy as in the batch normalization layer's case.

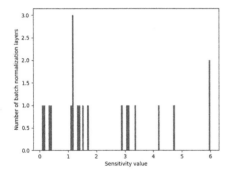

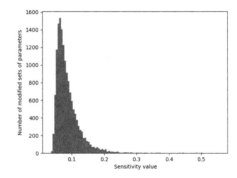

Fig. 7. Distribution of the sensitivity with respect to the second image of the CIFAR testing dataset over the batch normalization layers. For each batch normalization layer, the sensitivity Δ corresponds to the minimum value δ such that adding δ to all the γ parameters of the layer results in a change in the prediction. All Δ values greater than 6 are assimilated to 6.

Fig. 8. Distribution of the sensitivity with relation to the second image of the CIFAR testing dataset over the first convolutional layer. 64 parameters are selected at random among the layer's parameters, as explained in Sect. 4.3. For each selected set of parameters, the sensitivity Δ corresponds to the minimal value δ such that adding δ to the selected parameters results in a change in the prediction.

Let us note that even though the absolute increase in the accuracy does not seem critical, it still corresponds to an accuracy obtained after only 8 epochs in our case (instead of the full 13 epochs training).

4.4 Exhaustive Search FAR and FRR

We place ourselves in the attacker's shoes. We consider that we have full access to the implementation of a degraded NN and, according to Sect. 3, we know how to compute parameters given a certain PIN. Thus, we generate random PINs and compute the accuracy – FRR for FAR – associated with the deduced parameters instead of the optimal ones.

The minimal accuracy the attacker gets is the following for degraded parameters from the first convolutional layer (selected as in Sect. 4.3):

- For $FAR = 10^{-4}$, $FRR = 0.30\%$, representing a 25% relative increase compared to the original model.
- For $FAR = 10^{-5}$, $FRR = 0.94\%$, representing a 34% relative increase compared to the original model.

On average, the attacker gets:

- For $FAR = 10^{-4}$, $FRR = 0.87\%$, representing a 263% relative increase compared to the original model.

Table 1. Accuracy of the original model and of the model where some parameters have been replaced by random ones

	Number of protected parameters	FRR ($FAR = 10^{-4}$)	FRR ($FAR = 10^{-5}$)
Original model	0	0.24 %	0.70 %
Modification of one batch normalization (beginning of Sect. 4.2)	128	0.32 %	0.96 %
Modification of dynamic parameters (end of Sect. 4.2)	62	0.28 %	0.86 %
Modification of convolutional parameters (Sect. 4.3)	64	0.34 %	0.97 %

- For $FAR = 10^{-5}$, $FRR = 2.58\%$, representing a 269% relative increase compared to the original model.

For the second strategy on the batch normalization layers (Sect. 4.2), the attacker gets, on average, the following accuracies:

- For $FAR = 10^{-4}$, $FRR = 0.28\%$, representing a 16% relative increase compared to the original model.
- For $FAR = 10^{-5}$, $FRR = 0.82\%$, representing a 17% relative increase compared to the original model.

To gauge the accuracy of our system, we use again the LFW database and a proprietary setup. Each try takes around 15 min.

5   Conclusion

We introduce a premium mode for NN applications, for instance in mobile phones. Our defense strategy is threefold:

- we rely on a PIN only known by privileged users;
- the functionality of the NN is degraded by default;
- the attacker does not have access to a training dataset and has a limited testing facility and is therefore forced to blindly guess the correct PIN.

Each privileged user benefits from a dedicated training of the NN and is given a PIN which enables him to switch from a degraded mode to the premium one.

These protections can also be enforced by classical anti-reversing engineering techniques as well as OS and software security features.

We explain how for a facial recognition NN with more than 14 million parameters, we determine 64 sensitive optimal values for our proposal, showing its practicability. We followed two approaches. The first consisted in looking for parameters affecting the accuracy, based on [23]. The second can be applied when the attacker does not have a training database, based on [6]. Further research could focus on how to systematically select a small set of parameters with a high impact on the NN's accuracy. As a first step, we would like to determine a correlation between accuracy and the number of protected parameters.

Acknowledgments. The authors want to thank Vincent Despiegel and his team for their support.

References

1. Android enterprise security white paper (2020)
2. Bayerl, S.P., et al.: Offline model guard: secure and private ML on mobile devices. In: 23. Design, Automation and Test in Europe Conference (DATE 2020) (2020). http://tubiblio.ulb.tu-darmstadt.de/117658/
3. Browne, M., Ghidary, S.S.: Convolutional neural networks for image processing: an application in robot vision. In: Gedeon, T.T.D., Fung, L.C.C. (eds.) AI 2003. LNCS (LNAI), vol. 2903, pp. 641–652. Springer, Heidelberg (2003). https://doi.org/10.1007/978-3-540-24581-0_55
4. Collberg, C.: Engineering code obfuscation. In: Advances in Cryptology - Eurocrypt 2016. Lecture Notes in Computer Science, vol. 9666, p. 1 (2016). https://www.iacr.org/cryptodb/data/paper.php?pubkey=28982. abstract of invited talk
5. Denil, M., Shakibi, B., Dinh, L., Ranzato, M., de Freitas, N.: Predicting parameters in deep learning. In: Neural Information Processing Systems (2013)
6. Denil, M., Shakibi, B., Dinh, L., Ranzato, M., de Freitas, N.: Predicting parameters in deep learning. In: Burges, C.J.C., Bottou, L., Ghahramani, Z., Weinberger, K.Q. (eds.) Advances in Neural Information Processing Systems 26: 27th Annual Conference on Neural Information Processing Systems 2013. Proceedings of a meeting held December 5–8, 2013, pp. 2148–2156. Lake Tahoe, Nevada, United States (2013). http://papers.nips.cc/paper/5025-predicting-parameters-in-deep-learning
7. Frankle, J., Schwab, D.J., Morcos, A.S.: The early phase of neural network training. CoRR abs/2002.10365 (2020)
8. Gilbert, H.: On white-box cryptography (2016). invited talk
9. He, K., Zhang, X., Ren, S., Sun, J.: Deep residual learning for image recognition. In: 2016 IEEE Conference on Computer Vision and Pattern Recognition, CVPR 2016, Las Vegas, NV, USA, June 27–30, 2016. pp. 770–778. IEEE Computer Society (2016). https://doi.org/10.1109/CVPR.2016.90
10. He, K., Zhang, X., Ren, S., Sun, J.: Identity mappings in deep residual networks. In: Leibe, B., Matas, J., Sebe, N., Welling, M. (eds.) ECCV 2016. LNCS, vol. 9908, pp. 630–645. Springer, Cham (2016). https://doi.org/10.1007/978-3-319-46493-0_38
11. Hua, W., Umar, M., Zhang, Z., Suh, G.E.: Guardnn: Secure DNN accelerator for privacy-preserving deep learning. CoRR abs/2008.11632 (2020). https://arxiv.org/abs/2008.11632
12. Hua, W., Umar, M., Zhang, Z., Suh, G.E.: Mgx: Near-zero overhead memory protection with an application to secure DNN acceleration. CoRR abs/2004.09679 (2020). https://arxiv.org/abs/2004.09679
13. Huang, G.B., Mattar, M., Berg, T., Learned-Miller, E.: Labeled faces in the wild: a database forstudying face recognition in unconstrained environments. In: Workshop on Faces in 'Real-Life' Images: Detection, Alignment, and Recognition (2008). https://hal.inria.fr/inria-00321923

14. Ioffe, S., Szegedy, C.: Batch normalization: Accelerating deep network training by reducing internal covariate shift. In: Bach, F.R., Blei, D.M. (eds.) Proceedings of the 32nd International Conference on Machine Learning, ICML 2015, Lille, France, 6–11 July 2015. JMLR Workshop and Conference Proceedings, vol. 37, pp. 448–456. JMLR.org (2015). http://proceedings.mlr.press/v37/ioffe15.html
15. Krizhevsky, A.: Learning multiple layers of features from tiny images. Technical reports (2009)
16. Lambert, J., Sener, O., Savarese, S.: Deep learning under privileged information using heteroscedastic dropout. In: 2018 IEEE Conference on Computer Vision and Pattern Recognition, CVPR 2018, Salt Lake City, UT, USA, June 18–22, 2018. pp. 8886–8895. IEEE Computer Society (2018). https://doi.org/10.1109/CVPR.2018.00926, http://openaccess.thecvf.com/content_cvpr_2018/html/Lambert_Deep_Learning_Under_CVPR_2018_paper.html
17. Lidl, R., Niederreiter, H.: Finite Fields. Cambridge University Press (1997)
18. Mayrhofer, R., Stoep, J.V., Brubaker, C., Kralevich, N.: The android platform security model. CoRR abs/1904.05572 (2019)
19. Mueller, B.: Hacking soft tokens - advanced reverse engineering on android (2016)
20. Shelhamer, E., Long, J., Darrell, T.: Fully convolutional networks for semantic segmentation. CoRR abs/1605.06211 (2016). http://arxiv.org/abs/1605.06211
21. Simonyan, K., Zisserman, A.: Very deep convolutional networks for large-scale image recognition (2015). http://arxiv.org/abs/1409.1556
22. Sultana, F., Sufian, A., Dutta, P.: Advancements in image classification using convolutional neural network. CoRR abs/1905.03288 (2019). http://arxiv.org/abs/1905.03288
23. Suri, A., Evans, D.: One neuron to fool them all. CoRR abs/2003.09372 (2020). https://arxiv.org/abs/2003.09372
24. Tople, S., Grover, K., Shinde, S., Bhagwan, R., Ramjee, R.: Privado: practical and secure DNN inference. CoRR abs/1810.00602 (2018). http://arxiv.org/abs/1810.00602
25. VanNostrand, P.M., Kyriazis, I., Cheng, M., Guo, T., Walls, R.J.: Confidential deep learning: Executing proprietary models on untrusted devices. CoRR abs/1908.10730 (2019). http://arxiv.org/abs/1908.10730
26. Vapnik, V., Vashist, A.: A new learning paradigm: learning using privileged information. Neural Networks **22**(5–6), 544–557 (2009). https://doi.org/10.1016/j.neunet.2009.06.042
27. Wang, M., Deng, W.: Deep face recognition: a survey. CoRR abs/1804.06655 (2018)
28. Wei, L., Liu, Y., Luo, B., Li, Y., Xu, Q.: I know what you see: Power side-channel attack on convolutional neural network accelerators. CoRR abs/1803.05847 (2018). http://arxiv.org/abs/1803.05847
29. Xiang, Y., et al.: Open DNN box by power side-channel attack. CoRR abs/1907.10406 (2019). http://arxiv.org/abs/1907.10406
30. Xu, M., Liu, J., Liu, Y., Lin, F.X., Liu, Y., Liu, X.: A first look at deep learning apps on smartphones. In: WWW. pp. 2125–2136. ACM (2019)

An OWASP Top Ten Driven Survey on Web Application Protection Methods

Ouissem Ben Fredj[1](✉), Omar Cheikhrouhou[2,3], Moez Krichen[4,5],
Habib Hamam[6], and Abdelouahid Derhab[7]

[1] University of Sousse, Sousse, Tunisia
ouissem.benfredj@gmail.com
[2] Taif University, Taif, Saudi Arabia
o.cheikhrouhou@tu.edu.sa
[3] University of Monastir, Monastir, Tunisia
[4] Al-Baha University, Al Bahah, Saudi Arabia
[5] University of Sfax, Sfax, Tunisia
[6] University of Moncton, Moncton, Canada
[7] King Saud University, Riyadh, Saudi Arabia

Abstract. Web applications (WAs) are constantly evolving and deployed at broad scale. However, they are exposed to a variety of attacks. The biggest challenge facing organizations is how to develop a WA that fulfills their requirements with respect to sensitive data exchange, E-commerce, and secure workflows. This paper identifies the most critical web vulnerabilities according to OWASP Top Ten, their corresponding attacks, and their countermeasures. The application of these countermeasures will guarantee the protection of the WAs against the most severe attacks and prevent several unknown exploits.

Keywords: Survey · Security · Web · Attacks · OWASP top ten · Countermeasures

1 Introduction

During the latest period, the organizations have been using the web not only as a tool to advertise their images, product, and services, but also to perform their daily tasks, including sensitive data and complex workflows. Moreover, due to the popularity and the spread of sophisticated hand-held devices, several applications are moving from the regular desktop-based versions to the web-based ones to target more devices with low cost of portability [32]. On the other hand, the number attackers is continuously growing, and their attack techniques are becoming increasingly sophisticated and dangerous, which impose real security challenges on the organizations to secure their web applications (WAs). Hence, the security of WAs has become an important research area, and several solutions have been proposed to protect the WA.

From another point-of-view, the security administrators usually deploy WAFs (WA Firewalls) to protect the WAs. However, as will be shown later in this paper, the WAFs often use trivial protection methods instead of the advanced techniques suggested by the researchers (see Sect. 4). There is a large gap between

© Springer Nature Switzerland AG 2021
J. Garcia-Alfaro et al. (Eds.): CRiSIS 2020, LNCS 12528, pp. 235–252, 2021.
https://doi.org/10.1007/978-3-030-68887-5_14

the state of the art web protection methods and those employed by the existing WAFs. This paper tries to narrow down this gap by identifying the most severe web attacks as well as the appropriate countermeasures against each attack. The critical attacks are determined based on the most known web vulnerabilities, which were released by the OWASP project [2]. We have reviewed the security countermeasures to provide the readers with the smallest set of protection methods that prevent the broadest range of critical attacks.

The rest of the paper is organized as follows: In Sect. 2, the most critical vulnerabilities, as released by the OWASP project, are presented. For each vulnerability, the corresponding attacks are identified. Section 3 is tailored to the analysis of the most recent progress in the security countermeasures for each attack. A focus will be made on the runtime and server-side web protection methods. Section 4 deals with the use of Firewalls for the WA protection. Section 5 is dedicated for the adoption of formal methods for this same purpose. Section 6 concludes the paper and give future directions.

2   Security Attacks Against Web Applications

In this section, we describe the possible attacks that could target a Web Application (OWASP [2]).

2.1   Injection

The injection attacks consist in injecting (sending) untrusted information for an interpreter. This injection is a part of an instruction: command/query. By providing malicious information, the attacker can mislead the interpreter and cause unintended commands. The most critical injection attacks are the following:

- **SQL Injection:** It consists in injecting (inserting) SQL commands into input forms or queries to get access to a database (DB) or manipulate its data, for example: modification or deletion of database content.
- **Code Injection:** This attack consists in injecting code that the application interprets and runs, which exploits poor processing of untrusted data.
- **XPATH Injection:** This attack takes place when a WA uses user-input information for building an XPath query corresponding to XML data.

  For more information about SQL injection attacks, the reader can refer to [32].

2.2   Broken Authentication and Session Management

In case of broken authentication and session management attack, the intruder tries to exploit the vulnerabilities of the authentication procedure in order to access the WA or to use the credentials of other authorized users. This attack is classified into the following categories:

- **Brute Force Attack:** It consists in trying a combination of characters to guess the password of a given user.

- **Dictionary Attack:** If the attacker has some knowledge on the victim, he can prepare dictionary (set of valid words). Then, he combines these words to guess the victim password.
- **Credential Enumeration Attack:** Under this kind of attack, the intruder attempts to harvest valid usernames for a password-guessing campaign, by using verbose error of message telling whether the login is a valid username or not.
- **Session Fixation Attack:** In this attack, the hacker fixes the session ID, which will be used by user before the user logins into the server.
- **Cookie Poisoning Attack**: It consists in modifying a cookie by an intruder to obtain unauthorized information about the user for the purpose to perform for example identity theft.

2.3   Cross-site Scripting (XSS)

It consists in injecting malicious code/scripts into web responses, which are returned back by the trusted WA, to be executed by the web browser. The following three main kinds of XSS exist according to the way the malicious code is injected:

- **Stored XSS Attack:** It takes place when the user input (such as message forum, database data, comment field, visitor log, etc.) is stored on the WA server. Then, a victim may get back the stored data from the WA without making it safe.
- **Reflected XSS Attack:** It occurs when a client receives data in an HTTP request and uses the data in an unsafe manner within the immediate response.
- **DOM Based XSS Attack:** In this attack, the whole malicious data flow from source to sink occurs within the browser. It means that the data source is in the Document Object Model (DOM), the sink is in DOM as well, and the data flow does not leave the browser.

A recent survey about the XSS attacks can be found in [23].

2.4   Insecure Direct Object References

A Direct Object Reference takes place whenever a programmer presents references to internal implementation objects. It may be a database key, directory, or file. When there is no access control or other security measures, intruders may exploit such references to reach unauthorized data. This vulnerability may lead to the following several attacks:

- **Path Traversal Attack:** It is a kind of attack, in which insecure direct object reference to directories and files which are placed outside the web root folder or in hidden places including system and configuration files.
- **Direct Request Attack:** (also called forced browsing) It consists in using brute force procedures to access unlinked contents in the main directory. The attacker may use google crawler to list hidden pages and files.

– **Authorization Bypass Through User-Controlled SQL Primary Key Attack:** It occurs when the attacker manipulates a DB table primary key, which is used in an SQL statement, in order to reach inaccessible records.

2.5 Security Misconfiguration

Security misconfiguration problem occurs when one or more of the components of the system such as the applications, the frameworks, the application server, the web server, the DB server, the network router, and the platform are not well configured. Secure settings have to be defined, implemented, and maintained. Default settings are very often the cause of such a risk [50]. The attacker could exploit this flaw to perform several attacks. The severity of the attack depends on the misconfiguration level and place.

2.6 Sensitive Data Exposure

IT systems always store in a DB users personal data like passwords, home addresses, phone numbers, credit card details, etc. Once the systems are not properly secured from forbidden access, there is a strong likelihood of an attacker exploiting that vulnerability and stealing the information. There are three attacks, which are related to the sensitive data exposure:

– **Information Leakage Attack:** it occurs when a WA reveals sensitive data, such as error messages or developer comments. These sensitive data, which give an attacker useful guidance, can be exploited to attack the system [4–6,58].
– **Transmission Attack:** When the communication is not encrypted, all data exchanged between the client and the web server is sent in clear-text which leaves it exposed to interception, injection and redirection.
– **Database Theft:** when the sensitive data in the DB is not protected using strong encryption or access policies, attacker could steal this data. Three database attacks are possible: Brute-force attack; SQL injection and Privilege escalation.

2.7 Missing Function Level Access Control

Some WAs check access rights to function level before making the feature available to the user. Nevertheless, once each feature is accessed, applications must achieve the same access control check for the server. Whenever requests are not checked, attackers can access the features without proper permission. Examples of attacks that may exploit this vulnerability are the following:

– **Local File Inclusion Attack:** The attacker tries to find a page that receives as input a path to a file to be included in the calling page.
– **Remote File Inclusion Attack:** it is the same as the Local File Inclusion Attack but instead of including files located in the same server, the attacker manipulates the user input to include remote files.

– **Command Injection Attack:** it is another attack that accesses the OS functions with unauthorized manner. The attacker tries to find a piece of code in the WA that accepts untrusted input to build OS commands without proper sanitization.

2.8   Cross-site Request Forgery (CSRF)

According to [7], a WA is vulnerable to CSRF attacks (sometimes referred to as XSRF or Session Riding) when it does not verify that any request done by a trusted user has actually been intentionally done by that user only. There is a big difference between CSRF vulnerabilities and XSS vulnerabilities. The CSRF attack exploits an authenticated user to make a request on their behalf. Thus, a web site that uses cookies for authentication may be vulnerable, as well as those web application that use Basic or Digest authentications, because the browser automatically sends the cookies and the server will rely on that browser.

2.9   Using Components with Known Vulnerabilities

Software Components, like frameworks, libraries, and other kinds of modules, often execute with maximum privilege. Whenever a weak component is attacked, it may lead to serious threat. Depending on the vulnerabilities of the components, any kind of attack is eventually possible. For example, if a website is using a library vulnerable to SQL injection, the whole website will be vulnerable to such an attack. The open source libraries, framework, and content management systems (CMSs) are the source of many attacks.

2.10   Unvalidated Redirects and Forwards

WAs usually forward and redirect users to other websites and pages, and exploit input data to identify new potential destinations. Without proper checking and authentication of the input data, users can be redirected to malware or phishing. Attackers may also exploit forwards to reach unauthorized zones. For instance, http parameter can include, or part of, a URL value, which could be exploited by the WA to redirect the request to the considered URL. An attacker can execute a phishing scam and capture user information by changing the URL address to a hostile site. Since the server in the updated connection has the same name as the original (trusted) site attempts at phishing look more trustworthy.

3   Countermeasures Against Attacks

In this section, we present the main proposed solutions to mitigate web attacks described in the previous section.

3.1 Countermeasures Against Injection Attacks

Many solutions have been adopted to address the SQL Injection, as it presents the most widely spread attack [32]. The authors of [60] proposed a framework based on information theory for detecting SQLI attacks. The proposed framework statically estimates query's entropy based on the distribution of token probability of a query. First, the system computes the entropy of every query included in the program source code before the deployment of the application. Then, during the execution of the application, the system computes again the entropy of each invoked SQL query to detect if there is any change in the measured entropy. In [51], the authors proposed a WAF based on Artificial Neural Network (ANN) to avoid SQLIAs. The system consists of a pair of steps: Training step and Working step. During the training step, a collection of normal and malicious data is fed to the system to train the ANN. During the working step, the obtained ANN is integrated into the WA firewall to detect the WA attacks. The authors of [48] proposed a semantic comparison based scheme. The semantic comparison is made between the two syntax trees of a query during training and run-time. If the two trees are similar, then the query is evaluated as benign query, else it is evaluated as malicious one. Authors in [30] have proposed WASP, a tool for avoiding SQLIAs using the notion of positive tainting and on syntax-aware evaluation. The idea of positive tainting is to identify and track trusted data, instead of tainting untrusted data in traditional (negative) tainting approach. The advantages of the positive tainting over the negative one is that it generates false positives instead of false negatives, in case of incompleteness.

3.2 Countermeasures Against Broken Authentication and Session Management

For session hijacking, the traditional countermeasure technique consists in binding the client IP address. More precisely, in this technique, the web server binds a user's session to a fixed IP address, and then discard any request coming from a distinct IP address. This technique requires that each client possess a different and unchanging public IP address. However, a network generally uses NAT protocol to share the same IP address to multiple clients and, therefore, make this technique ineffective [25]. Another technique to mitigate session hijacking is based on tracking user browser fingerprint. A browser fingerprint consists of numerous characteristics of the user browser. Any modification of the user browser fingerprint might represent an attacker stealing a session [52]. Session-Lock [9] adds an integrity checks to every client request based on a secret shared with the server. If a session identifier is stolen, a valid request cannot be computed since the value of the secret is unknown. One limit of SessionLock is its vulnerability to script-based attacks. To mitigate session hijacking attacks and inspired by the concept of Kerberos service tickets, the authors in [24] proposed to replace the static session identifier with disposable tokens per request. Macaroons [33] targets cloud services and restricts access to cooki.e. Macaroons uses chains of nested Hash-based Message Authentication Codes (HMACs), constructed from a shared secret and a chain of messages.

3.3   Countermeasures Against XSS Attacks

A first defense line against XSS, at the server-side, is to adopt a user-input validation to enforce the security. Validation can use either blacklisting or whitelisting
techniques. Moreover, once user-input is found to be malicious, it can either
be sanitised or rejected [3]. However, the secure input handling method cannot
achieve full protection, especially for complex website.

A second defense line, which is becoming more and more implemented in
web-servers, is based on Content Security Policy, which generally defines trusted
origins that the browser is allowed to download resources (can be a script, a
style-sheet, an image, etc.) from them. Therefore, although an intruder is able
to inject vulnerable content into the website, the CSP method may block its
execution. Authors in [63] proposed a secure WA proxy for detecting and blocking
Cross Site Scripting (XSS) attacks. The proposed framework contains a reverse
proxy intercepting the returned HTML messages first, then using an altered web
browser to locate vulnerable scripts.

The authors in [59] proposed to use Kullback-Leibler Divergence (KLD) measure to provide a proxy-level detection methodology for the XSS attacks. The
idea is based on the intuition that legitimate WAs JavaScript code should remain
comparable or very similar to a rendered web page's JavaScript code. For this
purpose, the authors proceed to the tokenization of the considered script code
into unique elements and calculate the probabilities of their occurrences in order
to construct two sets P (legitimate JS code available in the application page)
and Q (observed JS code available in the response page). Then, KLD computes
the distance separating these two proposed probability distributions. An XSS
attack is detected in case of a significant divergence between the two sets.

3.4   Countermeasures Against Insecure Direct Object References and Missing Function Level Access Control

To secure the access to the resources and the utilization of internal functions of a
WA, most of security systems have used access control mechanisms. For instance
in Role-Based Access Control (RBAC) [27], programmers control objects by permissions, assign permissions to roles and assign roles to users. Permission autho-
rizes a user for a role in a given session. The Separation of Duty Constraints
prevent a user from acquiring two or more conflicting roles. For example, Cisco
ACE WA Firewall uses RBAC to define the administration roles of the WAF
itself. In [53], the authors describe an implementation of RBAC with role hier-
archies on the Web by secure cookies. The user's role information is injected
in a set of secure cookies and transmitted to the corresponding Web servers. In
order to verify the cookies, they use PGP (Pretty Good Privacy) to define
cookie-verification procedures.

In [12], the authors proposed an access control method for open web service
applications. Their work is based on the eXtensible Access Control Markup
Language (XACML) which belongs to the class of access control languages.

3.5 Countermeasures Against Sensitive Data Exposure

As presented in Sect. 1, the following three categories of sensitive data Exposure flaw exist:

- **Information Leakage:** As for this flaw, only the developer can improve security by paying attention to what he leaves in the code and to handle in a secure way the errors that can occur.
- **Transmission Attacks:** this kind of attacks is mainly avoided by a strong encryption mechanism and we do not know a well known approaches used in WAFs.
- **Database Thefts:** to deal with this attack, cryptography is a key solution together with a good security policy to access database. In [26], the authors proposed a dynamic database security policies as a solution for this kind of attack.

As conclusion, there are no known approaches that can be used by WAFs to overcome sensitive data exposure flaw.

3.6 Countermeasures Against CSRF

The are some countermeasures at the server-side to mitigate CSRF attacks [11, 26,36]. OWASP developed a project called CSRFGuard [1]. It is a library, which implements a variant of the Synchronizer Token Pattern to minimize the risk of CSRF attacks. The authors of [34] defined a server-side proxy named NoForge, which could be plugged into the considered system to discover and avoid CSRF attacks and it is transparent to users and applications. This proxy primarily detects and protects PHP applications against CSRF attacks. Zeller et al. in [64] enumerated the characteristics of server-side precautions to protect users. They also developed a plug-in at the server side for preventing users from the attacks.

3.7 Countermeasures Against Unvalidated Redirects and Forwards

The authors in [57] categorized the phishing countermeasures into four categories: blacklist-based, heuristic-based, visual similarity-based, and machine learning based. The blacklist-based techniques build a repository of discovered phishing URLs, which should be updated regularly. The most representative works under this category are the Google Safe Browsing API [8], PhishNet [54], which predicts the phishing URLs based on the known phishing URLs, and Automated Individual White-List (AIWL) [20] that keeps a list of trusted Login User Interfaces (LUI). However, this list suffers from the problem of untrusted LUI prediction. Generally, the blacklists offer good True-Positive (TP) rates but suffer from False-Positive (FP) rates. SPHERES [28] is a WAF implemented in the WA server based on behaviour, and prevents the phishing attack by defining a profile for each parameter provided by the web client.

Table 1. Attacks classification and their countermeasures

Attacks	Sources	Sinks	Countermeasure techniques
SQL injection	User input, cookies, server variables	Database	Information theory based; compare the query entropy before deployment and during execution
			Artificial neural network
			Semantic comparison
			Positive tainting and on syntax-aware evaluation
			Syntactic structures comparison of the programmer-intended query and the actual query
			Software-testing techniques
			The model is expressed as a grammar that only accepts legal queries
			Taint based approach
Code injection		System Web site	Technique based on multitier compilation
			Constructs a control flow graph for each function
Brute force attack, Dictionary attack, Credential enumeration	User input	Session	Picture-based
Session hijacking, Session fixation, Cookie poisoning	Cookies	Website, URL, Session	Time signature based
			Shared secret
			Token per request
			Chains of nested HMAC
Stored XSS, reflected XSS, DOM XSS	User input	Data base Website	Per-page security policies
			Probability distributions of tokens extracted from the script code
			Creation of shadow pages that reflects the set of scripts that a web application intends to create
			XSD schema file
			Reverse proxy
			Boundary injection and policy generation
CSRF	User input	Database	Server side changes and captcha
Privilege escalation	Use input	Database	Automatically instrument application source code program analysis to check for authorization state consistency in a web application
Transmission attacks	User input	ALL	Cryptography
Directory traversal attacks, Path Traversal attack, The direct request attack	User input	System, website	Access control using RBAC
			Simple filtering rule
			RBAC for cookies
			Security Policy Description Language
			Access control using RBAC for WS-BPEL processes
Authorization bypass through user-controlled key	User input	DB	Access control using RBAC
Local file inclusion, Command injection, Remote file inclusion	User input	System, DB, NET, website	Access control using RBAC
Phishing attack	User input	DB (user credentials)	Recognize fake URLs
			Recognize whitelist URLs

3.8 Discussion

The most severe, critical and widespread flaw as classified by the OWASP top ten is the injection flaw [2]. The main attack under this flaw is SQL injection. Several solutions were proposed to mitigate this attack and they can be classified mainly as grammar-based, entropy-based, machine learning-based and tainting-based. Grammar-based methods are efficient but require to write a grammar model for each possible query, which is error prone. Moreover, these methods can not discover stored procedure type attacks and database management systems (DBMS) specific subqueries. In addition, the time complexity of these methods is high, and hence it is impossible to discover the attack in real-time [47].

The entropy methods are based on probabilistic models and so far are unstable. Taint-based approaches are time consuming as they need to monitor every variable in the web site. Machine learning techniques are not well adapted to this context as they need a long training phase and the results can include several false negatives and positives [47].

The second severe flaw is related to authentication and session management. As for authentication, the value of the authenticated cookie must be updated each time the level of authorization of the user takes a new value to combat potential session vulnerabilities [16]. The web developer should enhance the authentication method using picture-based or time-signature-based authentication scheme. The common protection of session attacks prevents JavaScript access to session cookies. Another promising idea is based on defining a collection of security policies.

For the XSS attack, many defense solutions are adopted, and existing industrial approaches mostly rely on user input sanitizing [55]. Some approaches use probability distribution of tokens in a web page [59]. Other approaches are based on page code modification either by creation of shadow page [14], or by inserting a script ID [63], or using boundaries injection, [29].

The fourth and the seventh flaws lead to similar attacks. The fourth category encompasses attacks that lead to a misuse of the objects that exist in the web structure, and the seventh category encompasses the attacks that misuse the functions provided by the web application. Both categories could be secured by controlling and managing the roles, the objects and the permissions to handle both of them.

Regarding the fifth flaw, the web administrator should fine-tune the configuration entries of the web application during the deployment and use of the application. Thus, the default values usually known by the attacker will be minimized and the security of the component will be maximized. A static scan of the server configuration could help in this stage.

Regarding the sixth flaw, the web server must use secured connection when sensitive data are exchanged with the client (Emails, banking transaction, etc.). The system administrator must choose the right database access policies and a strong cryptography of sensitive data stored in database. The web developer must pay attention to what he leaves in the code source and must handle the system errors perfectly.

A good and very well known way to overcome the CSRF attacks, i.e., the eight flaw, is using captcha. We need to apply strong models to avoid bypassing it. Many others works are proposed to handle this attack. They add some code at the web server [64] and enhance also the client side by some routines.

Regarding the ninth flaw, the web developer should handle with care the external components used in the website especially the open source libraries and frameworks. The developer can minimize the risks produced by these components by rewriting their interface for example. However, it will be difficult to use a sub-sequential version of the component.

The tenth category in the top ten may lead to the phishing attach, which could be mitigated by blocking fake URLs using existing black lists [8,54] or white lists [20]. A summary of the studied approaches is given in Table 1.

4   Protection Methods for WA Firewalls

WA firewalls (WAFs) are the primary front-end protection mechanism for web-based applications which are continuously under attack. We can find two categories of WAF: open source and commercial.

4.1   Open Source WAF

Examples of open source solutions that can be used to deploy a firewall to protect web applications are the following:

- **AQTRONIX WebKnight**: It is an open source WA Firewall (WAF) for Internet Information Services (IIS). AQTRONIX WebKnight is an ISAPI filter that tries to secure the target web server by blocking certain requests. To do so, a scanning and processing of all requests is performed according to filter rules, which do not come from a dataset of attack signatures requiring regular updates.
- **ModSecurity:** It is a toolkit for real-time WA access control, logging and monitoring. This toolkit supports a pair of deployment options: reverse and embedded proxy deployment. This method enables protecting the WA against a wide range of attacks. It also offers the monitoring of HTTP traffic, its logging as well as the real-time analysis of it.

4.2   Commercial WAF

Examples of commercial solutions that can be used to deploy a firewall to protect web applications are the following:

- **dotDefender:** it is a WA Firewall installed on Apache or Microsoft IIS Server. This WAF claims preventing the following attacks: XSS, SQLIAs, Credit Card Disclosure, DoS, etc.

- **Imperva SecureSphere:** [31] it may be used as a reverse proxy or as a transparent bridge, and when deployed out-of-band, it operates passively as a sniffer, detection and alteration without protection against attacks.
- **Barracuda:** [13] it is designed to protect WA and Web sites from application vulnerabilities to instigate data theft, application-layer DoS attacks, or defacement of the Web site of an organization. Th WAF offers protection against attacks like XSS, Brute Force and SQL Injection.

5   Model-Based Testing and Formal Methods for Web Service Security

In this section, we give an overview on WA verification, i.e., model-based testing and formal methods, and present their applications for web applications. WA verification can be classified under the following two methods:

- **Model Based Testing (MBT):** It is a methodology [37–39] where the behavior of the System Under Test (SUT) is encoded by means of an abstract model. This methodology permits to automatically produce abstract test scenarios from the considered model. Regarding testing security aspects, the authors of [41] proposed an MBT methodology for validating security aspects of IoTs in Smart Cities. The proposed methodology takes advantage of the adoption of the standard testing language TTCN- 3 [44] and a cloud-oriented architecture [45]. Similarly, the authors of [42,43] proposed an MBT methodology in order to validate security properties of IoTs. In [40], a set of optimization techniques was adopted in order to diminish the complexity of MBT procedures.
- **Formal Methods (FM):** When establishing computer systems (CS), the complete detection and correction of design errors remain remarkably hard in the context of manual simple verification techniques and functional testing activities. Consequently, in the early 1980s, scientists [18,21,56] started to make CS verification methodologies more rigorous, specially by making them more automatic. In fact, with the emergence of new mathematical languages for the specification and description of dynamic systems, the first formal verification methodologies have appeared.

Model-based testing methods for WA security can be classified as follows:

- **Modelling HTTP Requests:** In [19], an approach named Chained Attack is proposed. The proposed approach considers HTTP requests as a starting point, produces models, and extracts scenarios of attacks from these models using model-checking procedures.
- **Formalizing Vulnerabilities into Test Purposes:** The authors of al [46] proposed an MBT security validation methodology, which allows to formalize vulnerability test patterns in form of test purposes. The authors defined the behavior of the considered web applications and purposes of tests, and adopted model-checking procedures in order to produce testing scenarios.

– **Consideration of an Attacker Model:** The authors of [15] adopted an MBT methodology, in which the formal models of attacker are considered to validate web applications and functionalities.
– **Technique Inspired by Mutation Testing:** In [17], the authors presented an MBT approach for validating security properties of WA. The proposed approach is closely inspired by mutation testing techniques.
– **Use of UMLsec Tool:** In [35], the authors proposed an MBT testing approach for the automatic production of security test-scenarios. The approach takes advantage of the UMLsec tool. It aims at testing the security properties of the Common Electronic Purse Specifications.
– **Use of Alloy Analyser:** In [10], a methodology using the Alloy Analyzer for inspecting several web applications and mechanisms was proposed. The authors adopted threat models such as an intruder taking control over a website or a whole part of the network.
– **Mobster Tool:** In [49], the authors introduced the MobSTer tool, which is a Model-based Security Testing Framework that may help security analysts in testing security aspects of WA. This framework combines model-checking procedures with the knowledge obtained from penetration testing guidelines and checklists.

Formal methods for WA security can be classified as follows:

– **Security by Construction:** Some works in the literature [61] aim at defining new formal languages and abstraction techniques in order to make the Web safer. For this purpose, these works attempt to identify the main limitations in the current conception techniques of the Web and suggest a paradigm evolution to ameliorate it. This set of suggestions is adequate for dealing with the principle source of security problems. However, they mostly need a deep change to current WA and technologies.
– **Modelling, Verification and Enforcement:** Some other research works adopt an other strategy which consists in considering appropriate algorithms and models for dealing with the FV of the security properties of modern Web technologies. These research works attempt to exploit available standards and frameworks as best as they can. This approach may be in many cases sub-optimal and not very effective. However, the main advantage is that this procedure does not impact a lot the existing Web technologies. For example with respect to scripting languages, different solutions [62] based on the adoption of rigorous semantics for the considered language were adopted.
– **An industrial Application:** In [22], the authors applied FV techniques for the security of Amazon Web Services (AWS). Two main goals were considered with this respect. The first one consists in raising the level of security of the provided products and the second one helping customers securing themselves against possible attacks.

6   Conclusions and Future Work

This paper presents an up to date survey about web applications vulnerabilities, attacks and server-side countermeasures. The main vulnerabilities and attacks, which targets current WAs according to the OWASP top 10 classification, have been described. After that we surveyed the countermeasures solutions proposed in the last decades to protect WAs against these attacks. The literature includes hundreds of works about server-side web protection methods, and many of them propose enhanced protection models. The existing WAFs include only simple protection rules, which does not take into account the advances in the field. There is a big gap between the research products and the WAF methods. The developers of WAFs try to propose a global protection tools that mitigate a wide range of attacks using simple methods that fail to deal with the complexity of new attacks. As a future work, we plan to design and develop a WA firewall that is lightweight and adaptable to current WAs needs.

References

1. Category: OWASP CSRFGuard project - OWASP. https://www.owasp.org/index.php/Category:OWASP_CSRFGuard_Project. Accessed 30 July 2020
2. Category: OWASP top ten project - OWASP. https://www.owasp.org/index.php/Category:OWASP_Top_Ten_Project. Accessed 230 July 2020
3. Excess XSS: A comprehensive tutorial on cross-site scripting. http://excess-xss.com/. Accessed 30 July 2020
4. Information leakage - OWASP. https://www.owasp.org/index.php/Information_Leakage. Accessed 30 July 2020
5. InfoSecPro.com - computer, network, application and physical security consultants. http://www.infosecpro.com/applicationsecurity/a52.htm. Accessed 30 July 2020
6. The web application security consortium/information leakage. http://projects.webappsec.org/w/page/13246936/Information%20Leakage. Accessed 30 July 2020
7. Website. https://lthieu.wordpress.com/2012/11/22/cross-site-request-forgery-a-small-demo. Accessed 30 July 2020
8. Website. https://developers.google.com/safe-browsing/. Accessed 30 July 2020
9. Adida, B.: Sessionlock: securing web sessions against eavesdropping. In: Proceedings of the 17th International Conference on World Wide Web, WWW 2008, New York, NY, USA, pp. 517–524. ACM (2008)
10. Akhawe, D., Barth, A., Lam, P.E., Mitchell, J., Song, D.: Towards a formal foundation of web security. In: 2010 23rd IEEE Computer Security Foundations Symposium, pp. 290–304, July 2010. https://doi.org/10.1109/CSF.2010.27
11. Anwar, D., Anwar, R.: Transparent data encryption-solution for security of database contents. Int. J. Adv. Comput. Sci. Appl. 2(3) (2011)
12. Ardagna, C.A., di Vimercati, S.D.C., Paraboschi, S., Pedrini, E., Samarati, P., Verdicchio, M.: Expressive and deployable access control in open web service applications. IEEE Trans. Serv. Comput. 4(2), 96–109 (2011)
13. Barracuda: Barracuda WAF. White paper (2019)
14. Bisht, P., Venkatakrishnan, V.N.: XSS-GUARD: precise dynamic prevention of cross-site scripting attacks. In: Zamboni, D. (ed.) DIMVA 2008. LNCS, vol. 5137, pp. 23–43. Springer, Heidelberg (2008). https://doi.org/10.1007/978-3-540-70542-0_2
15. Blome, A., Ochoa, M., Li, K., Peroli, M., Dashti, M.T.: Vera: a flexible model-based vulnerability testing tool. In: 2013 IEEE Sixth International Conference on Software Testing, Verification and Validation, pp. 471–478, March 2013. https://doi.org/10.1109/ICST.2013.65

16. Braun, B., Pauli, K., Posegga, J., Johns, M.: LogSec: adaptive protection for the wild wild web. In: Proceedings of the 30th Annual ACM Symposium on Applied Computing, pp. 2149–2156. ACM (2015)
17. Büchler, M.: Semi-automatic security testing of web applications with fault models and properties. Ph.D. thesis, Technical University Munich (2015). http://nbn-resolving.de/urn:nbn:de:bvb:91-diss-20151218-1273062-1-3
18. Bugliesi, M., Calzavara, S., Focardi, R.: Formal methods for websecurity. J. Log. Algebr. Methods Program. **87**, 110–126 (2017). https://doi.org/10.1016/j.jlamp.2016.08.006. http://www.sciencedirect.com/science/article/pii/S2352220816301055
19. Calvi, A., Viganò, L.: An automated approach for testing the security of web applications against chained attacks. In: Proceedings of the 31st Annual ACM Symposium on Applied Computing, SAC 2016, New York, NY, USA, pp. 2095–2102. ACM (2016). https://doi.org/10.1145/2851613.2851803. http://doi.acm.org/10.1145/2851613.2851803
20. Cao, Y., Ye, C., Weili, H., Yueran, L.: Anti-phishing based on automated individual white-list. In: Proceedings of the 4th ACM Workshop on Digital Identity Management - DIM 2008 (2008)
21. Clarke, E.M., Emerson, E.A.: Design and synthesis of synchronization skeletons using branching time temporal logic. In: Kozen, D. (ed.) Logic of Programs 1981. LNCS, vol. 131, pp. 52–71. Springer, Heidelberg (1982). https://doi.org/10.1007/BFb0025774. http://dl.acm.org/citation.cfm?id=648063.747438
22. Cook, B.: Formal reasoning about the security of amazon web services. In: Computer Aided Verification - 30th International Conference, CAV 2018, Held as Part of the Federated Logic Conference, FloC 2018, Oxford, UK, 14–17 July 2018, Proceedings, Part I, pp. 38–47 (2018). https://doi.org/10.1007/978-3-319-96145-3_3
23. Cui, Y., Cui, J., Hu, J.: A survey on XSS attack detection and prevention in web applications. In: Proceedings of the 2020 12th International Conference on Machine Learning and Computing, pp. 443–449 (2020)
24. Dacosta, I., Chakradeo, S., Ahamad, M., Traynor, P.: One-time cookies: preventing session hijacking attacks with stateless authentication tokens. ACM Trans. Internet Technol. **12**(1), 1:1–1:24 (2012)
25. De Ryck, P., Desmet, L., Piessens, F., Johns, M.: Primer on client-side web security. Springer, Cham (2014). https://doi.org/10.1007/978-3-319-12226-7
26. Doshi, J., Trivedi, B.: Sensitive data exposure prevention using dynamic database security policy. Int. J. Comput. Appl. Technol. **106**(15), 18600–9869 (2014)
27. Ferraiolo, D., Cugini, J., Kuhn, D.R.: Role-based access control (RBAC): features and motivations. In: Proceedings of 11th Annual (1995)
28. Fredj, O.B.: Spheres: an efficient server-side web application protection system. Int. J. Inf. Comput. Secur. **11**(1), 33–60 (2019)
29. Gupta, S., Gupta, B.B.: XSS-SAFE: a server-side approach to detect and mitigate cross-site scripting (XSS) attacks in javascript code. Arab. J. Sci. Eng. **41**, 897–927 (2015). https://doi.org/10.1007/s13369-015-1891-7
30. Halfond, W., Orso, A., Manolios, P.: WASP: protecting web applications using positive tainting and syntax-aware evaluation. IEEE Trans. Software Eng. **34**(1), 65–81 (2008)
31. Imperva: WAF gateway. White paper pp. 1–2 (2019)
32. Jemal, I., Cheikhrouhou, O., Hamam, H., Mahfoudhi, A.: SQL injection attack detection and prevention techniques using machine learning. Int. J. Appl. Eng. Res. **15**(6), 569–580 (2020)

33. Johns, M., Martin, J., Bastian, B., Michael, S., Joachim, P.: Reliable protection against session fixation attacks. In: Proceedings of the 2011 ACM Symposium on Applied Computing - SAC 2011 (2011)
34. Jovanovic, N., Kirda, E., Kruegel, C.: Preventing cross site request forgery attacks. In: Securecomm and Workshops, 2006. pp. 1–10. ieeexplore.ieee.org, August 2006
35. Jürjens, J.: Model-based security testing using UMLsec. Electron. Notes Theor. Comput. Sci. **220**(1), 93–104 (2008).https://doi.org/10.1016/j.entcs.2008.11.008
36. Kiernan, J., Jerry, K., Rakesh, A., Haas, P.J.: Watermarking relational data: framework, algorithms and analysis. VLDB J. Int. J. Very Large Data Bases **12**(2), 157–169 (2003)
37. Krichen, M.: Model-based testing for real-time systems. Ph.D. thesis, PhD thesis, PhD thesis, Universit Joseph Fourier, December 2007
38. Krichen, M.: A formal framework for conformance testing of distributed real-time systems. In: Lu, C., Masuzawa, T., Mosbah, M. (eds.) OPODIS 2010. LNCS, vol. 6490, pp. 139–142. Springer, Heidelberg (2010). https://doi.org/10.1007/978-3-642-17653-1_12
39. Krichen, M.: Contributions to model-based testing of dynamic and distributed real-time systems. Ph.D. thesis, École Nationale d'Ingénieurs de Sfax (Tunisie) (2018)
40. Krichen, M.: Improving formal verification and testing techniques for internet of things and smart cities. Mobile Netw. Appl. 1–12 (2019)
41. Krichen, M., Alroobaea, R.: A new model-based framework for testing security of IoT systems in smart cities using attack trees and price timed automata. In: 14th International Conference on Evaluation of Novel Approaches to Software Engineering - ENASE 2019 (2019)
42. Krichen, M., Cheikhrouhou, O., Lahami, M., Alroobaea, R., Jmal Maâlej, A.: Towards a model-based testing framework for the security of internet of things for smart city applications. In: Mehmood, R., Bhaduri, B., Katib, I., Chlamtac, I. (eds.) SCITA 2017. LNICST, vol. 224, pp. 360–365. Springer, Cham (2018). https://doi.org/10.1007/978-3-319-94180-6_34
43. Krichen, M., Lahami, M., Cheikhrouhou, O., Alroobaea, R., Maâlej, A.J.: Security testing of internet of things for smart city applications: a formal approach. In: Mehmood, R., See, S., Katib, I., Chlamtac, I. (eds.) Smart Infrastructure and Applications. EICC, pp. 629–653. Springer, Cham (2020). https://doi.org/10.1007/978-3-030-13705-2_26
44. Lahami, M., Fakhfakh, F., Krichen, M., Jmaiel, M.: Towards a TTCN-3 test system for runtime testing of adaptable and distributed systems. In: Nielsen, B., Weise, C. (eds.) ICTSS 2012. LNCS, vol. 7641, pp. 71–86. Springer, Heidelberg (2012). https://doi.org/10.1007/978-3-642-34691-0_7
45. Lahami, M., Krichen, M., Alroobaea, R.: TEPaaS: test execution platform as-a-service applied in the context of e-health. Int. J. Auton. Adapt. Commun. Syst. **12**(3), 264–283 (2019)
46. Lebeau, F., Legeard, B., Peureux, F., Vernotte, A.: Model-based vulnerability testing for web applications. In: 2013 IEEE Sixth International Conference on Software Testing, Verification and Validation Workshops. pp. 445–452, March 2013. https://doi.org/10.1109/ICSTW.2013.58
47. Lee, I., Jeong, S., Yeo, S., Moon, J.: A novel method for SQL injection attack detection based on removing SQL query attribute values. Math. Comput. Modell. **55**(1–2), 58–68 (2012). https://doi.org/10.1016/j.mcm.2011.01.050. http://www.sciencedirect.com/science/article/pii/S0895717711000689. Advanced Theory and Practice for Cryptography and Future Security

48. Mamadhan, S., Manesh, T., Paul, V.: SQLStor: blockage of stored procedure SQL injection attack using dynamic query structure validation. In: 2012 12th International Conference on Intelligent Systems Design and Applications (ISDA), pp. 240–245 (2012)
49. Meo, F.D., Viganò, L.: A formal approach to exploiting multi-stage attacks based on file-system vulnerabilities of web applications. In: Engineering Secure Software and Systems - 9th International Symposium, ESSoS 2017, Bonn, Germany, July 3–5, 2017, Proceedings, pp. 196–212 (2017). https://doi.org/10.1007/978-3-319-62105-0_13
50. Mnif, A., Cheikhrouhou, O., Jemaa, M.B.: An ID-based user authentication scheme for wireless sensor networks using ECC. In: ICM 2011 Proceeding, pp. 1–9. IEEE (2011)
51. Moosa, A.: Artificial neural network based web application firewall for SQL injection. Proc. World Acad. Sci. Eng. Technol. **64**, 12–21 (2010)
52. Nikiforakis, N., Kapravelos, A., Joosen, W., Kruegel, C., Piessens, F., Vigna, G.: Cookieless monster: exploring the ecosystem of web-based device fingerprinting. In: 2013 IEEE Symposium on Security and Privacy (SP), pp. 541–555. ieeexplore.ieee.org, May 2013
53. Park, J.S., Sandhu, R., Ghanta, S.L.: RBAC on the web by secure cookies. In: Atluri, V., Hale, J. (eds.) Research Advances in Database and Information Systems Security. ITIFIP, vol. 43, pp. 49–62. Springer, Boston, MA (2000). https://doi.org/10.1007/978-0-387-35508-5_4
54. Prakash, P., Kumar, M., Kompella, R.R., Gupta, M.: PhishNet: predictive blacklisting to detect phishing attacks. In: 2010 Proceedings IEEE INFOCOM, pp. 1–5. ieeexplore.ieee.org, March 2010
55. Prokhorenko, V., Choo, K.K.R., Ashman, H.: Web application protection techniques: a taxonomy. J. Netw. Comput. Appl. **60**, 95 – 112 (2016).https://doi.org/10.1016/j.jnca.2015.11.017. http://www.sciencedirect.com/science/article/pii/S1084804515002908
56. Queille, J.P., Sifakis, J.: Specification and verification of concurrent systems in CESAR. In: Dezani-Ciancaglini, M., Montanari, U. (eds.) Programming 1982. LNCS, vol. 137, pp. 337–351. Springer, Heidelberg (1982). https://doi.org/10.1007/3-540-11494-7_22. http://dl.acm.org/citation.cfm?id=647325.721668
57. Scott, D., Sharp, R.: Specifying and enforcing application-level web security policies. IEEE Trans. Knowl. Data Eng. **15**(4), 771–783 (2003)
58. Shabtai, A., Elovici, Y., Rokach, L.: A Survey of Data Leakage Detection and Prevention Solutions. Springer, Boston (2012). https://doi.org/10.1007/978-1-4614-2053-8
59. Shahriar, H., Hossain, S., Sarah, N., Wei-Chuen, C., Edward, M.: Design and development of Anti-XSS proxy. In: 8th International Conference for Internet Technology and Secured Transactions (ICITST 2013) (2013)
60. Shahriar, H., Zulkernine, M.: Information-theoretic detection of SQL injection attacks. In: 2012 IEEE 14th International Symposium on High-Assurance Systems Engineering (HASE), pp. 40–47 (2012)
61. Swamy, N., et al.: Gradual typing embedded securely in javascript. In: Proceedings of the 41st ACM SIGPLAN-SIGACT Symposium on Principles of Programming Languages, POPL 2014, New York, NY, USA, pp. 425–437. ACM (2014). https://doi.org/10.1145/2535838.2535889. http://doi.acm.org/10.1145/2535838.2535889
62. Taly, A., Erlingsson, U., Mitchell, J.C., Miller, M.S., Nagra, J.: Automated analysis of security-critical javascript APIs. In: 2011 IEEE Symposium on Security and Privacy, pp. 363–378, May 2011. https://doi.org/10.1109/SP.2011.39

63. Wurzinger, P., Platzer, C., Ludl, C., Kirda, E., Kruegel, C.: SWAP: Mitigating XSS attacks using a reverse proxy. In: 2009 ICSE Workshop on Software Engineering for Secure Systems, SESS 2009, pp. 33–39. IEEE (2009)
64. Zeller, W., Felten, E.W.: Cross-site request forgeries: Exploitation and prevention. NY Times, pp. 1–13 (2008)

Infrastructure Security and Malware Detection

Autonomous Vehicle Security: Literature Review of Real Attack Experiments

Siham Bouchelaghem[1](✉), Abdelmadjid Bouabdallah[2], and Mawloud Omar[3,4]

[1] Laboratoire d'Informatique Médicale, Faculté des Sciences Exactes,
Université de Bejaia, Bejaia, Algérie
bouchelaghemsiham@gmail.com
[2] Heudiasyc UMR CNRS 7253, Université de Technologie de Compiègne,
Compiègne, France
madjid.bouabdallah@hds.utc.fr
[3] LIGM, ESIEE Paris, Université Gustave-Eiffel, Noisy-le-Grand, France
mawloud.omar@univ-eiffel.fr
[4] Institut de Recherche Technologique SystemX, Palaiseau, France

Abstract. With recent advances in technology to bring about smarter cities, significant efforts are put forth to enhance living standards through efficient infrastructure and services. Smart mobility is a core aspect of the Smart City concept, looking for the design of smart solutions to the challenging urban traffic issues faced by modern cities. It is envisioned that vehicle automation will come to change our lives and society soon. Autonomous vehicles have been around for years now, driving around streets to test their ability to navigate real-world driving environments. In the long term, they are expected to improve road safety and increase citizens mobility, providing a suitable mode of transport for people who cannot drive. Although the technology is not yet mature, it has aroused the interest of both academia and industry to inherent security challenges that must be addressed before large-scale adoption. There has been a host of research efforts on the security of autonomous vehicles in terms of vulnerabilities, attacks and potential defenses. In this paper, we propose a novel taxonomy of attack surfaces in autonomous vehicles. Based on our taxonomy, we review a selection of relevant and recent research on real attack experiments carried out on many components and automated driving systems. We also perform threat modeling and risk assessment to support security aware design of autonomous vehicles.

Keywords: Smart mobility · Autonomous vehicle · Security · Attack surfaces · Threat modeling

1 Introduction

Several recent advances in embedded computing and sensor technology have led to an unprecedented interest in autonomous systems [1]. Autonomous Vehicles (AVs) that were deemed a futuristic project just few years ago are now a reality

© Springer Nature Switzerland AG 2021
J. Garcia-Alfaro et al. (Eds.): CRiSIS 2020, LNCS 12528, pp. 255–272, 2021.
https://doi.org/10.1007/978-3-030-68887-5_15

that is already upon us. These innovative vehicles designed to operate without any human intervention have drawn much attention from car manufacturers and leading technical companies for the development of sophisticated driverless vehicle prototypes [2,3]. In addition, the scientific community is increasingly investigating several issues and challenges that may hamper their future design and large-scale deployment. The major motive behind the emergence of AVs is the promise to improve the passenger experience on the roads by reducing traffic congestion, but above all to enhance road safety by reducing the risk of accidents. In fact, according to the recent report of the World Health Organization, about 1.35 million people die each year on road accidents worldwide [4]. The greater part of traffic accidents can be related to human errors and bad driving behavior as a result of inattention, distracted driving, carelessness, over-speeding, and so on. The automotive industry therefore plans to make AVs the newest reliable, safe, and fully automated means of transportation by reducing the number of human drivers behind the wheel.

The design of fully AVs nonetheless raises major concerns regarding safety, liability, interoperability, security and privacy which may slow down their wide deployment. In fact, citizens are wondering about their ability to willingly trust a vehicle they have no control on, especially because of the disastrous consequences in the event of a system failure. Although modern vehicles already have some automated features (e.g., lane departure warning, emergency braking), AVs are intended in the long term to perform various maneuvers on roads and highways without the need for drivers presence, even in unforeseen circumstances. As a result, citizens are extremely worried about their safety and that of their families, which may hinder the global marketing of AVs. Questions of liability are also required as who will be held responsible in the event of an accident. With the emergence of multiple European corridor projects, where AVs roam between multiple countries, stakeholders, infrastructures, and regulations, close cooperation is an important prerequisite to overcome heterogeneity issues and deploy innovative and interoperable autonomous driving technologies. Last but no means least, AVs are equipped with multiple sensors and communication capabilities, which provide external attackers with potential vulnerabilities and easily exploitable security breaches. This ubiquitous connectivity has in fact widened the attack surfaces of driverless vehicles. Communication and location privacy is therefore another important concern, since data collected by AVs and shared with other parties may hold personal information, which can seriously imperil citizens privacy if intercepted by malicious users.

There has been a significant body of work on security threats, exploitable vulnerabilities, potential attacks and associated countermeasures to address the security risks to AVs. This paper aims to provide a broad overview of the field by presenting a literature review of AV security issues. In particular, the main contributions of this paper are as follows:

– We analyze the AV functional architecture and propose a taxonomy of attack surfaces that can be used to enter the system and potentially cause damages;

– We survey some real security attack experiments existing in the literature and classify them based on the proposed taxonomy;
– We perform threat analysis and risk assessment on a system model of AV we developed. This could be used as a cornerstone principle toward building a security-by-design framework for AVs.

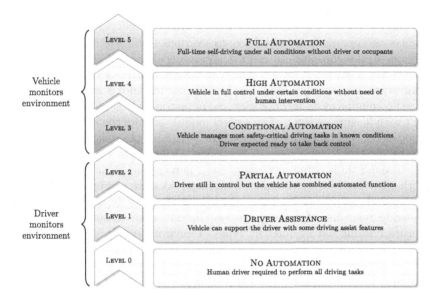

Fig. 1. SAE International levels of driving automation.

The remainder of this paper is organized as follows. In Sect. 2, we provide background on the AV technology, covering its main components and functional architecture. In Sect. 3, we propose a new taxonomy of attack surfaces and potential security threats to AVs. We also review some relevant security attacks performed on the main components of AVs and automated driving systems. In Sect. 4, we apply threat modeling approach to the AV system and analyze the risks posed by the identified threats. In Sect. 5, we discuss the main security requirements of AVs and potential threat mitigation derived from the previous analysis. Finally, we conclude the paper in Sect. 6.

2 Overview of AV Technology

With the growing awareness of high-end vehicles development trends, *automated* and *autonomous* are two terms often used interchangeably in reference to these vehicles, although there are some nuances in meaning. An *automated* vehicle refers to a vehicle controlled or operated by a machine to conduct driving tasks and monitor the roadway, but which may require a human driver to regain control in certain circumstances. An *autonomous* vehicle lies on actions and maneuvers performed independently by vehicles with higher levels of automation, without any human intervention. These definitions meet with the levels of driving automation identified by the Society of Automotive Engineers (SAE) [5]. Each level describes an increase in vehicle automation features and a decrease in driver involvement. Figure 1 illustrates the SAE standardization of driving automation levels, ranging from no automation to fully autonomous vehicles.

To carry out the mission of self-driving without hampering the safety of passengers and pedestrians, an AV requires various technologies that will enable it to perceive its environmental context and to decide accordingly how it should behave facing a given situation. These main components can be categorized into hardware and software modules. The former includes a myriad of sensors, advanced communication technologies and actuators, which allow the vehicle to interact with its surroundings. The second module enables the AV to understand and process collected information about the environment, make timely decisions and translate them into proper actions (e.g., whether to move, stop or slow down), through three core processes namely, perception, planning and control.

With their need for surrounding awareness, AVs are equipped with a range of sensors and imaging technology, which help them safely navigate the roads and provide real-time obstacle detection. Indeed, each sensor has the ability to capture information in different types of environment and specific ambient light conditions. To cope with the shortcomings of each sensor, the AV combines data from various sources to have a comprehensive view of the vehicle state and surroundings in a process called *sensor fusion* [6]. The aim is to provide AVs with data redundancy for more accurate environment perception and safer decision-making. AVs also contain an in-vehicle network of Electronic Control Units (ECUs), each responsible for a specific functionality such as unlocking the doors, opening a window, collision warnings, etc. Moreover, AVs leverage some connected vehicle technologies, namely, Vehicle-to-Vehicle (V2V) and Vehicle-to-Infrastructure (V2I) communication. V2X technology enables AVs to gather information from neighboring vehicles, roadside infrastructure, service providers, and so on, through Dedicated Short-Range Communication (DSRC) standard protocol, for enhanced driving automation and readily integration. Beyond pure Intelligent Transportation System technologies and in the 5G era, it is expected that AVs will leverage Cellular V2X (C-V2X) communication to benefit from advanced safety features, especially in high-density traffic environments.

3   Potential Threats and Practical Attacks

In this section, we provide a taxonomy of attack surfaces and potential threats to AVs, and present a review of real attack experiments performed on automated systems embedded in most AVs. Unlike the existing taxonomy of Thing and Wu [8], which relies on the type, skills and motivations of the attacker, the proposed taxonomy stems from our thinking and efforts to categorize potential attack surfaces from the analysis of the functional architecture of AVs. Furthermore, in addition to the in-vehicular threats, our taxonomy highlights environmental and application-related threats as new categories of attack surfaces in AVs.

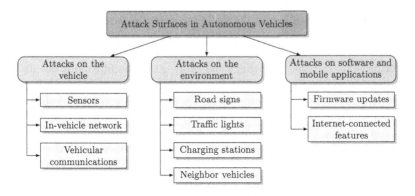

Fig. 2. Taxonomy of security threats and attack surfaces in AVs.

3.1   Attack Surfaces and Security Issues

As a key enabler for autonomous driving, modern vehicles are increasingly fitted with a range of sensing features and communication devices, which has brought to researchers and the automotive industry attention various new vulnerabilities and potential attack surfaces [7,8]. Just as connected vehicles, it is envisioned that AVs will leverage Vehicular Network (VN) technology, enabling V2V, V2I and, more recently, V2IoT communication for information sharing and service delivery. As it becomes more prevalent on the roads, vehicular communication promises to enlarge the AV attack surfaces, as the number of wireless interfaces increases. In this context, several security threats, vulnerabilities and well-known attacks have already been widely investigated in the VNs literature [9–12]. Likewise, the increased internal communications within AVs constitute a likely target for attackers to misuse with vehicle components. In fact, modern vehicles contain numerous ECUs interconnected via an in-vehicle network, exchanging data to provide control and maneuverability in the vehicle. Hence, this growing complexity in AV internal architecture rises new entry points to exploit such as ECUs software and bus network design vulnerabilities [13]. Moreover, wireless communications have also introduced a whole new range of security risks to the so far isolated in-vehicle network [14,15].

Currently, vehicle owners are increasingly looking for a connected experience while commuting, even placing their desire for more connectivity at the expense of more engine power and fuel efficiency. Hence, car manufacturers have explored ways to integrate mobile applications into modern vehicles, allowing consumers to interface with their vehicle and perform various functions such as unlocking the doors and starting the engine using their personal phones. While it creates passenger-centric experiences and improves driving convenience, increasing the connectivity also brings a lot of security vulnerabilities exposing AVs to severe damages due to malwares and potential personal data leakage. AVs will release their occupants from driving tasks, and give them more free time for listening to music, catching up on latest news, and playing games. Car manufacturers, application developers and service providers will be thus able to collect various data related to vehicle journeys and consumer preferences and habits, which may raise new privacy concerns. Another vulnerable attack point to look out for is the external environment as sensors fitted in AVs continuously capture information on its changing surroundings to allow reliable driving. Altering road objects such as road signs, traffic lights, or lane markings can tamper with the AV perception system, compromise the decision-making process and hamper passengers safety. Other traffic participants (i.e., neighboring cars) may be corrupted as well and give false traffic reports leading to traffic congestion and potential collisions.

In summary, we can classify potential attack surfaces in AVs according to the targeted vehicle components and driving elements as described in Fig. 2. Various practical tests have been performed to assess AV security against these different attacks. In what follows, we provide an extensive review of some experiments.

3.2   Survey of Real-World Experiments

With the intended increase in automotive sensors number and connectivity in future AVs, it is imperative to work on identifying security threats toward these new attack surfaces. Hence, several experiments have been conducted to analyze the feasibility of remote attacks on automated systems within self-driving vehicle prototypes. In Table 1, we summarize the main reviewed AV security attacks and identify potential safety implications.

Attacks on Sensors. Several new functionality that will be present in future AVs require various sensory features to provide an accurate depiction of the vehicle surroundings. These main components represent possible entry points for an attacker to compromise the vehicle. To study the feasibility and effectiveness of the attacks, multiple real experiments have been done on AV most critical sensors, both in laboratory and outdoor environments.

Petit et al. [16] have led an experimental study on remote attacks on camera-based and LiDAR systems using commodity hardware in different laboratory conditions. The authors have performed a blinding attack by emitting light into the camera with the aim to hide objects. In autonomous driving, preventing the camera from objects detection such as a vehicle ahead, the traffic light state or a speed limit signage can endanger passengers safety. The authors have also demonstrated the effectiveness of relay and spoofing attacks on a LiDAR sensor. Denial of Service attacks can affect the decision-making process and may even prevent the AV from detecting real obstacles.

Yan et al. [17] proposed a complementary work and conducted experiments on two other types of sensors widely used in AVs namely, ultrasonic sensors and radar. The authors have conducted outdoor experiments on a Tesla Model S to demonstrate the impact of jamming and spoofing attacks on autonomous driving. The authors have performed remote attacks and showed their destructive effect on the AV functioning and safety. In fact, jamming attacks makes the obstacles undetectable, which may lead to collisions while parking or maneuvering and impair pedestrians safety. Spoofing attacks deceive the sensors and disrupt their readings, which may cause the display of pseudo-obstacles and alter the distance of real ones.

Shoukry et al. [18] have demonstrated the impact of spoofing attacks on the Anti-lock Braking System (ABS) used in modern vehicles. The ABS is an automated safety system that maintains vehicle steerability and stability during emergency braking. The authors have experimented two non-invasive types of attacks namely, disruptive and spoofing attacks. In the former, the actuator placed near the wheel sensor corrupts the measured speed with a malicious signal overlying the original one. The second attack deceives the ABS by intercepting the original magnetic field and injecting a counterfeit signal such that the sensor reports an erroneous speed. Changing the ABS sensor readings can lead to life-threatening situations as the vehicle slips off the road.

Attacks on the In-Vehicle Network. Hoppe et al. [19] have performed several practical tests on recent CAN-bus-based automotive technology. The authors demonstrated that injecting a malicious code in the appropriate ECU allows attackers to easily eavesdrop on data or launch replay and spoofing attacks on different parts of the vehicle. Once a predefined condition met, the malicious code could replay CAN message for opening the driver window [20]. Another attack performed on warning lights could also switch the lights off as per the attacker request, which may lead to potential accidents when the vehicle breaks down. Hence, an attacker that gains control over the window may steal the vehicle or valuable items from the interior, unnoticed. Other experiments were performed on the airbag control system, where attackers can suppress several signs of system non-functionality and pretend the presence of operational airbags. Since the airbag system will be unavailable in emergency cases, severe injuries can be expected in case of accidents. Finally, attacks conducted on gateway ECU show that sensitive information can be disclosed.

Rouf et al. [21] have experimented attacks against modern vehicles embedded Tire Pressure Monitoring System (TPMS), where sensors inside each tire monitor their pressure in real time. The authors have found that pressure sensors unique identifiers can be eavesdropped at distance up to 40 meters from a passing vehicle and may be used for remote identification and tracking. Moreover, conducted tests suggest that the vehicle ECU managing TPMS data does not use any authentication nor input validation. From a nearby vehicle, attackers may be able to inject spoofed messages with erroneous tire pressure readings, thus triggering the low-pressure warning lights in target moving vehicle at inappropriate times. Such attacks could cause AV decision-making system confusion and may lead it to completely ignore TPMS-related warnings.

Kamkar [22] developed the RollJam device to compromise the vehicle door lock system without having the original key fob. Modern vehicles are equipped with a Remote Keyless Entry system that allows to wirelessly unlock the doors and disable the anti-theft alarm. The system generates a rolling code each time the user presses the key fob button and can be used only once to unlock the vehicle doors. Upon the first press on the key fob, the RollJam device jams the signal, intercepts and stores the rolling code. Since the doors fail to unlock, the user presses the key once again, which enables the RollJam device to jam and record the second code, while simultaneously broadcasting the first one. The vehicle doors successfully unlock leaving the attacker with a legitimate code able to unlock the doors later, once the user leaves.

Attacks on the Environment. Recent reported events have shown that greedy drivers may attempt to ease their daily commute by altering lane markings to redirect traffic and make the path toward their destination smoother or even get around parking issues creating their own spot [23,24]. Road objects alteration in autonomous driving may result in collisions and life-threatening situations. Sitawarin et al. [25] have proposed two novel security attacks against traffic sign recognition systems used in AVs. These attacks aim to deceive the traffic sign recognition mechanism through road sign alteration imperceptible to human eyes. Creating toxic signs causes misclassification that may influence vehicle dynamics leading to serious consequences such as large-scale traffic disturbances and life-threatening accidents.

Nassi et al. [26] have demonstrated how external attackers can exploit a new perceptual challenge to launch phantom attacks on Advanced Driver Assistance Systems (ADAS) and autopilots of semi-autonomous vehicles. A *phantom* object is a depthless object such as an obstacle (i.e., pedestrian, vehicle, motorcycle, etc.), lane, or road sign, which can be projected via a flying drone equipped with a portable projector or embedded in buildings and existing digital billboards located near roads. Phantom attacks aim to fool ADAS and autopilot systems to perceive these objects and consider them as real by exploiting the inability of semi-autonomous vehicles to validate their perception with a third party. Indeed, the delay in the large-scale deployment of vehicular communication systems has forced semi-autonomous cars to rely solely on sensor measurements to validate their perception of the surrounding environment. Considering phantoms as real objects can cause a car's ADAS or autopilot to perform reckless driving due to fake speed limits, deviate towards the lane of oncoming traffic, or end up in collisions due to sudden braking.

Ghena et al. [27] have performed a security analysis of a wireless traffic light control system deployed in the United States. The authors have discovered several vulnerabilities in both the wireless network and the traffic light controller, and leveraged these weaknesses to study the feasibility of remote attacks on such systems. Once on the network and after gaining access to the controller, an attacker can stop the normal traffic light functioning setting all lights to red. This would cripple the traffic flow and cause large-scale congestion if the attack spread over multiple intersections. Timing values of light states can also be modified, which may have an impact on road network management, trips duration and vehicle emissions. An attacker can even control and change the lights to be green along his route either for personal gain or to give his vehicle a clear passage through intersections as running away. Lights could also be maliciously changed to red when accidents or disasters happen to prevent emergency vehicles arrival.

Attacks on Software and Mobile Applications. Miller and Valasek [28] have exploited vulnerabilities in the Uconnect software, an Internet-connected feature that controls the entertainment and navigation systems of many Fiat Chrysler vehicles. Using a simple third-generation connection from Miller's house, they launched attacks on a Jeep Cherokee located on highway 10 mi away. Through the software vulnerability, they were able to remotely control innocuous functions of the vehicle such as air conditioning, radio and windshield wipers before cutting the brakes and sending the vehicle into a ditch [29]. In fact, the two researchers managed without physical access to rewrite the firmware of an adjacent chip in the vehicle head unit and send commands through the CAN bus to physical components like the engine and wheels.

Similar attacks were performed on the Mitsubishi Outlander Plug-in Hybrid Electric Vehicle (PHEV), exploiting the unusual method used to connect the PHEV mobile application to the vehicle [30]. Instead of using GSM module, the Outlander PHEV has a WiFi Access Point (AP) enabling user communication with the vehicle and the control over its various functions. The user must however disconnect from any other WiFi network and connect explicitly to the vehicle AP for remote control. Launching a man-in-the-middle attack, security researchers were able to replay various messages from the mobile application and figure out the binary protocol used for messaging. They succeeded then to flash the headlights, turn the air conditioning on and off, and more worryingly, disable the theft alarm system leaving the vehicle once unlocked vulnerable to many more attacks.

Nissan was forced to disable its Nissan Connect mobile application used to control some dedicated functions of its Leaf electric vehicles [31]. Through the discovered vulnerability, it has been shown that attackers can remotely hijack the air conditioning and heating system, control the temperature and drain the electric battery charge while the vehicle is not in motion. They only have to download the Nissan app and enter the Vehicle Identification Number (VIN) visible on the windscreen. Since VINs differ only in the last five digits, attackers can use every possible combination, gain access to a multitude of models, and turn the air conditioning on in every one.

Attacks on Vehicular Communications. Puñal et al. [32] have studied the impact of constant and reactive jamming attacks on V2V communication. The authors performed outdoor experiments for two different network topologies, following the relative position of transmitter, receiver and jammer placed inside standard vehicles. In the first topology, the two vehicles follow each other on a straight road with short and nearly constant distance, referred to as platooning. Whereas in the second topology, the two vehicles move along the same street in opposite directions heading to a crossroad, in an approaching configuration. The experiments show that jamming attacks can have negative impacts on VNs ranging from reduced packet delivery rate to large communication-blind areas creation, which may severely impact the supported safety critical applications failing to deliver warning and traffic coordination messages in a timely manner.

4   Threat Modeling of AVs

In this section, we model the security of AV systems to support the description of the surveyed attack scenarios. Based on the taxonomy and the three categories described in Sect. 3.1, we model the main components of the AV and their interactions, and map the attack scenarios on the developed model.

Security modeling of autonomous systems is a widely studied field. Different techniques have been used to model different aspects of these systems in order to find vulnerabilities and threats, and to further create attack models [33]. With numerous data connections and increasing connectivity to the outside world, AVs are exposed to a range of potential remote attacks. From a safety perspective, it is hence essential to address security concerns at the design phase, so as to avoid massive recalls of vehicles already on the road. In particular, threat modeling is a process that has been adapted to the automotive industry toward building secure road vehicles [34]. Not only will it strengthen security by early identifying and understanding the threats to the vehicle and its software, but it will also help assess the security risks to the AV and define the appropriate countermeasures. The absence of vulnerable areas can hardly be proven, only because no potential attack scenario has been found.

In this context, we apply the STRIDE threat modeling method [35] and the Common Vulnerability Scoring System (CVSS) technique [36] to identify and prioritize potential security issues that can compromise the AV safe operation. After analyzing the functional architecture of the AV and determining its main components, we have modeled the system as a Data Flow Diagram (DFD), using the Microsoft Threat Modeling Tool [37]. The DFD shows the information flows between the AV components and the environment, as illustrated in Fig. 3. The STRIDE method then analyzes the diagram and identifies security threats arising from the data flows so that mitigation strategies can be incorporated into the system design. These threats are categorized into six generic types: Spoofing, Tampering, Repudiation, Information disclosure, Denial of Service, and Elevation of privileges. Regarding the AV system, we characterize STRIDE threats as follows:

- Spoofing: an attacker masquerades a legitimate vehicle and/or disseminates fake information (e.g., geographical positions);
- Tampering: an attacker alters messages exchanged between vehicles, sensor data or ECUs firmware;

Table 1. Summary of experimented security attacks and potential safety implications.

Reference	Targeted component	Security attack	Exploited vulnerability	Safety implication
Petit et al. [16]	LiDAR	Relay and Spoofing	Physical signal reflection	Traffic disturbance due to fake objects detection
	Camera	Blinding (DoS)	Light sensitivity	Potential collisions due to unperceived obstacles
Yan et al. [17]	Ultrasonic sensors	Jamming and spoofing	Noise and interference sensitivity	Low-speed collisions due to undetected obstacles
	Radar			Traffic disturbance and pile-ups due to false obstacle distance measurements
Shoukry et al. [18]	Speed sensors	Spoofing	Physical exposure to magnetic field tamper	Traffic disturbance and accidents due to vehicle wrong trajectory and loss of control
Hoppe et al. [19]	Electric window lifts	Malicious code injection	CAN bus design	Potential accidents and theft
	Warning lights	Replay and spoofing	Lack of encryption and authentication	
	Airbag control system			Missing protection and severe injuries due to fake reported system status
	Central gateway	Eavesdropping	Gateway ECU implementation	Privacy breach due to personal information disclosure
Rouf et al. [21]	TPMS	Eavesdropping	ECU implementation	Privacy leak and tracking
		Spoofing	Lack of encryption, authentication and input validation	Passengers safety loss and potential robberies due to disregarded or fake warnings
Kamkar et al. [22]	RKE system	Jamming and Replay	ECU implementation	Vehicle or valuable items theft from interior
			Wireless sending of non-expiring rolling codes	
Sitawarin et al. [25]	Traffic sign recognition system	DARTS	Image classification	Traffic disturbance and collisions due to fake road signs recognition

(continued)

Table 1. (*continued*)

Reference	Targeted component	Security attack	Exploited vulnerability	Safety implication
Nassi et al. [26]	ADAS and autopilot systems	Phantom attacks	Validation gap	Reckless driving and traffic jams
				Collisions and deviation to lane of oncoming traffic
Ghena et al. [27]	Traffic light control system	DoS	Lack of encryption on wireless network	Traffic congestion due to poor road network management
		Timing values modification	Factory-default credentials use on network devices	
		Light control		Slow emergency vehicles response
Miller and Valasek [28]	Air conditioning	Code modification	Internet-connected software	Life-threatening collisions due to unauthorized access to critical driving systems
	Radio Windshield wipers Braking system Steering wheel			
Pentest Partners [30]	Headlights	Man-in-the-middle	WiFi access point	Vehicle or valuable items theft from interior
	Air conditioning Anti-theft alarm system			
Hull [31]	Heating system	Hijacking	Vehicle functions controlled via mobile phone	Electric battery drain
			Vehicle mobile app non-secure access via exposed VIN	
Puñal et al. [32]	V2V communications	Jamming	Wireless medium	Loss of safety due to timely warning dissemination failure

- Repudiation: a vehicle denies having performed a certain action (e.g., sending a message) or having been involved in a reported event;
- Information disclosure: an attacker gets unauthorized access to exchanged messages or to sensitive information (e.g., traveled positions, ECUs firmware);
- Denial of Service: an attacker prevents sensor data acquisition or timely message dissemination such as warnings and safety messages;
- Elevation of privileges: an attacker sends improper commands to the AV navigation system and gains unprivileged access to its critical functions.

The threat analysis part of the STRIDE method from a set of representative threats is summarized in Table 2. Once the threats are identified using STRIDE, we use the CVSS technique to perform risk assessment and prioritize the risks associated with each threat to the AV. The CVSS quantifies and prioritizes the amount of risk presented by each threat and associates it with vulnerabilities based on the following metrics [36]:

- Access Vector: reflects how the vulnerability can be exploited. The more remote an attacker can be, the higher the vulnerability score;
- Access Complexity: measures the complexity required for an attack to exploit the vulnerability;
- Confidentiality impact: measures the impact on confidentiality of a successful exploited vulnerability;
- Integrity impact: measures the impact on integrity of a successful exploited vulnerability;
- Availability impact: measures the impact on availability of the exploited vulnerability;
- Collateral Damage Potential: reflects how life-threatening the vulnerability can be and the potential for property damage.

The CVSS technique assigns a score to each metric and computes for each threat assessed an overall risk score ranging from 0 to 10. This value corresponds to a level of severity, which can vary from Low [0.0–3.9], Medium [4.0–6.9] to High [7.0 − 10.0]. Table 2 identifies the high risks that are inherent in sensor technology and highly safety-critical ECUs, since any failure in road objects detection or any arbitrary firmware issuance could have disastrous effects on safety, leading to vehicle control and stability loss, and passenger injuries.

5   Security Requirements and Threat Mitigation

From the previous threat modeling approach, we can easily infer that each STRIDE threat category can be mapped to a set of security requirements that the AV system must meet for proper and safe operation. In what follows, we put forward some details pertaining to these aspects and discuss possible threat mitigation.

- Authentication and trustworthiness: driving decisions should be made based on messages received from legitimate vehicles being actually at the claimed position, especially when related to safety applications and traffic congestion avoidance. AV decision-making system should hence verify during data fusion process that perceived data are consistent with environment-related data gathered from other sources, before coming to any wrong decision.
- Integrity: sensor data and ECU firmware should not be easily tampered with, so that an attacker cannot take control over the vehicle navigation and safety-related control features (i.e., braking, steering and speed control). Road objects physical alteration should also be prevented to ensure correct sensors measurement.

Table 2. Threat analysis and risk score of the AV system model.

Threat	Category	AV	AC	$Impact_C$	$Impact_I$	$Impact_A$	CDP	Risk score
Vehicle could be tracked	I	Network	Medium	Partial	None	None	High	3.5
Deliver malicious GPS data to cause drift off course	S	Network	High	Partial	Partial	None	Low	4.2
Using diagnostic line against the vehicle and denying the changes	R	Local	Medium	Partial	Partial	None	Low-Medium	5.1
Manipulate camera data in order to fake an object	S	Network	High	Partial	Partial	None	High	6.8
Reflash the ECU firmware in order to send arbitrary CAN messages	E	Local	High	Partial	Partial	Partial	High	6.9
Jam GPS signal received by the vehicle	D	Local	Low	None	None	Complete	Low-Medium	6.9
Manipulate the software configurations sent to the Brakes	T	Adjacent Network	Medium	Partial	Partial	Complete	High	8.2
Turning on/off the vehicle functions without passenger interaction	S	Adjacent Network	Medium	Partial	Partial	Complete	High	8.2
Sensor data can be attacked through DOS	D	Network	Low	None	None	Complete	High	8.9

- Non-repudiation and accountability: AVs bring new concerns in terms of lia-bility in case the vehicle is involved in an accident as future fully AVs are expected to move along without any occupant. Relevant authorities should hence have solid proofs (e.g., vehicle location, time and speed) about the claimed event.
- Confidentiality and privacy: sensitive information such as the vehicle owner identity and his/her successive travel positions must be protected, as it can be used for vehicle tracking and driving behavior prediction. ECUs firmware also contain confidential data (i.e., source code), which must not be accessed by malicious parties able to get control over vehicle critical functions.
- Availability: jamming the communication channel to delay safety messages should be prevented, as it can lead to traffic congestion and road accidents. Data acquisition should also be strengthened to improve automation and keep the system in a minimal risk functioning state. Hence, data redundancy should be ensured using different sensor types and V2X technology.
- Authorization: access control policies should be defined to prevent arbitrary actions or malicious firmware updates on safety-critical ECUs, such as the

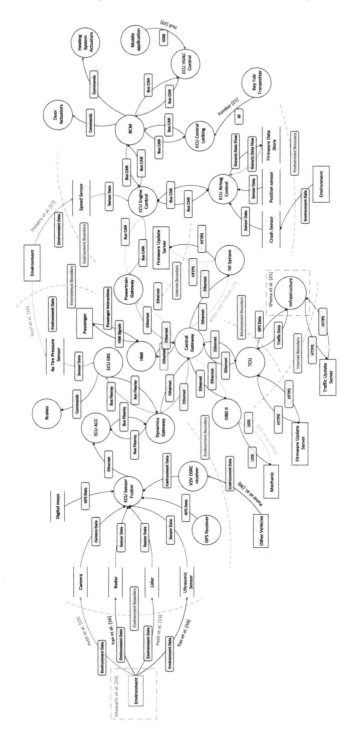

Fig. 3. DFD diagram representing the communication pattern in AVs.

engine management and transmission control (e.g., the brake system), and vehicle safety systems (e.g., ABS, TPMS), as they would allow an attacker to endanger the safety of passengers.

- Data freshness: messages generated or sent to ECUs must not be replayed to prevent an attacker from triggering critical commands, leading the AV to hazardous reactions or luckless decisions, beneficial to some malicious parties (e.g., opening the vehicle doors). Freshness of messages exchanged between cooperative AVs must also be ensured since traffic made decisions depend on timely environment-related data.

6   Conclusion

In this paper, we focused on the security issues of AVs. We have proposed a novel taxonomy of AV security threats related to different attack surfaces that can be targeted by external attackers. We believe that the proposed taxonomy provides a comprehensive insight over the vulnerabilities and the security threats to AVs known so far. Based on this taxonomy, we have then described and classified some relevant research works aimed at practically investigating the feasibility of remote attacks on AVs. After analyzing the AV functional components and the surveyed experiments, we have performed a threat analysis to identify potential points of attack and assess the risks posed by these threats to the functioning of AVs. The threat modeling approach outlined in this paper lies within an emerging research direction regarding security-by-design principles for AVs.

References

1. Wyglinski, A.M., Huang, X., Padir, T., Lai, L., Eisenbarth, T.R., Venkatasubramanian, K.: Security of autonomous systems employing embedded computing and sensors. IEEE Micro **33**(1), 80–86 (2013)
2. Waymo Homepage. https://waymo.com/. Accessed 23 Jun 2020
3. Tesla Autopilot. https://www.tesla.com/autopilot. Accessed 23 Jun 2020
4. World Health Organization, Global Status Report on Road Safety (2018)
5. SAE International Standard: Automated Driving: Levels of Driving Automation as per SAE **J3016**, (2018)
6. Kocić, J., Jovičić, N., Drndarević, V.: Sensors and sensor fusion in autonomous vehicles. In: 26th Telecommunications Forum, pp. 420–425. IEEE Belgrade (2018)
7. Petit, J., Shladover, S.E.: Potential Cyberattacks on Automated Vehicles. IEEE Trans. Intell. Transp. Syst. **16**(2), 546–556 (2015)
8. Thing, V.L.L., Wu, J.: Autonomous vehicle security: a taxonomy of attacks and defences. In: IEEE International Conference on Internet of Things and IEEE Green Computing and Communications and IEEE Cyber, Physical and Social Computing and IEEE Smart Data, pp. 164–170. IEEE (2016)
9. Jain, M., Saxena, R.: VANET: security attacks, solution and simulation. In: Bhateja, V., Tavares, J.M.R.S., Rani, B.P., Prasad, V.K., Raju, K.S. (eds.) Proceedings of the Second International Conference on Computational Intelligence and Informatics. AISC, vol. 712, pp. 457–466. Springer, Singapore (2018). https://doi.org/10.1007/978-981-10-8228-3_42

10. Hasrouny, H., Samhat, A.E., Bassil, C., Laouiti, A.: VANET security challenges and solutions: a survey. Veh. Commun. **7**, 7–20 (2017)
11. Bariah, L., Shehada, D., Salahat, E., Yeun, C. Y.: Recent advances in vanet security: a survey. In: 82nd Vehicular Technology Conference, pp. 1–7. IEEE, USA (2015)
12. Raya, M., Papadimitratos, P., Hubaux, J.P.: Securing vehicular communications. IEEE Wireless Commun. **13**(5), 8–15 (2006)
13. Cho, K. T., Shin, K. G.: Error handling of in-vehicle networks makes them vulnerable. In: Proceedings of the ACM SIGSAC Conference on Computer and Communications Security, pp. 1044–1055. ACM, Austria (2016)
14. Studnia, I., Nicomette, V., Alata, E., Deswarte, Y., Kaâniche, M., Laarouchi, Y.: Survey on security threats and protection mechanisms in embedded automotive networks. In: 43rd Annual Conference on Dependable Systems and Networks Workshop, pp. 1–12. IEEE, Hungary (2013)
15. Nilsson, D. K., Larson, U. E., Picasso, F., Jonsson, E.: A first simulation of attacks in the automotive network communications protocol FlexRay. In: Corchado, E., Zunino, R., Gastaldo, P., Herrero, Á., (eds.) Proceedings of the International Workshop on Computational Intelligence in Security for Information Systems CISIS 2008, Advances in Soft Computing, vol. 53, pp. 84–91. Springer, Berlin (2009) https://doi.org/10.1007/978-3-540-88181-0_11
16. Petit, J., Stottelaar, B., Feiri, M., Kargl, F.: Remote attacks on automated vehicles sensors: experiments on camera and LiDAR. In: Black Hat Europe, Amsterdam (2015)
17. Yan, C., Xu, W., Liu, J.: Can you trust autonomous vehicles: contactless attacks against sensors of self-driving vehicle. In: 24th DEFCON Hacking Conference (2016)
18. Shoukry, Y., Martin, P., Tabuada, P., Srivastava, M.: Non-invasive spoofing attacks for anti-lock braking systems. In: Bertoni, G., Coron, J.-S. (eds.) CHES 2013. LNCS, vol. 8086, pp. 55–72. Springer, Heidelberg (2013). https://doi.org/10.1007/978-3-642-40349-1_4
19. Hoppe, T., Kiltz, S., Dittmann, J.: Security threats to automotive CAN networks - practical examples and selected short-term countermeasures. Reliab. Eng. Syst. Saf. **96**(1), 11–25 (2011)
20. Hoppe T., Dittman, J.: Sniffing/Replay attacks on CAN buses: a simulated attack on the electric window lift classified using an adapted CERT taxonomy. In: 2nd Workshop on Embedded Systems Security, pp. 1–6. Austria (2007)
21. Rouf, I., et al.: Security and privacy vulnerabilities of in-car wireless networks: a tire pressure monitoring system case study. In: 19th USENIX Security Symposium, pp. 323–338. Washington (2010)
22. Kamkar, S.: Drive it like you hacked it: new attacks and tools to wirelessly steal cars. In: 23th DEFCON Hacking Conference (2015)
23. News From Elsewhere, Man Fined for Painting Road Signs to Aid his Commute (2017). https://www.bbc.com/news/blogs-news-from-elsewhere-42181263. Accessed 23 Jun 2020
24. South China Morning Post, The Thin White Line: Van Driver Eludes Chinese Traffic Cops by Chalking his own Parking Places (2017). https://www.scmp.com/news/china/society/article/2091872/thin-white-line-van-driver-eludes-chinese-traffic-cops-chalking. Accessed 23 Jun 2020
25. Sitawarin, C., Bhagoji, A.N., Mosenia, A., Chiang, M., Mittal, P.: DARTS: Deceiving Autonomous Cars with Toxic Signs. ArXiv preprint :1802.06430v3 (2018)

26. Nassi, B., Nassi, D., Ben-Netanel, R., Mirsky, Y., Drokin, O., Elovici, T.: Phantom of the ADAS: Phantom Attacks on Driver-Assistance Systems, IACR Cryptology ePrint Archive, Report p. 085 (2020)
27. Ghena, B., Beyer, W., Hillaker, A., Pevarnek, J., Halderman, J.A.: Green lights forever: analyzing the security of traffic infrastructure. In: 8th USENIX Workshop on Offensive Technologies, San Diego (2014)
28. Miller, C., Valasek, C.: Remote exploitation of an unaltered passenger vehicle. In: 18th Black Hat USA, pp. 1–91. Las Vegas (2015)
29. Greenberg, A.: Hackers Remotely Kill a Jeep on the Highway - With Me in It (2015). https://www.wired.com/2015/07/hackers-remotely-kill-jeep-highway/. Accessed 23 Jun 2020
30. Lodge, D.: Hacking the Mitsubishi Outlander PHEV Hybrid (2016). https://www.pentestpartners.com/security-blog/hacking-the-mitsubishi-outlander-phev-hybrid-suv/. Accessed 23 Jun 2020
31. Hull, R.: Nissan Disables Leaf Electric Car App after Revelation that Hackers can Switch on the Heater to Drain the Battery (2016). https://www.thisismoney.co.uk/money/cars/article-3465459/Nissan-disables-Leaf-electric-car-app-hacker-revelation.html. Accessed 23 Jun 2020
32. Puñal, O., Aguiar, A.: Gross: J.: VANETs we trust? characterizing RF jamming in vehicular networks. In: 9th International Workshop on Vehicular Inter-networking, Systems, and Applications, pp. 83–92. ACM, UK (2012)
33. Jahan, F., Sun, W., Niyaz, Q., Alam, M.: Security modeling of autonomous systems: a survey. ACM Comput. Surv. 52(5), 1–34 (2019)
34. Karahasanovic, A., Kleberger, P., Almgren, M.: Adapting threat modeling methods for the automotive industry. In: 15th ESCAR Conference, pp. 1–10. Germany (2017)
35. Hernan, S., Lambert, S., Ostwald, T., Shostack, A.: Uncover Security Design Flaws Using The STRIDE Approach. MSDN magazine (2006). Accessed 05 Jul 2020
36. Mell, P., Scarfone, K., Romanosky, S.: A complete guide to the common vulnerability scoring system. In: FIRST - Forum of Incident Response and Security Teams (2007)
37. Potter, B.: Microsoft SDL threat modelling tool. Netw. Secur. 2009(1), 15–18 (2009)

New Dataset for Industry 4.0 to Address the Change in Threat Landscape

Salwa Alem[1,2(✉)], David Espes[2(✉)], Eric Martin[1(✉)], Laurent Nana[2(✉)], and Florent de Lamotte[1(✉)]

[1] University Bretagne Sud, Lab-STICC (Laboratoire des Sciences et Techniques de l'Information de la Communicationet de la Connaissance), Lorient, France
{salwa.alem,eric.martin,florent.delamotte}@univ-ubs.fr
[2] University of Western Brittany, University of Brest, Lab-STICC CNRS, UMR 6285, 29200 Brest, France
{david.espes,laurent.nana}@univ-brest.fr

Abstract. Because of its connectivity and its convergence with the IT world, industry 4.0 has become one of the main target sectors of the attackers. These last few years, they improve their operating mode and hit with more sophisticated attacks. Anomaly-based Intrusions Detection Systems (IDS) use datasets to train the classification algorithms they use to detect these attacks. Their detection capacity is therefore strongly linked to the representativeness of these datasets and the attacks they address. Actually, few datasets focus on the specificities of Industry 4.0 and even less propose a realistic labeled dataset. Therefore, the main goal of this paper is to propose an industrial labeled dataset. It is characterized by several novelties consisting firstly in the fact that this data adds application features related to the industrial protocol Modbus. Then, it simulates twelve IT and OT attacks in a real environment. And finally in the labelling process, it contains 3 labels: one to characterize normal traffic, another for abnormal traffic and a specific label to distinguish the equipment reaction against an attack from the other types of data.

Keywords: Dataset · Neural networks · Artificial intelligence · Intrusion Detection System (IDS)

1 Introduction

After the Stuxnet, BlackEnergy, WannaCry and NotPetya attacks, the banking, maritime and industry sectors became the targets of cyberattacks. Attackers have begun hitting hard and massively these industries and they have left a lot of damage behind: the loss of dozens of millions of dollars by Indian banks, the total paralysis of three international ports in three countries in the world, etc.

The European Union Agency For Network and Information Security (ENISA) has shown in its report [6] that the maritime industry is sensitive to many cyberthreats and that industry 4.0 has to take cybersecurity measures to protect its equipment.

© Springer Nature Switzerland AG 2021
J. Garcia-Alfaro et al. (Eds.): CRiSIS 2020, LNCS 12528, pp. 273–288, 2021.
https://doi.org/10.1007/978-3-030-68887-5_16

With the emergence of digitalization in the industry 4.0, the convergence between Information Technology (IT) and Operation Technology (OT) worlds has become a reality. This reality brings a lot of benefits to industrialists like a quick time-to-market, reducing cost and also, on-demand manufacturing that business to consumer manufacturers experience on a daily basis [38]. However, it makes the industry vulnerable and its attack surface larger.

Today and more than ever, industry needs efficient means to protect its equipment and its communication. Malicious attacks have become more elaborate. The intruders have improved their operating mode and they use different evasion techniques to prevent detection by an Intrusion Detection System (IDS) [16]. Recently, hackers organize themselves and improve their cyberattack techniques by performing more zero-day attacks than using a simple malware. According to [34], Symantec Internet Security Threat mentioned in its Report published in 2017 that about four billion zero-day attacks were performed in 2016 and a 7% increase in zero-day vulnerabilities were reported in 2018 [35]. Therefore, the critical challenge today is the design and the development of an efficient IDS to protect ICS (Industrial Control System) rather than conventional security solutions.

Among the existing defenses, we notice anomaly-based IDS which are efficient enough to be used in either industry or IT environments. Unlike signature-based IDS, they can detect new threats because all events that differ from a normal behavior is considered as an attack. Many anomaly-based IDS have been proposed in the literature [7,12,28]. To evaluate the efficiency and the performance of an IDS, a benchmark dataset is required. Typically, a dataset comprises two parts: one for training and the other for testing. Training data is used in the learning phase to train the IDS then the testing data is used to evaluate the IDS performance.

Today, most of the proposed anomaly-based IDS use existing datasets like UNIBS [11], SSENET-2014 [4], URG'16 [20], CICIDS2017 [29], SSENET-2014 [36] or others to test the performance of their IDS. However, due to the complexity of a dataset generation and the effort required to capture, preprocess and label it, there are few public and free datasets. Therefore, we focus the purpose of this paper on the proposal of a publicly available industrial dataset whose novelty and added value are explained in Sect. 3.

This paper is organized as follows. Section 2 discusses related works. Section 3 presents the design and the architecture of the generation process of new dataset proposal. Section 4 describes the industrial platform and the attack scenarios used to build the dataset, while Sect. 5 exposes our dataset. The paper ends by a conclusion and perspectives in Sect. 6.

2   Related Works

This section reviews research works on network-based datasets for intrusion detection systems. Network traffic based datasets usually contain packet-headers and payloads. They can be classified into three categories: publicly available, non-publicly available and industrial datasets which are captured in industrial environment and contain industrial features.

- **Public datasets**: Among the most famous, we have DARPA 98 and DARPA 99 datasets from the MIT Lincoln Laboratory. Both datasets use network traffic captured from a simulated environment and lack actual attack data records [5, 13]. The KDD CUP 99 dataset improves DARPA98 version and is one of the most widely used datasets for NIDS evaluation. However, one of the criticisms made against the KDD CUP 99 dataset is the data duplication [36].
  In [36], the authors propose the NSL-KDD dataset which is based on KDD CUP 99 and mitigates the weaknesses of this latter.
  In [9], the authors proposed a malware dataset. It contains botnet, normal and background traffic generated from several malware scenarios. The authors labeled the malicious traffic based on the IP addresses used by the botnets.
  In [27], the authors expose a dataset called CIDDS-002. They emulated a small business environment using the OpenStack software platform. The authors simulate the internal, the real and up-to-date attacks from the internet. The criticism made to this dataset is the fact that it is not captured in a real environment and there is no heterogeneity and diversity in the simulated attacks as it is mentioned in [10].
  In [28], authors propose a reliable and publicly available dataset called CICIDS2017. It is captured in a real environment during 5 days. The dataset contains more than 80 features extracted and calculated from normal and malicious traffic. Authors use the CICFlowMeter software published by Canadian Institute for Cyber-security website [17] for this extraction. They provide a more exhaustive review of their dataset but it lacks the up to date attacks.
  In [20], UGR'16 dataset is presented. This dataset is designed for the anomaly-based detection algorithms that consider the cyclostationary nature of traffic data. The netflow traces are collected during 4 months in a real environment.
- **Non-public datasets**: Researchers propose a flow-based dataset called SANTA in [37]. Flow is defined by traffic that has the same 5-tuples (source IP, destination IP, protocol, source port, and destination port). Dataset contains real traffic and different attack scenarios. Its labelling was done by manual analysis and heuristics. In [39], authors present IRSC a dataset for IDS. It is also a flow-based dataset. The authors collected network flows as well as full packets. The criticism made to these both latter datasets is that they are not publicly available.
  In [30], authors expose a new labeled flow-based DNS dataset viz called PUF in order to detect compromised hosts in a network. It is captured in a real environment during three days. The labelling process was performed using logs generated by an Intrusion Prevention System (IPS). The criticism made to their dataset is the lack of a variety of attacks.
  [4] exposes a labeled dataset containing 28 attributes divided into host-based and network-based attributes. It contains 200,000 labeled data points. Its

data volume duration is 4 hours performed in an emulated environment. The dataset is not publicly available.

– **Industrial datasets:** Other researchers proposed industrial datasets. In [23], the authors propose two datasets. The first dataset contains transactions from the gas pipeline system. The second dataset contains transactions from the water storage tank system. Both of them contain network traffic features and payload content features. They include network traffic information and the current state of the process control system defined from the payload content. Both datasets are labeled.

Researchers generate in [18] a labeled dataset for Electric infrastructures that rely heavily on SCADA networks. Their system is implemented in a SCADA sandbox. Authors simulate some attacks and label the captured traffic. The environment configuration is detailed in their paper and the dataset is publicly available. The criticism made to this work is the lack of attacks diversity and their unrealistic experimentation environment.

Other researchers present their industrial evaluation dataset in [14] but they do not give details about the configuration environment, the simulated attacks or the capture duration. In addition, the dataset is not publicly available.

In [2], authors use eight datasets, five of them are proposed in other works and are publicly available and three of them are captured from a real urban waste water treatment plant. These latter are composed of raw sensors measurements related to the water level readings of a tank and the status of three pumps correlated with the temperature and the humidity. These measurements are transformed into a set of distributions to find the limit between normal and critical state. The datasets are labeled and consist of 38 process parameters and are not publicly available.

To propose an IDS based on neural networks, in [19], authors record five datasets composed of 20000 packets. In addition, dataset was captured only for normal traffic containing 100000 packets in a simulated environment. Several information related to the capture duration, simulated attacks and extracted features are missing. This dataset is not publicly available. There is no information about the labelling process.

In [8], authors use an industrial dataset composed of 19 features. It contains features related to network and others are a sensory data about a tank system. It is extracted in a simulated environment and contains normal and malicious traffic. The authors have labeled their dataset.

In [32] and [15], authors proposed an industrial dataset captured in an emulated testbed for a CPS process controlled by SCADA using Modbus/TCP protocol, their attacks are not varied and diverse. In [32], only the network captures are given. In [15], only some few features are extracted (6 features) with no feature related to Modbus protocol.

Table 1 gives an overview of the existing datasets:

Table 1. The existing dataset overview

Research work	Year	Public	Indus.	Durat	Packet	Flow	Envir.	label	Ref
DARPA98/99	98/99	Yes	No	7wks	Yes	No	Emul	Yes	[5, 21]
KDD-CUP99	99	Yes	No	n.m	Other	Other	Emul	Yes	[13]
NSL-KDD	2009	Yes	No	n.m	Other	Other	Emul	Yes	[36]
CIDDS-002	2017	Yes	No	14dys	No	Yes	Emul	Yes	[27]
CICIDS2017	2017	Yes	No	5dys	No	Yes	Emul	Yes	[28]
UGR'16	2016	Yes	No	4 mth	No	Yes	Real	Yes	[20]
Modbus_dataset	2016	Yes	No	n.m	Yes	No	Emul	Yes	[18]
Kyoto	2009	Yes	No	3 yrs	Other	Other	Real	Yes	[33]
UMASS	2011	Yes	No	7 wks	Yes	No	Emul	n.m	[26]
ISCX2012	2012	Yes	No	n.m	Yes	Yes	Emul	Yes	[31]
SANTA	2014	No	Yes	n.m	Other	Other	Real	Yes	[37]
IRSC	2015	No	Yes	n.m	Yes	No	Real	Yes	[39]
PUF	2018	No	Yes	3 dys	No	Yes	Real	Yes	[30]
-	2018	No	Yes	n.m	Yes	No	Emul	Yes	[14]
-	2015	No	Yes	n.m	Other	Other	Emul	Yes	[2]
-	2009	No	Yes	n.m	Yes	No	Emul	Yes	[19]
WUSTL-IIOT	2018	Yes	Yes	25 h	Yes	No	Emul	No	[15]
-	2019	No	Yes	n.m	Other	Other	Emul	Yes	[8]
-	2019	Yes	Yes	n.m	Yes	No	Emul	No	[32]

n.m: not mentioned

Several of these datasets propose a number of features used as inputs for machine learning algorithms. Most of them propose features describing only information technology (IT) communications and coming from transport layer of Open System Interconnection model (OSI) and not beyond, like the datasets proposed in [27,29] and [20].

None of the industrial proposed works deal with communications occurring between the different industrial levels and few of them propose datasets containing application features.

In order to fill some of the gaps mentioned above, we propose a publicly available industrial labeled dataset built from malicious and non-malicious data captured in a real industrial platform. Its novelty and the added value are explained in the next Section.

3   New Dataset Proposal

3.1   Dataset Novelty and Added Value

Several researchers propose datasets for machine learning algorithms. Most of them capture traffic from IT devices and disregard industrial environment. It is difficult to obtain real traffic from these environments due to the anonymization of sensitive information. Moreover, the proposed datasets are not complete and contain mainly transport features while many attacks occur at the application layer of the OSI model. As far as we know, there is no public dataset built from a convergent industrial control system i.e., attacks are launched from the Enterprise level to reach the industrial level. In this work, we propose a new dataset. Its novelties and added values are summarized as follows:

- **Complete**: it contains both transport layer features and application features allowing the detection of both attacks occurring through transport layer of the OSI model as well as application attacks. The extracted features are related to Modbus protocol which is a client-server type protocol. Consequently, the features are related to both the Modbus request and response. These features characterize either registers, memory or time. All of these application features are exposed in Table 2.
- **Real Environment**: it is extracted from a real industrial platform.
- **Labelled**: it contains labels to distinguish normal traffic from malicious traffic. To these labels, another label is added for the device reaction against an attack.
- **Available**: it is publicly available to allow its use and testing by researchers.
- **Attacks Diversity**: it contains malicious traffic simulated from 7 attacks between OT and IT attacks.

3.2   Design Criteria

According to [10], the evaluation of a reliable dataset requires many criteria to respect. Our dataset respects most of them as it is shown in Fig. 1. The supported criteria are summarized here:

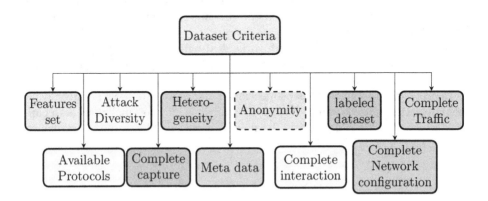

Fig. 1. Criteria of a reliable dataset

- **Complete Network Configuration**: our network topology (Fig. 3) includes various types of network equipment like switches and different operating systems. This topology integrates also industrial-specific equipment as industrial switches, Programming Logic Controller (PLC) such as M340 and M580 PLC and a real industrial Manufacturing Executive System (MES).
- **Complete Traffic**: we have three victim machines and three attacker machines which perform attacks on a real academic industrial platform.
- **Labeled Dataset**: the dataset is entirely labeled. Each sample is labeled as normal or with the type of attack or equipment reaction against an attack. The labelling procedure is described in Section V.
- **Complete Interaction**: internal and external flows are captured in the architecture.
- **Complete Capture**: probes are positioned at strategic places in the architecture in order to capture and record all the traffic.
- **Available Protocols**: this dataset deals with all common available protocols, such as TCP, ICMP, Modbus/TCP, HTTP and FTP.
- **Attack Diversity**: the simulated attacks are for the converging industry. Therefore, the dataset includes the most common attacks related to Information Technology (IT) world such as DoS, DDoS, Botnet, FTP Brute force, http flooding and others related to Operational Technology (OT) world like disturbance of the industrial process, Man In The Middle (MITM) against PLC and altering the data in the MES database through MSSQL server attack.
- **Heterogeneity**: malicious and non-malicious network traffics are captured from all victim machines.
- **Feature Set**: 134 features were extracted to build this dataset from network traffic thanks to the extractor developed during this work. These features will be described in Section V.
- **Labeled dataset**: Eight labels are given for each traffic kind (see Section V). One label for normal traffic, another for the reaction traffic and one label is used for each attack traffic.
- **Metadata**: this dataset contains application and transport layer features. Some of them are basic and others are statistically computed. Also more details on the type of attacks, the preprocessing and labelling processes are given later in this paper.
- **Anonymity**: All traffic will be provided with the payload and the used IP address.

3.3 Dataset Generation Process

In order to build the dataset, we start by performing the attacks, then capturing the traffic and finally extracting the features as shown in Fig. 2. All these steps have been performed on an academic platform hosted in Lab-STICC laboratory at University of Brest.

We carried out both IT attacks like DoS/DDoS, FTP and MSSQL brute force, but also attacks that are typically industrial like disturbing the production line and the MITM attack applied to a PLC (see Sect. 4).

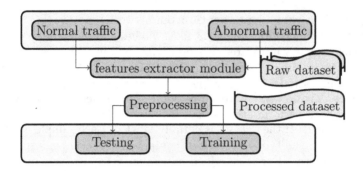

Fig. 2. Dataset extraction process

In the literature, datasets are either by flow (the traffic that has the same 5-tuples: source IP address, destination IP address, protocol, source port, and destination port) or by packet. Since dataset is intended to be used in a machine learning algorithm which requires a huge amount of data, each 2 s, a flow is split into sub-flows to generate enough samples to train any kind of machine learning algorithms.

3.4   Dataset Model

Our dataset model is composed of both networking and application features. It is composed of either basic features such as destination and source IP addresses, destination and source ports, protocols..., temporal features like RTT, TTL.. and an expressive features that require statistical calculation like avg, min, max, std. . .

The networking features are very helpful in our case because most attacks go through the network. Therefore, the nature of remote attacks can be established based on these features like RTT, duplication and retransmission packets to detect DoS attacks or MAC addresses and RTT to detect MITM attacks or based on application features like registers values, Modbus time to detect industrial attacks like disturbing process. The application features are related to Modbus protocol that we expose in Table 2 in Sect. 5. In our previous work [1], we identify 13 industrial attacks extracted from the industrial standard ISA95. They are divided into sequential, temporal or content attacks as explained hereafter:

1. Sequential attacks
   - PO (production order) request/response control: the attacker sends a response that matches no request.
   - WO (word order) sequencing control
   - Overlapping PO control
2. Temporal attacks
   - Planned/used total time control
   - Planned/used time per post control
   - Planned/used time between posts control

3. Content attacks
   - Planned/used PersonnelClass control
   - Planned/used EquipementClass control
   - Planned/used MaterialClass control
   - Produced quantity control
   - Equipment and data control
   - Sufficiency resources control
   - Consistency of launching PO control

Thanks to the Modbus application's features, an IDS can be trained to detect attacks on the intregrity of the system (i.e., sequential and content anomalies) and on its availability (i.e., temporal anomalies).

For each category, some attacks are performed in our dataset to offer the possibility to learn the specific pattern.

3.5   Data Acquisition: Extractor

An extractor tool has been developed in Python 3. Scapy, which is a Python library, is used for packet dissection. Scapy deals with packets using a class per protocol. For each protocol, a class is defined in a library which can be customized as per need basis.

A customized full duplex session extractor has been written to separate protocol sessions. Server and clients are then chosen based on addresses after separating session. It is assumed that sessions are initiated by clients.

Protocols data fields are processed after the extraction to give the required results like avg, max, min, etc. The processed protocols are TCP, HTTP, TLS, ICMP and Modbus.

This tool extracts more than 100 features every 2 s, some of them are extracted directly from the network packets and others are computed mathematically. These features are inspired from two other tools which are tstat [22] and tcptrace [24] that only extract the features related to the transport layer of the OSI model. The novelty of tool, proposed here, is the fact that it extracts also the application features related to Modbus protocol. The explanation of all these features is exposed in Table 2.

3.6   Dataset Approach Extension to Other Protocols

The methodology used in this paper is related to Modbus protocol which is the most widely used protocol in the industry today. However, this approach could be extended to other new emerging protocols like OPC-UA, MQTT. . . . For instance, if we consider the OPC-UA protocol, this latter uses two transport protocols which are OPC TCP and SOAP/HTTP(S). Therefore, we can extract some features related to the OPC-UA subscription step and other related to OPC-UA communication like MaxAge feature which gives the operation that the server has to perform, the NodeId Identifier feature used in the operation... OPC-UA is also a protocol which works in request/response mode as for Modbus protocol. Thus, we can extract some features related to OPC UA request and others related to the OPC-UA response like the elapsed time between OPC-UA request and response. Once the features are extracted, the next steps of our approach are the same.

4   Experimentation Environment

4.1   Description

Our experimentation platform is an academic production line, shown in Fig. 3, allowing the filling of bottles with balls and their capping. It is composed of:

- Material: Schneider Electric PLC (M340 and M580), 3 attackers laptops, one laptop dedicated to traffic capture and a victim computer.
- Software: Unity Pro, Ettercap, Metasploit, Wireshark.
- Manufacturing Executive System (MES): LINA.
- OS: Linux for the attacker, Windows 2012 server for the server, and Windows 10 for the port mirroring capture.
- Switch: one Alcatel-Lucent switch and two industrial switches with 3 Ethernet ports (resp. 5 Ethernet ports) embedded in the M340 (resp. M580) PLC.
- Protocols: TCP/IP, Modbus/TCP.

Depending on the attack, the victims could be either a PLC or a PC. A port mirroring setting is put in place to capture the whole traffic.

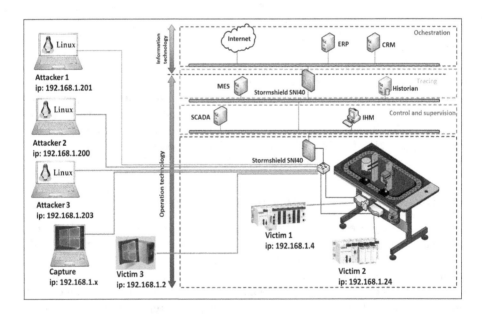

Fig. 3. Experimentation platform

4.2 Attacks Scenarios

As explained previously, our dataset model includes normal and attack traffic. For this work, twelve attacks are simulated on the experimentation platform. Among these attacks, some are typically IT and others are OT as described below:

1. **IT Attacks**:
   - **DoS/DDoS**: For theses attacks, we send a TCP SYN flood, TCP ACK (Acknowledgement) flood, TCP RST (Reset) flood or Xmax flood by setting all TCP flags (CWR, ECN, URG, ACK, PSH, RST, SYN, FIN). We simulate also UDP flood packets. The script implementing these attacks uses hping3. If hping3 is not found, it attempts to use the nmap-nping tool instead.
   - **FTP brute force**: It consists of using passwords and usernames dictionary method for cracking the FTP server connection.
     For this one, we start by getting the login and the password of the ftp server using either hydra or Metasploit tool then we connect to the server to retrieve some files and delete others.
   - **Web http DoS**: In this attack, a script written in Python called slowhttp-test is used to perform an application layer Denial of Service attacks (DoS). Its principle consists in the fact that requests are not processed before being completely received by the server. If the data is not complete or the speed sending packets is too low, the resource is kept busy till receiving the whole data. In this attack, Apache is targeted by causing very significant memory and CPU usage on it.
   - **Botnet**: The purpose of this attack is to control multiple compromised hosts. For that, Ares tool is used which is a remote administration tool (RAT) written in Python.
     It is composed of two programs:
     - Command and Control server (C&C), which is a graphical Web interface for the administration of agents (victims).
     - An agent (or backdoor), which runs on the compromised host ensuring communication with the C&C server.
2. **OT Attacks**:
   - **MSSQL attack**: It is composed of two steps. The first one is a MSSQL brute force to retrieve the MES database's login and password. The principle is the same as for the FTP brute force but using mssql_login module of Metasploit. Then, the second step consists in dropping or altering data thanks to taking control of the machine hosting the MES database.
   - **PLC disturbing process**: Two attacks are performed to disturb the PLC process. Their principle consists of disrupting the production line functioning by modifying either recipe scheduled by the operator, or by provoking a remote emergency stop. After studying and analyzing the registers configuration of the platform PLC, we chose to modify the registers responsible for the worst and the most widespread scenarios in industrial attacks, namely the complete shutdown of the production line and

the modification of the production line receipt. In our case, register 2 of M580 PLC is responsible for stopping remotely the conveyor and register 120 of M340 PLC is in charge of modifying seamlessly the number of balls. Therefore, bottles are filled, capped and removed to destocking without the operator noticing of the modification of his planned PO. To perform this, we properly connected to the PLC line and modified the Modbus registers. For this attack, we use the Metasploit attack tool and its Modbusclient module.

- **MITM**: For this attack, we get in the middle between the PLC and the server using Ettercap tool then we modify the content of the registers to disturb the line's nominal functioning. During this attack, either remote emergency stop is triggered or operation recipe is modified.

5 DATASET

To propose this dataset, several tasks are carried out from the extraction of features from pcap files to their finalization passing trough preprocessing and labelling steps. More details are given in the following paragraphs.

5.1 Preprocessing and Labelling

The first step for performing this work is the preprocessing process. The raw dataset is composed of several kinds of data like IP address, categorical data, digital data, and a list of values. Due to the variety of the data types, a preprocessing process is required to make data usable by any machine learning algorithm. Consequently, non-digital features like protocols are replaced by numerical values using the LabelEncoder class from the sci-kit learn library. The IP address dots are omitted to get one number instead of eight-digit number. The features which are in list format like register numbers or values are split into one value per row. Then the dataset is normalized and formatted to the same scale.

In literature, we find three options to label the data: manual labelling [39], semi-automatic labelling [25], and automatic labelling [3]. In view of the data simplicity (malicious and non-malicious data), we use the manual labelling in this dataset. We assign −1 to the normal traffic and for the malicious one, we distinguish each attack by assigning it a different label between 1 and n, where n is the number of attacks simulated in this work. The main novelty of this dataset is the fact that we add another label to characterize the equipment response to the attacks. We set this label to 0.

The dataset was captured so that normal traffic is separated from malicious traffic. This will facilitate the normal traffic labelling process. It remains to label malicious packets and distinguish them from those representing the reaction to an attack. To this end, we will use the different extracted features. Taking the example of a SYN flood attack, after several attempts and without receiving any ACK flag, the communication is cut, the RST flag is set at 1 and State_cnx_S0

Table 2. Application features for Modbus protocol

Features name	Meaning
Request_cnt_funcx	Number of the function code request x = 1, 2, 3, 4, 5, 6, 15 or 16 for the different Modbus function code
Response_cnt_funcx	Number of the function code response x = 1, 2, 3, 4, 5, 6, 15 or 16 for the different Modbus function code
Cmd address	Device ID in command
Resp address	Device ID in response
Cmd_memory_avg	Memory start position in Modbus request: includes internal memory addresses for read and write commands
Resp_memory_avg	Memory start position in response packet: includes internal memory addresses for read and write responses
Cmd_mry_cnt_avg	The average of the number of memory bytes for R/W response: includes field size for read and write responses
Resp_mry_cnt_avg	The average of the number of memory bytes for R/W response: includes field size for read and write responses
Cmd_length_avg	The average of total length of request packet: the lengths of the Modbus request
Resp_length_avg	The average of total length of response packet: the lengths of the Modbus response
Time_avg	The average of the time interval between two packets: the time between a Modbus query and its response.
Register_number	List of Modbus register numbers
Register_value	List of Modbus register values
Modbus_err_count	Modbus protocol error counter
Time_modbus_std	The time between a Modbus query and its response (Std)

and State_cnx_S1 are set at 1. Finally, we label all packets meeting these conditions as a reaction to SYN flood attack. Therefore, we label all attacks and reactions to attacks packets based on the suitable features.

5.2   Extracted Features

This dataset has been captured in Lab-STICC laboratory in Brest during three days. Normal traffic was captured for 2 h on the first day, then the attacks were captured for 30 min to 1 hour per attack during the first, the second and the third day. In Table 2, we made the choice to expose only the application features since they are one of the novelties. Thanks to these application metrics, we can detect attacks that belong to the three categories presented in Sect. 3. For example, an attack on the integrity of the receipt PO can be detected through the difference in the produced and planned quantities. In the same way, an attack that interrupts the process can be detected regarding the total production time.

6   Conclusion and Perspectives

In this paper, we propose a new industrial dataset filling some gaps of existing datasets. Its novelties consist in its completeness regarding the extracted features (transport and application features) and in their 3 added labels to distinguish normal traffic, malicious traffic and equipment reaction against an attack. This dataset is built from a real environment and contains a variety of attacks between IT and OT attacks. It will be publicly available.

In future works, more numerical details will be provided about the dataset composition. This dataset will be used to train a machine learning algorithm. A reduction features and/or selection features methods will be applied on this dataset to evaluate the most useful features for our study. We also intend to enrich the malicious traffic with other attacks and to use more other protocols.

In the rare research works proposed in the literature about datasets, authors propose datasets based on network traffic or on system processes parameters. To complete the loop, we plan to propose another dataset based on system processes parameters related to MES (Manufacturing Executive System) to detect illegal activities on the MES database.

References

1. Alem, S., Espes, D., Martin, E., Nana, L., De Lamotte, F.: A hybrid intrusion detection system in industry 4.0 based on ISA95 standard. In: 2019 IEEE/ACS 16th International Conference on Computer Systems and Applications (AICCSA), pp. 1–8 (2019)
2. Almalawi, A., Fahad, A., Tari, Z., Alamri, A., AlGhamdi, R., Zomaya, A.Y.: An efficient data-driven clustering technique to detect attacks in SCADA systems. IEEE Trans. Inf. Forensics Secur. **11**(5), 893–906 (2015)
3. Aparicio-Navarro, F.J., Kyriakopoulos, K.G., Parish, D.J.: Automatic dataset labelling and feature selection for intrusion detection systems. In: 2014 IEEE Military Communications Conference, pp. 46–51. IEEE (2014)
4. Bhattacharya, S., Selvakumar, S.: SSENet-2014 dataset: a dataset for detection of multiconnection attacks. In: 2014 3rd International Conference on Eco-friendly Computing and Communication Systems, pp. 121–126. IEEE (2014)
5. Brown, C., Cowperthwaite, A., Hijazi, A., Somayaji, A.: Analysis of the 1999 DARPA/Lincoln laboratory IDS evaluation data with netadhict. In: 2009 IEEE Symposium on Computational Intelligence for Security and Defense Applications, pp. 1–7 (2009)
6. Cimpean, D., Meire, J., Bouckaert, V., Vande Casteele, S., Pelle, A., Hellebooge, L.: Analysis of cyber security aspects in the maritime sector (2011)
7. Ferrag, M.A., Maglaras, L., Moschoyiannis, S., Janicke, H.: Deep learning for cyber security intrusion detection: approaches, datasets, and comparative study. J. Inf. Secur. Appl. **50**, 102419 (2020)
8. Gao, J., et al.: Omni SCADA intrusion detection using deep learning algorithms. arXiv preprint arXiv:1908.01974 (2019)
9. Garcia, S., Grill, M., Stiborek, J., Zunino, A.: An empirical comparison of botnet detection methods. Comput. Secur. **45**, 100–123 (2014)

10. Gharib, A., Sharafaldin, I., Lashkari, A.H., Ghorbani, A.A.: An evaluation framework for intrusion detection dataset. In: 2016 International Conference on Information Science and Security (ICISS), pp. 1–6. IEEE (2016)
11. Gringoli, F., Salgarelli, L., Dusi, M., Cascarano, N., Risso, F., Claffy, K.: GT: picking up the truth from the ground for internet traffic. ACM SIGCOMM Comput. Commun. Rev. **39**(5), 12–18 (2009)
12. Gurung, S., Ghose, M.K., Subedi, A.: Deep learning approach on network intrusion detection system using NSL-KDD dataset. Int. J. Comput. Netw. Inf. Secur. (IJCNIS) **11**(3), 8–14 (2019)
13. Hettich, S., Bay, S.D.: The UCI KDD archive [http://kdd.ics.uci.edu]. University of California, Irvine, CA. Department of Information and Computer Science 152 (1999)
14. Hijazi, A., El Safadi, A., Flaus, J.M.: A deep learning approach for intrusion detection system in industry network. In: BDCSIntell, pp. 55–62 (2018)
15. Teixeira, M., Zolanvari, M., Jain, R.: WUSTL-IIOT-2018 (2020). https://doi.org/10.21227/kzgp-7t84
16. Khraisat, A., Gondal, I., Vamplew, P., Kamruzzaman, J.: Survey of intrusion detection systems: techniques, datasets and challenges. Cybersecurity **2**(1), 20 (2019)
17. Lashkari, A.H., Draper-Gil, G., Mamun, M.S.I., Ghorbani, A.A.: Characterization of tor traffic using time based features. In: ICISSP, pp. 253–262 (2017)
18. Lemay, A., Fernandez, J.M.: Providing {SCADA} network data sets for intrusion detection research. In: 9th Workshop on Cyber Security Experimentation and Test ({CSET} 2016) (2016)
19. Linda, O., Vollmer, T., Manic, M.: Neural network based intrusion detection system for critical infrastructures. In: 2009 International Joint Conference on Neural Networks, pp. 1827–1834. IEEE (2009)
20. Maciá-Fernández, G., Camacho, J., Magán-Carrión, R., García-Teodoro, P., Therón, R.: UGR'16: a new dataset for the evaluation of cyclostationarity-based network IDSs. Comput. Secur. **73**, 411–424 (2018)
21. McHugh, J.: Testing intrusion detection systems: a critique of the 1998 and 1999 DARPA intrusion detection system evaluations as performed by Lincoln laboratory. ACM Trans. Inf. Syst. Secur. (TISSEC) **3**(4), 262–294 (2000)
22. Mellia, M., Carpani, A., Lo Cigno, R.: TStat: TCP STatistic and analysis tool. In: Marsan, M.A., Corazza, G., Listanti, M., Roveri, A. (eds.) QoS-IP 2003. LNCS, vol. 2601, pp. 145–157. Springer, Heidelberg (2003). https://doi.org/10.1007/3-540-36480-3_11
23. Morris, T., Gao, W.: Industrial control system traffic data sets for intrusion detection research. In: Butts, J., Shenoi, S. (eds.) ICCIP 2014. IAICT, vol. 441, pp. 65–78. Springer, Heidelberg (2014). https://doi.org/10.1007/978-3-662-45355-1_5
24. Ostermann, S.: Tcptrace (2005)
25. Pereira, L., Nunes, N.J.: Semi-automatic labeling for public non-intrusive load monitoring datasets. In: 2015 Sustainable Internet and ICT for Sustainability (SustainIT), pp. 1–4. IEEE (2015)
26. Prusty, S., Levine, B.N., Liberatore, M.: Forensic investigation of the oneswarm anonymous filesharing system. In: Proceedings of the 18th ACM Conference on Computer and Communications Security, pp. 201–214 (2011)
27. Ring, M., Wunderlich, S., Grüdl, D., Landes, D., Hotho, A.: Flow-based benchmark data sets for intrusion detection. In: Proceedings of the 16th European Conference on Cyber Warfare and Security (ECCWS), pp. 361–369. ACPI (2017)

28. Sharafaldin, I., Lashkari, A.H., Ghorbani, A.A.: Toward generating a new intrusion detection dataset and intrusion traffic characterization. In: ICISSP, pp. 108–116 (2018)
29. Sharafaldin, I., Gharib, A., Lashkari, A.H., Ghorbani, A.A.: Towards a reliable intrusion detection benchmark dataset. Softw. Netw. **2018**(1), 177–200 (2018)
30. Sharma, R., Singla, R.K., Guleria, A.: A new labeled flow-based DNS dataset for anomaly detection: PUF dataset. Procedia Comput. Sci. **132**, 1458–1466 (2018)
31. Shiravi, A., Shiravi, H., Tavallaee, M., Ghorbani, A.A.: Toward developing a systematic approach to generate benchmark datasets for intrusion detection. Comput. Secur. **31**(3), 357–374 (2012)
32. Frazão, I., Abreu, P., Cruz, T., Araújo, H., Simões, P.: Cyber-security modbus ICS dataset (2019). https://doi.org/10.21227/pjff-1a03. http://dx.doi.org/10.21227/pjff-1a03
33. Song, J., Takakura, H., Okabe, Y., Eto, M., Inoue, D., Nakao, K.: Statistical analysis of honeypot data and building of Kyoto 2006+ dataset for NIDS evaluation. In: Proceedings of the First Workshop on Building Analysis Datasets and Gathering Experience Returns for Security, pp. 29–36 (2011)
34. Swearingen, R.: Internet security threat report. Technical report, Symantec Security Center (2018)
35. Swearingen, R.: Internet security threat report. Technical report, Symantec Security Center (2017)
36. Tavallaee, M., Bagheri, E., Lu, W., Ghorbani, A.A.: A detailed analysis of the KDD CUP 99 data set. In: 2009 IEEE Symposium on Computational Intelligence for Security and Defense Applications, pp. 1–6. IEEE (2009)
37. Wheelus, C., Khoshgoftaar, T.M., Zuech, R., Najafabadi, M.M.: A session based approach for aggregating network traffic data-the SANTA dataset. In: 2014 IEEE International Conference on Bioinformatics and Bioengineering, pp. 369–378. IEEE (2014)
38. Williams, M.: The benefits and challenges of IT/OT convergence: rewriting the rules (2016). https://www.automation.com/en-us/articles/2016-2/the-benefits-and-challenges-of-itot-convergence-re
39. Zuech, R., Khoshgoftaar, T.M., Seliya, N., Najafabadi, M.M., Kemp, C.: A new intrusion detection benchmarking system. In: The Twenty-Eighth International Flairs Conference (2015)

Toward Semantic-Based Android Malware Detection Using Model Checking and Machine Learning

Souad El Hatib$^{(\boxtimes)}$, Loïc Ricaud, Josée Desharnais, and Nadia Tawbi

Laval University, Quebec City, Canada
{souad.el-hatib.1,loic.ricaud.1}@ulaval.ca,
{Josee.Desharnais,Nadia.Tawbi}@ift.ulaval.ca

Abstract. The ever-increasing presence of Android malware is accompanied by a deep concern about security issues in the mobile ecosystem. Android malware detection has received much attention in the research community. In fact, malware proliferation goes hand in hand with its sophistication and complexity. For instance, more elaborated malware, such as polymorphic or metamorphic malware, uses code obfuscation techniques to build new variants that preserve the semantics of the original code but modify its syntax and thus escape the usual detection methods. In the present work, we propose a model checking based approach that combines static analysis and machine learning. Mainly, from a given Android application we extract an abstract model expressed in terms of LNT, a process algebra language. This model is then checked against security related Android behaviors specified by modal μ-calculus formulæ. The satisfaction of a specific formula is considered as a feature. Finally, machine learning algorithms are used to classify the application as malicious or not. The use of temporal properties improves the classification performance.

Keywords: Malicious code detection · Model checking · μ-calculus · Android malware · Machine learning

1 Introduction

Google's Android operating system remains the most popular on mobile platforms. In fact, the platform prevails the mobile ecosystem with a market share of 86.1% in 2019 [1]. Android's openness and popularity attract a sheer number of developers including malware authors, hence lead to the proliferation of malicious applications. Signature-based techniques are among the mainstream Android malware detection techniques. However, these methods are overwhelmed by the huge number of applications added either to the official Android market or to third parties ones. The statistics portal [25] reports that approximately 1062 applications are uploaded to Google play on a daily basis. Moreover, effectiveness of signature based techniques relies on the regular updating of signature

© Springer Nature Switzerland AG 2021
J. Garcia-Alfaro et al. (Eds.): CRiSIS 2020, LNCS 12528, pp. 289–307, 2021.
https://doi.org/10.1007/978-3-030-68887-5_17

databases. Each signature syntactically identifies a specific malware, thus it fails to detect its variants. It is easy to circumvent these detection techniques by obfuscation. In practice, it is difficult to maintain continuous and regular updates of the signature database going hand in hand with the constant evolution of malware. In order to address these issues, research work presented in [6, 13, 30] propose static/dynamic data flow analysis tools to detect Android malware. These approaches provide an effective data leakage detection, but they fail to detect more elaborated malicious behaviors. Moreover, although promising, dynamic analysis techniques are time-consuming, while static analysis approaches are continually evolving to meet the challenge posed by undecidability [18]. There is clearly a need to implement more resilient detection techniques.

In this paper, we combine model checking and machine learning to classify Android applications as malicious or benign. In addition to features based on the presence or absence of API calls, we consider more complex features, based on the satisfaction of temporal logic formulæ. This allows an analysis closer to the semantics of the program, beyond its syntax.

In summary, this paper presents the following contributions:

- We propose APK2LNT, a Soot-based [26] tool that translates Android applications to LNT models. LNT is a process algebra language inspired by E-Lotos. The abstraction level of the generated model allows us to capture the semantics of Android malware (Sect. 4). This model takes into account concurrent constructions and their synchronizations.
- The features used in classification include temporal logic properties that encode Android security related behaviors (Sect. 5). The use of temporal logic allows to express sophisticated security behavior like the release of a message *after* the reading of sensitive information, instead of just the presence of these actions.
- We have built and tested multiple classifiers using a dataset of 5009 Android applications from a variety of Android markets (Sect. 6). The results show that the tool achieves an accuracy of 94,60% using a Random forest classifier. We compare the classification performance using two sets of features: the features consisting of API calls, and these features to which we join structured temporal logic formulæ representing unwanted behavior.

2   Related Work

The effervescent proliferation of Android malware has sparked great interest in developing efficient techniques allowing to automatically analyze and detect new threats. One of the most commonly used techniques is signature-based detection. Although it is very efficient in detecting known threats, this technique can be easily bypassed by obfuscation techniques. Therefore, there is a need to implement more robust techniques for malware detection. Shortcomings of this approach can be dealt with using semantic behavior models. In this context, many studies have been done.

2.1 Model Checking Based Malware Detection

Kinder et al. [16] present a model checking based approach to malware detection. Their tool models the control flow graph of an executable as a Kripke structure. An explicit model checking algorithm verifies the absence of malicious patterns. The latter were specified in Computation Tree Predicate Logic (CTPL), an extension of the computation tree logic considering register renaming.

Battista et al. [9] present an Android malware detection and classification approach using formal methods. Their main idea is to describe algebraically the behavior of an Android application using Calculus of Communicating System (CCS). Temporal properties encoding common malicious behaviors of a malware family, are specified in μ-calculus. They are verified on the models using Concurrency WorkBench (CWB) verification algorithms.

Mercaldo et al. [20] propose an approach to detect Android ransomware by means of model checking. Samples of Android ransomware were manually inspected to extract the ransomware malicious behaviors. These behaviors are then expressed in a branching temporal logic, namely the modal μ-calculus. An application is considered as an Android ransomware if it's CCS model, derived from the Java bytecode, satisfies the temporal logic properties.

Pommade [24] detects malware behaviors concealed in binary programs. Based on model checking algorithms, this tool models the program's stack using Push Down Systems (PDS). The resulting PDS's are checked against malicious behaviors specified in SCTPL or SLTPL. SCTPL (resp. SLTPL) is an extension of the computation tree logic (resp. linear temporal logic) with variables, quantifiers and predicates over the stack.

Song et al. [23] present a model checking based method for Android malware detection. Their tool is equipped with a model builder based on the disassembler Smali, that translates Android applications to PDS's. To decide whether or not a given Android application has some malicious behaviors, the tool applies SCTPL and SLTPL model checking for PDS's. To make malicious behavior specification more robust, the authors introduce a predicate encoding data dependencies between variables.

Cimino et al. [12] seek both detection and inhibition of Android malware behaviors. They derive processes in Language Of Temporal Ordering Specification (Lotos) from Android applications' Java bytecodes. The Construction and Analysis of Distributed Processes (CADP) [14] toolbox for model checking is then used to verify the logic rules expressed in μ-calculus. Once located, malicious behaviors are removed from the program.

2.2 Machine Learning Based Malware Detection

By combining static analysis and machine learning, Meng et al. [19] present an approach targeting both the detection and the classification according to attack patterns of Android malware. They extract the common malicious behaviors and patterns in a DSA (Deterministic Symbolic Automaton) from Android malware. They first identify suspicious applications using machine learning based on features extracted from the DSA, then they use Automata inclusion to classify these applications.

In [15], the authors propose a classification approach based on structured features, namely subgraphs of the functional call graph depicting malicious behaviors. In order to circumvent the graph isomorphism problem, the authors make use of graph kernels.

In their paper [17], Kwon et al. introduce the downloader-graph abstraction. The download graphs representing the download activity of hosts are constructed using telemetry from anti-virus and intrusion prevention systems. Properties of influence graphs such as the growth rate are used as features for classification.

Zhang et al. [29] present a semantic approach to Android malware classification. The semantics of Android applications are modeled by weighted contextual API dependency graphs. Graph based feature vectors are used to classify Android malware and benign applications.

DREBIN [5] is an Android malware detection tool performing static feature extraction. Indeed, the manifest file and the disassembled dex code of the application are both analyzed to extract the features. API calls, permissions and network addresses are among these features. Machine learning algorithms are used for a binary classification of Android applications.

Andrana [10] combines static analysis and machine learning to perform a binary classification of Android applications, which is obfuscation resilient. Namely, a set of features is determined, including the use of obfuscation techniques. Then, the application bytecode is disassembled and the presence of features in the disassembled application is checked. Ultimately, a machine learning classification is applied to decide whether an application is malicious or not.

3   Preliminaries

In this section, we briefly present the LNT language focusing only on essential elements related to process definition. Then, we present the syntax and semantics of the modal μ-calculus logic.

3.1   LNT Language

LNT is a high level formal specification language supported by the CADP verification toolbox [14]. It combines aspects from process algebra languages, functional languages and imperative languages. An LNT specification has both control and data components, i.e., types, functions, channels and processes which are defined within a module. In short, a system specification corresponds to a set of modules. Moreover, definitions from a module can be imported into other modules. Just as in other process algebra languages, system behaviors in LNT are expressed by means of processes. An LNT process is defined by an identifier, a behavior, an optional list of formal gates, an optional list of formal parameters and an optional list of process pragmas. Process pragmas are only used to give hints about how the translation of the source code to Lotos and C should be performed.

Process Definition. In the following grammar, *ap* stands for *actual parameter*, *fp* stands for *formal parameter*, *fg* stands for *formal gate*, *pp* stands for *process pragma*, *vd* stands for *variable declaration*, B_i denotes a behavior and G_i denotes a gate.

$\langle process\_definition \rangle$ ::= **process** Π [[$fg_0, \ldots, fg_m$]]
    [[$fp_1, \ldots, fp_n$]] **is**
    $pp_1, \ldots, pp_l$
    $\langle behavior \rangle$
    end process

$\langle behavior \rangle$ ::= **null**	no effect (with continuation)
| **stop**	(without continuation)
| B_1 ; B_2	sequential composition
| **var** $vd_0, \ldots, vd_n$ **in**	variable declaration
B_0	
end var	
| **loop**	forever loop
B_0	
end loop	
| Π [[actual_gates]] [$(ap_1, \ldots, ap_n)$]	process call
| **select**	non deterministic choice
B_0 [] ... [] B_n	
end select	
| **par** $[G_0, \ldots, G_n$ **in**]	parallel composition
[$G_{(i,0)}, \ldots, G_{(i,n_i)}$ ->] B_0	
|| ... ||	
[$G_{(i,0)}, \ldots, G_{(i,n_i)}$ ->] B_m	
end par	

Process Behaviors. For the sake of brevity and conciseness, we only present essential behaviors of an LNT process.

Non Deterministic Choice. Let P be a process whose behavior is **select** B_1 [] B_2 **end select**. P behaves either like B_1 or B_2. The interaction between P and its environment resolves the choice. In fact, the choice of a behavior B_i over B_1 and B_2 depends on the initial action offered by the environment and observable in B_i.

Parallel Composition. The parallel composition in LNT is defined by two sets, the global synchronization set $\{G_0, ..., G_n\}$ and the interface synchronization

$\{G_{(i,0)},...,G_{(i,n_i)}\}$. For every gate belonging to the global synchronization set, behaviors $B_0, \ldots, B_m$ can communicate through this gate only if this communication takes place simultaneously. Similarly, for every gate belonging to the synchronization interface, a behavior among $B_0, \ldots, B_m$ can communicate through this gate only if all behaviors $B_0, \ldots, B_m$ that contain this gate in their synchronization interface can make this communication simultaneously. For more details about the LNT language, see [11].

3.2 Modal μ-Calculus

The μ-calculus is an extension of Hennessy-Milner Logic with explicit minimal and maximal fixed points. It is used to describe properties of Labelled Transition Systems (LTS). A μ-calculus formula is defined using the following syntax, where K is a set of actions:

$\varphi ::= true \mid false \mid \neg\varphi \mid \varphi_1 \wedge \varphi_2 \mid \varphi_1 \vee \varphi_2 \mid [K]\varphi \mid \langle K \rangle \varphi \mid \mu Z.\varphi \mid \nu Z.\varphi$

The satisfaction of a formula φ by an LNT process P is defined as follows:

$P \models true$

$P \not\models false$

$P \models \neg\varphi$ iff $P \not\models \varphi$

$P \models \varphi_1 \wedge \varphi_2$ iff $P \models \varphi_1$ and $P \models \varphi_2$

$P \models \varphi_1 \vee \varphi_2$ iff $P \models \varphi_1$ or $P \models \varphi_2$

$P \models [K]\varphi$ iff $\forall Q \in \{P' \mid P \xrightarrow{a} P'$ and $a \in K\}.\, Q \models \varphi$

$P \models \langle K \rangle \varphi$ iff $\exists Q \in \{P' \mid P \xrightarrow{a} P'$ and $a \in K\}.\, Q \models \varphi$

$P \models \mu Z.\varphi$ iff $\exists n \in \mathbb{N}, P \models \mu Z^n.\varphi$

$P \models \nu Z.\varphi$ iff $\forall n \in \mathbb{N}, P \models \nu Z^n.\varphi$.

The recursive definition of the fixed point operators is as follows:

$$\mu Z^{n+1}.\varphi = \varphi[\mu Z^n.\varphi/Z] \text{ with } \mu Z^0.\varphi = false$$
$$\nu Z^{n+1}.\varphi = \varphi[\nu Z^n.\varphi/Z] \text{ with } \nu Z^0.\varphi = true$$

Intuitively, a process P satisfies the property $[K]\varphi$ if every process to which P evolves after carrying out any action in K has the property φ. A process P satisfies $\langle K \rangle \varphi$ if P can become a process that satisfies φ by performing an action in K.

4   Modeling Android Applications

Written in Java, our model builder, called APK2LNT, takes an Android application and outputs its corresponding LNT model. Algorithm 1 depicts the translation process. We first create the Inter-procedural Control Flow Graph (ICFG). In this graph a node corresponds to a bytecode instruction and a directed edge corresponds to a flow of control from the source node to the sink one. To do so, we create all the intra-procedural control flow graphs using Soot, then we collect and connect them in order to obtain the ICFG. Once created, we build its LNT model by visiting every node and creating a corresponding process. The process definition step depends on the statement's type. For instance, if it's an IF statement the non-deterministic choice behavior will be used to define the

---

Algorithm 1. Android to Apk translation

1: Construct the ICFG.
2: Create a stack with the first unit of the ICFG.
3: **while** stack is not empty **do**
4:     unit ← element on the top of the stack
5:     succs ← successors of unit
6:     **if** unit is an exit point ∨ (succs ≠ ∅ ∧ unit has not been defined) **then:**
7:         Define the process corresponding to the unit.
8:         Push succs on stack.

---

process behavior. The execution time of our model builder depends on the size of the input application. In order to accelerate the model-checking step, it is important that our model builder produce a precise and concise LNT model of an Android application. The translation process from APK to LNT described above is direct and unoptimized. In practice, we have applied the transformations described in the following paragraphs to this basic translation. These optimizations are important because they simplify the model, allow faster model checking and require complex reasoning to be sound.

4.1 Removal of Silent Chains

During the generation of an LNT model, the model builder extracts actions of interest from a file containing all the modal properties we want to verify. Non-relevant actions are replaced with silent actions, denoted by "i" in LNT. The goal is to reduce the model size in order to mitigate the state explosion problem, namely by compacting silent action chains in a safe way (keeping internal choice). Let P_1 be the following process:

process P_1 **is** i;P_2 **end process**
process P_2 **is** i;P_3 **end process**
...
process P_{n-1} **is** i;P_n **end process**

After compacting silent actions, process P_1 is specified by:

process P_1 **is**   i;P_n **end process**

4.2 Synchronization Mechanisms

Many Android applications run multiple threads. Taking into account the synchronization mechanisms is crucial for an accurate model. Since we are looking for the presence of bad behaviors, a safe approximation is to consider all possible action interleavings. However this introduces impossible behaviors, which may lead to wrong feature evaluations, and false positives.

Two types of synchronization are supported: lock synchronization and synchronized methods.

Synchronization with Locks. A *lock* is a synchronization mechanism used to address mutual exclusion problem in conflicting critical sections. For each Java/Android lock API, for example the "lock" and "unlock" methods of the ReentrantLock class, we build an action that concatenates the object of the synchronization as well as the synchronization method in question. For instance, let's consider two threads P_1 and P_2 running in parallel and synchronizing on the same object o. In particular, the run() methods of these two threads execute a block similar to the one below:

```
ReentrantLock o = new ReentrantLock();
try{
    o.lock();
    a_i;
    b_i;
}finally{
    o.unlock();
}
```

Expressions a_i, b_i represent Java instructions guarded by the object o in P_i, $i = 1, 2$. For the LNT model with synchronization, we use the specification below

```
type M_ACTION is LOCK, UNLOCK end type
channel MONITOR is (M_ACTION, NAT) end channel
channel ACTION is (NAT) end channel

process P[O : MONITOR, A, B : ACTION](id : NAT) is
    loop
        O(LOCK, id);
        A(id);
        B(id);
        O(UNLOCK, id)
    end loop
end process

process MO[O : MONITOR] is
    loop
        var pid : NAT in
            O(LOCK, ?pid);
            O(UNLOCK, pid);
        end var
    end loop
end process

process MAIN[O : MONITOR, A, B : ACTION] is
    par O in
        MO[O]
    ||
        par
            P[O, A, B](1)
        ||
            P[O, A, B](2)
        end par
    end par
end process
```

The resulting LTS is illustrated in Fig. 1.

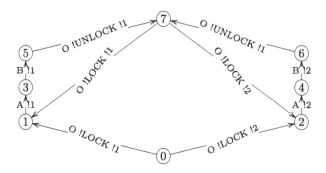

Fig. 1. Pictorial representation of the LTS associated with the process MAIN related to synchronization with locks.

Synchronized Methods. In Java, a method is declared as synchronized by only adding the key word synchronized to its declaration. Synchronized methods are modelled in the same way as lock synchronization, the only difference being that the synchronization object becomes the instance of the class where the synchronization block was declared.

5   Security Related Android Behaviors

Many classification approaches targeting Android applications are based on features related to API calls. This likely increases the rate of false positives. Our key insight to defeat more elaborated malware without inducing unacceptable rates of false positives is to use temporal properties that encode structured malicious behaviors. In fact, instead of using Android API calls only, we focus on the relationship between these calls as indicators of malicious behavior.

A first set of features is built by statically extracting Android methods that require a specific permission in order to be invoked. For the mapping between Android API methods and permissions we used Pscout's [7] mapping. A second set of features, which is complementary to the first one, comes from the specification of suspicious Android behaviors in modal μ-calculus formulæ. Both sets are used by machine learning algorithms to classify Android applications. The relevance and effectiveness of these features are left to the machine learning algorithms.

The focus of this section is to present a few of our security related features as well as their specifications.

5.1   Evasion Technique

A significant part of Android malware incorporate evasion techniques to evade detection. Malware authors can tap the difference between real device and emulator environments to bypass dynamic analysis tools, namely by detecting the emulator and shutting down functionalities related to malicious behaviors. To detect virtualization, one can use the TelephonyManager methods to retrieve relevant information about the execution environment. For instance, the value of getdeviceId() is null in case of emulator. Vidas and Christin [27] provide several Android API methods that return particular values when running under an emulated device. An evasive malware attempts to spot the difference between emulators and real devices by checking these values using Android String comparison methods. Afterwards, it hides the malicious behavior by remaining dormant, which can be done using the class javautilTimer. This behavior can be specified using the following formula:

DormantFunctionality = **mu** X.((DetectionOfVirtualization **and** $\varphi2$) **or** $\langle$true$\rangle$(X))

DetectionOfVirtualization = **mu** X.((($\langle$androidosBuildgetRadioVersion$\rangle$true **or** $\langle$androidtelephonyTelephonyManagergetDeviceID$\rangle$true **or** $\langle$androidtelephony-TelephonyManagergetNetworkCountryIso$\rangle$true **or** $\langle$androidtelephonyTelephony-ManagergetLine1Number$\rangle$true **or** $\langle$androidtelephonyTelephonyManagergetNetworkType$\rangle$true **or** $\langle$androidtelephonyTelephonyManagergetNetworkOperator$\rangle$ true **or** $\langle$androidtelephonyTelephonyManagergetPhoneType$\rangle$true **or** $\langle$android-telephonyTelephonyMangergetSimCountryIso$\rangle$true **or** $\langle$androidtelephonyTele-phonyManagergetSimSerialNumber$\rangle$true **or** $\langle$androidtelephonyTelephonyMana-gergetSubscriberId$\rangle$true **or** $\langle$androidtelephonyTelephonyManagergetVoiceMail-Number$\rangle$true) **and** $\varphi1$) **or** $\langle$true$\rangle$(X))

$\varphi1$ = **mu** X.((($\langle$javalangStringEquals$\rangle$true **or** $\langle$javalangStringcontains$\rangle$true **or** $\langle$ javalangStringstartsWith$\rangle$true) **or** $\langle$true$\rangle$(X))

$\varphi2$ = **mu** X.((($\langle$javautilTimerschedule$\rangle$true **or** $\langle$javautilTimercancel$\rangle$true **or** $\langle$javautilTimerscheduleAtFixedRate$\rangle$true) **or** $\langle$true$\rangle$(X))

5.2   Block Incoming SMS

SMS Trojans like Opfake family are known by their background subscriptions to SMS premium services. They send SMS messages to premium rate numbers without the consent of users and then intercept and block incoming SMS messages, so that the user is not notified. Using the androidtelephonygsmSmsManagerSend-TextMessage method, the malware sends an SMS to a premium rate number. Afterwards, it monitors incoming messages by verifying that the value of android-contentIntentgetAction equals "android.provider.Telephony.SMS_RECEIVED", and then blocks the SMS using androidcontentBroadcastReceiverabortBroad-cast.

BlockIncomingSms = **mu** X.((($\langle$androidtelephonygsmSmsManagerSendTextMes-sage$\rangle$true **and** $\psi1$) **or** $\langle$true$\rangle$(X))

$\psi 1 = \mathbf{mu}\ X.(((\langle \text{androidcontentIntentgetAction}\rangle \text{true}\ \mathbf{and}\ \psi 2)\ \mathbf{or}\ \langle \text{true}\rangle(X))$

$\psi 2 = \mathbf{mu}\ X.(((\langle \text{javalangStringequals}\rangle \text{true}\ \mathbf{and}\ \psi 3)\ \mathbf{or}\ \langle \text{true}\rangle(X))$

$\psi 3 = \mathbf{mu}\ X.((\langle \text{androidcontentBroadcastReceiverabortBroadcast}\rangle \text{true}\ \mathbf{or}$
$\langle \text{true}\rangle(X))$

5.3   Ransomware

Android ransomware pose a serious security threat to smartphones. This type of malware has the ability to compromise user's data. Such malware target the user by either locking the victim's device or encrypting its data. The aim of ransomware attacks in general is to coerce victims to pay ransoms in order to regain access to their data. For device locking, malware authors can make use of the method androidappadminDevicePolicyManagerlockNow to lock the device immediately and make the display go to sleep as if the lock screen timeout has expired at the point of this call.

LockTheDevice $= \mathbf{mu}\ X.(((\langle \text{androidcontentContextgetSystemService}\rangle \text{true}\ \mathbf{and}$
$\theta 1)\ \mathbf{or}\ \langle \text{true}\rangle(X))$

$\theta 1 = \mathbf{mu}\ X.((\langle \text{androidappadminDevicePolicyManagerlockNow}\rangle \text{true}\ \mathbf{or}$
$\langle \text{true}\rangle(X))$

The second behavior is accomplished by encryption. It consists in accessing storage directories, and then encrypting all the files contained in these directories. Encryption can be done using the Android cryptography APIs. Afterwards, the malware deletes the original files and keeps only their encrypted version.

UsesCryptoApis $= \mathbf{mu}\ X.(((\langle \text{javaxcryptoCiphergetInstance}\rangle \text{true}\ \mathbf{or}\ \langle \text{javaxcryptoCipherdoFinal}\rangle \text{true}\ \mathbf{or}\ \langle \text{javaxcryptospecDESKeySpecDESKeySpec}\rangle \text{true}\ \mathbf{or}$
$\langle \text{javaxcryptospecSecretKeySpec}\rangle \text{true}\ \mathbf{or}\ \langle \text{javasecurityMessageDigestgetInstance}\rangle \text{true}\ \mathbf{or}\ \langle \text{javasecurityMessageDigestupdate}\rangle \text{true}\ \mathbf{or}\ \langle \text{javasecurityMessageDigestdigest}\rangle \text{true})\ \mathbf{or}\ \langle \text{true}\rangle(X))$

ExternalStorageEncryption $= \mathbf{mu}\ X.(((\langle \text{androidosEnvironmentgetExternalStorageDirectory}\rangle \text{true}\ \mathbf{and}\ \theta 2)\ \mathbf{or}\ \langle \text{true}\rangle(X))$

$\theta 2 = \mathbf{mu}\ X.((\langle \text{javaioFileFile}\rangle \text{true}\ \mathbf{and}\ \theta 3\ \mathbf{or}\ \langle \text{true}\rangle(X))$

$\theta 3 = \mathbf{mu}\ X.(((\langle \text{javaioFileInputStream}\rangle \text{true}\ \mathbf{and}\ \theta 4)\ \mathbf{or}\ \langle \text{true}\rangle(X))$

$\theta 4 = \mathbf{mu}\ X.(((\langle \text{javaioInputStreamread}\rangle \text{true}\ \mathbf{and}\ \theta 5)\ \mathbf{or}\ \langle \text{true}\rangle(X))$

$\theta 5 = \mathbf{mu}\ X.((\langle \text{javaxcryptoCipherOutputStream}\rangle \text{true}\ \mathbf{or}\ \langle \text{true}\rangle(X))$

DeleteExternalStorageData $= \mathbf{mu}\ X.(((\langle \text{javaioFileFile}\rangle \text{true}\ \mathbf{and}\ \theta 6)\ \mathbf{or}$
$\langle \text{true}\rangle(X))$

$\theta 6 = \mathbf{mu}\ X.(((\langle \text{androidosEnvironmentgetExternalStorageDirectory}\rangle \text{true}\ \mathbf{and}$
$\theta 7)\ \mathbf{or}\ \langle \text{true}\rangle(X))$

$\theta 7 = \mathbf{mu}\ X.((\langle \text{javaioFiledelete}\rangle \text{true}\ \mathbf{or}\ \langle \text{true}\rangle(X))$

Therefore, to specify ransomware behaviors we use the following formula:

Ransomware = ((UsesCryptoApis **or** ExternalStorageEncryption) **and** Delete-externalstoragedata) **or** LockTheDevice

5.4 Spyware

Android spyware is a major cause of privacy leakage in Android devices. In fact, spyware manage to stealthy take pictures and record videos without the victim's consent. As explained in [23] calling the method androidhardware-CameraTakePicture without previously calling androidhardwareCameraSetPreviewDisplay or androidhardwareCameraSetPreviewTexture will take a picture without informing the user about the camera access. Similarly, by not calling the method androidmediaMediaRecorderSetPreviewDisplay the user won't be notified when recording videos or audio tracks.

TakingPictures = **mu** X.((⟨androidhardwareCameraopen⟩true **and** ω1) **or** ⟨true⟩(X))

ω1 = **mu** X.(((⟨androidhardwareCameraTakePicture⟩true) **or** ((**not** (⟨androidhardwareCameraSetPreviewDisplay⟩true **or** ⟨androidhardwareCameraSetPreviewTexture⟩true)) **and** ⟨true⟩(X)))

BackgroundRecording = **mu** Y.((⟨androidmediaMediaRecorderSetAudioSource⟩true **or** ⟨androidmediaMediaRecorderSetVideoSource⟩true) **or** ([androidmediaMediaRecorderSetPreviewDisplay]false **and** ⟨true⟩(Y)))

5.5 Native Code

The Android platform provides support for native code. In order to improve application's performance, the Android Native Development Kit (NDK) [2] can be used to implement optimized parts of code in C and C++ and to incorporate it through the JNI interface. Native code isn't malicious in itself, however, its use helps to evade static analysis tools. Hence, the execution of native code poses a security threat. At Android API-level, Android applications can load native libraries using the method javalangSystemloadLibrary. In the same fashion, javalangProcessBuilderstart and javalangRuntimeexec can be used to execute native code. Thus we use the following formula:

NativeCode = **mu** X.(((⟨javalangSystemloadLibrary⟩true **or** ⟨javalangRuntimeexec⟩true **or** ⟨javalangProcessBuilderstart⟩true) **or** ⟨true⟩(X))

5.6   Use of Obfuscation

Unquestionably, malware authors seek to defeat security analysis. In fact, one of the common techniques used to evade detection is code transformation, namely by rewriting existent malware with the intention to make it difficult to analyze statically. This can be done through code obfuscation techniques, which enable developers to change the syntax of the program while preserving its semantics. Although code obfuscation also aims at protecting intellectual property of programs, malware writers take advantage of it to bypass security analysis tools. With this in mind, we included the use of code obfuscation in our features. Authors of [22] explain a variety of transformations techniques used to obfuscate code. Reflection and dynamic code loading are among these techniques.

Reflection. Through Java reflection, one can inspect classes, interfaces, fields and methods at runtime. Thus, invoking methods through reflection makes it difficult for static analysis to track invoked methods. We use the following formula to detect method calls through reflection.

Reflection = **mu** X.((⟨javalangClassforName⟩true **and** ψ1) **or** ⟨true⟩(X))

ψ1 = **mu** X.(⟨javalangClassgetMethod⟩true **or** ⟨true⟩(X))

Dynamic Code Loading. The Android platform offers the possibility to dynamically load external code during runtime. Sebastian et al. [21] show that there is a significant security risk arising from the use of dynamic code loading (DCL). It's not only helpful for malware authors to escape detection, but the improper use of DCL also makes benign applications vulnerable to code injection attacks. The methods DexClassLoader and classloader are used to perform dynamic class loading.

Dynamicclassloading = **mu** X.((⟨dalviksystemDexClassLoaderDexClassLoader⟩ true **or** ⟨javalangClassLoaderClassLoader⟩true) **or** ⟨true⟩(X))

5.7   Check Ip Address

Some Android malware collect sensitive information about the victim's device. For instance, information about networks. Indeed, the Acnetdoor Trojan sends the Ip address to a remote server after opening a backdoor on the infected device [3].

CheckIpAddress = **mu** X.((⟨javanetNetworkInterfacegetNetworkInterfaces⟩true **and** ω1) **or** ⟨true⟩(X))

ω1 = **mu** X.(((⟨javautilEnumerationhasMoreElements⟩true **or** ⟨javanetNetworkInterfacegetInetAddresses⟩true) **and** ω2) **or** ⟨true⟩(X))

ω2 = **mu** X.((javanetInetAddressisLoopbackAddress⟩true **or** ⟨javanetInetAddressgetHostAddress⟩true) **or** ⟨true⟩(X))

5.8 Domain Name Server (DNS) Lookup

Network communication plays an important role in malware functioning. Fengguo Wei et al. [28] observe that 64% of malware varieties and 90% of malware applications in their dataset of 24,650 malware application samples have C&C servers. Android malware has multiple strategies to communicate with remote servers. In addition to Hardcoded Ip addresses, DNS lookups can be used to establish connection with the C&C server. In fact, malware programs carry out DNS queries to obtain the Ip address of the remote server. In Android, the methods getByName and getAllByName of the java.net.InetAddress class can be used to perfom DNS lookups.

DnsLookups = **mu** X.(⟨javanetInetAddressgetByName⟩true **or** ⟨javanetInetAddressgetAllByName⟩true **or** ⟨true⟩(X))

Table 1. The range of hyperparameter values

Classifier	Hyperparameter	Values
Random forest	n_estimators	{100, 200, 300, 400, 500, 600, 700, 800, 900, 1000, 1100, 1200, 1300, 1400, 1500}
	max_depth	{10, 20, 30, 40, 50, 60, 70, 80, 90, 100, 110, None}
SVM	gamma	{0.01, 0.1, 1,10, 100}
	C	{0.001, 0.01, 0.1, 2, 10, 100}
KNN	n_neighbors	{5, 7, 9, 11, 13, 15, 17, 19, 21, 25, 31, 35, 41, 45, 51, 55, 61, 66, 71, 77, 80, 85, 91, 99}
GBC	n_estimators	{100, 200, 300, 400, 500, 600, 700, 800, 900, 1000}

6 Machine Learning

The task of building a good classification model is often carried out empirically using a few machine learning algorithms and comparing their performance. Accordingly, we conducted a series of evaluations using multiple supervised machine learning algorithms namely the K-Nearest Neighbors, Random Forest, Gradient boosting and Support Vector Machine. For training and testing of our machine learning models, we used a dataset of 5009 Android applications, with a size of up to two megabytes, from Androzoo [4] which is a growing collection of Android Applications collected from several sources. Namely, in our dataset, applications were collected from Google play market, Appchina market, Anzhi market and Genome dataset. Our malware samples represent 63% of our dataset and were flagged as malicious by at least 10 antivirus products.

We randomly split the dataset in two disjoint partitions: the training set representing 67% of the total samples was used to build the learning model, whereas the remaining samples, i.e., 33% of the dataset was used to evaluate the performance of the model on unseen data. The sampling was done in a stratified manner to guarantee that the proportion of benign and malicious applications would be the same in both train and test sets. To choose the appropriate hyper-parameters of the learning models, 5-fold cross-validation over the training set has been used. Considering all possible combinations of hyperparameter values in Table 1, we selected the combination reporting an optimal average F1-score.

We conducted this experiment using two different sets of features, one with only permission-guarded API call features, and one that contains also features about the satisfaction of structured μ-calculus formulæ. Note that many Android applications turned out to return exactly the same features, and this was even more frequent for the smallest set of features. Thus, to prevent overfitting we have split the dataset so that the train and test sets remain disjoint for both features sets. Table 2 shows the classification results using permission-guarded API calls. In the second set of features, we use both permission-guarded API calls and security related behaviors specified in μ-calculus formulæ. As shown in Table 3, there is a slight improvement compared to the first set of features. We note a decrease in the false negative rate and the false positive rate. For further comparison, we use the ROC (Receiver Operating Characteristic) curve. The area under the curve measures the model discriminative ability. In fact, the closer the ROC curve is to the upper left corner, the better the model is at discriminating between benign and malicious Android applications. Figure 2 shows the ROC curve corresponding to each classifier using the second set of features. Overall the random forest classifier outperforms the other learning algorithms with an accuracy of 94.60% and an F1-score of 95.94%.

Table 2. Classification results using Api calls

	Accuracy %	FNR %	FPR %	TPR %	TNR %	F1-score %
RF	94.29	5	6	95	94	95.72
SVM	92.76	6	9	94	91	94.59
KNN	92.39	7	10	93	90	94.31
GBC	93.07	6	9	94	91	94.82

Table 3. Classification results using Api calls and μ-calculus formulæ

	Accuracy %	FNR %	FPR %	TPR %	TNR %	F1-score %
RF	94.60	5	6	95	94	95.94
SVM	92.94	5	11	95	89	94.77
KNN	93.62	5	9	95	91	95.24
GBC	94.17	5	7	95	93	95.64

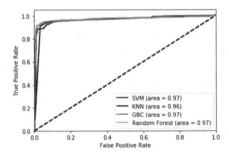

Fig. 2. Receiver operating characteristic curves

In order to collect the features, there are two phases, the translation from the APK to an LNT model, and one where we check the μ-calculus properties against this model. The translation is done in a few seconds for some applications, in minutes for other, with a mean of 62.88 s per application. Similarly, although the model verification can be done in two minutes for some applications, this duration fluctuates considerably depending on the model size. In some cases, it takes up to 30 min per application. To mitigate this problem, the computations were made on a supercomputer to simultaneously verify multiple applications.

7   Discussion and Futur Work

The presented approach has its own advantages and disadvantages. To begin with, a semantic approach, as proposed here, should yield better results than the usual syntactical approaches as it analyses the behaviour of the application rather than just its syntax which can be easily obfuscated. On the other hand, this approach relies heavily on formulae. Therefore, formulating relevant temporal properties play a significant role in improving the effectiveness of the approach.

Despite the encouraging results, our prototype is still subject to improvements. Due to the state explosion problem, we limited the size of our Android application samples to 2 megabytes. This limitation allows us to lighten and accelerate the verification process but it prevents comparison with the state-of-the-art tools. Unsurprisingly, the time taken for verification depends on the model size, which in turn depends on the application size. Mitigating this limitation will enhance the classification performance as it will allow to train the algorithms using varied applications and will also enable comparison with existing malware detectors. The LNT model will be made more precise by taking into account more synchronization constructions such as synchronization barriers. Finally, we plan to extend the set of temporal logic formulæ in order to cover more malicious behaviors. This will help at reducing false positives and false negatives.

8   Conclusion

In this paper, we propose a semantics based malware detection tool for Android. From an Android application, we extract a formal model that describes the application behavior in a non-ambiguous manner. The formal model is checked against security related properties expressed in μ-calculus. In addition to other statically extracted features, namely permission-guarded API calls, the satisfaction of these properties is fed to a machine learning algorithm predicting whether a given Android application is malicious or not. The current prototype of our tool detects Android malware with an accuracy of 94,60%.

Acknowledgment. We would like to thank Andrew Bedford for his help all along the project. The Computations were made on the supercomputer "Graham" from the university of Waterloo, managed by Calcul Québec and Compute Canada, along with the Grid'5000 testbed [8].

References

1. IDC Smartphone OS Market Share. https://www.idc.com/promo/smartphone-market-share/os. Accessed 31 Oct 2019
2. Android NDK | Android Developers. https://developer.android.com/ndk/. Accessed 08 Dec 2019
3. Current Android Malware (2018). https://forensics.spreitzenbarth.de/android-malware/
4. Allix, K., Bissyandé, T.F., Klein, J., Le Traon, Y.: Androzoo: collecting millions of android apps for the research community. In: Working Conference on Mining Software Repositories (MSR), pp. 468–471. IEEE (2016)
5. Arp, D., et al.: DREBIN: effective and explainable detection of android malware in your pocket. Ndss. **14**, 23–26 (2014)
6. Arzt, S., et al.: Flowdroid: precise context, flow, field, object-sensitive and lifecycle-aware taint analysis for android apps. Acm Sigplan Notices **49**(6), 259–269 (2014)
7. Au, K.W.Y., Zhou, Y.F., Huang, Z., Lie, D.: Pscout: analyzing the Android permission specification. In: Proceedings of the 2012 ACM Conference on Computer and Communications Security, pp. 217–228. ACM (2012)
8. Balouek, D., et al.: Adding virtualization capabilities to the grid'5000 testbed. In: Ivanov, I.I., van Sinderen, M., Leymann, F., Shan, T. (eds.) CLOSER 2012. CCIS, vol. 367, pp. 3–20. Springer, Cham (2013). https://doi.org/10.1007/978-3-319-04519-1_1
9. Battista, P., Mercaldo, F., Nardone, V., Santone, A., Visaggio, C.A.: Identification of android malware families with model checking. In: ICISSP, pp. 542–547 (2016)
10. Bedford, A., et al.: ANDRANA: quick and accurate malware detection for android. In: Cuppens, F., Wang, L., Cuppens-Boulahia, N., Tawbi, N., Garcia-Alfaro, J. (eds.) FPS 2016. LNCS, vol. 10128, pp. 20–35. Springer, Cham (2017). https://doi.org/10.1007/978-3-319-51966-1_2
11. Champelovier, D., et al.: Reference Manual of the LNT to LOTOS Translator (2017)
12. Cimino, M.G.C., Vaglini, G.: Localization and inhibition of malicious behaviors through a model checking based methodology. In: ICISSP, pp. 644–652 (2017)

13. Enck, W., Gilbert, P., Han, S., Tendulkar, V., Chun, B.G., Cox, L.P., Jung, J., McDaniel, P., Sheth, A.N.: Taintdroid: an information-flow tracking system for realtime privacy monitoring on smartphones. ACM Trans. Comput. Syst. (TOCS) **32**(2), 5 (2014)
14. Garavel, H., Lang, F., Mateescu, R., Serwe, W.: CADP 2010: a toolbox for the construction and analysis of distributed processes. In: Abdulla, P.A., Leino, K.R.M. (eds.) TACAS 2011. LNCS, vol. 6605, pp. 372–387. Springer, Heidelberg (2011). https://doi.org/10.1007/978-3-642-19835-9_33
15. Gascon, H., Yamaguchi, F., Arp, D., Rieck, K.: Structural detection of Android malware using embedded call graphs. In: Proceedings of the 2013 ACM Workshop on Artificial Intelligence and Security, pp. 45–54. ACM (2013)
16. Kinder, J., Katzenbeisser, S., Schallhart, C., Veith, H.: Detecting malicious code by model checking. In: Julisch, K., Kruegel, C. (eds.) DIMVA 2005. LNCS, vol. 3548, pp. 174–187. Springer, Heidelberg (2005). https://doi.org/10.1007/11506881_11
17. Kwon, B.J., Mondal, J., Jang, J., Bilge, L., Dumitras, T.: The dropper effect: insights into malware distribution with downloader graph analytics. In: Proceedings of the 22nd ACM SIGSAC Conference on Computer and Communications Security, pp. 1118–1129. ACM (2015)
18. Landi, W.: Undecidability of static analysis. ACM Lett. Program. Lang. Syst. (LOPLAS) **1**(4), 323–337 (1992)
19. Meng, G., Xue, Y., Xu, Z., Liu, Y., Zhang, J., Narayanan, A.: Semantic modelling of android malware for effective malware comprehension, detection, and classification. In: Proceedings of the 25th International Symposium on Software Testing and Analysis, pp. 306–317. ACM (2016)
20. Mercaldo, F., Nardone, V., Santone, A., Visaggio, C.A.: Ransomware steals your phone. formal methods rescue it. In: Albert, E., Lanese, I. (eds.) FORTE 2016. LNCS, vol. 9688, pp. 212–221. Springer, Cham (2016). https://doi.org/10.1007/978-3-319-39570-8_14
21. Poeplau, S., Fratantonio, Y., Bianchi, A., Kruegel, C., Vigna, G.: Execute this! analyzing unsafe and malicious dynamic code loading in android applications. NDSS. **14**, 23–26 (2014)
22. Rastogi, V., Chen, Y., Jiang, X.: Droidchameleon: evaluating Android anti-malware against transformation attacks. In: Proceedings of SIGSAC Symposium on Information, Computer and Communications Security, pp. 329–334. ACM (2013)
23. Song, F., Touili, T.: Model-checking for Android malware detection. In: Asian Symposium on Programming Languages and Systems, pp. 216–235 (2014)
24. Song, F., Touili, T.: Pushdown model checking for malware detection. Int. J. Softw. Tools Technol. Transf. **16**(2), 147–173 (2014)
25. Statista, The Statistics Portal: Number of available applications in the google play store from december 2009 to June 2018. https://www.statista.com/statistics/266210/number-of-available-applications-in-the-google-play-store/. Accessed 08 Dec 2019
26. Vallée-Rai, R. Co, P., Gagnon, E.M., Hendren, L.J., Lam, P., Sundaresan, V.: Soot - a java bytecode optimization framework. In: CASCON (1999)
27. Vidas, T., Christin, N.: Evading android runtime analysis via sandbox detection. In: Proceedings of the 9th ACM Symposium on Information, Computer and Communications Security, pp. 447–458. ACM (2014)
28. Wei, F., Li, Y., Roy, S., Ou, X., Zhou, W.: Deep ground truth analysis of current android malware. In: Polychronakis, M., Meier, M. (eds.) DIMVA 2017. LNCS, vol. 10327, pp. 252–276. Springer, Cham (2017). https://doi.org/10.1007/978-3-319-60876-1_12

29. Zhang, M., Duan, Y., Yin, H., Zhao, Z.: Semantics-aware Android malware classification using weighted contextual API dependency graphs. In: Proceedings of the 2014 ACM SIGSAC Conference on Computer and Communications Security, pp. 1105–1116. ACM (2014)
30. Zhang, Y., et al.: Vetting undesirable behaviors in Android apps with permission use analysis. In: Proceedings of the 2013 ACM SIGSAC Conference on Computer and Communications Security, pp. 611–622. ACM (2013)

Short Papers

Augmented Voting Reality

Hervé Chabanne[1,2], Emmanuelle Dottax[1(✉)], and Denis Dumont[1]

[1] Idemia, Courbevoie, France
{Herve.Chabanne,Emmanuelle.Dottax,Denis.Dumont}@idemia.com
[2] Télécom Paris, Paris, France
Herve.Chabanne@telecom-paris.fr

Abstract. We show how to enhance a classical ballot box to enable automatic tally, while keeping the voter experience as close as possible to the one she already knows. We describe the physical add-on, based on off-the-shelf infrared technology, as well as the cryptographic aspects, for which we rely on self-enforcing e-voting systems by Hao et al.

1 Introduction

In view of the next presidential election, US voting system has been evaluated and evidence of vulnerabilities has been found [2,3]. As stressed by [1], audit capacity is paramount, and physical ballots should remain to enable manual tally in case of contest of results (see also [13]). As a result, [10] asks for paper ballots and audits. Paper-based systems are indeed more resilient against hacking. They are also very familiar, and more trusted by citizens in general. However, they suffer long and tedious tallies. As explained in [12], the time-gap between (possibly tampered) preliminary results and final ones can be exploited, for example, to benefit from stock market reaction. In this work, we introduce a paper-based voting system that enjoys an immediate, automatic tally feature. We make limited modifications to the conventional process, minimizing changes in the voters experience, and achieving the same security properties.

Our solution leverages the principles of the "self-enforcing e-voting system" used in the DRE-i (Direct Recording Electronic with integrity) proposal [7]: electronic ballots are encrypted in advance, and the tally does not involve any trusted authority. This is achieved thanks to a "self-cancellation" property, first introduced in [9]. The DRE-i system has been extended in [11] to get rid of the need for tamper-resistant hardware. It should be noted that this extension has served on May, 2019, during the UK local elections, for an e-voting trial at Gateshead [8]. While the original system relies on DRE machines, we embed the same principle into a paper-based vote.

There have been other attempts to embed a cryptographic voting system into physical paper; for instance, Scantegrity II [4,5] makes use of invisible ink.

As a running example, we consider a referendum which offers the voters a choice of accepting or rejecting a proposal. Paper ballots are written "Yes" or "No", and voters choose between these two options in a voting booth, where they put their paper ballot inside an envelope. Then they drop their envelope in

© Springer Nature Switzerland AG 2021
J. Garcia-Alfaro et al. (Eds.): CRiSIS 2020, LNCS 12528, pp. 311–316, 2021.
https://doi.org/10.1007/978-3-030-68887-5_18

the voting box. At the end of the referendum, we want to know the number of "Yes" votes. We differentiate three "parties": the voters, the assessors who are in charge of the referendum at the polling station, and the printer who issues the paper ballots.

Section 2 explains how a classical voting box needs to be equipped to support our solution. Section 3 is devoted to the description of the property which enables self-enforcing e-voting systems and Sect. 4 describes our proposal. Section 5 concludes.

2   Physical Embodiment of the Setup

2.1   Voting Box

We equip classical voting boxes (see Fig. 1) with the capability of capturing data in the infrared field (IR). To do so, a transparent, mechanical rail guides the paper ballot towards the box slot; while moving through this rail, the envelope will be scanned: sufficient lighting (e.g. LEDs) and a camera are present to this end. A system to record the scanned values in a memory is also added.

Fig. 1. A classical voting box

Remark 1. We do not claim that our modified voting box cannot be tampered with. Nevertheless, it should be simpler to audit than DRE machines, which are targets of choice for hackers [2,3]. scanned values. Indeed, it offers very basic features and does not embed any user interface, which can be painful to analyze.

2.2   Ballots

Each paper ballot will embed a cryptogram (next section explains the content of this cryptogram): in the visible field, a ballot is a classical one, but the cryptogram is printed in the IR. Hence, cryptograms are invisible without special equipment, while they will be recorded by the voting box during the vote. This will be used for an automatic tally process. Still, paper ballots can be used for traditional tally in case of dispute.

To limit the information available to an IR spectrum eavesdropper, e.g. to ensure confidentiality of the vote in the presence of malicious assessors, the cryptograms are somehow encrypted. How this is done is described in the next sections.

3 Self-cancellation Property

We here recall the so-called "self-cancellation" formula, on which the protocol [7] relies.

Let p and q be two large primes, with $q|p-1$, and let G_q be the subgroup of order q of the group $\mathbb{Z}_p^*$. Let g be a generator of G_q. We assume that the Decision Diffie-Hellman problem in G_q is intractable.

Let $N > 0$ be an integer (standing hereafter for the number of ballots). For $i \in \{1, \ldots, N\}$, we take x_i at random in $\{1, \ldots, q-1\}$, and compute y_i such that $g^{y_i} = \prod_{j=1}^{i-1} g^{x_j} / \prod_{j=i+1}^{N} g^{x_j}$. We have the following result (see [9] for a proof):

Lemma 1 (Self-cancellation Property). $\prod_{i=1}^{N} g^{x_i y_i} = 1$.

In [7], for each vote $i \in \{1, \ldots, N\}$, the DRE computes and casts the corresponding cryptogram v_i as follows: $v_i = g^{x_i} g^{y_i} g^{c_i}$, with $c_i = 1$ for a "Yes", and $c_i = 0$ for a "No". At the end of the election, the tally amounts to computing:

$$\prod_{i=1}^{N} v_i = \prod_{i=1}^{N} g^{x_i} g^{y_i} g^{c_i} = \prod_{i=1}^{N} g^{c_i} = g^{\sum_{i=1}^{N} c_i} \tag{1}$$

Even if the Discrete Logarithm is hard in G_q, one can obtain the results from (1) as the number of "Yes" votes is limited.

If all N votes have not been casted, the self-cancellation is not enabled, but the result can still be obtained by multiplying with the remaining "No" cryptograms. Note this can also be used to get partial results.

Interestingly, and as explained in [7], the cryptograms alone do not leak the value of the vote. This provides confidentially without having to manage a secret key, hence without having to rely on a third party for the tally.

4 Our Proposal

We "embed" the previous voting process into paper-based voting, using the physical add-ons described in Sect. 2.

4.1 Referendum Preparation

For each polling station, a sufficient number N of pairs of "Yes"/"No" paper ballots is printed in advance. Each pair is associated with an index i, $i \in \{1, \dots, N\}$. For each pair, the cryptograms for both options are computed: v_i^0 for "No" and v_i^1 for "Yes". We thus have $v_i^0 = g^{x_i} g^{y_i}$ and $v_i^1 = g^{x_i} g^{y_i} g$, where x_i, y_i have been generated as exposed in the previous section.

To prevent forgery of ballots, the printer is equipped with a private key and generates signatures on the values (i, v_i^c), $c \in \{0, 1\}$. For each ballot, the value v_i^c as well as the signature are printed in IR. The public key of the printer is integrated to the voting boxes (see Sect. 4.2).

The paper ballots corresponding to the "No" choice are printed twice. The first set will be used for the voting process. The second set is slightly different: the indexes i are now printed – for convenience – in the visible field. This set is not accessible to voters, and will be used only for the tally hereafter.

The paper ballots must verify the following:

- there are N pairs of genuine paper ballots;
- values in visible and IR fields correspond to the same choice;
- the whole set of paper ballots verifies the self-enforcing property.

More precisely:

- for the two sets of ballots where a "No" is written, the one kept by the assessors and the one given to the voters:
  - for each given index $i \in \{1, \dots, N\}$, the cryptogram values v_i^0 must be identical,
  - moreover, the self-cancellation formula should stand, i.e. $\prod_{i=1}^{N} v_i^0 = 1$;
- for each index i, the values v_i^0 and v_i^1 written respectively on the "No" ballot and "Yes" ballots, must verify $v_i^1 / v_i^0 = g, i \in \{1, \dots, N\}$.

To give assurance on this, the ballots could be produced via a process similar to the one currently deployed in the smart cards industry, where certified Hardware Security Modules (HSMs) are used to enforce compliance with specified methods. These HSMs would compute cryptograms at high-speed. In addition, a secure mailing system, like the one used today to securely distribute banking cards and PINs to their owners, could be used to send paper ballots to voting stations.

Still, audits could be required to check the material actually deployed. All the above mentioned properties can be verified via non-destructive procedures that could be automated (like scanning all the ballots). Details on how this would be organized are left open at this stage.

Extra precautions against the assessors and other people physically present in the polling stations can also be taken to prevent eavesdropping. For instance, the second set of "No" paper ballots can be placed in a sealed box until the tally. Also, pairs of paper ballots "Yes" and "No" could be wrapped together in an envelope to enforce the resistance against IR spying before the vote.

4.2   Referendum and Tally Procedures

Voters follow a widely deployed procedure, without modification: they choose one or more paper ballots, go inside a voting booth to place their vote inside an envelope (and discard the other paper ballots), and finally, put the envelope in the voting box.

Remark 2. If the pair of "Yes"/"No" paper ballots is delivered to the voters inside an envelope as mentioned above, there should be two different colors to clearly differentiate the envelopes which serve to transport the ballots from the ones which are used for voting.

When the vote is inserted into the voting box, the value written in the IR on the paper ballot is scanned through the still-closed envelope. The validity of the signature of the cryptogram v_i and the fact that its index i has not be used before are checked. If so, an assessor enables the fall of the envelope inside the box. At the same time, the values v_i and i are recorded in the memory, together with their signature.

At the end of the referendum, it is expected that not all indexes are present in the box. To ensure the self-cancellation and perform the tally, the cryptograms v_i^0 for all missing indexes i have to be added. The assessors can got the list of missing indexes, and get the corresponding paper ballots from their set of copies. Introducing these ballots into the voting ballot box ensured preservation of the self-cancellation property, and the result of the poll can be computed.

5   Conclusion

We have presented the idea of replacing DRE machines in the Hao et al. voting systems [7–9,11] with paper ballots and voting scanners, to enable automatic tally. We print paper ballots in the infrared field to achieve this without modifying the voters experience. We protect ourselves against infrared eavesdroppers in the polling station by using the technique of Hao et al. voting systems, which provides confidentiality without requiring usage of a private key to get the result.

As a further step, we would like to produce a draft implementation. This would allow us to build a more detailed hardware model setup; in particular, regarding the IR technology to use (active or passive sensors, ...). We shall also identify the risks of such a solution and formally analyse the security of our proposal. The events in the voting station could be modeled to prove the achieved security properties, following [6].

Another extension would be to generalize our work to multi-candidate elections and complicated voting rules (see [9] for details) as well as taking into account large-scale voting with our scheme.

References

1. Bernhard, M., et al.: Public evidence from secret ballots. In: Krimmer, R., Volkamer, M., Braun Binder, N., Kersting, N., Pereira, O., Schürmann, C. (eds.) E-Vote-ID 2017. LNCS, vol. 10615, pp. 84–109. Springer, Cham (2017). https://doi.org/10.1007/978-3-319-68687-5_6
2. Blaze, M., Braun, J., Hursti, H., Hall, J.L., MacAlpine, M., Moss, J.: Report on Cyber Vulnerabilities in U.S. Election Equipment, Databases, and Infrastructure. DEFCON 25 Voting Machine Hacking Village (2017)
3. Blaze, M., Braun, J., Hursti, H., Jefferson, D., MacAlpine, M., Moss, J.: Report on Cyber Vulnerabilities in U.S. Election Equipment, Databases, and Infrastructure. DEFCON 26 Voting Village (2018)
4. Carback, R., et al.: Scantegrity II municipal election at Takoma Park: the first E2E binding governmental election with ballot privacy. In: USENIX Security Symposium, pp. 291–306. USENIX Association (2010)
5. Chaum, D., et al.: Scantegrity II: end-to-end verifiability for optical scan election systems using invisible ink confirmation codes. In: EVT. USENIX Association (2008)
6. Cortier, V.: Electronic voting: how logic can help. In: Demri, S., Kapur, D., Weidenbach, C. (eds.) IJCAR 2014. LNCS (LNAI), vol. 8562, pp. 16–25. Springer, Cham (2014). https://doi.org/10.1007/978-3-319-08587-6_2
7. Hao, F., et al.: Every Vote Counts: Ensuring integrity in large-scale electronic voting. In: EVT/WOTE. USENIX Association (2014). https://www.usenix.org/system/files/conference/evtwote14/jets_0203-hao.pdf
8. Hao, F., et al.: End-to-End Verifiable E-Voting Trial for Polling Station Voting at Gateshead. Cryptology ePrint Archive, Report 2020/650 (2020)
9. Hao, F., Zieliński, P.: A 2-round anonymous veto protocol. In: Christianson, B., Crispo, B., Malcolm, J.A., Roe, M. (eds.) Security Protocols 2006. LNCS, vol. 5087, pp. 202–211. Springer, Heidelberg (2009). https://doi.org/10.1007/978-3-642-04904-0_28
10. Engineering National Academies of Sciences and Medicine. Securing the Vote: Protecting American Democracy. The National Academies Press (2018)
11. Shahandashti, S.F., Hao, F.: DRE-ip: a verifiable e-voting scheme without tallying authorities. In: Askoxylakis, I., Ioannidis, S., Katsikas, S., Meadows, C. (eds.) ESORICS 2016. LNCS, vol. 9879, pp. 223–240. Springer, Cham (2016). https://doi.org/10.1007/978-3-319-45741-3_12
12. Sommer, D.M., Schneider, M., Gut, J., Capkun, S.: Cyber-Risks in Paper Voting. CoRR, abs/1906.07532 (2019)
13. Stark, P.B., Wagner, D.A.: Evidence-Based Elections. IEEE Secur. Priv. **10**(5), 33–41 (2012)

Malicious Http Request Detection Using Code-Level Convolutional Neural Network

Ines Jemal[1]([✉]), Mohamed Amine Haddar[2,3], Omar Cheikhrouhou[1,3], and Adel Mahfoudhi[1,3]

[1] University of Sfax, ENIS, CES, LR11ES49, 3038 Sfax, Tunisia
ines.jemal@stud.enis.tn
[2] ReDCAD Laboratory, University of Sfax, Sfax, Tunisia
[3] College of Computer and Information Technology, Taif University, Taif, Saudi Arabia

Abstract. Http requests represent the main component of a web navigation system. These requests, once received by the server, need to be analyzed to guarantee that they are attack-free. Attacks carried by Http requests can have disastrous effects. Due to the importance of Http requests, it is crucial to design an efficient and robust Http request analyzer that guarantees the detection of malicious ones and prevent them from being processed. In this paper, we propose a new technique to process the Http request called Code Embedding. The proposed method was integrated within the Convolutional neural network to provide an efficient and robust web attack detection tool. The experimental results prove that our method outperforms the previous works and reaches an accuracy of 98.125%.

Keywords: Web security · Web attacks · Convolutional neural network · ASCII code

1 Introduction

Web security is one of the most challenging research fields due to the increasing number of web attacks. Researchers and developers have been proposing different techniques and solutions to mitigate these web threats. Some of these methods are signatures based, others are anomalies based. However, these methods are unable to detect the zero-day attacks.

Nowadays, deep learning techniques are widely used in web security to perform classification tasks. The Convolutional neural network (CNN) is one of the competitive deep neural techniques. It has a typical architecture that can learn on a big scale. In our case, CNN can learn from a huge number of Http requests. Although CNN is a powerful classifier tool, the detection accuracy highly depends on the pre-processing of the input data. Therefore, pre-processing the data input is an important step to increase the CNN performance.

© Springer Nature Switzerland AG 2021
J. Garcia-Alfaro et al. (Eds.): CRiSIS 2020, LNCS 12528, pp. 317–324, 2021.
https://doi.org/10.1007/978-3-030-68887-5_19

In this paper, we propose a new technique to process Http request that we called Code Embedding. We evaluated our technique using CNN. To show the ability of our CNN model with our Code embedding technique in detection web attacks, we used the CSIC 2010 dataset [1]. The experimental results show that Code embedding outperforms the existing techniques (Words and Characters embedding approaches) and it increases the CNN performances. Our technique performs better than the existing approaches, it fulfills 98.125% of accuracy.

The remainder of this paper is organized as follows: The second section presents the state of the art of neural networks pre-processing techniques. Our technique Code embedding and our designed CNN are presented in Sect. 3. Section 4 compared our approach to the existing one. The last section concludes this paper and briefly explains our future work.

2   Related Works

To detect the web attacks at the server-side, many works proposed the use of deep learning techniques especially the Convolutional neural network (CNN).

Zhang et al. [2] used the CNN to detect web attacks using CSIC 2010 [1] data-set. They dissected the Http request into words and deleted the non-alphanumeric characters. Their CNN model achieved 96.49% of accuracy. The authors claim that the embedding vectors generated by words embedding approach are among the best ways to detect web attacks.

Jane et al. [3] used two neural networks multilayer Feed Forward networks. The first neural network checks the trained web application data, while the second neural network checks the trained data of the user behavior. The input of the first neural network (ANN1) is defined by a set of collected information from several sections of Http request. The second neural network (ANN2) stores data about user behavior. The two neural networks ANN1 and ANN2 achieved 92% and 95% of accuracy, respectively.

Joshua et al. [4] used the eXpose neural network based on a character embedding approach to detect malicious URL, they investigated the automatic extraction of features for a short string. Their model achieved a 92% detection rate.

Erxue et al. [5] used CNN to improve intrusion detection systems. The authors used the word embedding approach to detect malicious payloads. Their model achieved 95.75% of accuracy.

The previously presented works used either the word embedding or the character embedding approaches to process the Http requests. Trying to enhance the attack detection rate, we propose a new embedding approach called Code Embedding, which is presented in the next section.

3   CNN Based Code Level

The web application attack detection mechanism is presented in Fig. 1. A user consults a web application and sends a request to the webserver. Before the request arrives at the server, it must be processed by our prototype web application firewall based on a Convolutional Neural Network (CNN) that takes as input all the Http requests and treats them using the proposed code embedding technique. Our designed CNN makes a binary decision: If the request is malicious then it must be rejected automatically, else it will be sent to the webserver.

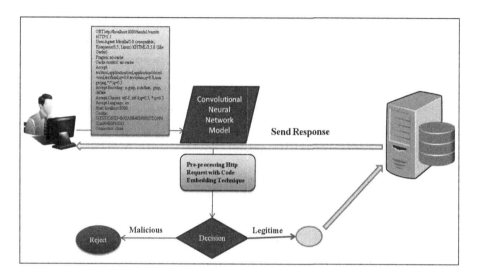

Fig. 1. Web attack mechanism

In what follows, we detail the Code embedding technique that presents a new pre-processing way of the CNN data input.

3.1 Http Request Pre-processing

The Http request has a standardized form and is composed of different parts that contain words, characters, and symbols (Fig. 2).

```
GET http://localhost:8080/tienda1/carrito HTTP/1.1
User-Agent: Mozilla/5.0 (compatible; Konqueror/3.5; Linux) KHTML/3.5.8 (like Gecko)
Pragma: no-cache
Cache-control: no-cache
Accept: text/xml,application/xml,application/xhtml+xml,text/html;q=0.9,text/plain;q=0.8,image/png,*/*;q=0.5
Accept-Encoding: x-gzip, x-deflate, gzip, deflate
Accept-Charset: utf-8, utf-8;q=0.5, *;q=0.5
Accept-Language: en
Host: localhost:8080
Cookie: JSESSIONID=B92A8B48B9008CD29F622A994E0F650D
Connection: close
```

Fig. 2. A real Http request

An attack is a malicious form of the Http request. The attackers add or inject additional information to the Http request in order to modify its interpretation according to their needs. Processing the input is a necessary step, it influences the CNN accuracy. In the security study with deep learning, the most used techniques in pre-processing the Http request are words and characters embedding. The words embedding dissects the Http request into words. The characters embedding approach dissects the fully Http requests into characters. The main drawback of these techniques is the unpredictable behavior of the neural network for new characters or words. In this paper, we propose a new technique to process the Http request called Code Embedding. It is an interpolation of the characters embedding to the ASCII code value level. The idea of Code embedding comes from the successful results of CNN in image recognition when the input are integers (the RBG values of the image pixels). The Code embedding consists of three steps:

- First, dissecting the whole Http request into words.
- Second, each word is dissected into characters.
- Finally, we replaced each character or symbol with its integer value (the machine integer value like the ASCII code).

The result of these steps is a vector V of integers (ASCII code values).

3.2   The Designed CNN

The Convolutional neural network (CNN) is a very popular technique used for deep learning. It is widely used in many domains and has realized attractive results. It is one of the most popular algorithms for deep learning. It can learn directly from the data input and eliminates the need for manual features engineering selection and extraction. CNN has a typical architecture, it is composed of different layers that aim to extract and select the features automatically. Figure 3 presents the different layers that shape the CNN.

The Embedding Layer: It receives the data input (Code ASCII) after the processing operation. Each code ASCII value is embedded into a digital vector of dimension d. We chose d equal to 128. The output is a digital matrix of dimension $l * d$ while l presents the number of ASCII code values.

The Convolutional Layer: It convolves the digital matrix based on the kernel size. Each kernel scrolls through the digital and convolves with a local area of size $n * k$. After many experiences done, we are convinced to use 4 kernel size (k1, k2, k3, k4) = (3, 4, 5, 6), and for each kernel size, we use $n = 128$ filters. The output is a feature map, which size is less than the digital matrix size.

The Max-pooling Layer: Based on the activation function, the Max-pooling Layer extracts and selects the features engineering from the features map. It reduces the number of neurons that the network must learn. We chose the Rectified Linear Unit (ReLU) function that has the following definition $f(x) = Max(0, x)$.

The Fully Connected Layer: All neurons of the fully connected layer are connected to each neuron in the Max-pooling layer. It makes the reasoning operation at a high level.

The Softmax Layer: It makes the binary decision. In our context, it classifies the Http request into two classes benign or malicious. So, it has two neurons that are connected to all the neurons in the fully connected layer.

These layers are based on parameters that are essential in the precision measurement of the CNN model. To build our designed Convolutional neural network, we have worked on several hyper-parameters that shape the CNN: We chose Adam as an optimizer that permits to constantly update the network weights of neurons in each backward and forward step. We chose Relu as an Activation function that decides the value of each neuron in the CNN. We chose 4 kernel sizes 3, 4, 5, 6, and for each kernel size, we used 128 filters. We tuned 0.5 dropout that helps to drop certain neurons chosen arbitrary to reduce the network over-fitting. We chose cross-entropy as a loss function, it measures the performance of the classification model. Table 1 summarizes the hyper-parameters values of our model CNN.

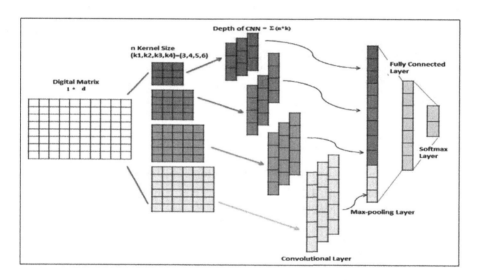

Fig. 3. Implementation of code embedding technique using CNN.

4   Experiments and Results

In order to evaluate our Code Embedding technique in web attack detection, we conduct our experiment using the train/test method with the CSIC 2010 dataset [1].

Table 1. CNN model hyper-parameters

Hyper-parameters	Value
Embedding vector size	128
Optimizer	Adam
Activation function	Relu
Kernel size	4, 5, 6, 7
Number of kernel size	128
Dropout	0.5
Batch size	64
Loss function	Cross entropy

4.1 Large Scale Dataset

We chose the CSIC 2010 [1] dataset to show the performance of the Code Embedding technique. It is close to reality since it contains 36000 normal traffic Http requests and 25065 malicious traffic that described the most serious attacks as SQLI [6]. We split our data input into two parts. The first is used to train our CNN model, it presents 80% of the whole dataset. The second part (20%) is used to test it. Table 2 shows the distribution of the CSIC 2010 dataset using the Train/Validation/Test method. 63288 Http requests are used to train the CNN and 19413 Http requests to test it and to show its performance to detect new attacks (from the test set).

Table 2. Experimental dataset distribution.

Http requests	Training & validation phase	Testing phase
Normal	43236	14400
Abnormal	20052	5013
Total number	63288	19413

4.2 Evaluation Metrics and Results

To evaluate the performance of the Code Embedding technique with our designed CNN in the detection of web attacks, we use four criteria: the Accuracy, the Precision, the Recall, and the F1-Score. These metrics are presented using the True Positive rate (TP), True Negative rate (TN), The False Positive rate (FP), and False Negative rate (FN).

$$Accuracy = \frac{TP+TN}{TP+TN+FN+FP}$$
$$Recall = \frac{TP}{FN+TP}$$
$$Precision = \frac{TP}{TP+FP}$$
$$F1\text{-}Score = 2 * \frac{Precision*Recall}{Precision+Recall}$$

We implement our proposed CNN with the programming language Python3.6 [7] which is rich in libraries to manage the deep learning techniques as Tensorflow [8] and Keras [9]. Using the free cloud service Google Colaboratory [10], we trained the CNN model about 6000 steps. In every 100 steps, we recorded the rates of loss and accuracy training. We remark that the accuracy training rate increases and the loss rate decreases towards zero.

4.3   Results and Comparison Study

After 6000 steps of training, we tested the new Code embedding technique within the CNN using 19413 Http requests. Table 3 presents the value of the different metrics obtained. The accuracy reached 98.125%, the precision rate is 94.833%, the Recall rate achieved 97.779%, and the F1-Score is 96.284%. These results reveal that based on the Code embedding technique, our designed CNN performs better in detecting web attacks compared to the existing embedding techniques.

Table 3. Performance of code embedding.

Metrics	Accuracy	Recall	Precision	F1-score
Rate	98.125%	97,779%	94,833	96,284%

Table 4. Comparison web-security based works accuracy

References	Approach	Accuracy
Zhang et al. [2]	Word embedding	96.46%
Jane et al. [3]	Word embedding	95%
Joshua et al. [4]	Character embedding	92%
Erxue et al. [5]	Word embedding	96.75%
Present work	Code embedding	98.125%

As shown in Table 4, the accuracy of previously existing web security work using word and character embedding approaches did not overtake 96.75% and 92%, respectively. We proved by experiments that our CNN based on Code embedding achieved better accuracy (98.125%) compared to Zhang et al. [2], Joshua et al. [4], Erxue et al. [5] and Jane et al. [3] that used the CNN to detect server-side web attacks.

5   Conclusion

In this paper, we investigated a new technique to pre-process the Http request called Code Embedding. Through experiments, we demonstrated that our technique increases the performance of the Convolutional neural network in the detection of web application attacks. In the experiments, we noted an extra overhead time in the training and testing phases compared to the existing embedding techniques. In future works, we will investigate this problem and we will use our pre-processing technique with other well-known neural networks.

References

1. Dataset csic-2010. http://www.isi.csic.es/dataset/
2. Zhang, M., Xu, B., Bai, S., Lu, S., Lin, Z.: A deep learning method to detect web attacks using a specially designed CNN. In: Liu, D., Xie, S., Li, Y., Zhao, D., El-Alfy, E.-S.M. (eds.) ICONIP 2017. LNCS, vol. 10638, pp. 828–836. Springer, Cham (2017). https://doi.org/10.1007/978-3-319-70139-4_84
3. Stephan, J.J., Mohammed, S.D., Abbas, M.K.: Neural network approach to web application protection. Int. J. Inf. Educ. Technol. 5(2), 150 (2015)
4. Saxe, J., Berlin, K.: eXpose: a character-level convolutional neural network with embeddings for detecting malicious URLs, file paths and registry keys. arXiv preprint arXiv:1702.08568 (2017)
5. Min, E., Long, J., Liu, Q., Cui, J., Chen, W.: TR-IDS: anomaly-based intrusion detection through text-convolutional neural network and random forest. In: Security and Communication Networks, vol. 2018 (2018)
6. Jemal, I., Cheikhrouhou, O., Hamam, H., Mahfoudhi, A.: SQL injection attack detection and prevention techniques using machine learning. Int. J. Appl. Eng. Res. 15(6), 569–580 (2020)
7. Van Rossum, G., et al.: Python programming language. In: USENIX Annual Technical Conference, vol. 41, p. 36 (2007)
8. Abadi, M., et al.: TensorFlow: a system for large-scale machine learning. In: 12th USENIX Symposium on Operating Systems Design and Implementation, OSDI 2016, pp. 265–283 (2016)
9. Manaswi, N.K.: Understanding and working with keras. Deep Learning with Applications Using Python, pp. 31–43. Apress, Berkeley (2018). https://doi.org/10.1007/978-1-4842-3516-4_2
10. Bisong, E.: Google colaboratory. Building Machine Learning and Deep Learning Models on Google Cloud Platform, pp. 59–64. Apress, Berkeley (2019). https://doi.org/10.1007/978-1-4842-4470-8_7

Enhancement of a Business Model with a Business Contextual Risk Model

Zakariya Kamagaté[1,2]([✉]), Jacques Simonin[1], and Yvon Kermarrec[1]

[1] IMT Atlantique – Lab-STICC UMR CNRS 6285, Technopôle Brest Iroise,
29238 Brest cedex, France
{zakariya.kamagate,jacques.simonin,yvon.kermarrec}@imt-atlantique.fr
[2] LASTIC-DRIT, ESATIC,
18 BP 1501 Abidjan 18, Abidjan, Côte d'Ivoire

Abstract. In this paper, we propose an approach of security risk-driven contextual model for software systems development. The approach is model-driven using enterprise business architecture as the basis for the contextual models definition, associating security risk concerns. Enterprise Architecture (EA) enables the description of an organisation's structure, its business and its underlying Information System. By using a Model-Driven Engineering (MDE) approach such as Model-Driven Architecture (MDA), we dene an architecture for models, and we provide a set of guidelines for structuring specications expressed as (EA) contextual models. Then these models are enhanced to integrate security aspects in the overall development process. The proposal aims to analyse enterprise security from a business-oriented view and define security requirements inherited by the lower architectures, particularly IS architecture. The approach provides a meta-model of business contextual risk with a security management process, consisting on a systematic method, guiding to risk modelling and risk treatment strategies.

Keywords: Risk · Models · Business scenario · Security · Threats · Software engineering · Enterprise architecture · Model-Driven Engineering · Model-driven architecture

1 Introduction

Model-Driven Security (MDS) has emerged as a specialized Model-Driven Engineering (MDE) [1,2] approach for supporting the development of security-critical systems. MDE consists of using models and their transformations as primary artefacts for each stage of system development process. Model-Driven Architecture (MDA) [7], an MDE approach, that uses models, promotes a vertical separation of concerns at a high level of abstraction, without any considerations about the target platform. These specicity can be integrated (semi) automatically to produce code compliant with each platform. Throughout its process, MDE gives the possibility to define contextual models as constraints definition

J. Garcia-Alfaro et al. (Eds.): CRiSIS 2020, LNCS 12528, pp. 325–334, 2021.
https://doi.org/10.1007/978-3-030-68887-5_20

[4]. This is a prevailing solution to define system architecture applying gradual constraints by refining the initial system specification [3]. This methodology
directly inspired several MDS proposals [15] that applied this paradigm to information security engineering, bringing several benets to the domain. Nevertheless,
many attacks toward organisations have success because of issues associated with
how systems within organizations are structured. In this context, it is necessary
to examine security by taking into account all components that influence the
organization's systems, including business, application and technologies. Enterprise Architecture (EA) fulfils this need. EA can be defined as an approach that
clearly shows how the enterprise's structures (business processes, Information
Systems, applications, technologies...) are integrated. Also, it reduces organization's complexity by providing specic viewpoints on an integrated entire model
[5]. However, "true integration of security in Enterprise architecture requires a
system engineering approach. Then security and risk are considered as soon as
possible in the system engineering development lifecycle" [6]. In this context,
MDA instances are ideal solutions for EA security integration by dening an
architecture for models, providing a set of guidelines for structuring specications
expressed as models. The goal of this paper is to present a security risk-driven
contextual approach, based on the concepts of well established EA frameworks
such as TOGAF [11] and its compositional layers (e.g., business and IS) by leveraging the related-context concept of MDE. As main contribution, we defined
contextual models related to TOGAF (business, Information system) architectures with security risk concerns. Then, these models integrate the model-driven
Architecture (MDA) process at the CIM stage with a transformation chaining to
the Platform Independent Model (PIM) stage. The result is a PIM instance of
risk-driven logical architecture of business tasks. The paper is organised as follows. Section 2 is the Background, and next, the related works regarding MDS is
describing in Sect. 3. The proposed approach of business contextual risk-driven
modelling is dened in Sect. 4, with subsections describing the meta-model and
the security management process. We present the Model-driven integration with
enhancement of a business contextual risk model into MDA approach in Sect. 5,
and finally we end with conclusion and future work in Sect. 6.

2   Background

Model-driven Architecture (MDA) deals with models and uses different levels of
abstraction to address the problem and the solution domain. It defines methodologies to lower the level of abstraction by defining relationships between the
participating models. The goal of MDA is to create an Enterprise Architecture
(EA) modeling capability helping analysts and developers to describe a company's business and software assets [21]. Model-driven Security (MDS) takes
advantage of the (MDA) techniques by providing guidelines to support the construction of systems with security mechanisms integration. [18] defines (EA)
as "a coherent whole of principles, methods and models that are used in the
design and realization of the enterprise's organizational structure, business processes, information systems, and infrastructure". A large number of frameworks

for enterprise architectures have been proposed. Among the most, important ones are the Zachman Framework [9], the Department of Defense Architecture Framework [10] and the Open Group Architectural Framework (TOGAF) [11]. TOGAF is considered as one of the best frameworks concerning business and technical layers, as it provides many structures and details for these. At the core of TOGAF is the Architecture Development Method (ADM), eight phases that provide an iterative process of continuous architecture development. In this paper we combine TOGAF and MDA for enterprise architecture development, with security concern. The approach is a Model-Driven security oriented Enterprise Architecture.

3   Related Works

In a white paper published in 2016 [6], The Open Group analyses different approaches to integrate risk and Security within a TOGAF Enterprise Architecture. It examines a selection of risk and security modelling paradigms and extracts a set of core concepts for them. Then it maps most of the concepts to ArchiMate language elements. Contrary to this white paper, our approach uses UML for graphical representation of security concerns as contextual models. We create an enterprise architecture modeling capability based on MDA approach. Then we generate specific applications to implement the architecture. In [12], the authors proposed an integration of security risk management and enterprise architecture management. The integration is in the form of concepts mapping between Information System Security Risk Management (ISSRM) and the Enterprise Architecture Management (EAM) metamodels. The approach leverages enterprise architecture modelling to support the identification of business and IS assets. It also proposes to model the treatment of the risk, especially in relation with the value of the risk. However, contrary to our, this approach does not give real support in the identification of the threats and risk associated with the elements of the architecture. In our proposal, threats and risk are analysed with the STRIDE [19] method, as a basis for security requirements from business point of view. The model-driven security provides supports for modelling security requirements as a concern from the requirements stage. Here, security relevant information are provided at the right level of abstraction as contextual models. Then, model transformation mechanisms are useful to integrate these models into the overall system architecture. The following section describes the risk-driven business contextual model proposed within our approach.

4   Risk-Driven Business Contextual Model

This section is dedicated to the introduction of the business contextual risk model supported by a security management process. Our main contribution of risk-driven business model is based on the Open Group guide that describes how the TOGAF architecture development can be used to create security risk-driven system's architecture [6]. We use UML as a modelling language to describe the architecture artifacts in the meta-modelling. Our approach is a Transformation Contextual Model (TCM) defined by a risk expert to inuence the development process from the early stage (Computation Independent Model) of the development life cycle. Next, the description of the business contextual risk meta-model.

4.1 Business Contextual Risk Metamodel

The TCM-BR (TCM - Business Risk) model (see Fig. 1) corresponds to the business risk model in the TOGAF Enterprise Architecture related to Risk and Security integration. Business Risk model is the result of threat/risk analysis from the business scenario model. **Threat** is based on threats identification, risk likelihood of materializing, and impact of an incident on business assets (business tasks). NIST defines threat as "Any circumstance or event with the potential to adversely impact organizational operations (including mission, functions, image, or reputation), organizational assets, or individuals through an information system via unauthorized access, destruction, disclosure, modification of information, and/or denial of service". [16] A threat is always related with a specic business task (sequence) and is evaluated measuring its probability and potential impact resulting in a measurement of its risk. **Risk process** is risk identified from threat analysis in the organisation's business in the context of business scenarios. Risk is the combination of a threat with one or more vulnerabilities leading to a negative impact harming one or more of the assets. **Risk Treatment measure** is an action, device, procedure, or technique that reduces a threat, vulnerability, or an attack. It comprises two steps: -Risk Treatment decision: consisting on action against risk (i.e.: risk mitigation, risk elimination, risk transfer or risk acceptation); and -security requirements: defines security objectives (in term of CIA, authentication, authorisation...) considered to select corresponding security strategies (services) and appropriate control measures to implement. The following paragraph presents the process guiding to security management.

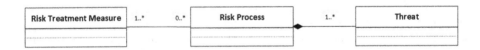

Fig. 1. Business contextual risk meta-model.

4.2 Security Management Process for Business Contextual Risk Model

The security risk management process proposed below is compliant with ISO 27005 [14] and ISO 31000 risk management standards, defined by ISO. The method comprises the classical steps of risk management: Context Establishment, risk assessment and risk treatment. Our approach presents the particularity to execute the actions of the process with the basis of contextual enterprise architecture models supported by the model-driven architecture (i.e.: CIM level). The process described below (see Fig. 2) puts the focus on how the enterprise architecture can support each action of the process from the enterprise business scenario and the IS supporting the business. Here the description of each action:

Fig. 2. Security management process.

- **Context and assets identification:** consists in knowing the field of the organization, its environment, determining precisely its limits and identifying its resources, assets and services. An Asset (business assets and IS assets) is considered as anything that has value to the organisation and contributes for achieving its goals [12].
- **Security goals:** Security goals also known as security properties are criteria that act as indicators to assess the signicance of a risk [13]. It is generally defined in term of condentiality; integrity; availability, non-repudiation, accountability.
- **Threat and Risk analysis:** In our approach, we use STRIDE [20] threat modeling method to support threat and risk analysis by providing a checklist of threat models with the corresponding security property violated. In this way, security objectives are defined based on the need to guarantee these security properties. To each security property, correspond a security strategy (service) proposed to mitigate risk as security requirement. In addition, for each mitigation strategy, a list of controls or mitigation techniques are proposed for the implementation. STRIDE [20] method is a mnemonic for things that go wrong in security. It stands for Spoofing, Tampering, Repudiation, Information Disclosure, Denial of Service, and Elevation of Privilege (see definition in Table 1).

Assumed, the following threats/attacks in the context of an online shopping that can lead to loss of money (business financial loss). We defined a list of risks as (R1 to R6) to characterise each threat:

- R1 (Risk 1): Credentials spoofing; R2 (Risk 2): Phishing; R3 (Risk 3): Sniffing; R4 (Risk 4): Session hijacking; R5 (Risk 5): Buffer Overflow; R6 (Risk 6): Unauthorized.

The mitigation methods listed in the table (see Table 1) are intended to serve as examples to illustrate ways to address threats for threat analysis, risk process, and Risk Treatment in the online shopping context: As shown in the Table 1, the column (1) describes STRIDE threat model, which corresponds to threat element in TCM-BR.Column (2) is the definition of each element. Each threat model corresponds in column (3) to a security property (goals/drivers). The column (4) is the security services proposed as threat mitigation strategy. Threat mitigation strategy corresponds to threat treatment measure (decision) taken to how to treat threat. From this decision, a security requirement is defined based on violated security properties that determine security objectives in term of CIA, authentication, authorization... and the corresponding strategy controls as security services. The column (5) proposes some technical means that can be applied to tackle threats. The corresponding elements of STRIDE helps identify risks related to a specific domain (e.g.: risks to online shopping) and propose a treatment measure. A threat is always related with a specic business task (or sequence of tasks) and the underlining IS components (applications and operations). A threat is evaluated, measuring its probability and potential impact resulting in a measurement of its risk.

- **Security requirements**: Security requirements are the security needs to treat identified risks. It is defined by the decision of how to treat risk designed as risk treatment decision. There are four types of measures (related decisions) to treat risk: risk mitigation or reduction (decision), risk avoidance (decision), risk transfer (decision) and risk acceptance (decision). Risk mitigation (reduction) decisions lead to security requirements.
- **Security control engineering**: Control (also called countermeasure or safeguard) is a designed means to improve security, specied by a security requirement, and implemented to comply with it. The column (5) of Table 1 corresponds to control techniques for threats mitigation.

A model of logical components, composed by logical operations, which supports the core business of the company, represents a view of the logical architecture. This consists in a static view made up of logical application components and logical risk management components, which supports the business model described in CIM and the contextual business model described just before in (TCM-BR). The following section describes the logical architecture and presents the overall model-driven integration architecture of our approach.

5   Business Contextual Risk Model Integration into MDA Approach

This section presents our approach of integrating a contextual risk model into a Model-Driven Engineering process with business architecture of the Enterprise Architecture. The proposal aims to extend the CIM model, representing business context models of EA with an enhancement transformation using the MDA approach mechanisms. Model-driven architecture (MDA), comprises three levels of abstraction: computation independent model (CIM) or (requirements), platform independent model (PIM) or (design and architecture) and platform

Table 1. STRIDE threat models and mitigation measures (adapted from [20]).

Threat model	Definition	Security property	Strategy (Security service)	Mitigation techniques	Example: Risks of online shopping
Spoofing	Impersonating something or someone else	Authentication	Authentication	Passords, Tokens, Biometrics, HTTPS, Ipsec, Crypto tunnels, Digital signatures or authenticators	R1, R4, R6
Tampering	Modifying data or code	Integrity	Integrity, permissions	Digital Signatures, Keyed MAC, IPSEC, HTTPS, ACLs/permissions, Crypto tunnels	R6
Repudiation	Claiming to have not performed an action.	Non repudiation	Fraud prevention, logging, signatures	Digital signatures, Logging	R2, R3, R6
Information Disclosure	Exposing information to someone not authorized to see it	Confidentiality	Permissions, encryption	SSL : IPSEC, HTTPS, Permissions, File encryption, Disk encryption (FileVault, itLocker)	
Denial of Service	Deny or degrade service to users	Availability	Availability	Fail over, Load balancing, Elastic cloud, design more capacity	
Elevation of privilege	Gain capabilities without proper authorizaLon	Authorization	Authorization, isolation	Roles, privileges, Input validation (fuzzing*), Sandboxes, firewalls	R1, R4, R6

specic model (PSM) or (implementation). A CIM presents what the system is expected to do, a PIM represents how the system reaches its requirements out specific platform details and a PSM combines the specication in PIMs with details required to describe the system implementation on a particular type of platform. A series of transformations are performed to build a software system: transformation from CIM to PIM, transformation from PIM to PSM, and transformation from PSM to code. Our approach concerns a CIM enhancement with a transformation of CIM to PIM. The overall development process integrates the dierent models involved (including the business contextual risk model described previously) in the architecture, by a model transformation chaining in a MDA compliant development process. A contextual transformation for enhancement (CTe) and enhancement transformation (ET) are useful for this purpose. At each stage of the transformation chaining, a new contextual model is created by a TCM integration during the enhancement process, taking into account the previous model. These models are used to build a PIM model that is a risk-driven logical architecture of business tasks. The models description instances are illustrated with a scenario of two tasks of an online shopping performed by a customer:

1. Read customer login and password
2. Open a customer session

As follow the description of the overall architecture and the composing model

The CIM is a model of a business scenario. The CIM concepts target the description of business task(s) composing a business scenario:

- **"Business Scenario"** (close to the Business Service concept defined in the TOGAF meta-model) describes a business scenario (*BSCustomerAuthentification*).
- **"Business Task"** specifies the name of a task composing a business scenario (Read customer login and password and Open a customer session business tasks of the *BSCustomerAuthentification* business scenario).
- **"Business Task Sequence"** represents a temporal sequence of two tasks (Read customer login and password before Open a customer session).

The CICM-R (CICM – Risk) meta-model shows a mapping relationship between a task of a business scenario and business risks. This mapping is achieved by a business expert and a security risk expert with the instantiating of the "Contextualized Business Task with Business Risk" concept that links (represented below by the "→" symbol) a "Business Task" instance and a "Business Risk" instance *(Read customer login and password → R1 and R6)*.

TCM-LIS (TCM – Logical Information System) is the contextual model in relation to integration with enhancement. This enhancement by a logical architecture model of the IS (which is designed by Enterprise Architects) needs the following concepts:

- "Logical Application Component" defined in the TOGAF meta-model (*LACUserManagement* and *LACSessionManagement*).
- "Logical Application Component Dependency" (*LACSessionManagement depends on LACUserManagement*).
- "Logical Application Operation", which composes a logical application component (*LAOReadCredentials* in *LACUserManagement*, *LAOCreateSession* in *LACSessionManagement*).

A Logical Application Component (*LAC*) is dedicated to risk management. This component designed as *LACRiskManagement* encapsulates operations that treat each risk: *LAOProcessR1* and *LAOProcessR6* in our illustration.

The CICM-L (CICM – Logical) meta-model is a mapping relationship ("Contextualized Business Task with Logical Application Operation" concept) between a business task and IS logical application operations packaged into logical application components ("Logical Application Operation" concept) designed by the Enterprise Architects (*Read customer login and password→ LAORead-Credentials and Open a customer session→ LAOCreateSession*). A sequence of business tasks involves a possible mapping with a logical application component dependency between components owning the operations mapped with the business tasks (*Read customer login and password* before *Open a customer session*) → *LACSessionManagement* on *LACUserManagement*).

LACRiskManagement depends on A business scenario is generally a sequence of tasks consisting in "request" and "access" operations of resources (e.g: data). Thus, in one hand, a Logical Application Component depends on a Risk Logical Application Component when the "request" operation is identify as critical (risky) and requires a treatment before its execution. In addition, in the other hand, a Risk Logical Application Component depends on a Logical Application Component when the "access" operation is identify as critical (risky) and requires a treatment after its execution. Hence, a representation of logical data provided by logical operation can give details of business operations and help to identify precisely the resources concerned by the related risks. In this case, risk process can be highlight dynamically by an UML sequence diagram to perform a better analysis and management of risk.

6 Conclusion and Future Works

In this paper, we proposed a business contextual risk-driven model integration into the MDA approach based on TOGAF Enterprise Architecture. A contextual enhancement transformation was useful to achieve the contextual models integration within the CIM to PIM model. Then we leveraged the concepts of model-driven security paradigm by analyzing information security risk from a business (scenario) point of view. The integration results into a PIM instance of risk-driven logical architecture of business tasks. The PIM describes a static architecture of the model that illustrates the logical application components and the logical risk management component. We are currently working on the dynamic logical contextual risk model that defines rules for the dynamic management of logical application components, composed by logical operation risks.

References

1. Selic, B.: MDA manifestations. Eur. J. Inform. Prof. **9**(2), 12–16 (2008)
2. Kleppe, A., Warmer, J., Bast, W.: MDA Explained the Model-Driven Architecture: Practice and Promise. Addison-Wesley, Boston (2003)
3. Davies, J., Gibbons, J., Milward, D., Welch, J.: Compositionality and refinement in model-driven engineering. In: Gheyi, R., Naumann, D. (eds.) SBMF 2012. LNCS, vol. 7498, pp. 99–114. Springer, Heidelberg (2012). https://doi.org/10.1007/978-3-642-33296-8_9
4. Simonin, J., Puentes, J.: Automatized integration of a contextual model into a process with data variability. Comput. Lang. Syst. Structures **54**, 156–182 (2018)
5. Innerhofer-OBerperfler, F., Breu, R.: Using an enterprise architecture for IT risk management. In: ISSA, pp. 1–12 (2006)
6. Open Group Guide: Integrating Risk and Security within a TOGAF® Enterprise Architecture ISBN: 1-937218-66-9 Document Number: G152 Published by The Open Group, January 2016
7. Kleppe, A.G., Warmer, J., Warmer, J.B., et al.: MDA explained: The Model Driven Architecture: Practice and Promise. AddisonWesley Professional, Boston (2003)

8. Asnar, Y., Giorgini, P., Massacci, F., et al.: From trust to dependability through risk analysis. In: The 2nd International Conference on Availability, Reliability and Security (ARES 2007), pp. 19–26. IEEE (2007)
9. Zachman, J.A.: A framework for information systems architecture. IBM Syst. J. **38**(2/3), 454–470 (1999)
10. Department of Defense Architecture Framework Working Group: DoD Architecture Framework, version 1.5. Department of Defense, USA (2007)
11. The Open Group: TOGAF 2007 edition, Van Haren Publishing, Zaltbommel, Netherlands (2008)
12. Grandry, E., Feltus, C., et Dubois, E.: Conceptual integration of enterprise architecture management and security risk management. In: 17th IEEE International Enterprise Distributed Object Computing Conference Workshops, vol. 2013, pp. 114–123. IEEE (2013)
13. Dubois, É., Heymans, P., Mayer, N., et al.: A systematic approach to define the domain of information system security risk management. In: Intentional Perspectives on Information Systems Engineering, pp. 289–306. Springer, Berlin, Heidelberg (2010)
14. Hervé S.: Consultants ISO/IEC 27005:2011 Information technology - Security techniques - Information security risk management (2010)
15. Lucio, L., Zhang, Q., Nguyen, P.H., et al.: Advances in model-driven security. In: Advances in Computers, pp. 103–152. Elsevier (2014)
16. threat-Glossary — CSRC, Arpil 2020. https://csrc.nist.gov/glossary/term/threat
17. Chowdhury, M.J.M.: Security risk modelling using SecureUML. In: 16th International Conference Computer and Information Technology, pp. 420–425. IEEE (2014)
18. Jonkers, H., Lankhorst, M.M., Ter Doest, H.W.L., et al.: Enterprise architecture: management tool and blueprint for the organisation. Inf. Syst. Front. **8**(2), 63–66 (2006)
19. Myagmar, S., Lee, A.J., et Yurcik, W.: Threat modeling as a basis for security requirements. In: Symposium on Requirements Engineering for Information Security (SREIS), pp. 1–8 (2005)
20. Shostack, A.: Threat Modeling: Designing for Security. John Wiley & Sons, Indianapolis (2014)
21. https://www.omg.org/mda/mda_files/09-03-WP_Mapping_MDA_to_Zachman_Framework1.pdf

Secure Data Processing for Industrial Remote Diagnosis and Maintenance

Walid Arabi[1]([✉]), Reda Yaich[1], Aymen Boudguiga[2], and Mawloud Omar[3]

[1] Institut de Recherche Technologique SystemX, 91120 Palaiseau, France
{walid.arabi,reda.yaich}@irt-systemx.fr
[2] Université Paris-Saclay, CEA-List, 91120 Palaiseau, France
aymen.boudguiga@cea.fr
[3] LIGM, ESIEE Paris, Université Gustave-Eiffel, Noisy-le-Grand, France
mawloud.omar@gmail.com

Abstract. In this work, we study the digitization of the industrial maintenance process, and its mutation towards new methods such as remote diagnosis (i.e., over the air) and preventive maintenance. First, we describe the advantage of remote and preventive maintenance. Then, we apply it to a reference industrial architecture and investigate its security vulnerabilities. Finally, we propose a secure framework that ensures the confidentiality of maintenance data during its life-cycle. We do so by using homomorphic encryption which not only ensures the confidentiality of maintenance data at transit and rest, but also their confidentiality in use. We give some implementation results regarding simple maintenance operations and discuss the viability of the approach.

Keywords: Industry 4.0 · Remote maintenance · Data confidentiality · Homomorphic encryption.

1 Introduction

Recent developments of manufacturing digitization technologies, such as Industrial Internet of Things (IIoT), cloud systems, data analytic and machine learning, drive emergence of highly smart architectures integrating device and service networks. These technologies enabled remote monitoring, remote operation, and remote maintenance of modern manufacturing systems. Modernized maintenance under the term of Smart Maintenance occurred over the time, and rapidly evolved using new Big Data Analytics. However, integration of these technologies in industrial systems raised new challenges. One of main challenges is the required high security. Indeed, integration of such complex manufacturing technologies increases the threat range from potential attackers targeting, to industrial data surveillance and/or disruption.

Problem Statement– Remote monitoring and maintenance raise confidentiality and privacy issues regarding industrial data collection and analysis.

© Springer Nature Switzerland AG 2021
J. Garcia-Alfaro et al. (Eds.): CRiSIS 2020, LNCS 12528, pp. 335–346, 2021.
https://doi.org/10.1007/978-3-030-68887-5_21

Indeed, collected data characterize originating site and disclose sensitive information about IT architecture, equipment configuration and operating regime. These data are critical and interest hackers as they carry details about plant's devices and manufacturing site vulnerabilities. Fortunately, classical encryption tools provide confidentiality of maintenance data during transit from analyzed site to original equipment manufacturer (OEM) and their contractors or subcontractors. Indeed, OEMs and contractors/subcontractors are in charge of remote maintenance and diagnostics in practice. However, industrial sites and plants Managers cannot allow the OEM to decipher equipment configuration data to analyze and process it. Indeed, maintenance data are considered as a confidential property for the industry brand image safeguard. Consequently, privacy of these data during their analysis by OEMs must be preserved.

Contribution– In this work, we propose to use homomorphic encryption to ensure the confidentiality of industrial data used for remote and preventive maintenance. Indeed, we propose to extend the remote maintenance infrastructure with a cloud service that runs maintenance algorithms over homomorphically encrypted data on behalf of different maintenance monitors. As such, the industrial devices data remains confidential during its transmission, storage and analysis. Our proposed solution makes remote maintenance compliant with the National[1] and European regulations[2] regarding the governance and processing of sensitive data that may convey confidential industrial information or personal information. In addition, we evaluate some simple maintenance functions using Microsoft `SEAL` homomorphic encryption library. The evaluated functions are averaging and variance computation.

Paper Organization– The remainder of this paper is structured as follows. In Sect. 2, we review the maintenance process of critical infrastructures. In Sect. 3, we present the homomorphic encryption. In Sect. 4, we present the detailed description of our proposed protocol for a privacy preserving remote maintenance. In Sect. 5, we describe a simple example of a maintenance algorithm and give some implementation results using Microsoft `SEAL` library. Finally, Sect. 6 concludes the paper and gives ideas for future work.

2   Secure Maintenance of Critical Infrastructures

Equipment maintenance is one of the key elements of manufacturing systems. Equipment maintenance is part of the production life-cycle, reaching 60%–70% of the total production cost. Therefore, being able to forecast machine maintenance operations and perform them in a short time period, can lead to successful troubleshooting and simultaneously increase industrial devices availability. Additionally, since replacement of damaged components can be as high as 70% of total maintenance cost, it is thus considered as one of the high priorities for

---

[1] Such as the Military programming law or the French glossary on data protection (CNIL).

[2] Like the NIS directive or the General Data Protection Regulation.

manufacturing firms to discover alternative policies for reducing maintenance costs to increase incomes.

Recent advances of industry digitization and IIoT platforms brought out remote maintenance. With these technologies, the service providers are able to identify the problem and the solution before moving on site. There are two common types of maintenance: predictive and preventive. Preventive maintenance is a scheduled maintenance, performed even when industrial machines are out of failure in order to prevent any future breakdowns. Preventive maintenance helps to extend lifespan of machines and increases efficiency and productivity. Predictive maintenance is used to determine condition of machines during service in order to estimate when maintenance must be carried out. This mode induces cost saving, because maintenance tasks are carried out only when necessary. The efficiency of these two maintenance modes depends highly on the flexibility of data collection process. The data gathered from shop floor and machines allow added value data-driven services such as diagnosis (faults detection) and prognosis (prediction of future faults).

The remote maintenance architecture contains three main entities: industrial device, cloud service and the OEM or one of contractor/subcontractor. Indeed, OEM or contractor/subcontractor represents the maintenance operator. The latter recovers the results of analysis of device confidential data in order to provide device owner with recommendations regarding device state of wear. In practice, industrial device provides cloud service with maintenance data. The cloud service runs different maintenance algorithms on the received data. Then, outputs of these algorithms are transmitted to maintenance operator (e.g., the OEM).

3   Homomorphic Encryption

Homomorphic Encryption (HE) schemes allow performing computations directly over encrypted data. That is, with a fully homomorphic encryption scheme E, we can compute $E(m_1 + m_2)$ and $E(m_1 \times m_2)$ from encrypted messages $E(m_1)$ and $E(m_2)$. The first constructions of HE schemes, allowing either multiplication or addition over encrypted data back to the seventies [13]. Then, in 2009, Gentry [9] proposed the first Fully Homomorphic Encryption (FHE) scheme able to evaluate an arbitrary number of additions and multiplications over encrypted data. Starting from Gentry breakthrough, many Leveled HE and FHE schemes are proposed in literature [2,3,5,6,8,11,17].

In practice, a public key homomorphic encryption scheme $HE = (HE.Keygen, HE.Enc, HE.Dec, HE.Eval)$ is defined by the following probabilistic polynomial-time algorithms with respect to the security parameter k:

- $(pk, evk, sk) \leftarrow HE.Keygen(1^k)$: outputs an encryption key pk, a public evaluation key evk and a secret decryption key sk. The evaluation key is used during homomorphic operations. evk key corresponds to the relinearization key in leveled homomorphic schemes such as BFV [8] or to the bootstrapping key in gate boostrapped schemes such as TFHE [6].

- c ← HE.Enc$_{pk}$(m): encrypts a message m into a ciphertext c using the public key pk,
- m ← HE.Dec$_{sk}$(c): decrypts a message c into a plaintext m using the public key sk.
- c$_f$ ← HE.Eval$_{evk}$(f, c$_1$, . . . , c$_k$): evaluates the function f on the encrypted inputs c$_1$, . . . , c$_k$ using the evaluation key evk.

Currently, several FHE schemes (e.g. BFV, TFHE, CKKS [5], etc.), which can be mixed together using CHIMERA framework [1]. As for the overhead induced by the size of the homomorphic ciphertexts during transmission and storage, transciphering can be used [4]. This cryptographic technique changes data encryption algorithm from classical symmetric encryption to HE scheme, without decrypting the data. Let m be a plaintext, SYM a symmetric scheme with key k, SYM.Enc$_k$(m) the encryption of m with SYM, and HE a homomorphic encryption scheme. With the transciphering, it is enough to run in homomorphic domain the decryption circuit of SYM.Dec using homomorphic encryption of the symmetric key HE.Enc$_{pk}$(k) to obtain the message encrypted with pk:

$$HE.Eval_{evk}(SYM.Dec_{HE.Enc_{pk}(k)}(SYM.Enc_k(m))) = HE.Enc_{pk}(m)$$

Another interesting notion in HE is batching. It serves to perform the same operation on a set of ciphers for a cost of one single operation. It allows Single Instruction Multiple Data (SIMD) processing of homomorphically encrypted data as initially proposed by Smart and Vercauteren [15]. It consists in packing several values of the clear message in the same encrypted one, thus making it possible to reduce expansion factor between the clear and encrypted messages.

Beside theoretical research, field of homomorphic encryption has been strongly active regarding implementation efforts. Several practical libraries are released over the last years. HElib [10] is maintained by Halevi and Shoup. It implements the BGV scheme and allows packing of ciphertexts and SIMD computations. As such, it is able to perform additions and multiplications in an efficient way, but bootstrapping operation is significantly slow. Microsoft SEAL is another library [14] that implements BFV and CKKS schemes. SEAL provides an easy API for setting the security parameters and supports batching. TFHE [16] is an open-source implementation for the TFHE scheme. The library features an efficient operation of bootstrapping. The latter has to be applied after computing every gate of the circuit. This library is more efficient than HElib, however, for lightweight operations, HElib is used as a somewhat homomorphic encryption scheme. The current implementation of TFHE does not provide batching and SIMD computations.

4 Privacy Preserving for Remote Maintenance Infrastructure

In this section, we present our solution for providing a privacy preserving maintenance infrastructure. First, we define our adversary model with respect to the maintenance architecture specified in Sect. 2. Then, we describe our proposed protocol for the private treatment of maintenance data thanks to the use of homomorphic encryption. Our main idea is to make the cloud service run different maintenance algorithms over industrial devices data that are encrypted using a homomorphic cryptosystem. Then, the obtained result is sent to the maintenance operator for decryption.

4.1 Threat Model

In this work, we consider a honest-but-curious model (also called the semi-honest model). In this model, many entities $(e_1, \ldots, e_n)$, having as secret information $(s_1, \ldots, s_n)$, participate to a protocol P to compute a function $F(s_1, \ldots, s_n)$. Each entity $e_{i,i\in[1,n]}$ is honest and must follow each step of P. However, $e_{i,i\in[1,n]}$ is curious. That is, $e_{i,i\in[1,n]}$ will try to find information about other entities secrets $s_{j,j\neq i}$. P is secure in the honest-but-curious model if each $e_{i,i\in[1,n]}$ has no other information than $F(s_1, \ldots, s_n)$ at the end of the protocol.

In the honest-but-curious model, the adversary cannot inject modified message as in the Dolev and Yao model [7]. Even when compared to passive Dolev and Yao adversaries, a honest-but-curious adversary cannot eavesdrop on communication channels as she will deviate from the protocol P [12]. In addition, using a honest-but-curious adversary avoids message modification attacks against homomorphically encrypted data. Indeed, as homomorphic encryption schemes are malleable by definition, a malicious adversary is able to modify the content of encrypted data.

For our solution, we consider that industrial devices are honest. Meanwhile, the cloud service and the maintenance operator are honest-but-curious. In addition, we require that the cloud service and the maintenance operator do not collude. Indeed, if they collude, they recover the industrial device data. In the following, the cloud service runs maintenance algorithms over homomorphically encrypted data and provides the maintenance operator with the encrypted outputs.

4.2 Privacy-Preserving Protocol for Remote Maintenance

The data collected from the industrial device is secret and sensitive, and represent intellectual property. That is why, we use homomorphic encryption to ensure its confidentiality even during its treatment within the cloud service. That is, we ensure that the device data will not be disclosed in clear to the hosting server at any moment. However, we must ensure that this server has no access to any decryption key (i.e., secret keys of maintenance operators). As such, an attacker seeking to exfiltrate industrial device data by compromising the cloud service provider will, at most, be able to exfiltrate encrypted data. Moreover, she will have no choice but to attack the cryptosystem (a difficult task by construction) or to attack yet another entity holding a decryption key to be able to decrypt ciphertexts.

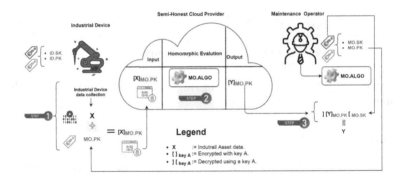

Fig. 1. The High-Level Architecture of the homomorphic encryption based infrastructure for Remote diagnosis and Maintenance

Figure 1 depicts the high-level view of our proposed privacy-preserving maintenance architecture. Indeed, Each entity has a public and a private key. Those keys are identified in Fig. 1 by the initials of the entity followed by "PK" for public key or "SK" for secret key. Moreover, the maintenance operator has to share its algorithm for maintenance data analysis with the remote cloud service. The chosen maintenance algorithm is identified by the entity initials followed by "$ALGO$". In practice, maintenance algorithms consist in averaging and computing the standard deviation of the input data and mainly in checking a predefined set of rules and inequalities.

First, the industrial device encrypts its maintenance data X with the public key of the maintenance operator "$MO.PK$", and sends it to the cloud service provider. The latter runs the algorithm of the concerned maintenance operator "$MO.ALGO$" over the encrypted data "$[X]_{MO.PK}$". Finally, the cloud service provider sends the algorithm result "$[Y]_{MO.PK}$" to the maintenance operator that deciphers it with "$MO.SK$" and recovers a set of responses to different evaluation criteria (Y). Based on the obtained responses, the maintenance operator sends recommendations to the manager of the industrial device.

4.3   Protocol Optimization with Transciphering

As mentioned in Sect. 3, transciphering solves the problem of bandwidth consumption when transmitting homomorphically encrypted data $[X]_{MO.PK}$ from a device to the cloud service provider. Indeed, all HE schemes proposed so far suffer from a very large ciphertext expansion, and therefore the transmission of the data between industrial devices and cloud service providers become a significant bottleneck in practice. Transciphering relies on recryption and the combination of two encryption schemes; one symmetric and the other one homomorphic, to solve this problem of bandwitdh consumption.

Let's enhance our protocol with the use of transciphering. First, the industrial device encrypts some data X under a homomorphic friendly symmetric encryption scheme with a key SK and obtains $[X]_{SK}$. In addition, it encrypts

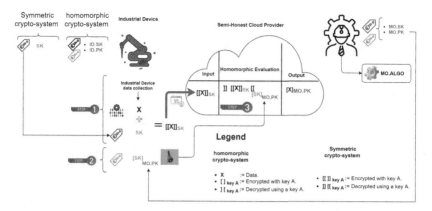

Fig. 2. Transciphering optimization

SK with the maintenance operator public key $[SK]_{MO.PK}$. Then, it sends $[X]_{SK}$ and $[SK]_{MO.PK}$ to the cloud service. Transmitting $[X]_{SK}$ and $[SK]_{MO.PK}$ is less cumbersome than transmitting $[X]_{MO.PK}$. The cloud service deciphers $[X]_{SK}$ with $[SK]_{MO.PK}$ and obtains $[X]_{MO.PK}$ and then proceeds with the computation of $MO.ALGO$, the maintenance algorithm, as discussed in the previous Sect. 4.2.

Another advantage of transciphering is allowing targeted encryption of maintenance data. That is, if we have more than one maintenance operator which are interested in an industrial device data, transciphering is a simple way of sharing these data between the different operators. In this case, the industrial device encrypts its data with the symmetric key SK and obtains $[X]_{SK}$. Then, it sends $[X]_{SK}$ with $\{[SK]_{MO_1.PK}, \ldots, [SK]_{MO_k.PK}\}$ to the cloud service where $MO_i.PK$ is the public key of the maintenance operator identified by i. The cloud service transciphers the industrial device data in demand of the maintenance operator i to get $[X]_{MO_i.PK}$ and then runs $MO_i.ALGO$. As such, we have a simple and efficient way of sharing the same encrypted data with multiple maintenance operators owning different public and private keys.

5   Implementation

In this section, an example of maintenance functions that can be computed in practice is given. Two simple functions: averaging and computing standard deviation over homomorphically encrypted data are considered. These two functions represent the most used aggregation functions in the context of our use-case. Furthermore, the presented implementation is discussed regarding two homomorphic cryptosystems provided in Microsoft SEAL library, namely BFV and CKKS. BFV works with integers, while CKKS supports the use of real numbers with limited precision.

5.1 Homomorphic Calculus of an Average

Encoding Integers with BFV Scheme. Let $A = (X_1, X_2, \ldots, X_N)$ the sample provided from which we the mean is calculated. In order to compute the average of this sample, $N - 1$ additions and a division have to be homomorphically evaluated. The first problem in evaluating such an operation in the homomorphic domain is the representation of the division operator. This problem is avoided by performing a pre-calculation at the level of sample supplier. The entity requester divides the whole sample on the cardinal N, such as:

$$B = \frac{A}{N} = (\frac{X_1}{N}, \frac{X_2}{N}, \ldots, \frac{X_N}{N}). \tag{1}$$

According to the required decimal precision, the sample supplier and the destination entity pre-share a precision k, such as:

$$C = \lfloor B \cdot 10^k \rfloor = (\lfloor \frac{X_1}{N} \cdot 10^k \rfloor, \lfloor \frac{X_2}{N} \cdot 10^k \rfloor, \ldots, \lfloor \frac{X_N}{N} \cdot 10^k \rfloor). \tag{2}$$

This step allows to normalize the sample toward a set of integers. We get the final sample $D = (X_1', X_2', \ldots, X_N')$ with

$$X_i' = \lfloor \frac{X_i}{N} \cdot 10^k \rfloor. \tag{3}$$

In order to compute the sample mean M, first the data will be encrypted with destination entity public key by performing homomorphic sum on D, such as

$$M' = \sum_{i=1}^{N}(X_i') = [M \cdot 10^k]_{MO.PK} \tag{4}$$

To get M, it is enough for the destination entity to decrypt M' with its private key and to divide the result by 10^k.

In order to protect secrecy of the sample cardinal N, the maximum size of samples N' is fixed, such as $N' > N$. The sample is completed by a set of $Enc(0)$ so as to reach N'. Hence, the samples provided to the Cloud will be of the form:

$$[X_1'], [X_2'], \ldots, [X_N'], [(0)], \ldots, [(0)] \tag{5}$$

Encoding Real Numbers with CKKS Scheme. It is possible to encrypt real numbers with CKKS. So, computing the average becomes easy as we have just to sum up the ciphertexts of the samples $A = (X_1, X_2, \ldots, X_N)$ as $[M]_{MO.PK} = \sum_{i=1}^{N}[X_i]_{MO.PK}$. Then, we multiply $[M]_{MO.PK}$ by the encrypted inverse of the cardinal N.

5.2 Homomorphic Calculus of a Standard Deviation

Let $A = (X_1, X_2, \ldots, X_N)$ the sample provided and from which the standard deviation is calculated. As a reminder, the standard deviation of a discrete variable composed of N observations is the positive square root of the variances and is defined as follows:

$Var(A) = \mathbf{E}([A - \mathbf{E}(A)^2])$, so standard deviation wich will be denoted S is simply $S = \sqrt{Var(A)}$.

Let $\bar{X} = \frac{1}{N} \sum_{i=1}^{N}(X_i)$, then by developing, we have:

$$S = \sqrt{\frac{\sum_{i=1}^{N}(X_i - \bar{X})^2}{N}} \tag{6}$$

In practice, the variance (V) is considered instead of the standard deviation (we remind that the variance is the square of the standard deviation (S)). Working with the variance releaves us from computing the square root in the homomorphic domain. Indeed, computing the square root in the homomorphic domain is possible as we can approximate the square root using a polynomial calculated via interpolation. However, this approximated polynomial works well for small data around zero and diverges for larger inputs (as the polynomial limit at infinity will be infinity).

$$V = S^2 = \frac{1}{N} \cdot \sum_{i=1}^{N}(X_i - \bar{X})^2 = \sum_{i=1}^{N} \frac{1}{N^2} \cdot (X_i - \bar{X})^2 = \sum_{i=1}^{N} \frac{1}{N} \cdot \frac{(X_i - \bar{X})^2}{N} \tag{7}$$

As previously done for calculation of the average, transformations made on sample A to obtain D are repeated. Keeping the same notations we have:

$$V = \sum_{i=1}^{N} \frac{1}{N} \cdot (X_i' - M)^2. \tag{8}$$

Since we cannot evaluate a division with the BFV scheme, the solution is to make a local pre-calculation on the industrial device which consists in multiplying $1/N$ by variance inputs and take the integer part, exactly as we did for the sample for the average calculation. $\lfloor (\frac{1}{N}) * 10^K) \rfloor = N'$.

$$V = \sum_{i=1}^{N} \frac{1}{N}(X_i' - M)^2 = \sum_{i=1}^{N} N' \cdot (X_i' - M)^2 \tag{9}$$

The calculation of the variance with the BFV scheme is still feasible, but scaling the samples and the $\frac{1}{N}$, may distort the result. For this reason, only CKKS scheme is used for implementation.

Implementing a variance using CKKS is quite easy as we can encrypt directly real numbers while ensuring a predefined precision level. In addition, CKKS has the advantage of avoiding rescaling of values to big integers as in BFV. Indeed, using big integers in BFV impacts the choice of security parameters and we end up encrypting data in big polynomials with large coefficient. Working with these big polynomials impacts naturally the timing performance of the evaluated algorithm in the homomorphic domain.

5.3   Performance

In this section, the timing performance of average and variance calculus using CKKS with Microsoft SEAL library is described. In addition, it is proposed to use batching to compute several mean and variance values with SIMD. Using batching is quite interesting in practice as it allows the cloud service to compute the average and variance of several maintenance metrics coming from different industrial devices, simultaneously.

Our averaging and variance computation algorithms are implemented on an Intel Core i7 and tests are run in 1 CPU cadenced at 3,9GHz. The used security parameters respect the default security level provided by SEAL which is equal to 128 bits.

For each experiment, we batched 8192 slots of plain-text data where plain-texts are vectors of 10 or 100 inputs. For 10 input vectors, computing the average takes 49.62 ms and the variance takes 465.976 ms. Meanwhile, for 100 input vectors, computing the average takes 74.61 ms and the variance takes 3.874361 s. That is, if the maintenance data is a vector of 10 inputs, computing an average takes 5,69 μs (i.e. 49.62 ms/8192) while computing a variance takes 56.881 μs. If the maintenance is a vector of 100 inputs, computing an average takes 9.107 μs and computing a variance takes 472.944 μs.

With these preliminary results, it is assumed that the overall approach reveals to be practical in real settings even for larger volumes of data. Data used for remote diagnosis and/or predictive maintenance are generally collected at a daily base and very limited values are needed to monitor the state of an industrial asset.

6   Conclusion and Future Work

We presented in this work a homomorphic encryption based infrastructure to preserve the confidentiality of sensitive data in the context of industrial remote diagnosis and/or preventive maintenance.

The approach relies on a "semi-honest" third party cloud services to run maintenance algorithms over homomorphically encrypted data. Our solution is simple and ensures industrial data confidentiality at transit, storage and in use.

We implemented as example an averaging and a variance computation functions as they are used frequently for maintenance data analysis. The obtained times are acceptable and allow us to confirm that homomorphic encryption is a serious candidate for providing remote data analysis.

Our initial results from a realistic use-case example clearly demonstrate that practical homomorphic encryption is achievable in reasonable industrial contexts with very limited computation and bandwidth overhead.

As future works, it is planned to implement a full maintenance infrastructure to simulate data transmission delays, evaluate transciphering timing and implement more complex maintenance algorithm in the homomorphic domain. We are particularly interested in evaluating the relevance of the approach in the context of machine learning based predictive maintenance process.

Acknowledgments. This research is funded by the European Union's Horizon 2020 research and innovation programme under the Secure Collaborative Intelligent Industrial Automation (SeCoIIA) project, grant agreement No 871967. Additionally, part of this work was done as part of IRT SystemX project PFS (Security of Smart Ports). The authors want to thanks Renaud Sirdey for his insightful advises.

References

1. Boura, C., Gama, N., Georgieva, M., Jetchev, D.: Chimera: combining ring-lwe-based fully homomorphic encryption schemes. Cryptology ePrint Archive, Report 2018/758 (2018). https://eprint.iacr.org/2018/758
2. Brakerski, Z., Gentry, C., Vaikuntanathan, V.: (Leveled) Fully homomorphic encryption without bootstrapping. In: Proceedings of the 3rd Innovations in Theoretical Computer Science Conference. ITCS 2012, pp. 309–325 (2012)
3. Brakerski, Z., Vaikuntanathan, V.: Fully homomorphic encryption from ring-LWE and security for key dependent messages. In: Rogaway, P. (ed.) CRYPTO 2011. LNCS, vol. 6841, pp. 505–524. Springer, Heidelberg (2011). https://doi.org/10.1007/978-3-642-22792-9_29
4. Canteaut, A., et al.: Stream ciphers: a practical solution for efficient homomorphic-ciphertext compression. Cryptology ePrint Archive, Report 2015/113 (2015). https://eprint.iacr.org/2015/113
5. Cheon, J.H., Kim, A., Kim, M., Song, Y.: Homomorphic encryption for arithmetic of approximate numbers. Cryptology ePrint Archive, Report 2016/421 (2016). https://eprint.iacr.org/2016/421
6. Chillotti, I., Gama, N., Georgieva, M., Izabachène, M.: Faster fully homomorphic encryption: bootstrapping in less than 0.1 seconds. In: Cheon, J.H., Takagi, T. (eds.) ASIACRYPT 2016. LNCS, vol. 10031, pp. 3–33. Springer, Heidelberg (2016). https://doi.org/10.1007/978-3-662-53887-6_1
7. Dolev, D., Yao, A.C.: On the security of public key protocols. In: Proceedings of the 22nd Annual Symposium on Foundations of Computer Science. SFCS 1981, IEEE Computer Society, USA, pp. 350–357 (1981). https://doi.org/10.1109/SFCS.1981.32
8. Fan, J., Vercauteren, F.: Somewhat practical fully homomorphic encryption. IACR Cryptol. ePrint Archive 2012, 144 (2012)
9. Gentry, C., et al.: Fully homomorphic encryption using ideal lattices. STOC **9**, 169–178 (2009)
10. Homomorphic encryption library (release 1.0.2) (2020). https://github.com/homenc/HElib

11. López-Alt, A., Tromer, E., Vaikuntanathan, V.: On-the-fly multiparty computation on the cloud via multikey fully homomorphic encryption. In: Proceedings of the Forty-Fourth Annual ACM Symposium on Theory of Computing, pp. 1219–1234. ACM (2012)
12. Paverd, A., Martin, A., Brown, I.: Modelling and automatically analysing privacy properties for honest-but-curious adversaries (2014). https://www.cs.ox.ac.uk/people/andrew.paverd/casper/casper-privacy-report.pdf
13. Rivest, R.L., Adleman, L., Dertouzos, M.L.: On data banks and privacy homomorphisms. Found. Secure Comput. **4**(11), 169–180 (1978)
14. Microsoft SEAL (release 3.5). https://github.com/Microsoft/SEAL Microsoft Research. Redmond, WA (2020)
15. Smart, N.P., Vercauteren, F.: Fully homomorphic SIMD operations. Des. Codes Crypt. **71**(1), 57–81 (2012). https://doi.org/10.1007/s10623-012-9720-4
16. Fast fully homomorphic encryption library over the torus (release 1.1). https://github.com/tfhe/tfhe (2020)
17. van Dijk, M., Gentry, C., Halevi, S., Vaikuntanathan, V.: Fully homomorphic encryption over the integers. In: Gilbert, H. (ed.) EUROCRYPT 2010. LNCS, vol. 6110, pp. 24–43. Springer, Heidelberg (2010). https://doi.org/10.1007/978-3-642-13190-5_2

Towards Attacker Attribution for Risk Analysis

Elena Doynikova[1]([✉])[iD], Evgenia Novikova[1,2][iD], Diana Gaifulina[1][iD],
and Igor Kotenko[1][iD]

[1] St. Petersburg Federal Research Center of the Russian Academy of Sciences,
14ya liniya V.O., St. Petersburg, Russia
{doynikova,novikova,gaifulina,ivkote}@comsec.spb.ru
[2] Saint Petersburg Electrotechnical University "LETI", 5 Prof. Popov Street,
St. Petersburg, Russia

Abstract. An attacker model is one of the key models in risk analysis and other security related tasks. The goal of the research is the attacker model specification in the form of attacker profile, i.e. as a set of attributes. In the paper we introduce the formal attacker model and its attributes, we describe the input data for the experiments and the process of their handling, and, finally, we describe the conducted experiments demonstrating an appropriateness of the selected attributes. In the future research we plan to extend the experiments and to introduce the risk analysis technique using the proposed attacker model.

Keywords: Attacker model · Attacker attribution · Attacker profile · Attributes · Risk analysis · Data analysis

1 Introduction

An attacker model determination is one of the essential stages for risk analysis. To date, different attacker models are proposed. From our point of view, they can be classified into low-level and high-level models.

We name a model as a high-level if it operates with high-level attributes for the attacker class determination. In this case possible attributes include an attacker goal, location of the attacker, and complexity of the exploited vulnerabilities. Possible classes of attackers are hackers, spies, terrorists, corporate raiders, professional criminals, vandals, and voyeurs. This type of models is usually used in the techniques of attacker type determination and risk analysis based on attack graph analysis [1–3].

We name a model as a low-level if it uses low-level attributes (or features) for the attacker specification. In this case possible attributes are as follows: destination port, alert signature, host, etc. This type of models is usually used in the risk analysis techniques based on hidden Markov model [4,5] and on fuzzy inference [6,7]. It is also utilised in attributing cyber attacks using data mining methods [8,9]. These techniques look preferable relative to the attack graph

© Springer Nature Switzerland AG 2021
J. Garcia-Alfaro et al. (Eds.): CRiSIS 2020, LNCS 12528, pp. 347–353, 2021.
https://doi.org/10.1007/978-3-030-68887-5_22

based techniques as soon as they allow determining high-level attack and attacker characteristics based on the objective low-level characteristics. But development of such techniques is limited by the complexity of revealing of the relationships between the high-level and low-level attributes and the lack of consistent datasets for the model training.

In [10] we formulated the set of questions related to the attacker model: (1) how to specify the attacker model; (2) how to calculate automatically the values of attributes constituting the attacker model using not an expert technique but the technique based on the dynamic data gathered from logs and traffic while target system operation; (3) where to get the appropriate initial data for the experiments; (4) do we really need the attacker model to analyse information security risks. We research the first three questions in this paper. As an answer to the first two questions we introduce the formal attacker model, attributes of the attacker model and preliminary mapping between the high-level and low-level attributes. We describe input data for the experiments and the process of their processing as the answer to the third question.

In the future research we plan to extend the experiments, to answer the last question specified above and to introduce the risk analysis technique using the proposed attacker model.

Contribution of the paper is as follows: the formal attacker model that links low-level attributes calculated from raw data and high-level attacker characteristics; classification of attacker attributes and preliminary attempt to link high-level and low-level attributes; determination of the requirements and analysis of the datasets for the experiments, as well as the variants of the datasets for attacker attribution; the first experiments with the subset of attacker attributes and algorithms for determining attacker types in a dataset.

The paper is structured as follows. Section 2.1 specifies the formal attacker model, introduces classification of its attributes, and gives preliminary mapping between low-level and high-level attacker attributes. Section 2.2 describes the input data for the experiments, the selected attributes and the conducted experiments. The paper ends with the conclusion and future work prospects.

2   Attacker Attribution

In this research we make our first steps towards attacker attribution aimed at specifying the attacker model. On the basis of the analysis of the related research we specify the attacker model (or profile) and outline high-level attacker characteristics as well as features extracted from network traffic and events logs that can be used for its specification. The model and attributes are given in Sect. 2.1. Then we conduct the experiments to check if the selected features allow us to outline different types of attackers. The requirements to the datasets for the experiments, the datasets themselves, and the experiments using different methods are presented in Sect. 2.2.

2.1   Attacker Model and Classification of Attributes

We specify attacker model At as follows:

$$At = hf_1, ..., hf_k,$$

where hf_i – the high-level attacker characteristics, $i \in [1, k]$, k – number of high-level attacker characteristics. They are calculated on the basis of the low-level attributes: $hf_i = func(lf_1, \ldots, lf_m)$,

lf_j – the low-level objective attacker characteristics obtained from the raw data, $j \in [1, m]$, m – number of low-level attacker characteristics,

$func()$ – a function for calculating the high-level characteristic on the basis of low-level characteristics.

We divided the attributes of each class on semantically meaningful groups describing different aspects of attacker behaviour.

The High-Level Attributes are attributes that can not be obtained directly from raw data gathered while monitoring the system under analysis. These attributes are usually evaluated using expert methods and, thus, are usually subjective. The first group incorporates inherent attacker characteristics including skills, motivation, intention. The second group characterizes an attacker capabilities and incorporates such characteristics as used resources. Used resources and attacker skills are connected in terms of complexity of used resources. The third group connects an attacker and a system under attack and includes an attacker location, privileges, goals (aims), access, and knowledge. An attacker location, privileges and access are connected with the system via the objects the attacker has access to, type of access and privileges, and detected activity (events and incidents). An attacker goals are connected with the system via the objects the attacker aims to compromise and the type of privileges the attacker aims to obtain. An attacker knowledge is connected with the system via the objects he/she accessed before, type of access and privileges, and detected activity. The fourth group connects an attacker and attack and includes the attack steps.

The Low-Level Attributes are attributes that can be obtained directly from the raw data gathered while monitoring the system under analysis. Thus, we can consider such attributes as objective. The low-level attributes can be classified by their source, namely, event logs and network traffic.

In [8] Fraunholz et al. proposed the following classification of network traffic characteristics: origin characteristics, target characteristics, content characteristics and temporal characteristics. We applied the same classification to the network and log based characteristics and we added one additional class – observable attack characteristics. Origin characteristics describe an attack (or normal action) source used by an attacker. Target characteristics describe an attacker goal or destination of the attack or normal action. Content characteristics specify an attack (or normal action) content or payload. Temporal characteristics incorporate frequency and time characteristics of attacks (or normal actions) on the selected time interval. Observable attack characteristics incorporate observable characteristics of the attack not included in other four classes (e.g. alert signature or category from events log [9]).

The next step is to link low-level attributes and high-level attributes. Thus, the high-level attribute "attacker skills" can be determined considering an attacker visibility in process of attack, complexity of the used tools and his/her knowledge. In their turn, visibility can be specified using low-level attributes "frequency of alerts" and "distribution of alerts", tools complexity can be determined considering "number of used exploits" and "severity of used exploits", and attacker knowledge can be specified using "frequency/distribution of alerts", "number of ports/protocols", etc. Further determination of algorithms for calculating the high-level metrics (or attributes) based on the low-level attributes is rather challenging task. The possible solution is to implement consequent mapping of the low-level events to the middle level activities and then to determine the high-level attributes of the attacker such as skills, resources and motivation.

2.2   Source Data for Attacker Attribution and Experiments

In general case the object attribution is a classification task and it requires the labeled data. In order to implement the attacker attribution and fine-tuning of features used in the analysis process it is required: 1) to have a dataset that contain a lot of attack actions against one information system performed by the attackers with different skills, resources, intention and motivation; 2) the dataset has to be labeled as we need to know what actions were performed by what attacker. In general case the datasets gathered in scope of the capture the flag (CTF) competitions satisfy the requirements listed above. The only problem is that this kind of datasets does not contain explicit labels for the high-level attacker features. However, some information about contest winners could be used to know the most efficient teams.

We outlined two datasets for our experiments, namely, network traffic from DEFCON 25 and DEFCON 26 CTF [11]. In scope of the DEFCON CTF the participants exploit the vulnerabilities of the information system deployed for the CTF, compromise the opponent computers and protect their own assets.

We analysed the network traffic from DEFCON 25 and DEFCON 26 CTF [11] and divided it on the subsets by teams. For each subset we calculated the following low-level features: the intensity of receiving and sending network packets; bytes per time or the intensity of receiving and sending bytes; TCP dialogs; TCP-points from network traffic, i.e. pairs IP address and port; IP-points; number of ports; number of protocols; IP dialogs; IP-address.

All these features could be used to analyse the high-level attacker skills attribute. In the experiments we were interested in establishing if there are groups of attackers that have similar level of skills. We implemented statistical assessment of the parameters and applied clustering techniques for the DEFCON 26 CTF dataset first. We tried t-SNE and metric-MDS algorithms. t-SNE algorithm is a nonlinear projection of the multidimensional space into two-dimensional space, it converts similarity between data points into a probability that these points are in neighborhood relationship, and tries to minimize the Kullback-Leibler divergence between the joint probabilities of the low-dimensional embedding and high-dimensional data. Metric-MDS algorithm is a linear data reduction technique that tries to preserve the original dissimilarity metrics that could be calculated as pairwise distances for numerical data. Though t-SNE and metric-MDS algorithms showed approximately similar results, the application of metric-MDS algorithm revealed possible number of clusters more clearly. After we detected a number of possible clusters, we applied k-means algorithm with defined number of clusters.

Figure 1 shows projection of feature vectors used to form team profiles onto two-dimensional space produced by MDS algorithm. The color of nodes shows the distribution of teams among clusters, while their size depends on total amount of sent and received packets. It is clearly seen that there is one outlier, three teams expose rather similar behaviour, while the profiles of the rest teams are very similar as they form rather dense region of points.

Fig. 1. MDS projection of features characterizing team behaviour during DefCON 26.

These results are rather expectable, as it is possible to assume that all teams participating in the CTF final possess rather similar high level of skills. Unfortunately, we did not obtained final scores of the teams, and, therefore, could not correlate these kind of data with results obtain. Though it is not possible to assume, whether the outlier is a winner or no, it is possible to conclude that selected features allows establishing the skill level of the attacker.

We also analyzed network traffic generated by teams within DEFCON 25 CTF. Unlike to DEFCON 26 CTF, it was possible to match attributes extracted from network traffic to the teams' scores. The results of experiments showed that the used attributes are not enough to determine the skill level of the team as some teams who received high scores were clearly seen as outliers, while the winning team did not exhibit any extraordinary network behavior and was always among teams with average scores.

3   Conclusion

In the conducted research we analysed the attacker model concept. We provided the formal specification of the attacker model based on the high-level and low-level attributes. We classified existing high-level and low-level attributes and made preliminary mapping between them. We specified the requirements to the datasets for the experiments and named two suitable for attacker attributing datasets. We conducted the experiments on clustering of attacker types by high-level skills attributes using these datasets and determined the set of low-level attributes. The experiments approved differences between the selected attackers.

In the future work we plan to enhance the set of low-level attributes and linking between the low-level and high-level attacker attributes, to develop the algorithms for calculating high-level attacker metrics on the basis of low-level attributes and to develop the technique for application of our attacker model in risk analysis.

References

1. Kheir, N., Cuppens-Boulahia, N., Cuppens, F., Debar, H.: A service dependency model for cost-sensitive intrusion response. In: ESORICS Proceedings, Athens, Greece (2010)
2. Kotenko, I., Stepashkin, M.: Attack graph based evaluation of network security. In: Leitold, H., Markatos, E.P. (eds.) CMS 2006. LNCS, vol. 4237, pp. 216–227. Springer, Heidelberg (2006). https://doi.org/10.1007/11909033_20
3. Doynikova, E., Kotenko, I.: Countermeasure selection based on the attack and service dependency graphs for security incident management. In: Lambrinoudakis, C., Gabillon, A. (eds.) CRiSIS 2015. LNCS, vol. 9572, pp. 107–124. Springer, Cham (2016). https://doi.org/10.1007/978-3-319-31811-0_7
4. Oosterhof, G.M.: Cowrie-Medium-Interaction Honeypot. https://github.com/micheloosterhof/cowrie. Accessed 18 July 2020
5. Katipally, R., Yang, L., Liu, A: Attacker behavior analysis in multi-stage attack detection system. In: CSIIRW Proceedings, Oak Ridge, TN, USA. ACM, New York (2011)
6. Shyla, S., Sujatha, S.: Cloud security: LKM and optimal fuzzy system for intrusion detection in cloud environment. J. Intell. Syst. **29**, 1626–1642 (2019)
7. Orojloo, H., Abdollahi Azgomi, M.: Predicting the behavior of attackers and the consequences of attacks against cyber-physical systems. Secur. Commun. Netw. **9**, 6111–6136 (2016)
8. Fraunholz, D., Krohmer, D., Duque Antón, S., Schotten, H.D.: YAAS-on the attribution of honeypot data. J. Int. J. Cyber Situat. Aware. **19**, 31–48 (2017)
9. Perry, I., et al.: Dierentiating and predicting cyberattack behaviors using LSTM. In: DSC Proceedings, Kaohsiung, Taiwan (2018)

10. Doynikova, E., Novikova, E., Kotenko, I.: Attacker behaviour forecasting using methods of intelligent data analysis: a comparative review and prospects. Information **11**, 168 (2020)
11. DEFCON 26 CTF Homepage. https://media.defcon.org/DEF%20CON%2026/ DEF%20CON%2026%20ctf/. Accessed 19 July 2020

Modelling and Verification of Safety of Access Control in SCADA Systems

Inna Vistbakka[1] and Elena Troubitsyna[2(✉)]

[1] Åbo Akademi University, Turku, Finland
inna.vistbakka@abo.fi
[2] KTH - Royal Institute of Technology, Stockholm, Sweden
elenatro@kth.se

Abstract. Modern safety-critical systems become increasingly networked and interconnected. To ensure their safety, the designers should guarantee not only that the critical parameters are accessed and modified by authorised users and components but also that the permitted operations should not violate safety. Traditionally, the designers rely on Role-Based Access Control (RBAC) to define the access to the system parameters. In this paper, we define a safety-aware RBAC model that takes into account current system state and safety of intended actions. Our approach relies on contract-based reasoning and formal modelling in Event-B. The approach is illustrated by a case study – a supervised control of a power switch.

1 Introduction

Modern safety-critical Supervisory Control and Data Acquisition (SCADA) systems becomes increasingly open and interconnected. Monitoring and control of the required processes is typically performed by several interacting components as well as in collaboration with human users. The use of networked technologies offers the attractive opportunities for developing advanced monitoring and control capabilities and services. However, this also makes the task of ensuring safety increasingly more challenging. On the one hand, the system design should guarantee that the authorised users have an access to the eligible system resources, especially in the emergency situations. On the other hand, the critical system parameters should be protected from an access by the unauthorised users and erroneous modifications by the authorised users. This aspect of the system behaviour is addressed by the access control policy.

Role-Based Access Control (RBAC) [2] is a widely used access control model. It regulates users' access to computer resources based on their role in an organisation. In the context of this paper, the term "user" is treated broadly and designated both human system operators as well as system components. The standard RBAC framework adopts a static, state-independent approach to define the access rights to the system resources. However, in safety-critical systems the static model is insufficient for ensuring system safety and should take into account current system state and safety of intended access to the critical parameters. In this paper, we propose a safety-aware model of RBAC. The proposed

J. Garcia-Alfaro et al. (Eds.): CRiSIS 2020, LNCS 12528, pp. 354–364, 2021.
https://doi.org/10.1007/978-3-030-68887-5_23

model allows a designer to explicitly define the rights to access a certain system parameter based on its criticality with respect to system safety, current state of the system and safety of intended access operation. We formalise the safety-aware RBAC and propose a systematic contract-based approach to defining the rights to access the system parameters. We rely on the design-by-contract approach [7] to explicitly define the safety-aware access rights for each role over the system parameters. We not only define a generic pattern for specifying system functions according to RBAC and safety constraints but also demonstrate how to implement the proposed patterns in Event-B [1]. The approach is illustrated by a case study – a supervised control of a power switch.

2   Safety-Aware RBAC

RBAC: Basic Concepts. Role-Based Access Control (RBAC) [2] is one of the main mechanisms for ensuring data integrity in a wide range of computer-based systems. The authorisation model defined by RBAC regulates users' access to computer resources based on their role in the organisational context of the system.

RBAC is built around the notions of users, roles, rights and protected system resources. A *resource* is an entity, e.g., data, access to which should be controlled. In SCADA systems, the resources are the monitored, controlled and analysed system parameters. The system parameters typically include the measurements provided by the sensors, the settings of the actuators, the mode of system operation, logs etc. A user can access a parameter based on an assigned role. In case of a human user – a system operator – a role is usually seen as a job function performed by the user. In case of a subsystem, a role defined the set of operations that the subsystem in a certain role performs. In their turn, rights define the specific actions that can be applied to the parameters. RBAC can be defined as a table that relates roles with the allowed rights over the resources. RBAC in the context of SCADA systems has the following elements:

- USERS is a set of users;
- ROLES is a set of available user roles;
- PARAMETERS is a set of protected system parameters;
- RIGHTS is a set of all possible rights over the parameters;
- PERMISSIONS is a set of permissions over the parameters.

Moreover, US_ASSIGN defines a *user assignment* to roles, while RO_PERM is *permission assignment* to roles. Next we discuss all these notions in details.

Access control in traditional (i.e., static) RBAC is realised in terms of (static) *permissions*. A permission is an ability of a holder of a permission to perform some action(s) in the system. To formally define all possible permissions, we introduce the relation PERMISSIONS as follows:

$$\text{PERMISSIONS} : \text{PARAMETERS} \leftrightarrow \text{RIGHTS}$$

It describes relationships between a certain system parameter and the rights that can be applied to it.

Permission assignments to a role are defined based on the job authority and responsibilities within the job function. To formally define permissions that are provided by the system to the different user roles, we define the function RO_PERM that maps each user role to a set of allowed rights over the parameters:

$$RO\_PERM : ROLES \rightarrow \mathbb{P}(PERMISSIONS).$$

In our work, we consider rights to be basic operations over the parameters, such as *Read* and *Write*. The operation defines a certain system function. An operation would usually require certain rights to be exercised over a resource. For instance, an operation "Delete log" would require a *"Write"* right over the log status parameter, i.e., changing its value from *Open* or *Locked* and back to *Open* as well as *"Delete"* right over the parameter *Log file*.

Traditionally, RBAC gives a static view on the access rights associated with each role, i.e., it defines the permissions to manipulate certain parameters "in general", i.e., without referring to the system state. Therefore, rights define the necessary conditions for an operation to be executed. However, we argue, that these conditions are insufficient for SCADA systems and should take into account the dynamic state of the system. For instance, assume that a human operator would like to manually change the setting of an actuator from *OFF* to *ON*. Moreover, let the operator has the *Write* right over the *switch setting* parameter. From the (static) RBAC point of view, such an operation is legitimate. However, if the controller parameter value is high then such an operation would put the system into the hazardous state, and hence, should not be allowed.

It is easy to see that while defining the access rights for SCADA systems, we should rely not only on the permissions defined by a role but also on the state of the other system parameters. Therefore, the static view on RBAC should be complemented with an explicit definition of the *state-dependant* conditions taking into account safety constraints.

Dynamic RBAC. Let us now discuss a formalisation of the dynamic view on RBAC. Each parameter can be characterised by its state, i.e., we can introduce the set STATES $= \{st_1, ..., st_j\}$ defining all possible states of the resources. Then we can define *dynamic (state-dependant) permissions* as the following function:

$$DYN\_PERM : PARAMETER \times STATES \rightarrow \mathbb{P}(RIGHTS).$$

For each parameter and its specific state, DYN_PERM returns access rights applicable to the parameter in each of its states. Let us note, that DYN_PERM is defined for all allowed access rights that can be applied to the parameter. Then *dynamic role permissions* can be defined as the function DYN_RO_PERM:

$$DYN\_RO\_PERM : ROLES \rightarrow \mathbb{P}(DYN\_PERM).$$

The dynamic and static views on RBAC are intrinsically interdependent. The permissions defined by the static and dynamic constraints constitute the necessary and sufficient constraints the user has over the operations execution.

```
Operation  oper_i
  params  us, res, ro
  pre  Resource_State(res) = state
       US_ASSIGN(us) = ro
       rights(ro) ∈ DY_RO_PERM(ro)(res, state)
       safety(state') = TRUE
  post Resource_State(res) = state'
       rights' [roles] = DY_RO_PERM[roles](res, state')
  end
```

Fig. 1. A generic operation implementation for RBAC

Safety-Aware RBAC. The safety-aware view on RBAC, advocated in this paper, aims at defining conditions enabling a valid and safe execution of system functions operation with respect to both – static access rights defined by RBAC and state-dependant dynamic constraints defined by safety conditions.

The behaviour of SCADA systems is often described using the notion of functions. A function, often called an operation, by using the corresponding permissions changes the states of the system parameters. The users performing an operations must have all the permissions required to complete all required manipulations with the parameters. Thus we should verify consistency between the defined RBAC and access rights required by an operation. We define the correctness conditions as the *contract for operation*. We follow the design-by-contract approach [7], i.e., define each contract as a combination of a *precondition* (the conditions on the operational input) and a *postcondition* (conditions to be satisfied as a result of the operation execution). The operation is a state transition resulting in the change of the variables values from v to v'.

To ensure, that an execution of an operation is permitted also from the safety point of view, we should guarantee that all final reachable states satisfy safety conditions *safety*, i.e.,

$$\forall\, s \in \sigma \;\implies\; (s \in safety)$$

The generic structure of an operation description is given in Fig. 1. In the RBAC context, an operation defines user action over a system parameter. Upon an operation execution, the state of the parameter might be changed. Therefore, we need to add a clause that explicitly checks whether the operation is also permitted from safety point of view. Thus, in the context of safety-aware RBAC, we can define an operation as shown in Fig. 3.

The user operation over the system resource has following parameters: a user *us*, a user role *ro* and a resource *res*. They are defined in **params** clause. The **pre** clause contains the predicates over the current state of the resource *res*, required access *rights* of the role *ro* over the resource *res* to perform the operation, and the reachable states of the operation (to verify that the safety is preserved by the operation execution). The **post** clause defines the postcondition as the predicates over the modified *state* of a resource and revised access *rights* for all *roles* over the resource *res*. In the definition of the operation, we used the term "resource" in order to avoid a confusion with the parameters of the operation.

The precondition aims at verifying that the resource is in the correct state before the operation execution, the user has a role that makes him/her eligible for executing this operation, the operation can be executed with respect to the current resource state and the role as well as it does not violate safety.

The postcondition postulates that the state of the resource might change as well as the dynamic rights for the system roles in the safety-preserving way, i.e.,

$$state' \in Post(oper_1) \implies safety(state') = TRUE$$

Let us observe, that the input parameter role ro does not change as a result of the operation execution. However, it should be defined since the same operation would typically have different contracts for different roles.

3   Overview of Event-B

Event-B is a state-based formal approach that promotes the correct-by-construction development paradigm and formal verification by theorem proving [1]. In Event-B, a system model is specified as an *abstract state machine*. An abstract state machine encapsulates the model state, represented as a collection of variables, and defines operations on the state, i.e., it describes the dynamic behaviour of a modelled system. The variables are strongly typed by the constraining predicates that, together with other important system properties, are defined as model *invariants*. Usually, a machine has an accompanying component, called a *context*, which includes user-defined sets, constants and their properties given as a list of model axioms.

The dynamic behaviour of the system is defined by a collection of atomic *events*. Generally, an event has the following form:

$$e \mathrel{\widehat{=}} \textbf{any } a \textbf{ where } G_e \textbf{ then } R_e \textbf{ end,}$$

where e is the event's name, a is the list of local variables, G_e is the event *guard*), and R_e is the event action.

The guard is a state predicate that defines the conditions under which the action can be executed. The action is a parallel composition of deterministic or non-deterministic assignments. We can transform the operation representation in the pre- postcondition format into Event-B form, as we did in [12]. This would allow us to establish the correspondence between the definitions of an operation contract and an Event-B event. To perform it we rely on our previous work presented, e.g., in [6]. Let us now demonstrate the proposed approach by a case study – a control of the power switch of a boiler system.

4   Case Study – Monitoring and Control of a Power Switch

In this paper, we consider an industrial boiler – a large tank, which produces steam for an industrial process by boiling the water supplied into it. The pressure inside of the steam boiler is controlled by a power switch which should be kept between predefined safety boundaries. Moreover, it should never exceed *MAXCRIT* value due to the danger of an explosion. The pressure is maintained by switching the power switch of the heater ON and OFF. A sensor measures pressure inside of a boiler and sends its measurements as a payload of a packet over a network to the controller. The controller analyses the sensors readings and assign the heater the values required to maintain the desired functionality and safety.

The boiler is operated it two modes – automatic and manual. In automatic mode, the controlling software performs control cycle – it checks the value of the sensor and based on it, switches the actuator (heater) ON and OFF. An operator can change an mode of operation to manual. In the manual mode, the operator can directly send the commands to the actuator.

The operator can also change mode from manual to maintenance. In the maintenance mode, a maintenance worker can calibrate the sensor, as well as read and delete the log. The operator can also change the mode from manual or maintenance to automatic.

The are three roles in the systems: *Controller*, *Operator* and *Technician*. For each role we define the set of operations that a user in the corresponding role can perform as shown in Table 1.

Table 1. Examples of operations for role and permissions over resources

Role	Operation	Mode	Parameter	Permission
Controller	SWITCH-ON	automatic	sensor	read, w-calibrate
Operator	SHUTDOWN	manual	actuator	read, w-ON, w-OFF
Operator	MODECHANGE	any mode	mode	read, w-A, w-M, w-Ma
Technician	READLOG	maintenance	log	read, write, delete

The safety condition that the system should preserve is derived from the requirement that the pressure should not exceed *MAXCRIT* bars. The functional requirements are derived from the requirements on switching on and off the heater and mode changes. Based on the defined role-based access control policy and safety requirements, next we present contracts for several operations.

The operation *SWITCH-ON* results in increasing the pressure in the boiler. The operation has safety constraint – the pressure after an execution of this operation should not exceed *MAXSAFE* bars (Fig. 2).

In the precondition of the operation, we check that the parameter *act* – the actuator is in the appropriate state, i.e., it is switched off. Then we check that the operations is to be executed by the users with the role controller – *C* or operator *O* and the mode is either automatic *A* or manual *M*. To ensure, in the precondition we also check that after changing the state of the actuator the safety condition would not be violated. In the postcondition, the state of the actuator parameter is changed accordingly.

The operation *SWITCH-OFF* can be defined in a similar way. Since this operation cannot violate safety condition, the precondition would contain only

```
Operation SWITCH-ON
   params us, sen, act, ro, mode
   pre   Resource_State(act) = write_OFF
         US_ASSIGN(us) = ro
         ro ∈ {C, O}
   mode ∈ A, M
         rights(ro) ∈ DY_RO_PERM(ro)(act, write_OFF)
         sen + Δ < MAXSAFE
   post  Resource_State(act) = write_ON
end
```

Fig. 2. A generic operation implementation for RBAC

```
Operation MODECHANGE
   params us, ro, mode
   pre   Resource_State(mode) = write_A
         US_ASSIGN(us) = ro
         ro = O
         rights(ro) ∈ DY_RO_PERM(O)(mode, write_A)
   post  Resource_State(mode) = write_M
end
```

Fig. 3. A generic operation implementation for RBAC

the check of the permissions to execute the operation by the roles and the corresponding state of the resource.

Another example of an operation is $MODECHANGE$. This operation can be executed by the operator only and depends on the current mode state, as shown below:

Below we present the specifications of several operations in Event-B. We start by specifying the states of each system parameter using the function $parameter\_state$:

$$parameter\_state \in PARAMETERS \rightarrow STATES.$$

Next we link each role with the set of operations that correspond to it. Moreover, for each role, we also define the required basic access rights, e.g, *Create, Read, Write, Delete* abbreviated as *C, R, W, D* values, respectively.

To specify dynamic permissions for the introduced roles, we define a variable $dPerm$ with the following properties:

$$dPerm \in ROLES \times PARAMETERS \rightarrow \mathbb{P}(RIGHTS),$$
$$dPerm(\text{Operator}, sen) \subseteq \{R, D\} \wedge$$
$$dPerm(\text{Operator}, act) \subseteq \{R, Write\_OFF, Write\_ON\} \wedge$$
$$dPerm(\text{Operator}, mode) \subseteq \{R, Write\_A, Write\_M, Write\_Ma\} \quad etc.$$

The variable $dPerm$ is a function that assigns to each role and a report a set of possible access rights that can be associated with the role.

Obviously, for each role, the set of available access rights to a parameter depends on the current state of this parameter and safety conditions. Let us note that the variables *dPerm* and *report_state* together represent the *dynamic role permissions* RO_DYN_PERM discussed in Sect. 2. We use these two variables instead of one just to avoid nested data structures (function of function) in Event-B specification. An excerpt from Event-B specification is given in Fig. 4. It The shows the specifications of events specified according to the proposed operation contract. By relying on Event-B provers, we were able to demonstrate the desirable safety properties.

5 Related Work and Conclusions

Recently the problem of modelling and analysing the access control policies has attracted a significant research attention. Milhau et al. [8] have proposed a methodology for specifying access control policies using a family of graphical frameworks and translating them into the B. The main aim of the work has been to formally specify an access control filter that actually regulates access control to the data. In this work, the dynamics is mainly considered with respect to the operation execution order, while, in our work, the dynamic view on the

---

Machine Heater_abs
Events...
SWTICH_ON_OPERATOR $\hat{=}$
  any *act, u*
  where *act_state*(*act*) = *WRITE_OFF*
    US_ASSIGN(*u*) = Operator
    WRITE_ON $\in$ *dPerm*(Operator, *act*)
    mode = *M*
    sen + Δ < 61
  then
    act_state(*rep*) := *WRITE_ON*
    dPerm(Operator, *act*) := {*WRITE_OFF*}
  end
SWTICH_OFF_CONTROLLER $\hat{=}$
  any *act, u*
  where *act_state*(*act*) = *WRITE_ON*
    US_ASSIGN(*u*) = Controller
    WRITE_ON $\in$ *dPerm*(Controller, *act*)
    mode = *A*
  then
    act_state(*rep*) := *WRITE_OFF*
    dPerm(Controller, *act*) := {*WRITE_OFF*}
  end
Delete_LOG $\hat{=}$
  any *log, u*
  where *log_state*(*log*) = *write*
    US_ASSIGN(*u*) = Technician
    R $\in$ *dPerm*(Technician, *log*)
  then
    log_state(*rep*) := *WRITE*
    dPerm := *dPerm* $\lhd\!\!\!-$ ({Operator $\mapsto$ *rep* $\mapsto$ {*R*}} $\cup$
                     {Controller $\mapsto$ *rep* $\mapsto$ {*R*}})
  end
  ...

Fig. 4. Event-B specification of RMS (with possible inconsistencies)

access policies depends on the system state, in particular, on the state of the corresponding system parameters and safety conditions.

A number of works uses UML and OCL based domain specific language to design and validate the access control model. For instance, a domain-specific language for modelling RBAC and translating graphical models in Event-B was proposed in [17].

Verification of behaviour aspects of software models defined using the design-by-contract approach has been also discussed in the context of security requirements and graphical modelling. An approach to integrating UML modelling and Event-B to reason about behaviour and properties of web-services was proposed in [10]. A contract-based approach to modelling and verification of RBAC for cloud was proposed in [9]. In our work, the defined operational contracts are used as a generic specification that is implemented in Event-B.

A data-flow oriented approach to graphical and formal modelling has been proposed in [13,14,18] and [15,16]. These works use the graphical modelling to represent system architecture and the data flow. The diagrams are translated into Event-B, to verify the impact of security attacks on the invariant system properties.

In this paper, the behaviour of the components is modelled within a single monolithic specification. To overcome this abstraction and represent the constraints for each component and a resource in an explicit way, we can rely on the modularisation approach [3] and Event-B extension proposed in [5] and demonstrated in [4] to support compositional reasoning and specification patterns [11].

In this paper, we have proposed a novel formal model of safety-aware dynamic RBAC. In our formalisation, we relied on a contract-based approach to define the constraints required to verify correctness of operations with respect to the static and safety-enforced dynamic RBAC constraints. In this work, have proposed also demonstrated how to specify behaviour of SCADA systems in Event-B according to the safety-aware RBAC policies.

In this paper, we relied on theorem proving to verify correctness of the desired safety-aware RBAC policy. By explicitly defining assumptions and constraints about system domain, we were able to prove that the defined safety-aware RBAC constraints ensure safety. Event-B and the Rodin platform have offered us a suitable basis for the formalisation and automation of our approach. The provers have been used to verify correctness of the data structure definitions and invariant preservation by the operations. We have validated our approach by a case study – monitoring and control of a pressure in an industrial boiler. We believe that the proposed approach facilitates an analysis of complex access control policies.

As a future work, we are planing to consider more complex variants of dynamic RBAC. For instance, we will model the situations when several users can get simultaneous or partial access to some parts of a data resource depending on their roles and resource states. Moreover, we are planing to work on an extension of the proposed approach for modelling and verification of dynamic RBAC and formalise it as Event-B specification patterns.

References

1. Abrial, J.R.: Modeling in Event-B. Cambridge University Press, Cambridge (2010)
2. Ferraiolo, D.F., Sandhu, R.S., Gavrila, S.I., Kuhn, D.R., Chandramouli, R.: Proposed NIST standard for role-based access control. ACM Trans. Inf. Syst. Secur. 4(3), 224–274 (2001)
3. Iliasov, A., et al.: Supporting reuse in event B development: modularisation approach. In: Frappier, M., Glässer, U., Khurshid, S., Laleau, R., Reeves, S. (eds.) ABZ 2010. LNCS, vol. 5977, pp. 174–188. Springer, Heidelberg (2010). https://doi.org/10.1007/978-3-642-11811-1_14
4. Iliasov, A., et al.: Verifying mode consistency for on-board satellite software. In: Schoitsch, E. (ed.) SAFECOMP 2010. LNCS, vol. 6351, pp. 126–141. Springer, Heidelberg (2010). https://doi.org/10.1007/978-3-642-15651-9_10
5. Iliasov, A., et al.: Developing mode-rich satellite software by refinement in Event-B. Sci. Comput. Program. 78(7), 884–905 (2013)
6. Laibinis, L., Troubitsyna, E.: A contract-based approach to ensuring component interoperability in Event-B. In: Petre, L., Sekerinski, E. (eds.) From Action Systems to Distributed Systems - The Refinement Approach, pp. 81–96. Chapman and Hall/CRC (2016)
7. Meyer, B.: Design by contract: the Eiffel method. In: Proceedings of Tools 26, p. 446 (1998)
8. Milhau, J., Idani, A., Laleau, R., Labiadh, M., Ledru, Y., Frappier, M.: Combining UML, ASTD and B for the formal specification of an access control filter. ISSE 7(4), 303–313 (2011)
9. Rauf, I., Troubitsyna, E.: Generating cloud monitors from models to secure clouds. In: DSN 2018. IEEE Computer Society (2018)
10. Rauf, I., Vistbakka, I., Troubitsyna, E.: Formal verification of stateful services with REST APIs using Event-B. In: IEEE ICWS 2018. IEEE (2018)
11. Tarasyuk, A., Troubitsyna, E., Laibinis, L.: Formal modelling and verification of service-oriented systems in probabilistic Event-B. In: Derrick, J., Gnesi, S., Latella, D., Treharne, H. (eds.) IFM 2012. LNCS, vol. 7321, pp. 237–252. Springer, Heidelberg (2012). https://doi.org/10.1007/978-3-642-30729-4_17
12. Tarasyuk, A., Troubitsyna, E., Laibinis, L.: Integrating stochastic reasoning into Event-B development. Formal Asp. Comput. 27(1), 53–77 (2015)
13. Troubitsyna, E., Laibinis, L., Pereverzeva, I., Kuismin, T., Ilic, D., Latvala, T.: Towards security-explicit formal modelling of safety-critical systems. In: Skavhaug, A., Guiochet, J., Bitsch, F. (eds.) SAFECOMP 2016. LNCS, vol. 9922, pp. 213–225. Springer, Cham (2016). https://doi.org/10.1007/978-3-319-45477-1_17
14. Troubitsyna, E., Vistbakka, I.: Deriving and formalising safety and security requirements for control systems. In: Gallina, B., Skavhaug, A., Bitsch, F. (eds.) SAFECOMP 2018. LNCS, vol. 11093, pp. 107–122. Springer, Cham (2018). https://doi.org/10.1007/978-3-319-99130-6_8
15. Vistbakka, I., Troubitsyna, E.: Towards a formal approach to analysing security of safety-critical systems. In: EDCC 2018, pp. 182–189. Computer Society (2018)
16. Vistbakka, I., Troubitsyna, E.: Pattern-based formal approach to analyse security and safety of control systems. In: Papadopoulos, Y., Aslansefat, K., Katsaros, P., Bozzano, M. (eds.) IMBSA 2019. LNCS, vol. 11842, pp. 363–378. Springer, Cham (2019). https://doi.org/10.1007/978-3-030-32872-6_24

17. Vistbakka, I., Barash, M., Troubitsyna, E.: Towards creating a DSL facilitating modelling of dynamic access control in Event-B. In: Butler, M., Raschke, A., Hoang, T.S., Reichl, K. (eds.) ABZ 2018. LNCS, vol. 10817, pp. 386–391. Springer, Cham (2018). https://doi.org/10.1007/978-3-319-91271-4_28

18. Vistbakka, I., Troubitsyna, E.: Modelling and verification of dynamic role-based access control. In: Atig, M.F., Bensalem, S., Bliudze, S., Monsuez, B. (eds.) VECoS 2018. LNCS, vol. 11181, pp. 48–63. Springer, Cham (2018). https://doi.org/10.1007/978-3-030-00359-3_4

Security Assessment and Hardening
of Autonomous Vehicles

Samir Ouchani[1]([✉]) and Abdelaziz Khaled[2]

[1] CESI LINEACT, Aix-en-Provence, France
souchani@cesi.fr
[2] Evina, Paris, France

Abstract. In recent years, experts have noted the risks of hacking the autonomous vehicles. Since the latter become more complex, the number of potential vulnerabilities and the constraints on security algorithms increase. This paper proposes a model checking based framework that relies on a set of pre-defined attacks and counter measures from where the security requirements are used to assess how well the model is secure. First, we formalize a system, a case of cyber physical systems, using UML class and activity diagrams. Further, we use UML to develop a meta language for autonomous vehicle systems, cyber attacks, and cyber counter measures. The framework instantiates the dependent-application diagrams for the domain application of autonomous vehicles, searches for the existing attack surfaces; then it generates the possible attacks that might exploit the found vulnerabilities/weaknesses. Further the proposed framework generates the proper java code for the composition counter measures, attacks, and smart vehicle models. Finally to show the effectiveness of the proposed solution, we model, analyze, harden, and evaluate our framework on a real use case.

Keywords: Cyber security · Domain specific language · Autonomous vehicles · Threat behavior · Attack graphs · Countermeasures · UML · JAVA

1 Introduction

The arrival of autonomous vehicles on our roads opens up a new cybersecurity challenges with the threat of hackers capable of accessing the vehicle remotely and penetrating on-board systems and networks. One of the main challenges in development of autonomous vehicles is the discovering vulnerabilities and weaknesses at early stage of development. Whereas the second is about assessing efficiently and quantifying the precise degree of vulnerability of an existing system when this is exposed to known attacks.

An answer to the first challenge requires to check whether a model of the system satisfies a set of relevant security properties. This check is performed in the presence of an attacker, usually a Dolev Yao adversary with a considerable power that controls all the system's communication channels to interfere with the system's functionalities. This technique of analysis is known as *model checking*. It has been successfully applied to

© Springer Nature Switzerland AG 2021
J. Garcia-Alfaro et al. (Eds.): CRiSIS 2020, LNCS 12528, pp. 365–375, 2021.
https://doi.org/10.1007/978-3-030-68887-5_24

discover insidious attacks and anomalies for the risk analysis and security assessment of the model-based systems [19]. However, although efficiently implemented in specific cases, model checking's worst-case time complexity is exponential in the size of the system's and of the property's models. Large systems may be beyond reach for this type of analysis. The response to the second challenge, instead, is more pragmatic [18].

Considering only documented attacks—that is, patterns of actions known to be used to gain unauthorized access to the system's services, resources, or information, or to compromise the system's integrity, availability, and confidentiality [1]—it consists in estimating the system's degree of vulnerability looking at the system's *attack surfaces* [14]. An attack surface is roughly the set of system's actions that are accessible externally and the system's resources which can be modified via those actions. The more extensive the attack surface is, the more vulnerable the system can be. Detecting attack surfaces requires to inspect a system's model and to find out if known attacks can reach the system's core procedures via the system's exposed actions. The literature offers a variety of ways to describe attacks: attack tree, attack graph, and network attack graph [17].

Such models are used by many organizations that have a special interest in collecting, describing, and classifying attack patterns. For instance, this paper's work is about this second challenge. It proposes a formal framework to detect attack surfaces *automatically* on systems modeled in UML. The latter is a general-purpose, graphical, modelling language for specifying, designing, and verifying complex hardware and software systems, as well as organizative and procedural workflows. UML2.0-based formalism is a prominent object-oriented graphical language which has become *de facto* a standard in software and systems modelling. Assuming that a system modeled in UML is therefore a pragmatic choice, in order to be compliant with the current engineering practices. UML covers the perspectives of a system's modeling, especially its structure and behavior, with its extended profiles MARTE and SysML. Particularly, *class and activity diagrams* are the specific formalism that this work adopts, can express a qualitative and quantitative elements of a system's behaviour and at various levels of abstraction [8].

In general a strong system [16] is one in which the cost of an attack is greater than the potential gain to the attacker. Conversely, a weak system is one where the cost of an attack is less than the potential gain. The cost of an attack should take into account not only money, but also time to recovery and potential punishment for criminal. This paper proposes a model checker based framework that automatically finds attacks that exist in a given autonomous vehicle system. The schema of the framework is depicted in Fig. 1. First it develops a meta model specific to Autonomous Vehicles (AV), their related threats, attacks, and counter measures. It takes as input a system modeled as a set of classes and activity diagrams that are instantiated from the developed meta language. Further, it generates the attacks dependent to the system under test using the attack templates that have impacts on the attack surfaces of the system. Then, the framework composes the instantiated model, the generated attack, and the proper countermeasure. Based on this composition, the framework produces secure implementation by transforming the autonomous vehicles system to Java.

The remainder of this paper is organized as follows. Section 2 reviews the existing related work. Then, Sect. 3 present the security assessment of autonomous vehicles system. The implementation of secure systems is given in Sect. 4. The experimental results are described in Sect. 5. Finally, Sect. 6 concludes this paper and provides hint the future research directions.

2   Related Work

In this section, we survey the existing initiatives related to system attacks modeling, attack detection, counter measures, and their application on autonomous vehicles.

Attack Modeling. A risk-based approach [17] has been proposed to create modular attack trees for each component in the system [7]. These trees are specified as parametric constraints, which allow quantifying the probability of security breaches that occur due to internal and external component vulnerabilities. Another approach models probability metrics based on attack graphs as a special Bayesian network [5]. Each node of the network represents vulnerabilities as well as the pre and post conditions. [12] and [9] extracted specific cryptography-related information from UMLsec diagrams. Moreover, the Dolev-Yao model of an attacker is included with UMLsec to model the interaction with the environment. Further, [22] extended UMLsec to model peer-to-peer applications along with their security aspects. They rely on the concept of abuse cases defined as UML use cases and state machine diagrams to represent attack scenarios. [15] generated attack scenarios from the threat model of the wireless security protocol. First, they collect attacks from vulnerabilities databases. Then, they classify them in terms of violated properties. Finally, they generate the protocol attack tree by relying to SecurelTree tool.

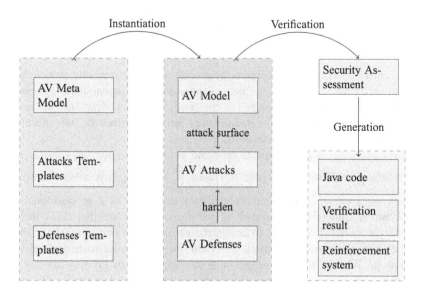

Fig. 1. Secure autonomous vehicles systems.

Attack Surfaces Detection. [6] identified security vulnerabilities in code level by tailoring attack patterns based on the software components. These patterns take the form of regular expressions that are generic representations of vulnerabilities. [10,20] distilled attack surfaces of an attack graph by shifting out the minimum cost in the graph. They use SAT solver to view the minimum effort of an attack to conquer critical assets in the system. [23] developed an approach based on runtime analysis to compute attack surfaces by finding the system adversaries in order to determine which program entry points access is an adversary controlled objects. They use the system's access control policy to distinguish adversary controlled data from trusted ones. [13] identified the communication attack surfaces by considering intent-based attacks on applications that do not hold common signature-level permissions. Any component of the correct type with a matching intent filter can intercept the intent. The possible attacks enabled by such unauthorized intent receipt depend on the type of the intent. [3] analyzed the external attack surface of modern automobile systems. Systematically, they synthesize the set of possible external attack vectors as a function of the attacker's ability to deliver malicious input via specific modalities. For each modality, they characterize the attack surface exposed in current automobiles with their set of channels.

Security Autonomous Vehicles. [11] proposed to guarantee location privacy to mobile users through an architecture that develops: a system epochs, a labeled transition based threat model, and a query measuring the location sensitivity. [4] analyzed both safety and security by integrating a six steps based method to analyze safety and security including with ISO standards 26262 and SAE J3061. [21] showed the relation between a threat, attack, vulnerability, and its impact on autonomous vehicle. [2] designed autonomous vehicle for securing sensitive areas from any type suspicious activities by relying on self-governing navigation and recursive path.

3   AV Security Assessment

For the security assessment, we rely on the probabilistic and symbolic model checker PRISM to verify the security requirements expressed in the probabilistic computation tree logic (PCTL). A PRISM program is a composition of a set of *modules* defined as a set of variables and commands. The evaluation of variables defines the state of a module whereas commands define their transitions.

PRISM expresses a probabilistic command as $[\alpha]\ g\ \rightarrow\ p_1\ :\ u_1 + ... + p_m\ :\ u_m$, where p_i is a probability value ($p_i \in]0,1[$ and $\sum_{i=0}^{m} p_i = 1$), α is a label that names the action α, g is the guard over all variables expressed as a propositional logic formula, and u_i describes the *update* of variables. An update that takes the form $(v'_j = val_j) \& \cdots \& (v'_k = val_k)$ to assign the value val_i to only a local variable v_i. So, for a given action α, if the guard g is valid, then the update u_i is enabled with a probability p_i. When $p = 1$, it is simple command expressed by $[a]\ g \rightarrow u$.

Syntactically, a module named M is delimited by two keywords: the module head "module M", and the module termination "endmodule". Further, we can model costs with reward module R delimited by keywords "rewards R" and "endrewards". A reward module is composed from a *state reward* or a *transition reward*. A state reward associates a cost (reward) of value r to any state satisfying g and it is expressed by $g : r$. A transition reward is specified by $[a]\, g : r$ to express that the transitions labeled a, from states satisfying g, are acquiring the reward of value r.

For an automatic assessment of security in AV, we develop $\mathcal{T}_P$ (Listing 1.1) that transforms the structural and behavioral diagrams of a given AV model into a PRISM code. The security requirements are expressed in PCTL as follows.

$$\phi ::= \top \mid ap \mid \phi \wedge \phi \mid \neg\phi \mid P_{\bowtie p}[\psi]$$
$$\psi ::= X\phi \mid \phi U^{\leq k}\phi \mid \phi U\phi$$

The term "$\top$" means *true*, "ap" is an atomic proposition, $k \in \mathbb{N}$, $p \in [0,1]$, and $\bowtie \in \{<, \leq, >, \geq\}$. The operator "$\wedge$" represents the *conjunction* and "$\neg$" is the *negation* operator, and P is the probabilistic operator. Also, "X", "$U^{\leq k}$", and "U" are the *next*, the *bounded until*, and the *until* temporal logic operators, respectively.

Listing 1.1. PRISM Code Geneation.

```
T : A → P
T(A) = ∀n ∈ A,  L(n = ι) = ⊤, L(n ≠ ι) = ⊥,  Case(n) of
l : ι ↦ N  ⇒  in  {[l]l ⟶ (l' = ⊥)&(L(N)' = ⊤); } ∪ T(N)  end
l : M(x, y) ↦ N  ⇒  in  {[lx]lx ⟶ (l'x = ⊥)&
    (L(N)' = ⊤); }∪{[ly]ly ⟶ (l'y = ⊥)&(L(N)' = ⊤); } ∪ T(N)end
l : J(x, y) ↦ N ⇒ in  {[l]lx ∧ ly ⟶ (l'x = ⊥)&(l'y = ⊥)&(L(N)' = ⊤); }cupT(N)end
l : F(N₁, N₂) ⇒  in  {[l]l ⟶ (l' = ⊥)&(L(N₁)' = ⊤)&(L(N₂)' = ⊤); } ∪ T(N₁) ∪ T(N₂)  end
l : D(A, p, g, N₁, N₂) ⇒ Case (p) of ]0, 1[ ⇒ in
{[l]l ⟶ p : (l' = ⊥)&(l'g = ⊤) + (1 − p) : (l' = ⊥)&(l'¬g = ⊤); } ∪ {[l¬g]l g ∧ ¬g ⟶ (l'¬g = ⊥)&
    (L(N₂)' = ⊤); }
∪{[lg]lg ∧ g ⟶ (l'g = ⊥)&(L(N₁)' = ⊤); } ∪ T(N₁) ∪ T(N₂)end
Otherwise in  {[l]l ⟶ (l' = ⊥)&(l'g = ⊤); } ∪ {[l]l ⟶ (l' = ⊥)&(l'¬g = ⊤); }
∪{[lg]lg ∧ g ⟶ (l'g = ⊥)&(L(N₁)' = ⊤); } ∪ {[l¬g]l g ∧ ¬g ⟶ (l'¬g = ⊥)&(L(N₂)' = ⊤); }∪
    T(N₁) ∪ T(N₂)end
l : aB ↦ N, Case (B) of↑ Aᵢ ⇒ in  {[l]l → (l' = ⊥); }
∪{[L(E(Aᵢ))]L(E(Aᵢ)) → (l' = ⊥)&(L(N)' = ⊤); } ∪ T'(Aᵢ);  end
ε ⇒  in  {[l]l ⟶ (l' = ⊥)&(N' = ⊤); } ∪ T(N')  end
l : ⊗ ⇒  in  [l]l ⟶ (l' = ⊥);  end
l : ⊙ ⇒  in  [l]l ⟶ &ₗ∈ℒ(l' = ⊥); end
```

4   AV Code Generation

This section generates the Java code for the presented class diagrams.

Listing 1.2. Class diagram to Java Code.

```
Λc : C → J
Λc (c) = ∀c, c1, c2 ∈ C,  Case (c) of
c ⟹ in public final class c {}end
p ⟹ in package p.name; end
a ∈ Att(c) ⟹ in public class c { vis(a) type(a) _a; } end
g ∈ c1 × c2 ⟹ in public abstract class c1 {}
public final class c2 extends c1 {} end
r ∈ c1 × c2 ⟹ in public abstract class c1 {}
public final class c2 implements c1 {} end
s ∈ c1 × c2 ⟹ in public final class c1 {private c2 _c1,2;}
    public final class c2{} end
c ∈ c1 × c2 ⟹ in public final class c1 {private final c2;
    private c1() {_c2 = new c2();}
public final class c2 {} end
d ∈ c1 × c2 ⟹ in public final class c1{public use(c2 c2){}}
public final class c2{public void method(){C c;}} public final class C {}
else ⟹ in {} end
```

5   Experimental Results

In this section, we present the specification of an autonomous vehicle system and threat behavior with our MML as well the requirement properties.

Model's System

In the specification with our MML, the base class is *Vehicle* who was instantiated from *Object* class, where the methods of the class represent its behavior, *Vision* and *Lidar* classes are objects where their task is to detect, create a 3d map and send it to the *Controller*. The localization system is presented by three classes, *GPS* represents the device in the vehicle and was instantiated from *Device* class, *GSM* is a protocol of communication was instantiated from *Protocol* class and finally *GPS Server* represents the station of GSM network and was instantiated from *Protocol* class. Also the driver that is presented with *Driver* is instantiated from *Social Actor* class to control the vehicle manually or through voice order because the vehicle has voice detector which is presented by *Voice* and was instantiated from *Object* class (Fig. 2).

Attackers Behavior

In our case study, we presented two types of attackers, the first is a drone with a laser and his objective is to do DDos attack. The second attacker is a malware on the smartphone of the driver which allows the attacker to control the car through the smartphone.

First Attacker. Figure 4 presents the model of the attacker, the class *KLidar* describes his knowledge, and it contains the information about Lidar sensor like the communication frequency. Class *VLidar* present the vulnerability of Lidar sensor. For the skills of the attacker are presented by the class *Dos Attack* which it means that the attacker can do only Dos attack. The diagram of the attack under the name *Resource Depletion (CAPEC-119)* (Fig. 3).

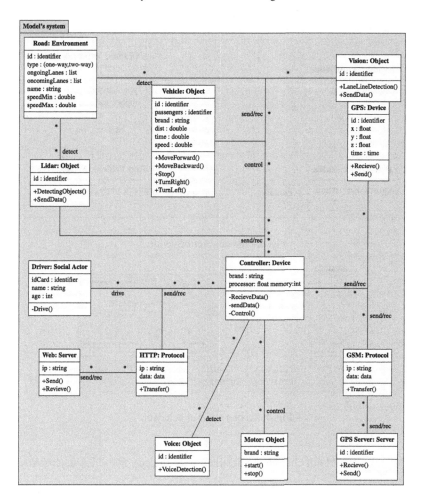

Fig. 2. Model's system of autonomous vehicle.

Second Attacker. Figure 4 presents the model of the attacker, the class *Network:Knowledge* presents his knowledge, and it contains the information about the deployed communication protocols. The class named *Network:Vulnerabilty* presents the vulnerabilities of the protocol's network. The skills of the attacker are presented by the class *Network:skills* which it means that the attacker can do attacks related to the network.

Requirement Properties

We have defined three properties to see if the attacker may violate the properties or not.

– The attacker could not stop the car. $P =?[\Box((CurentPosition \neq destinitation) \wedge (Run = \top))]$

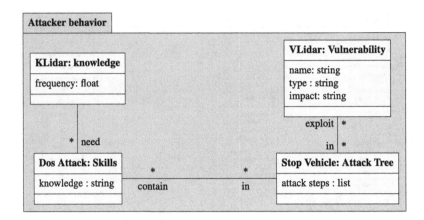

Fig. 3. First attacker behavior.

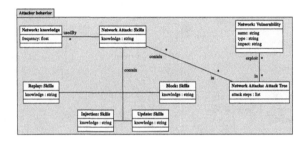

Fig. 4. Second attacker behavior.

- The attacker could not change the destination of the car. $P =?[\Box(destinitation = target)]$
- Could the car know when to stop. $P =?[\Box(Time2Destinitation = EstimedTime)]$

Verification Result

The results, obtained from the verification are summarized in Table 1 where the symbol ✓ means an attack has been found and the symbol ✗ means that the property is safe. The experiments were carried out on a Intel(R) Core(TM) i5-2450M CPU @ 2.50 GHz with 4 GB of RAM.

The first attacker can violate only Φ_1 because his knowledge and skills are limited, it will go near to the vehicle and send signals with the laser to saturate the channel to cause denial-of-service of the Laser and that will stop the vehicle.

The second attacker can violate all the properties, because he is inside the network and he uses the smartphone of the victim which allows him to control totally the car, he needs only to install the malware on the smartphone by a fishing e-mail.

Table 1. The verification results.

Property/Attacker	First attacker	Second attacker
Φ_1	✗	✗
Φ_2	✓	✗
Φ_3	✓	✗

Reinforcement Recommendation

Figure 5 shows the counter-measure used to monitor and detect abnormal behavior, it adds physical solutions to absorb signals attacks in addition to a secure channel.

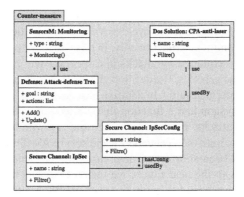

Fig. 5. Counter-Measure.

Secure Vehicle Implementation

Listing 1.3 presents the java code for the class diagram of the vehicle, the attack, and the counter measures.

Listing 1.3. Vehicule-System Java Code.

```
public class Vehicle {
private String id ;...
public void start () ;...
public void stop () ;...
private Vision _vision ();
private Road _road ();
private Lidar _lidar ();
private Controller _controller () ;...   ' }
public class Ddos {
private String id ;
private String goal ;...
```

```
private StopVehicle _stopvehicle;
private KLidar _klidar;}
public class DefenseDos {
private String goal;
private action list actions;...
public void add();
public void update();...
private PhysicMeasures _physicmeasure;
private SensorsM _sensorm;}
```

6 Conclusion

One way to ensure security in cyber physical systems, like autonomous vehicle, and to reduce the cost related to those systems products is to detect vulnerabilities to attacks, at early stages of the development life-cycle as well as to provide a correction mechanism that ensure their continuous functionality. In this paper, we presented a framework to detect vulnerabilities exploited by attacks in a special environment of cyber physical systems, autonomous vehicles. We developed a UML based meta-models dedicated to AV, attacks and counter measures. In addition, we devised an algorithm that detects attack surfaces of the system and a function that assigns for each attack surface a set of potentially harmful attacks. Further we harden the AV with a set of counter measures and finally we generate the java code for the secure AV. The effectiveness of the proposed approach has been shown on a real case of smart autonomous vehicle in a malicious environment. In the near future, we intend to extend the presented work in many directions. First, we intend to apply our framework on different real cases. Further, we would like to achieve more complete catalog that covers more type of attacks and counter measures such that related to product chain. In addition, as a next task is to implement and prove the correctness of the proposed approach.

References

1. Abrams, M.D.: NIMS information security threat methodology. Mitre Technical report MTR 98 W000009, MITRE, Center for Advanced Aviation System Development, McLean, Virgini, August 1998
2. Ayub, M.F., Ghawash, F., Shabbir, M.A., Kamran, M., Butt, F.A.: Next generation security and surveillance system using autonomous vehicles. In: 2018 Ubiquitous Positioning, Indoor Navigation and Location-Based Services (UPINLBS), pp. 1–5, March 2018
3. Checkoway, S., et al.: Comprehensive experimental analyses of automotive attack surfaces. In: Proceedings of the 20th USENIX Conference on Security (SEC 2011), p. 6. USENIX Association (2011)
4. Cui, J., Sabaliauskaite, G., Liew, L.S., Zhou, F., Zhang, B.: Collaborative analysis framework of safety and security for autonomous vehicles. IEEE Access **7**, 148672–148683 (2019)
5. Frigault, M., Wang, L.: Measuring network security using Bayesian network-based attack graphs. In: Proceedings of the 32nd IEEE International Computer Software and Applications Conference (COMPSAC 2008), pp. 698–703 (2008)

6. Gegick, M., Williams, L.: On the design of more secure software-intensive systems by use of attack patterns. Inf. Softw. Technol. **49**, 381–397 (2007)
7. Grunske, L., Joyce, D.: Quantitative risk-based security prediction for component-based systems with explicitly modeled attack profiles. J. Syst. Softw. **81**, 1327–1345 (2008)
8. Holt, J., Perry, S.: SysML for Systems Engineering. Institution of Engineering and Technology Press, January 2007
9. Houmb, S.H., Islam, S., Knauss, E., Jürjens, J., Schneider, K.: Eliciting security requirements and tracing them to design: an integration of common criteria, heuristics, and UMLsec. Requir. Eng. **15**, 63–93 (2010)
10. Huang, H., Zhang, S., Ou, X., Prakash, A., Sakallah, K.A.: Distilling critical attack graph surface iteratively through minimum-cost SAT solving. In: ACSAC 2011, pp. 31–40 (2011)
11. Joy, J., Gerla, M.: Internet of vehicles and autonomous connected car - privacy and security issues. In: 2017 26th International Conference on Computer Communication and Networks (ICCCN), pp. 1–9, July 2017
12. Jürjens, J., Shabalin, P.: Automated verification of UMLsec models for security requirements. In: Baar, T., Strohmeier, A., Moreira, A., Mellor, S.J. (eds.) UML 2004. LNCS, vol. 3273, pp. 365–379. Springer, Heidelberg (2004). https://doi.org/10.1007/978-3-540-30187-5_26
13. Kantola, D., Chin, E., He, W., Wagner, D.: Reducing attack surfaces for intra-application communication in android. In: Proceedings of the 2nd ACM Work. on Security and Privacy in Smartphones and Mobile Devices (SPSM 2012), pp. 69–80. ACM (2012)
14. Manadhata, P.K., Wing, J.M.: An attack surface metric. IEEE Trans. Soft. Eng. **37**(3), 371–386 (2011)
15. Morais, A., Hwang, I., Cavalli, A., Martins, E.: Generating attack scenarios for the system security validation. Netw. Sci. **2**(3–4), 69–80 (2013)
16. OGorman, L.: Comparing passwords, tokens, and biometrics for user authentication. Proc. IEEE **91**(12), 2021–2040 (2003)
17. Ouchani, S., Mohamed, O.A., Debbabi, M.: A security risk assessment framework for SysML activity diagrams. In: 2013 IEEE 7th International Conference on Software Security and Reliability, pp. 227–236 (2013)
18. Ouchani, S.: Ensuring the functional correctness of IoT through formal modeling and verification. In: Abdelwahed, E.H., Bellatreche, L., Golfarelli, M., Méry, D., Ordonez, C. (eds.) MEDI 2018. LNCS, vol. 11163, pp. 401–417. Springer, Cham (2018). https://doi.org/10.1007/978-3-030-00856-7_27
19. Ouchani, S., Ait Mohamed, O., Debbabi, M.: Efficient probabilistic abstraction for SysML activity diagrams. In: Eleftherakis, G., Hinchey, M., Holcombe, M. (eds.) SEFM 2012. LNCS, vol. 7504, pp. 263–277. Springer, Heidelberg (2012). https://doi.org/10.1007/978-3-642-33826-7_18
20. Ouchani, S., Lenzini, G.: Attacks generation by detecting attack surfaces. Procedia Comput. Sci. **32**, 529–536 (2014.) The 5th International Conference on Ambient Systems, Networks and Technologies (ANT-2014), the 4th International Conference on Sustainable Energy Information Technology (SEIT-2014)
21. Plosz, S., Varga, P.: Security and safety risk analysis of vision guided autonomous vehicles. In: 2018 IEEE Industrial Cyber-Physical Systems (ICPS), pp. 193–198, May 2018
22. Siveroni, I., Zisman, A., Spanoudakis, G.: A UML-based static verification framework for security. Requir. Eng. **15**, 95–118 (2010)
23. Vijayakumar, H., Jakka, G., Rueda, S., Schiffman, J., Jaeger, T.: Integrity walls: finding attack surfaces from mandatory access control policies. In: Proceedings of the 7th ACM Symposium on Information, Computer and Communications Security (ASIACCS 2012), pp. 75–76. ACM (2012)

Author Index

Printed in the United States
By Bookmasters